CRITICAL REFLECTIONS ON ECONOMY AND POLITICS IN INDIA, VOL. 1

Studies in Critical Social Sciences Book Series

Haymarket Books is proud to be working with Brill Academic Publishers (www.brill.nl) to republish the *Studies in Critical Social Sciences* book series in paperback editions. This peer-reviewed book series offers insights into our current reality by exploring the content and consequences of power relationships under capitalism, and by considering the spaces of opposition and resistance to these changes that have been defining our new age. Our full catalog of *SCSS* volumes can be viewed at https://www.haymarketbooks .org/series_collections/4-studies-in-critical-social-sciences.

CRITICAL REFLECTIONS ON ECONOMY AND POLITICS IN INDIA, VOL. 1

A Class Theory Perspective

RAJU J. DAS

Haymarket Books
Chicago, IL

Published in paperback in 2021 by
Haymarket Books
P.O. Box 180165
Chicago, IL 60618
773-583-7884
www.haymarketbooks.org

ISBN: 978-1-64259-360-0

Distributed to the trade in the US through Consortium Book Sales and
Distribution (www.cbsd.com) and internationally through Ingram Publisher
Services International (www.ingramcontent.com).

This book was published with the generous support of Lannan Foundation and
Wallace Action Fund.

Special discounts are available for bulk purchases by organizations and
institutions. Please call 773-583-7884 or email info@haymarketbooks.org for more
information.

Cover design by Jamie Kerry and Ragina Johnson.

Printed in the United States.

10 9 8 7 6 5 4 3 2 1

Library of Congress Cataloging-in-Publication data is available.

Contents

Acknowledgements

I have benefitted from my conversations (online and offline) with many scholars in different parts of the world who take the class perspective seriously. I have discussed with them various issues, including fascistic tendencies and Left politics. They include: Greg Albo, Himani Bannerji, Tom Brass, Patrick Bond, Joseph Choonara, Kevin Cox, Jamie Gough, Kevin Hewison, Sándor John, Robert Latham, David Laibman, Deepak Mishra, Bertell Ollman, Hira Singh, Murray Smith, Mohanakumar S., Steven Tufts, and many others. My current and former graduate students at York University, have been, of course, a permanent source of comradely suggestions, criticisms and encouragement. Yvonne Yim at York University has kindly provided assistance numerous times.

A grant from Canada's Social Sciences and Humanities Research Council in 2006 (*grant* number: 510441) made it possible for me to collect some of the empirical evidence reported in the book to illustrate its theoretical arguments. This is gratefully acknowledged. I am grateful to the men, women and children in various localities in India who have freely shared with me their thoughts about their lives and about their struggles.

I made rough drafts of the diagrams used in the book, but it was Ashley Chen, a former graduate student of mine and now a teacher, who deciphered these drawings and who converted these into their publishable form. I do not know who else can do this. She also produced the graphs based on the statistical data I supplied to her, and she has saved me from many typographical errors as well. I cannot thank her enough.

I imagine this book as a concrete 'application', theoretically and empirically, of the ideas laid out in my *Marxist class theory for a skeptical world* published in 2017. I have wanted to write a book on India from the theoretical perspective of class, but I would not have written that book at this moment, if it was not for the constant encouragement received from Professor David Fasenfest, the editor of Brill's Critical Social Science Book Series. He encouraged me in part because he saw my desire to write such a book. He is incredibly patient, kind and supportive, and like a true comrade, he is never unwilling to offer criticisms when they are due and in my own interest. I am extremely grateful for his unflinching support for unfashionable ideas in my work (and in the writings of many others in the world). I hope that the book meets David's expectation to some extent.

Finally, I am grateful to all those who have kept alive class analysis, both theoretically, and politically.

Illustrations

Figures

Tables

Maps

Photo

Preface

Critical Reflections on Economy and Politics in India is a book on political economy and the politics of the Right and the Left in post-independence India.
Originally published in 2020 by Brill as a single volume (658 pages), this book
is now being published by Haymarket as two volumes for the convenience of
the reader. Volume 1 of this edition contains chapters 1-7 from the original, and
Volume 2 covers the remaining chapters 8-14. All in-text references to different
chapters can be found in the respective Haymarket volumes. The Introduction
to the complete work is found in Volume 1, and the Conclusion in Volume 2
refers to all the material in the Haymarket paperback volumes.

These two volumes present a class-based interpretation of the economic
and political situation in contemporary India within a globalizing world. The
first Haymarket volume deals with such topics as: the importance of class analysis of the Indian society and the state, the specificities of India's capitalism
and neoliberalism, as well as the dynamics of poverty, geographically uneven
(and combined) development, technological change, and nature-dependent
export-oriented production.

Volume 2 concerns itself with more explicitly political matters. Given the
sufferings of workers and petty-producers, it is not surprising that India has had
one of the strongest Left movements in the world. Indeed, Left-led struggles in
the form of workers' strikes in urban areas and the Naxalite/Maoist movement
in rural areas have been a long-standing part of the political landscape of India.
But all is not well with Left theory and practice, so this book offers a critical discussion of the Left. Interestingly, and dialectically speaking, the political-economic processes that have adversely impacted the masses which therefore
necessitated Left-led struggles at local, regional and national scales, have also
been the ones that are responsible for the emerging politics of the Right. There
now exist in India 'fascistic tendencies' (i.e. the mechanisms that *can* produce
a fully-fledged fascist state), part of a global trend, which are nurtured and supported by certain political and so-called cultural organizations. Right-wing politics is blatantly pro-big-business and against the fundamental interests of the
exploited masses. India's right-wing politics reflects the identity politics of the
ruling classes materialized in the form of Hindu nationalism and supremacism.
It seeks to preserve a crisis-ridden capitalist system through physical coercion
and ideological manipulation by the fascistic elements both from within and
outside the state. In India, the democratic rights of religious minorities (especially, Muslims), democrats, Leftists, trade union leaders, progressive intellectuals, and millions of ordinary secular-minded workers and petty-producers are

increasingly under attack; millions live in fear or intimidation. The world's largest democracy has become a 'half democracy' even by the traditional standards of capitalism. Not surprisingly, the politics of the Right is explicitly anti-Left, raising the question of 'what is to be done' by the Left. Volume 2 takes up this question in greater detail.

If class relations, especially under capitalism, are behind the problems of the masses, as is the case in India and elsewhere, then the response should be a political project. The goal of this political project must be to create not a more democratic, more egalitarian and more developed *capitalism* but a society that practices popular democracy and operates without the rule of capital and other forms of class relation. The political mobilization for such a project as a protracted process requires workers and small-scale producers to militantly combat the identity politics of the Right, and to defend democratic and economic rights.

The two volumes apply *abstract* theoretical ideas to the *concrete* situation in India, prompting a rethinking of certain abstract ideas. In general terms, the analysis in these volumes demonstrates the necessity of abstract theories for the study of concrete situations underssptood as 'the concentration of many determinations'. More specifically, this analysis applies a materialist and dialectical class theory (see my *Marxist Class Theory for a Skepitcal World,* Brill 2017 and Haymarket 2018) to the Indian context in a manner that takes seriously the matter of the 'tyranny, oppression, violence, and abuse' that have become the fate of ordinary men and women belonging to religious minorities and lower castes in India.

The struggle of the masses in defense of hard-won democratic rights and for a secure and sustainable livelihood is quite literally a matter of life and death. People are dying because of hunger, malnutrition, economic insecurity, poverty and poverty-inducted illnesses, and they are dying because of lynching and riots orchestrated by fascistic elements. Given India's growing global importance, the success or failure of the struggle of the masses in India will influence the success and failure of such struggles elsewhere. Theoretically-informed critical reflections on the current situation are a necessary tool in such struggles for a just society, in India and in other countries.

Raju J Das
Professor
York University, Toronto
April 19, 2021

CHAPTER 1

Introduction

The Indian society can be characterized by a complex set of inter-connected processes. These include: its relatively low labor productivity, combined with a slow and uneven technological change, its turn to neoliberalism, its emphasis on export-oriented production offering a low-wage platform of global capitalism, and the fact that the majority of its population are in absolute poverty or are very vulnerable to falling in it, while there is a massive on-going concentration of wealth and income in the hands of a tiny minority. These processes also embrace the fact that the post-colonial capitalist state has, more or less, failed to meet the economic needs of the masses irrespective of which political party manages the affairs of the state, while the state has succeeded in maintaining capitalist property relations and creating conducive conditions for capitalist accumulation. India has also been experiencing lower-class struggles led by the Left, and the recent emergence of right-wing/'fascistic' tendencies. Understanding these relatively concrete processes requires a critical theoretical reflection.

This critical reflection must be based on certain principles. For a start, to critically reflect on the concrete political and economic situation in India, one needs relatively general concepts that reflect a set of processes and relations. To understand India, one needs to understand much more than India. Secondly, this set of concepts must be informed by an emphasis on class (more on this below). Thirdly, while it is true that to understand India, one needs general theoretical ideas, a study of India, given its enormous social and geographical complexity, can potentially contribute to the production of general ideas and/ or to the critical scrutiny of existing general ideas. Understanding India – indeed, understanding any country or place – requires a two-way interaction between more general ideas and more specific ideas. One needs general ideas in part because Indian society shares some common traits with many other countries. One needs specific ideas because India has a degree of specificity relative to other countries. The ways in which the *general* attributes of the capitalist economy and the capitalist polity are *combined* elsewhere are different from those in India; also, a given general process (e.g. capitalist exploitation) takes a specific form in India, and this partly explains why what happens in India does not quite happen elsewhere (or does not happen to the same extent and in the same way). To reiterate the features of Indian society mentioned above: India is capitalist, India is neoliberal, India experiences uneven technological changes, India experiences export-oriented production, India has a state that fundamentally supports the rich propertied classes vis-à-vis lower classes, India has seen massive and militant lower-class movements, and India faces fascistic tendencies. Many other countries can be said to have experienced all these. But the forms in which these processes are played out in India are different from those elsewhere. India's capitalism is not exactly like that of America's or Canada's, although there are profound similarities. India's neoliberalism shares some common traits with neoliberalism elsewhere, and yet there is something that I will call neoliberalism with Indian characteristics. And so on. So, this is a book on India which is more than about India. And, once again, this book is informed by a class-based general theoretical approach. But one might ask why class?

1   Why Class?

In fact, it is argued that class approach is not that relevant to India because of India's complexity and specificity (its history, its caste relations, etc.). M.N. Srinivas, one of India's well-known sociologists, says that: Indian reality is 'far too complex, regional and sectional differences very real', therefore 'the studies of sociologists seemed to make sense to non-Marxists', and not to Marxists (Srinivas, 2012: 181). Even if some scholars do not reject class analysis, they will not accept the idea that class has a degree of primacy over other social divisions such as caste. The view of Andre Beteille, another well-known sociologist of India, is not atypical of the liberal intelligentsia: Beteille (2007) says that 'Classes are undoubtedly important, but they are not important in the way Marx, or even, Lenin, thought them to be' (p. 9) and that class has no primacy over caste or occupation or income as categories of analysis. This view is shared by even left-leaning scholars.

Subir Sinha (2009) says that Marxist class analysis pays too much importance to the economic and as a result fails to see the worker as embodying many non-economic identities. Herring and Agarwala (2006) lament the decline in class analysis, and yet they say that the sole emphasis in the traditional class theory on the material forms of property deflects attention from cultural capital and the beneficial role of the state for common people. Chakrabarti and Cullenberg (2003) following a postmodernist-Marxist perspective on class say that: contrary to traditional class analysis, class as a social force representing class interests does not exist, and that there is no reason to believe that the working class can have a spark of consciousness.

John Harriss (1988) says that: there are 'limitations of existing paradigms and of the various ways in which essentialist constructs (like "peasant economy" or even "capitalism") have been substituted for specific contextual analysis' (p. 55). This criticism of class analysis echoes that of Gidwani, for whom capitalism operates on the basis of what is merely an assemblage of contingent and interrupted logics, without any structural regularities (Gidwani, 2008). Spivak argues that given the erosion of the factory-based stable work, there are no workers in the traditional sense, and that no class consciousness is possible, and therefore, there is no need for class analysis (Spivak, 2000).

Class analysis is also criticized, because its prediction of class polarization and proletarianization has been apparently disproved. This criticism comes not only from liberal scholars but also from many Marxists such as Byres, Harriss, and others. The critics also draw a political conclusion: given incomplete polarization and partial proletarianization, the proletariat is a small section of the population and cannot be assigned the political importance that class analysis has assigned it (Lerche and Shah, 2018: 942). The emphasis on labor *as a class* in class analysis is increasingly replaced by the concept of 'classes of labor' (Bernstein, 2007).

Class analysis, including by Marx himself, is also faulted for ignoring class struggle outside of production (Herring and Agarwala, 2006; also see Chandra and Taghioff, 2016; Omvedt, 1993). Marxist class analysis is also regarded as inadequate because it offers the 'centralized revolutionary party' performing 'vanguard-functions' on behalf of the working class (Sinha, 2009: 157).

While all these criticisms have been mounted, there *are* studies on India's social-economic problems that do not ignore class. Some of the studies are explicitly class-based analysis (see Pattenden, 2016; Sathyamurthy, 1996; see also Desai, 1975). There are studies that pay some attention to class without class being given any special causal significance. For example, scholars such as Amartya Sen (2006) take an intersectionality type approach to class, or an approach in which class is one of several divisions. In fact, for Sen, class is a part of a bigger picture (which concerns inequality), while other scholars subsume it under marginality (Bhattacharyya and Basu, 2018). And, of course, a large number of scholars focus on the dispossession of small-scale producers as a class issue: studies on dispossession have become a cottage industry. There are others who focus on figuring out how many classes there are, while many examine class agency, especially, of precariously employed people.

2   Why Not Class – Why Not a Class-Based Analytical Framework?

It is important to the respond to the criticisms against class analysis of India and to the existing approaches to class analysis, and outline an alternative approach developed in part through a critical and respectful dialogue with those who have problems with class analysis. I begin to do this initially in Chapter 2, and develop the nature of my response and show the relevance of an alternative approach to class analysis, in the remainder of the book.

The book is an attempt to 'apply' to the Indian context, some of the general ideas developed over the years and presented in my *Marxist class theory* (Das, 2017a; also, Das, 2012a). This book is based on the idea that class relations do exist objectively, at a more abstract level and at a more concrete level, and form the context within which non-class relations work and shape class relations. Human beings need 'things' (food, and shelter as well as education, health-care, software and theatre, etc.) to meet their material and cultural needs. These things need to be produced and shared. Production is a material activity based in a set of *processes*, and can only happen within given social *relations*. These are, above all, the relations and the processes involving those who control the means of production and those who do not (direct producers). These are class relations:[1] these are relations of exploitation, which is why these are also relations of conflict and struggle, whether covert or overt. The class relations have impacts on how classes (e.g. workers, capitalists and small-scale producers), class-fractions and individuals relate to one another, and on the ways in which human beings relate to nature: exploitative class relations of capitalism, based on the unceasing pursuit of profit, adversely impact not only the economic and social lives and the material bodies of members of lower classes, but also the environment. Because class relations prompt conflict of interests between classes, political power is generally mobilized in the economic and political interest of those who control means of production to: (a) persuade the direct producers to accept the arrangements more or less as they are, including by giving some material concessions as well through various methods of deception and illusion, and (b) to suppress their struggle, when necessary. In keeping the direct producers under control, mechanisms of oppression are deployed such that direct producers are not only economically exploited but also socially oppressed on the basis of caste, gender and religion, etc. The matter of social oppression, in the sphere of ideology and material practices, is too important to be left out of concrete class analysis.

---

1   Class relations, and indeed, all relations, are to be seen as relations *and* processes.

These are relatively well-known and very simple ideas in class analysis,[2] and have relevance to India as to any other society. This means that in examining India's economy and polity, one must bear in mind the mutually antagonistic interests of those who control society's productive resources, and the toiling masses (wage-workers and small-scale producers). Economic development processes and political processes are to be seen as ultimately class processes.

It *is* important to talk about individual classes. However, the examination of how many classes exist and how different groups within the working class experience life differently must be a part of a larger consideration in which the emphasis should be given to the fact that there is class as a relationship (with its contradictions), that affects politics, economy and culture and how we relate to nature and one another. It is *that* relationship which form the class-context, and which underlies how classes, class-fractions and individuals of specific classes, as well as state agencies and state elites, function,or do not function, and how they exercise their agency or how they do not.

The class analysis concerns the *entire* society, including the state. The class-perspective on India (and other countries) can prompt theoretically rigorous and empirically-corroborated research on a wide variety of topics. Only a few are covered in this book. These include: nature of India's capitalism as a form of class society; nature of neoliberalism with Indian traits; technological change in relation to direct producers; production for the world market and a dual metabolic rift and their implications for workers of different oppressed categories; the social character of the capitalist state in relation to dominant and subordinate classes; lower-class struggles, and fascistic tendencies as a ruling class response to the capitalist crisis, a response that combines a ruthless pursuit of capitalism as well as oppression of religious minorities, and the potential and actual role of Left politics in social transformation. These themes are slightly elaborated below.

3 Components of a Class-Based Framework for Understanding Contemporary India

3.1 India's Capitalist Class Relation, and Neoliberal Capitalism

One must begin by asking what is the nature of capitalist class society of India? Interestingly, the nature of the economic development process in most parts of India, and especially, in the countryside, does not appear to support Marx and Engels's (1848) optimism in *The Communist Manifesto* that the bourgeoisie

---

2 This is not to say that these ideas are widely accepted in India or elsewhere.

(or, the capitalist mode of production led by this class) constantly revolution-izes the mode of production. If capitalism revolutionizes the development of productive forces, and yet if labor productivity per hour is still so low, then could it be that India is not (dominantly) a capitalist country? Conversely, if India *is* a capitalist country, why does it have such a low level of labor produc-tivity? Indeed, the question of whether or not India is a capitalist country proper and the question of what the barriers are to its further development, if capitalism does exist, are not yet settled. It is interesting that there is a lack of a consensus on the meaning of capitalism itself (Wood, 2007). There is a need to conceptualize capitalism as a class relation in the specific context of India.

Like everything else in the world, capitalism comes in multiple forms. The capitalist class relation, in India or elsewhere, exists in different forms: formal and real subsumption of labor, for example. The formal subsumption is the most general form of capitalism, and in this sense India is decidedly capitalist in terms of class relations. The formal subsumption has four traits including, commodification of labor power and of the means of production and subsis-tence, and exploitation of labor in the workplace, on the basis of the appro-priation of absolute surplus value. While overall India is characterized by the dominance of formal subsumption of labor, in specific areas and sectors, there is a transition to real subsumption of labor, a transition that is unevenly shaped, in part by, the changing balance of power between capital and labor. More concretely, India's class structure is characterized by the combination of for-mal and real subsumptions of labor, coexisting with relations that are not capi-talist in terms of *production* relations.

While from one vantage point, India's capitalism can be seen in terms of subsumption of labor (i.e. the way in which labor is integrated into production under capitalist class relation), from another angle (i.e. the way in which and the extent to which the state regulates capitalism), the stages, or the chrono-logical forms, through which capitalism has developed can be expressed, for example, as Keyenesian/developmentalist and neoliberal. The neoliberal form/stage of capitalism in India has rightly attracted much attention but not always in an entirely adequate manner. Indian neoliberal capitalism, with its specific traits and consequences, requires a critical examination.

3.2 *Class Character of Technological Change*

In capitalism, whether it is in its neoliberal form or not, and despite the struc-tural obstacles to technological changes, partly stemming from the formal subsumption of labor, technological changes, whether in mechanical or bio-chemical, etc. forms, do happen. Technological change happens, even if not in a systemic manner, and is expected to be a means of bringing about development. For the less developed world, technological change is a means of catching up with advanced countries as well. There is a widespread belief that technological change can solve society's problems, so it is important to examine the social nature of technology. This question can be asked in the context of many different forms of human activity (e.g. agriculture, industry, services). It is useful to ask the question in the context of agriculture which has trans-historical and capitalism-specific importance (production of food and raw materials, and production of surplus value) and which has been going through many technological revolutions in the last 10,000 years or so.

Given that those who depend on agriculture for a living tend to be poor (they cannot satisfy their basic needs), what is the relation between technology and poverty? These issues are discussed in the context of the Green Revolution technology that began to be widely used in the 1960s in India (and elsewhere). The world has seen four agricultural revolutions, all having resulted in a dramatic acceleration of growth (Lipton, 1989: 316). The Green Revolution (GR), which is more than half a century old now, is the last but one of these (the GR is followed by the genetic – biotechnological – revolution). Its speed, scale and spread have 'far exceeded those of any earlier technological change in food farming' (ibid.: 14–15). Indeed, the GR triggered off an extremely important debate in studies on India, including in the form of the celebrated mode of production debate, that focused on the nature and the extent of capitalist development in India.

The relation between the GR and poverty/inequality is among the most widely researched topics. The literature on the GR–poverty relation has been almost polarized between the 'GR enthusiasts' who see favorable impacts of the GR on poverty/inequality and 'GR sceptics' who take almost an opposite view. Separating the poverty issue from the inequality issue, it can be said that there is a near consensus that the GR has caused an increase in inequality.

The GR–poverty relation, the intellectual construction of which has changed over time, is an interesting issue more generally. It can be considered to be a part of the larger literature on the relation between technology and society (Smith, 2010), including the poor people in society. An influential strand is neo-Malthusianism of which Michael Lipton is arguably a representative, and which needs a robust Marxist class-theoretic response. Lipton is one of the most widely cited researchers on the GR and poverty topic. He wrote a book in 1989, *New Seeds and Poor People*. Lipton's work, like much of the massive amount of research on the GR–poverty relation, is firmly within a paradigm which gives much more causal power to technology and to population than they can possibly bear. Lipton's view that the GR has a *necessary* poverty-reducing property, that the poor would be necessarily poorer without the technology, is mistaken. Against Liptonian views, I argue that capitalism as a class relation shapes possibilities for technological change, and it also shapes how technological change benefits the common people or not. Capitalism induces technological change which can increase production, but whether this can benefit the workers is a different matter.

3.3   Capitalist Production for the World Market and a Labor-Environmental Metabolic Rift

To understand such matters as the nature of capitalism as well as prospects of economic development and poverty alleviation, it is important to understand technological change. However, understanding these matters requires a broader perspective, one that is focused on the entire process of capitalist production. Indeed, how capitalist production happens under neoliberalism sheds important light on the social character of production, including the class relation between capital and labor. Capitalism exists in neoliberal forms, and neoliberalism has its specific national traits such as those in India. A specific form of neoliberal capitalism is agrarian neoliberalism.

Crucial to the neoliberal project have been agricultural exports as a source of foreign exchange and fiscal stability. The policy has led to India becoming a member of a group of nations that Harriet Friedman (1993) calls 'New Agricultural Countries' (NACS). Counterpoised to the Newly Industrialized Countries (NICS) of recent decades (Brohman, 1996), the emergence of the NACS represents a quintessential strategy of Third World development under neoliberalism, which has occurred, 'paradoxically, with heavy state support'. 'New agriculture' refers to the production, for the world market, of high-value non-traditional crops (e.g. flowers and shrimps), as compared to the traditional crops produced under colonialism and during the immediate post-colonial period (Maitra, 1997). New Agriculture signifies a dialectics of articulation and disarticulation. It *articulates* local social production relations in NACS directly to the world market – and to its price signals – more closely than achieved during the era of the Green Revolution, when national food self-sufficiency was emphasized (Nanda, 1995). New agriculture also *disarticulates* agricultural production from the requirements of local populations and environments (Teubal, 2000): products of new agriculture are not affordable by the ordinary families.

Thus the situation today is that whilst NACS, such as India, are increasingly specializing in luxury and niche-market crops, fish farming, and animal feeds in order to pay back their debts, and are under pressure from evolving World Trade Organization rules, developed countries have specialized in the

intensive export of heavily subsidized basic wage goods. This trend is indicative
of an emergence of a new international division of labor in agriculture (McMichael, 2000). This new division of labor signifies, among other things, the relatively deregulated production of commodities for export, based on a low-paid,
unorganized working class that is increasingly deprived of government welfare
benefits: in other words, neoliberal capitalism in agrarian/rural contexts.

Like many other countries of the South, India is a low-wage platform of
global neoliberal capitalism. Such a platform works in industries, services as
well as in agriculture, of which aquaculture is an important part. Aquaculture
is the fastest growing food-producing sector in the world (World Bank, 2007).
Shrimp culture is an important part of aquaculture. Shrimp production is a
specific form of new agricultural production. If shrimp-culture is being promoted, we must understand whether the men, women and children who produce shrimps as wage-workers benefit. When explored through a materialist
and dialectical class perspective, the issue of shrimp wage laborers reveals the
nature of a specific kind of 'metabolic rift' that is generally not talked about
in the existing literature. This is a rift that characterizes the relation between
wage labor and capital, where capital takes a lot more out of labor than it
gives it. This rift co-exists with the ecological metabolic rift (Foster, 2007)
where capital takes more out of nature than it gives nature. This approach also
shows how place-specific relations of social difference – social oppression
mechanisms – along with biophysical conditions of production, influence the
more general social relations of capitalism.

3.4   *The Class Relations of the Capitalist State*

The general social relations of capitalism affect not only economic matters
(e.g. technological change, working conditions, etc.) but also political matters.
It is in fact a truism that in order to understand the economic issues such as
poverty and development that confront India (or any other country, for that
matter), one must investigate the nature of the state, for the economic is a deeply political matter and the political is, to borrow a phrase from Lenin, 'concentrated economics'. It is not surprising that the state in a large, under-developed,
capitalist country such as India, has been the subject of much discussion. Thus,
for example, the Rudolphs look upon the state as a third actor which has seemingly marginalized both capital and labor (Rudolph and Rudolph, 1987). However, their approach substantially underestimates the dominant class bias
of the state, a bias that exists structurally and instrumentally (i.e. as a result
of the use of state institutions by the capitalist class as an instrument). Bardhan (1998) characterizes the state as an 'above the fray' arbiter between dominant classes, including the landed. Adopting a problematic approach to class

(within so-called analytical Marxism), this view does not say much about the actual exploitative class relations and the role of the Indian state in reproducing them. Nor is Chibber's (2003) recent analysis convincing. Chibber (2003) says that the capitalist class accepted, and benefitted from, import-substituting industrialization, which ensured protection from external competition, but it thwarted state initiatives to regulate industrial activity which were thought necessary for rapid industrial transformation. It is not clear to me why the capitalist class would subordinate itself to the state to any significant extent and without complaint, except in exceptional cases. Whether or not the Indian capitalist class refused to be controlled by the Indian state via the latter's planning mechanisms, becomes an important question, not for Marxists, but mainly for those who take – and took – the claim that India has a socialist regime and that was a barrier to economic development. Marxists do not need to be convinced that ultimately it is capital that decides what the state does or does not do. Basically, the state-class relation cannot be understood adequately within any framework including that of Chibber, that abstracts from (a) the *totality* of the relations between all the proprietary classes and the classes they exploit, *including in rural areas*, and (b) the global situation (e.g. imperialism's connection to an economy, both during colonial times and after formal decolonization). It is also important to avoid politicism: explaining state's action in terms of its own capacity (Das, 1999a). Class analysis of the state must prioritize the relation between proprietary classes, and between them and the exploited classes, and see the state and the capitalist class, more or less, as two arms of capital-as-a-class-relation, within which disagreements, including over who should listen to whom and how much, are intra-family matters.

The cultural turn (as exemplified in the work of Stuart Corbridge, Akhil Gupta, Partha Chatterjee, etc.) also fails to appropriately examine the Indian state. Its underlying notion of the state is that it is merely a power relation, but why is there a need for state actors to exercise power relations and in whose interests? Might there be a relation between power relations and the class character of the state? This literature complements the macro, national level structuralist treatment of the state, in which the state appears to be disembodied and working without the involvement of social agents. But it comes at a cost: this literature, influenced by the post-turn (or the cultural or discursive turn) is largely silent on the materiality of the state, on its solidity, its coherence, all of which come mainly from its class logic. It is the latter which one should be able to infer from, and which in turn determines, everyday interaction.

Against the existing views on the Indian state is needed a thoroughgoing historical materialist interpretation, based on class. Just as political-economic processes are class processes and concern class relations, so do the fundamental aspects of the state. What is necessary is an emphatic reassertion of the validity of class analysis, now out of academic fashion, with particular reference to the formation, reproduction and agency of the state. Such an approach says that the state cannot but reflect – and is thus driven by – class interests, albeit in ways that are sometimes contradictory. The material fact of class is the most important social context affecting the conditions under which lower classes (i.e. workers and small-scale producers in urban and rural areas) live and work. Capitalist relations, along with what are taken to be 'pre'/'non'-capitalist relations in rural areas where they exist, define this class context. And the ways in which capitalist and other class relations shape the state are in turn shaped by non-class relations.

The class relation shapes the relation between the rulers and the ruled, and the latter relation shapes the class relation, within a system of relations in which the class relation, ultimately, is fundamental. And the relation between class and the state itself is shaped by various empirically-existing conditions, including mechanisms of social oppression (e.g. caste), external connections such as economic globalization, and so on. Class does not (and cannot) operate in a vacuum: it is accordingly reproduced and impinged on – among other things – both by ideologies and practices of caste, ethnicity, nationality, region and gender and by the political form of the state itself (i.e. democratic form; federal form). Since capitalism is the dominant mode of production in India, the state is predominantly a capitalist apparatus, and as such an agent of capitalist development nationally and locally. For this reason, the state and rural/urban capital are the two arms of what is an overarching capitalist social relationship. The actions of both capital and the capitalist state – class struggle from above – are in turn influenced politically by struggles conducted against them by lower classes.

3.5   *Lower-Class Struggles*

Implicit in the class view of (Indian) society is an interesting dialectical connection. This connection is between the conditions of existence and class struggle. Conditions of existence include what Marx (2000: 425), in *Preface to the Critique of Political Economy*, referred to as 'material productive forces' and 'relations of production' (and the empirical effects, such as various forms of deprivation emerging partly from the contradiction between the two). Because these conditions are exploitative, they *require* (necessitate) class struggle for their alleviation and eventual transcendence, and they *prompt* (make possible) class struggle from below for this purpose. The second aspect of the dialectic is that: these conditions not only prompt lower-class struggle, but also condition, or set limits on, class struggle. The conditions of existence also include ideas of 'people' as well as the actions of the state that seeks to create order in a class society. The state seeks to create an order not only by interventions in support of the dominant classes, but also by *repressing* exploited classes and seeking to elicit their consent to the system's reproduction, including through selective bribes. State policies often take the form of 'development', on the ground and on paper. State policies must be construed partly as a form of class struggle from above, launched on behalf of the propertied, to reproduce the social order.

India's capitalist political system and its capitalist political economy have failed to meet the needs of the masses. Such a failure has prompted not only trade union struggles, which have inflicted a cost on the capitalist economy, about which the capitalist associations complain about. It has also led to the Maoist struggle that has been going on in a quarter of the country's territory for almost half a century. It is also known as the Naxalite struggle because it started in the Naxalbari region of the West Bengal province. The Naxalite movement is a part of the worldwide Maoist movement. It is the longest surviving revolutionary movement in the history of peasant resistance in India. The former Prime Minister of India, Mr. Manmohan Singh, of the centrist Congress Party, called the Naxalites the single biggest national security threat.

The Naxalite movement has mobilized poor people against sections of the propertied class (e.g. landlords, traders; mining companies) for social justice in India. The movement has conferred limited benefits upon the poor in some places. It is not averse to using violence to get these benefits and to stop them from being taken away. The Indian state seeks to violently repress it, killing thousands. Anyone suspected of having any links with the Naxalite movement, and especially, with that faction of it which the state has banned, can be jailed or killed. This raises wider conceptual questions about the relation between 'social movements' (broadly, movements against injustice in a class-society) and the state. Why does a state kill its citizens? The answer lies in the legitimacy threat from the militant Naxalite movement to the state: it does things for the poor that the state has failed to do, and it is not unwilling to defend its gains where necessary by force. Of course, a critique of the Indian state's violent response to the Maoist movement does not *at all* mean an endorsement of how Maoists understand society and seek to change it. The long-term structural changes in society require active participation of politically conscious masses in cities and villages in a process of political mobilization against class exploitation and social oppression. Emphasizing violent methods of destruction as a *strategy* cannot construct the conditions for such mobilization, even though such methods may yield short-term localized results.

3.6   *Fascistic Tendencies as a Form of Class Struggle from Above*

The failure of the bourgeois political economy and of the bourgeois state to meet the needs of the masses, which has been behind lower-class struggle, however uneven and weak, is the context in which a serious threat has emerged to the democratic and social rights of the people, a threat that is posed by right-wing forces in India.

The Bharatiya Janata Party (BJP), a right-wing party, which is supported by fascistic movements and people, won India's 2014 general election partly by promising development or *vikas* for all (and also by stoking hatred against non-Hindus). (The BJP has also won the 2019 election, which will not be covered in this book; on this topic see, Das, 2019b.) Major promises (e.g. a massive creation of jobs, crackdown on black money hidden away in foreign banks) made by the party in power have turned out to be, more or less, false promises but the government keeps repeating them. The government spends millions on publicity to make people believe to be true what is not true, and, in particular, that good days (achhe din) are upon them. As far as the well-being of the masses is concerned, there has been little change, in part because the right-wing government is wedded to pro-business interventions. Yet, many have started understanding the real intentions of the right-wing government, which are both communal (religious-sectarian) and pro-business, and therefore, against the toiling classes. Among those who initially fell for emotionally-charged appeals from the right-wing forces supporting the government, to national and religious pride based on distorted representations of the past (and present), many are now understanding that what is really important is access to decent employment and standard of living, social peace, and so on, and that false pride cannot meet such needs. This is evident in the electoral defeat of the BJP in the by-elections for the Lok Sabha (Lower House of the Parliament) and for provincial legislatures in 2018. (That these disappointments did not produce the BJP's defeat in 2019 is a different matter, on which see Das, 2019b.)

The phenomenon of the right-wing regime in India goes beyond the failure of the government to meet the economic needs of the people. The country is indeed experiencing something like a national emergency. This is in the form of persistent attacks on the basic democratic rights of ordinary citizens, by hyper-nationalist Hindu-supremacist forces, which are supported by, and which support, the right-wing BJP. Religious minorities, especially, Muslims, have become 'near-exact equivalent of the Jew' (Sarkar, 2016: 143). The right-wing forces are bent on creating a Hindu state, where religious minorities will remain subservient to the majority religion, and where Dalits (ex-untouchables) will continue to be oppressed by the higher castes in the Hindu social order. The capitalist class society has always made use of mechanisms of social oppression based on caste, gender and indigeneity; now a new axis of social oppression has been added to the mix: oppression based on religion. Furthermore, the Hindu-nationalist forces are targeting not only religious minorities and *dalits*, but also Leftists as well as rationalists and secularists, who oppose their Hindu-tva (Hindu-ness) ideology and their assault on democratic rights.

The rise of the BJP is a part of the world-wide right-wing bourgeois political trend moving on (or towards) a 'fascistic path'. Contrary to what some believe (e.g. Vanaik, 2017), I argue that there *are* 'fascistic tendencies' – as a form of bourgeois politics or an extreme tendency toward the breakdown of bourgeois politics – in both richer and poorer countries. To the extent that such a danger exists, whether it is in rich countries or in poorer countries such as India, the question is how do we understand the threat as we face it, from the standpoint of removing it?

There *is*, undoubtedly, a fascistic threat in India. This is a threat to India's Left and progressive culture and to the idea of India as a country in which there has traditionally been a large amount of support for secularism and democracy. The fascistic threat has strong material conditions. The development of fascistic tendencies is a class project, more than anything else. The dominance of right-wing forces represents a most extreme form of the latent tendency towards an attack on democracy, the tendency that exists in capital-ist societies when there is massive inequality and where the most basic needs of the masses remain unmet while a tiny class basks in obscene amounts of wealth and income, under conditions of capitalist crisis of growth. India, the largest democracy of the world, is home to the largest number of people in absolute poverty. The emergence of fascistic tendencies points to a curious case of ideological and political inversion of sorts whereby the relation of an-tagonism between the working people and capital, which is their real enemy, is transformed into an antagonistic relation between the working people and their manufactured, or fake, enemies, i.e. minorities, communists, etc. A per-son can be killed for eating beef or for dealing in beef. Non-human beings (cows) have come to have more value than humans. Could there be a connec-tion between kowtowing to the capitalist market as a holy cow and the extra-ordinary amount of religious-sectarian reverence for cows?

While the ideology of fascism has been in India at least since the 1920s, the same time when the communist party was also born, its political success has come since the early 1990s. There are at least three political-economic pro-cesses behind the rise of the fascistic forces:

1.   Like many other countries, India – especially, its bottom 70–80% – faces numerous pressing problems: low wages, un-/under-employment, inse-cure employment, reduction in government's welfare, forcible loss of

access to land or other means of livelihood, crisis of rural economy, ecological degradation, lack of quality health care, education and shelter, etc. These problems are fundamentally caused by the nature of capitalist class relation and exacerbated by its neoliberal form. While the masses have not been doing well, the top 1–10% of the wealth-owning class began doing extremely well, especially, since late 1980s.

2.   Ordinary people are engaged in recurrent protests and struggles, which are often organized by the Left, against exploitation, oppression, dispossession and immiserization/inequality. In India, the intensity of strikes (e.g. person-days lost per strike) is actually increasing, and strike is a top risk factor for Indian business associations. So, there is a pressure on the enterprise-owners to reduce not only wage-costs of workers but also the possibility of strikes which inflict an economic cost. To reduce these costs, they need help from political party leaders. This help comes in the form of repression and deception/consent-making. The need for repression is often expressed as admiration for authoritarianism and for a strongman who could solve problems. The deception works in part on the basis of the creation of illusory differences based in religion, etc.

3.   Capitalism indeed does not only create the *structural* condition for fascistic tendencies by creating economic problems for the masses, who then blame their conditions on an imaginary enemy (e.g. religious minority; those critical of the system of exploitation and oppression). It also creates the *agencies* through which the fascistic project, including its violence aspect, as a mass movement, is carried out. Here the role of economically frustrated petty bourgeois and lumpenproletarian, and even some proletarian, elements is important as fascistic movement's storm troopers.

Of course, a fuller understanding of fascistic tendencies must take us beyond the sphere of the political-*economic*. We must pay attention to the sphere of politics in a bourgeois society. The political dynamics of the fascistic tendency have been different in different countries. One needs to pay attention to the fascistic tendencies as they are manifested in the *concrete political situation* in India, by remaining mindful of the canvas of the *general* political economic dynamics of the fascistic tendencies.

The Congress Party, and the Communist parties (which are social-democratic *in practice*) constitute the combined forces of the 'Center' and the Left, and can be called, with *some* justification, 'reformist democracy'. There are various failures of 'reformist democracy' – the failures on the economic front and the failures to protect democracy and secularism – which have produced a situation for the right-wing forces to become stronger, electorally and otherwise. In other words, the entire political system – not just the BJP – is responsible for the fascistic tendencies.

3.7   *What Can the Left Do?*

The fascistic forces constitute a very powerful obstacle to, and reflects relative weakness of, the progressive and the Left movement. In several parts of India, communists and their offices are being physically attacked, and communists are being killed or harmed by the fascistic forces. So, the fascistic forces will have to be stopped, and stopped right now. These forces must be the target of an all-out fight, a fight on economic, political and ideological fronts. The question is how, and what role the Left has in this? To answer this, we must begin with the Marxist theory of Left politics, according to which the Marxist Left must mobilize its *basic classes* (skilled and unskilled workers, self-employed small-scale producers, and unemployed people, of all castes and religions) with help from politically progressive ('de-classed') intellectuals, against the fascistic brigade, mainly in the *extra-electoral* sphere, as a part of the struggle to transcend the capitalist class relations that are at the origin of the fascistic tendencies. This should be *the dominant approach* to fighting the fascistic movement. On the basis of their large numbers as well as rallies and general strikes, and local-level people's committees, Marxist forces must take the lead, where possible, in directly countering the fascistic movement and stop it from physically intimidating people.

But how does the power of the Marxist theory of politics relate to India's empirical context? The Indian Left – all the Left parties from the right to the left – must mobilize its forces extra-electorally against the fascistic movement at local, regional and national scales. But to the extent that the electoral arena is also an important area of political struggle in a liberal democracy, the Left must use that sphere as well.

4   The Chapter Outline

The book is divided into 12 main chapters, apart from the introduction and the conclusion. Many of these chapters were written over a number of years in the form of journal articles (as well as progressive electronic online magazines) and have been thoroughly revised.

Chapter 2 is, effectively, a continuation of this Introduction chapter and sets the context for the Chapters 3–13. It begins with the various criticisms raised against class analysis of India and then discusses how class analysis has been conducted in the Indian context. The chapter makes a series of criticisms against (a) the criticisms against class analysis and (b) some aspects of the extant class analysis. It then provides an outline of how class analysis of India should look like.

Chapter 3 is an examination of India's capitalism as a form of class relation. It begins with the famous Indian mode of production debate, critically discussing how certain scholars define capitalism in general and capitalism in the Indian context (including in Indian agriculture), and then presents an alternative approach. In doing so it builds on Marx's discussion in *Capital* volume 1 on subsumptions of labor, a discussion that is often neglected or misinterpreted. It argues that capitalism can exist when formal subsumption prevails and that India is a dominantly capitalist country. It also argues that the transition to real subsumption, with attendant technological change, can be a very long process, and, that *notwithstanding* Marx's view about 'spontaneous' transition to real subsumption, it is anything but spontaneous. That transition is mediated by the changing balance of power of capital and labor, which occurs in a context of a whole host of geographically-specific factors such as capitalist state interventions. I provide some empirical discussion to corroborate my argument about the relation between the balance of power between capital and labor, and the transition from formal subsumption. Thus, I discuss how class struggle can prompt real subsumption though not in any unilinear, straightforward, way, and I show how property owners can respond to class struggle against formal subsumption by way of *reinforcing* formal subsumption and/or introducing hybrid subsumption (exploitation based on mercantile-usury-rental extraction). While there are technical and other reasons for a transition to real subsumption (for example, in the industrial sector), there are limits to such a transition, within the context of peripheral capitalism, operating within the constraints of the imperialist world market.

While Chapter 3 deals with the form of capitalism in India from the vantage point of the subsumption of labor under capital, Chapter 4 deals with the form of capitalism from a different standpoint: neoliberal vs state-directed form of capitalism. It makes some brief conceptual observations on the neoliberal phase of capitalism in general, and examines neoliberal capitalism as it operates, and impacts people's lives, in India.

If Chapter 3 partly deals with the ways in which formal subsumption can be an obstacle to technological change, Chapter 5 asks: when technological change does happen under capitalism (with state-support), how does it benefit the working class? More specifically, Chapter 5 presents a 'slice' of the global intellectual discussion on the social character of technological change in the form of the famous Green Revolution (GR): it discusses Michael Lipton's and others' views on the supposed positive and negative benefits of the GR for the poor. It then critiques this literature for its underlying neo-Malthusianism and for its abstraction from class issues. The chapter goes on to present an alternative statement on the GR and poverty relation putting at the center the nature of the capitalist class relation, a statement that views the relation as contingent and not necessary. It also provides an empirical analysis of the GR–poverty relation in India, which was one of the 'model' GR countries in the mid-1990s. The chapter also very briefly reflects on the genetic (biotechnological) revolution in terms of its proponents' claim about its pro-poor benefits, the claims that are similar to the claims made about the GR's pro-poor effects.

As mentioned, Chapter 4 deals with neoliberalism – neoliberal form of capitalism – with Indian traits at a very general level. A specific form of neoliberal capitalism is agrarian neoliberalism, which, in turn, is expressed in a more concrete form: export-oriented aquaculture. This is the topic of Chapter 6. This Chapter briefly outlines the current state of the analysis of shrimp culture, and offers Marxist criticisms of this analysis, and maps out the contours of a different framework. It then presents the empirical discussion on shrimp farm laborers, including their socio-geographical character, and reflects on the ways in which class relations, social oppression and natural conditions of production are inter-connected.

Chapter 7 deals with the capitalist state in India. It examines the ways in which the Indian state is influenced by its 'base' in the dominant classes, and the coalition character of relations between property-owning classes and between them and the upper bureaucracy which has had a degree of autonomy. It then deals with the relation between the state and lower classes, and the state-form (territorial and liberal-democratic form) and lower-class struggles. Implications of the politically contradictory nature of state intervention in relation to uneven development and neoliberalism are also outlined.

Chapter 8 briefly looks at some of the exploitative and oppressive material conditions in India's rural areas, and also considers the failure of the post-colonial capitalist-landlord state to counter these conditions. The chapter shows how it is the unjust conditions of living that have created a situation 'ripe' for class struggle, one instance of which is the Naxalite movement. The chapter discusses the uneven growth and spread of the movement and presents a theoretical-political critique of the movement.

Chapter 9 is a continuation of Chapter 8 and also builds on Chapter 7. Its focus on the state's repressive response to the Naxalite Movement. It begins by critically discussing the existing conceptual literature on state repression of social movements, and presents a preliminary attempt at an alternative approach to the topic. It then provides some empirical evidence on what the

Naxalite Movement actually does for the poor, and examines the state's ideological-repressive response to the movement. The chapter explains why the state deploys violent means against it. The state is repressive towards the Naxalite movement not just because the movement uses violence. The state is also repressive because the movement seeks to create an alternative landscape of development which potentially poses a crisis of legitimacy.

Chapter 9 is followed by a series of four chapters on the right-wing forces in relation to India's political economy and its Left movement. Using content from media, and data from national and international institutions, Chapter 10 empirically examines India's development under the post-2014 right-wing regime, in terms of its economic and social-political aspects. It discusses the record of the BJP government in promoting economic development and inequality. It shows how the ultra-rich, the class basis of the right-wing government, are benefitting from the government enormously, and how the poorer segments are, more or less, losing under this government. It also shows the government's record of political development, including democracy and social harmony. It discusses how the dismal record of development is slowly getting registered in the minds of people who are getting disillusioned with the government. This disillusionment is an embryonic consciousness against right-wing thinking and policies, but whether it will further develop in a progressive direction and how it will shape electoral and extra-electoral battles against right-wing forces, no one can tell with certainty.

Chapters 11–12 interpret the rise of right-wing forces on the basis of a framework in which the concept of fascism – or, what I call fascistic tendencies – plays a central role. Chapter 11 deals with some definitional/conceptual issues concerning fascism and introduces the topic of the fascistic threat in India and sheds light on its importance to India's Left and progressive culture. It deals with the political economy of fascism and fascistic tendencies, at a general theoretical level, but with an eye towards India, relating the fascistic tendencies to class society, to capitalist class-society and to India's capitalist society. It considers the *economic* as well as *cultural-political* processes, and class *agency* involved in the fascistic movement.

Chapter 12 deals with the failures of 'reformed democracy' (centrist and Left forces) in India to protect democracy and secularism and social-economic rights. This has allowed a political space, within the overall logic of the failure of the capitalist system to meet the needs of the masses, a space within which the BJP and its forces then deploy a battery of political techniques to strengthen fascistic movement and implement right-wing economic policies by capturing power.

Chapter 13 deals with the question of what is to be done about the fascistic threat? It begins with the Marxist theory of Left politics, outlining how the Left anywhere in the world must fight against fascistic tendencies as a part of the fight for socialism. It then discusses the Indian situation in relation to this general theory: it outlines the strengths and weaknesses of the Indian Left movement, and shows how the Left can fight the fascistic tendencies on the basis of extra-electoral mobilization of the toiling masses as well as class-based electoral politics, putting the accent on the first method. Whether the existing Left movement is up to the task is a different matter. I remain skeptical of this possibility (see Das, 2019b).

Class in India

The discussion in this book on India's political economy and politics (of the Right and of the Left) is informed by a class-based theoretical approach. But one might ask: why does one need such an approach? Is Indian society not too complex for the class analysis to be useful? A continuation of the introduction to the book, Chapter 2 deals with this question in a relatively rudimentary manner, on the basis of the general ideas about class proposed in Das (2017a), while the relevance of a class perspective on India will be clearer in the subsequent chapters (Chapters 3–13) on the basis of further development of specific themes.

This Chapter has four sections. In Section 1, I deal with some common criticisms against class analysis (or, Marxist class analysis). In Section 2, I present how class has been treated by various scholars studying India. In Section 3, I critique these views as well as the criticisms against Marxist class analysis. In Section 4, I outline a very broad approach to class analysis of India, anticipating many of the themes discussed in the remainder of the book.

1   Existing Criticisms against Class Analysis of India

1.1   *India Too Complex for Class Analysis*

For some, the Indian society is to be seen in terms of categories defined on the basis of not only caste, which is said to define India's specificity, but also gender, indigeneity, income, occupation, region, religion, community, and so on. If there are so many divisions, one may say: why use the class perspective? In fact, it is often said that Indian society is too complex for class, which is an analytical category from the Western industrial society, to be useful. M.N. Srinivas, one of India's well-known sociologists, says that Indian reality is 'far too complex, regional and sectional differences very real, and the studies of sociologists seemed to make sense to non-Marxists', and not Marxists (Srinivas, 2012: 181).[1]

---

1 Srinivas (2012) says this in a talk delivered at the All India Sociological conference held in 1997: 'the country has been undergoing rapid cultural and social change since the 1940s... Marxism of the more dogmatic variety seemed to help a large number of Indian intellectuals

1.2   *Primacy Assigned to Class Mistaken*

Even if some scholars think that class analysis has something to contribute to the study of Indian society, the fact that it assigns primacy to class has been a problem for them. Consider the view of Andre Beteille, another well-known sociologist of India. He says that in the 1970s when he began studying India's social structure, he was 'attracted by the Marxian approach' (i.e. by Marxian class analysis), and yet he remained 'sceptical about it' throughout his entire academic life (Beteille, 2007: 1–2). Why? Beteille says that 'Classes are undoubtedly important, but they are not important in the way Marx, or even, Lenin, thought them to be' (p. 9).[2] More specifically, according to him, class analysis (of Marx, Lenin and other Marxists) gives primacy to class over other divisions, so 'for this reason I have been attracted to the more open, flexible, and pluralistic approach of Max Weber' (pp. 7–8).

1.3   *Too Much Autonomy to the Economic in Class Analysis*

Sinha (2009) criticizes Marxists for treating class as an economic category, autonomous from politics and culture. He says that 'continued and insisted-upon separation of culture and identity from questions of class poses challenges to the Marxist framework in approaching contemporary movements' (Sinha, 2009: 160). Marxist class analysis reduces class to an economic concept.[3] It also fails to 'address the whole set of factors that produce subordination'; in other words, it fails to 'see the worker as embodying a range of identities that are not only not reducible to the economic, but more accurately, which allow us to unravel the cultural underpinnings of the economy' (Sinha, 2009: 171).

From a related standpoint, Herring and Agarwala (2006) say that class analysis has problematically paid much more attention to the material/economic forms of property than it should:

> [The] emphasis [in old or traditional class theory] on the material forms of property alone deflects attention from the importance of cultural capital and the role of the developmental state in distributing life chances. (p. 348)

---

understand what was happening and where India was heading, but not everyone was satisfied with it' (p. 181).

2   'The work of Marx provided the most important initial stimulus for the analysis of classes. But one has to make a distinction between the historical significance of that work and its contemporary significance' (ibid.: 12).

3   Orthodox Marxists should 'either scale back their notion of "class" so that it is not "economic" in the last instance, or ... broaden their concept of the "economic" itself' (p. 171).

1.4   *No a priori Existence of Class*

Marxism is also wrong to think of class as an a priori category, and it ignores the fact that the 'constitution' of class occurs on 'the shifting contours of an unstable and fluid socio-cultural terrain' (Sinha, 2009: 168). Sinha seems to think that class is an identity like caste or gender is (p. 163). According to Fernandes (1994), class is a contested category, one that is constituted by conflict and exclusion. As well, class analysis is said to ignore the fact that the making of class politics represents a continual process of reconstruction and conflict rather than a predefined teleology. The author says that the study of working class politics in India suffers from essentialism. Sanchez and Strumpell (2014), in a similar vein, argue for re-centering class analysis, and discuss the historically contingent emergence of Indian working classes through different types of labor, gender and ethnic struggles.

This strand of critique is continued in John Harriss (1988), who himself researches class in his empirical work on India. He appears to support the idea that 'the 'social' is not an autonomous domain but, in important respects, is created by politics' (p. 47). Harriss says: 'Western models of class are applied with great difficulty in South Asia. ... It would help, and assist the elucidation of gender and ethnic relations, to focus on the labour process [read: the struggle for a share of the social product]...rather than starting with particular concepts of class, or modes of production' (p. 51). Harriss also says that: there are 'limitations of existing paradigms and of the various ways in which essentialist constructs (like "peasant economy" or even "capitalism") have been substituted for specific contextual analysis' (p. 55).

This sort of criticism anticipates Henry Bernstein's (2007) implied – and not-so-implied criticism – of classical class theory in the context of the Global South, that informs the view of many scholars working on India:

> [T]here is no "homogeneous proletarian condition" within the "South", other than that essential condition [which is] the need to secure reproduction needs (survival) through the (direct and indirect) sale of labour power. The ways in which this is done defy inherited assumptions of fixed (and uniform) notions of "worker", "peasant", "trader", "urban", "rural", "employed" and "self-employed".

Both Harriss's and Bernstein's views of class analysis are echoed in the thinking of Gidwani, for whom class analysis is too structural and law-given: contrary to the claims of Marxism, he says, capitalism, is not a frame of economic organization based on the consistent operation of laws, but rather an assemblage of contingent and interrupted logics (Gidwani, 2008). This implies that what is

interesting about class can be figured out only locally, conjuncturally. One reason for this, one could infer, is that what is interesting about class inheres in
the cultural realm which exhibits enormous local variations, and that therefore there can be no general perspective on class.

1.5   Too Many Changes in the Working Class for Class Analysis
          to Be Useful

Subalternists argue that the erosion of the factory-based stable work has meant
that there are no workers in the traditional sense, and that no class consciousness is possible, and therefore, there is no need for class analysis (Spivak,
2000).[4] Likewise, Subir Sinha (2009) says, Marxist class analysis has not responded to the fact that the Indian work force is mobile, precarious and infor-
malized, that it is differentiated economically, and that it is also differentiated
politically (it has both party-based unions and independent unions).

1.6   Non-existent Polarization, Contrary to Class Analysis

While the previous criticism is that society has changed too much for class analysis to be useful, there is another argument according to which the society is
not changing as per the premise of class analysis. Class analysis is criticized
because its prediction of class polarization and proletarianization has been
disproved. A reason for Beteille's skepticism of class analysis is that contrary to
the prediction of Marx and Lenin, class polarization is not happening. In
fact, the anti-polarization thesis is held by those who claim to be Marxists. They
say that there is not polarization but 'partial polarization' (Byres, 1981). This is
because small-scale producers can subsist on the basis of self-exploitation,
government support, remittance money, etc. (Byres, 1981; Bhaduri, 1986; Harriss-
White and Janakarajan, 2004; see also Parthasarathy, 2015). Harriss (2011) says:

> [I]t is clear that Byres' (1981) argument that what was taking place was
> rather "partial proletarianisation", with small and marginal producers
> continuing to reproduce themselves, partly by virtue of labouring outside
> agriculture, was substantially correct.

The partial polarization ideas have even led some to say that class analysis is
too determinative in its theoretical expectation. In fact, to them, not only has
full-scale proletarianization not happened but also this fact has a political implication which is contrary to class theory: the proletariat is a small section of

---

4   On how subaltern studies is associated with the decline of class analysis, see Chibber (2006).
    For more recent work on this topic, see Brass (2017): Brass importantly refers to 'the culturalist
    displacement of class categories in India by the Subaltern Studies project' (p. 24).

the population and cannot be assigned the political importance that class analysis has given it:

> [I]n India, class struggle from below is not being led by the proletariat understood as a class fully reproduced inside a capital – labour relation. The proletariat in India is small, it is not expanding, and the main sections of it are relatively privileged when compared to the majority who are informal workers.
>
> LERCHE and SHAH, 2018: 942

Many scholars working on India take seriously Bernstein's (2007) idea that because polarization has not happened and therefore because direct producers are not wage-earners, there are 'classes of labor', indicating the absence of a 'homogenous proletarian condition'. The term, 'classes of labor', encompasses 'various and complex combinations of employment and self-employment': all those who have to earn their living on the basis of 'insecure and oppressive … wage employment and/or a range of likewise precarious small-scale and insecure, "informal sector"' (Bernstein, 2007: 6; see also Breman, 2003). If there are not many workers, it is then futile to expect class-based action. In fact, Patnaik (1999: 205–206), like Lerch and Shah (2018), says, as capitalist contradiction in India has not been deep enough, this leads to a situation where the exploited classes (poor peasants and landless agricultural laborers) are not yet a decisive majority in most regions of the country, which weakens potential organization against the exploiting classes.

1.7   *Inadequacy of Class Analysis on Political Grounds*
There are at least three types of argument here. One is that class analysis ignores class struggle outside of production as it pays too much attention to economic capital, or more generally, to economic aspects of class. Class analysis is problematic because it cannot uncover the struggles in civil society:

> Old class analysis was not so interested in these struggles in civil society. Marx himself was convinced that the point of production was decisive as a determinant of class formation and collective action.
>
> HERRING and AGARWALA, 2006: 347–348

The popularity of new social movements, as opposed to class-based movements, is taken to be indicative of the irrelevance of class-based politics and of class analysis (see Chandra and Taghioff, 2016; Omvedt, 1993). Capitalists and workers are divided into many categories, so they – and especially, workers – are not a cohesive group capable of political action.

Marxist class analysis is inadequate politically on an additional ground: Marxist attempts to offer the "centralized revolutionary party" performing 'vanguard-functions' as 'the privileged agent of mediation' are problematic (Sinha, 2009: 157). Sinha rightly says that Marxist-party managers (as in Bengal) have discouraged strike and support the capitalist path that China is following, and from this, he, however, concludes that class analysis itself is wrong (p. 158) rather than subjecting the communist movement to class analysis.

For Chakrabarti and Cullenberg (2003), contrary to class analysis, class as a social force representing class interests does not exist. There is no reason to believe that the working class can have a spark of consciousness. They are against 'any concept of a centered totality of the subject'. They are against concepts of 'false consciousness' and 'vanguard party' (p. 94). They critique the assumption in class theory that the class consciousness of the working class in line with its class interest will be a reality and that it will trickle down to individual members of that class. They say that neither the working class knows, nor the vanguard party knows, what the interests of the working class is. The objective interest cannot be the basis for any knowledge.[5] The working class does not have one subject position but many, so the subjectivity of its members cannot be reduced to a simple class interest. Yet, Chakrabarti and Cullenberg (2003) are deeply critical of the leftist program for small peasantry and labor: their argument is that the Left mistakenly thinks of these classes as being unable to act on their own and as being dependent on it for help. This argument contradicts their idea that the masses cannot correctly know their interests.

Interestingly, while some scholars say that class analysis (and indeed Marxism as such) is problematic because practicing Marxists (communists in power in Indian provinces) have acted in a way that is contrary to Marxism, according to others, class analysis crosses the boundary between analysis and action, so it is not a proper scholarly enterprise: 'Srinivas was inclined to view Marxism and class analysis as motivated by political as against scholarly interests', so he rejected class approach (quoted in Beteille, 2007: p. 3).

2   Existing Approaches to Class in India

Given all these alleged problems with class analysis, different scholars have pursued different analytical paths. Some have (almost) rejected class altogether

---

5   Then why will anyone think that post-modernists know anything about class, even if they have been involved in much academic practice (e.g. reading) and political practice (social democratic action over the redistribution of surplus)?

(e.g. Roy, 2005). This strand of thinking includes the work of those, including Srinivas, who talk about all kinds of social divisions and oppressions *but* those that are based in class.[6] There are others who have engaged in class thinking, assigning to it a variable degree of significance. In terms of the latter, there are at least four approaches which can be briefly mentioned below.[7]

2.1   *Class + (or 'Inter-sectionality' Type) Approach*

For some, class is important but it is not *that* important: class is one of several other 'things', and class-based politics is merely one among many different forms of political activity. Class is no more important as an analytical category than any other.

As in the West, often the argument, sometimes implicit and sometimes, explicit, is that: one cannot talk about class unless one talks about non-class categories such as gender or ethnicity. For example, 'There is no point to talk about class without making it clear that it is backward to talk about class without speaking about gender and race' (Yates, 2006, in Gimenez, 2018: 263). And as we have seen, similarly, Sinha (2009: 171) says that one must view the worker, 'as embodying a range of identities' that are not 'reducible to the economic'. A major problem with this sort of views is that it conflates the more abstract level at which the worker exists with the less abstract level, and it misses the point that what exists at more abstract level is real.

Critical of those who emphasize ideas at the expense of interests, Andre Beteille (2007), says that class in terms of property relations is important, but so is caste, and they are mutually irreducible. If property is important, so is education and income as well (p. 11). And he suggests that class theory must be divorced from historical materialist theory of society.

In a chapter entitled 'Class in India' in his influential *Argumentative Indian*, Amartya Sen (2006) usefully emphasizes the importance of class.[8] He thinks about 'class as a source of disparity' or of inequality (or injustice or deprivation; he uses all these terms). He says that 'class is not the only source of inequality' and that 'interest in class as a source of disparity has to be placed within a bigger picture that includes other divisive influences: gender, caste,

---

6   See the recent work on caste, which, more or less, ignores the explanatory framework of class (see: Shah et al., 2006; Sharma, 2002; Judge, 2014; Verma, 2005). On recent work on women's issues, see the collection of articles in Fernandes, 2014 (this is a 350-page book on gender which hardly has any discussion on class issues confronting women; cf. Menon, 1999a).

7   I generally focus on the literature dating from the 1990s.

8   For example, he says that: 'class is not only important on its own, it can also magnify the impact of other contributors to inequality' (Sen, 2006: 206).

region, community and so on' (Sen, 2006: 205). Using a language that is close to the language of intersectionality, Sen says: one should treat different forms of inequality together, making more explicit room for their extensive *interdependencies*' and 'their *complementarity*' (p. 205; italics added). He argues for an '*integrated* understanding of the functioning of class *in alliance* with other causes of injustice' (ibid.; italics added). He talks about: 'interactive presence' of different features of deprivation (e.g. class and gender) (p. 207).

Just as Sen subsumes class to inequality (or injustice or deprivation), other scholars subsume it under marginality: economic deprivation (a proxy for class); dispossession and non-class relations constitute marginalities (Bhattacharyya and Basu, 2018). Or, to elaborate on this point: hunger + forcible land acquisitions + material deprivation of minority groups and tribes + caste discrimination + regional disparities + gendered forms of exclusion, etc. = marginalities.

There is a large amount of literature which treats class, more or less explicitly, in terms of its interaction/intersection with non-class relations: class is seen in the 'multiple matrices of inequality' mode of thinking. For example, Thara (2016) says that as a concept, intersectionality is important to understand how gender is intertwined with experiences that derive from, and shape, caste and class. Focusing on the subjectivities of Dalits across India and on their continued socio-economic and political marginalization, Anandhi and Kapadia (2017) explore what they call the political economy of gender, caste and class in India. Chakrabarti (2001) talks about the inter-connection between the social power wielded by members of the dominant land-owning caste of the capitalist class, and about how class and social power are conditioned by caste. Heller and Fernandes (2006) integrate class analysis with the politics of caste, religion, and language. Lerche and Shah (2018) expand Philippe Bourgois's concept of conjugated oppression 'to express how multiple axes of oppression based on social relations such as race/caste/tribe/ethnicity/ region or gender and sexuality, etc. are co-constitutive of and shape class relations, potentially producing extreme relations of oppression, inseparable from each other in capitalist accumulation' (p. 931).[9] Similarly, in the context of informal workers, Agarwala (2019) talks about the 'intersectional nature of class, caste, and gender identities' (p. 410).

Fernandes (1994) says that the structural and ideological/cultural components of class are constructed through the politics of gender and community. Chatterjee (2012) points to the existence of an assemblage in an Indian city,

---

9   They add that: 'For India we argue that the spread of capitalism has been marked by class
       relations that are mutually constituted with caste, tribe, gender and region-based oppres-
       sion' (p. 951).

where gender, class, caste and ethnicity intersect in myriad ways creating pos-sibilities for resistance (see also Clarke, 2017; Kapadia, 1997; Velaskar, 2016). All the discussion on so-called 'caste-class dominance', more or less, speaks to the intersectionality mode of thinking without necessarily assigning any primacy to class (Frankel, 1994; Harriss, 2013).

2.2   *The Post-modern-Marxist Approach to Class*

While there is much in this approach that one can agree with (e.g. the empha-sis on the surplus value appropriation in the conceptualization of capitalist class relation), there is a lot that is simply troublesome. Influenced by Stephen Resnick and Richard Wolff, as well as Barry Hirst and Ernst Laclau, Chakrabarti and Cullenberg (2003), commenting on the Indian mode of production, ar-gue against the property-relations-focused definition of class. They say that class must be seen solely in terms of the appropriation of surplus labor. The capitalist class, like the working class, is disaggregated in terms of process of performance, appropriation, distribution, and receipts of surplus value. Those (e.g. toy manufacturers) receive surplus value and are productive capitalists. Money-lenders, merchants or landlord capitalists receive a part of this surplus value and are called unproductive capitalists. An individual can be both ex-ploiter and exploited.

2.3   *A Weaker, Agency-Based, Approach to Class*

Those who subscribe to what I advisedly call a weaker, agency-based theory of class emphasize the importance of class, but they make important criticisms of classical class theory of Marx, and argue for a less ambitious class analysis.

Critical of Marxism's focus on economic aspects capital, there is an attempt to add to 'economic capital', social and cultural capitals, on the basis of Bour-dieu's theory (Upadhya, 1997; see also Jeffrey et al., 2005).

Herring and Agarwala (2006) do emphasize the significance of class very well:

> Class analysis always takes the material world seriously.... [Class] is never simply a construction or an imaginary. Class structures relations among people; these relations are critical for understanding not only life chanc-es, but also political behavior. (p. 324)

They go on to add that:

> Class structure defines positions for individuals, based on their relation-ship to economic assets; these class positions in turn differentiate

objective material interests: landlords and tenants, workers and owners. Under certain conditions, these interests may be recognized, mobilized, and acted upon – thus ultimately explaining collective action in which people attempt to improve their life chances through politics and policy: land reform, minimum wages, welfare transfers, income redistribution. (p. 331)

But there is a need to do class analysis differently, according to the two authors. This means that: 'Uncovering mechanisms takes priority, and the uncovering must be an *empirical process*. How do things actually work?' (p. 347; italics added). The mechanisms in question are, however, not the causal mechanisms that lie in social relations, as causal mechanisms, ultimately, should: they are not structural mechanisms. Rather: 'Mechanisms focus attention on *agency* of historical actors' (e.g. informal workers), and this would allow 'recovering in the process human agency' (Herring and Agarwala, 2006: 347; italics added). But the agency is not a macro-scale agency. It operates at the local scale: 'At the micro level, where all of us live, are the day-to-day practices through which classes define and reproduce themselves' (ibid.). So, the implication is that: classes are how classes define themselves and not given a priori, i.e. prior to how individuals think and behave empirically.[10]

Given that most of the workers in India work in the informal sector without government benefits, it is important to notice the ways in which they engage in struggles:

> The informal economy illustrates the necessity of original class analysis and possibilities for *rethinking theory*. It is not that informal-sector workers fail to organize for class interests, but rather that new structures of production alter their strategies.
>
> HERRING and AGARWALA, 2006: 346; see also ROY CHOWDHURY, 2015; italics added

And the struggle of the classes happens in the sphere of civil society, locally, in communities and local institutions, and they have important material effects. Informally employed workers are not permanently employed in a place, so they struggle for government benefits rather than for higher wages and better working conditions from their employers. The old class theory has ignored

---

10   This appears to contradict their own view that 'Class structure defines positions for indi-
      viduals, based on their relationship to economic assets' (ibid.).

these struggles over benefits outside of production, the struggles where class interests intersect with non-class identities:

> In pursuing these ends [in civil society], individuals are strategic, and objects of larger strategies; struggles often take highly euphemized forms, as in struggles over caste, identity, and culture, that are then often interpreted as Indian exceptionalism.
>
> HERRING and AGARWALA, 2006: 348

Given all this, there is said to be a need to *rethink* class theory:

> In recovering class, we find a useful rethinking of the deductivist and macro-historical logic of dominant versions of European class analytics.
>
> [...] We find that complexities of class structures, and their interpretations from specific class positions, necessitate a less determinative intellectual architecture than The Communist Manifesto. (p. 347)

And, rethinking the old class theory leads to the conclusion that: the gap between the Marxist relational approach and Weber's gradational approach is less than it is thought to be:

> Class analytics itself can and does evoke theological permutations among pure theorists, but the essential perspective is both straightforward and commonsensical. Though much has been made of distinguishing Marxian from Weberian class analysis, for example, both emphasize the primacy of economic assets as differentiating people across classes.
>
> HERRING and AGARWALA, 2006: 324

So, in the weaker version of class theory, several inter-related claims are made. (1) Marxism does not have the specificity vis-à-vis Weberianism. This is a conclusion that the late Erik Wright, a well-known class theorist, reaches (see Wright, 2015: Chapter 1). (2) Class theory must give up on its greater analytical ambition (be 'less determinative'), as 'bold claims to a universalist framework making strong predictions rendered class theory uniquely vulnerable' (Herring and Agarwala, 2006: 351). This is also a conclusion that Wright reaches (see Wright, 2015).[11] (3) Class analysis must be less theoretical (more 'commonsensical'), according to Herring and Agarwala and similar other authors such as

---

11   See Chapter 2 in Das (2017a) for a detailed presentation of Wright's class theory, and Chapter 4 for a comprehensive critique.

Beteille for whom class analysis must be divorced from the wider historical-materialist theory of society. (4) Correspondingly, class analysis must be more oriented towards the local scale and the everyday life, and it must be more agency-focused. Marxism is also obsessed with the nation as the stage of politics (p. 163) apparently ignoring the local scale struggles. (5) Much more attention needs to be paid to workers who are not stably employed (who are informally employed) and to their struggles, *outside* of production/workplace, over state-benefits.

2.4   *A Multi-class Approach to Class*

In this approach, there are many different classes (and not just many different fractions of a class), beyond the two-class model of class analysis, and they have different life experiences and opportunities and levels of living, etc. So class (as an analytical category, as a thought-object) matters because class*es* matter in the real world. The obverse of the stress on the multiplicity of classes is the idea that class polarization does not happen as quickly as class theory has predicted.

Thorner (1973) talks about the rural society in terms of: malik (big land-owners), mazdoor (workers), kisan (peasants). In part influenced by Lenin and Mao, there is a lot of empirical work that has revealed how in different areas a multiplicity of classes exists. Utsa Patnaik, a prominent Indian political economist, uses what she calls labor exploitation index to produce an analytical map of many different classes that the rural society is divided into.[12] This can be, and has been, useful to understand how different classes have different kinds of economic experience (including opportunities for accessing credit).

To the extent that class position can be determined at the family level, a family's class position is a function of the following apart from its ownership of

---

12   The index measures the extent of the use of outside labor or conversely the extent of working for others, relative to the extent of self-employment. The index for a household is defined as:

$E = [(HI-HO) + (LO-LI)]/F$, where,

   E = exploitation index;

   HI = Labor days hired on property including leased-in property. (Labor is defined as manual labor);

   HO = Family labor days hired out to others;

   LO = Family and hired labor days used on leased-out property;

   LI = Labor days similarly worked on leased-in property;

   F = Labor days worked by the household on its property, including leased-in property, is an indicator of self-employment. The index is a ratio which can be positive or negative depending on whether the household is a net employer of outside labor or is itself on balance working for others.

property: available quantity of family labor deployed in production; quantity of work the family does for other members of society for a wage (which could vary between zero and a positive number); and the quantity of work other members of society perform for the family (Patnaik, 1999, 1987). Given these conditions, there can be, as Patnaik shows: a multiplicity of classes. Landlords perform no manual labor in self-employment and they employ others. Rich peasants are involved in as large an employment of others as self-employment. Middle peasant are involved in smaller employment of others' labor than self-employment. Small peasants do not employ others and they either do not work for others, or they work for others to a smaller extent than self-employment. Poor peasants work for others to a greater extent than self-employment. Landless laborers are not self-employed and they work entirely for others (Patnaik, 1999: 236). Landlords and rich peasants are primarily exploiting others. Middle and small peasants are neither exploited nor do they exploit: they are mainly self-employed. Poor peasants and landless laborers are primarily exploited by others.

Bhaduri's (1983) class map has fewer classes than Patnaik's: agricultural capitalist class; money-lending and merchant class; small peasantry (including those who work as part-time wage-earners); and farm labor. For Rudra (1988), a class refers to a group of people defined in terms of their common relation to the means of production, who have a non-antagonistic relation among themselves, and who have an antagonistic relation with members of other classes. There may be conflict of interest within a class, but that is less important than inter-class conflict in interest. In the rural context, on the one hand, there are big landlords (including rich peasants, capitalist farmers and feudal landowners) who constitute the ruling class, and whose power comes from the ownership of productive resources, and on the other, there are laborers (including those who may own small amounts of land) who are the subordinate class. While the latter class exists in an objective sense, they lack class consciousness, because of the geographical isolation of the members of this class from one another.

Similarly, Rudolph and Rudolph (1987: 341) talk about bullock capitalists: they are the self-employed commercial owner-cultivators, with land holdings large enough to support a pair of bullocks (in the 1970s). They are neither capitalists nor workers. They are neither exploiters nor the exploited. They hold more land than any other 'land-holding class' in rural areas. Mention may be made of the view of a liberal political scientist, Ashutosh Varshney. Varshney (1994) talks about class (e.g. farmers as a class), but his view of class is primarily based on the exchange relations as opposed to the production/property relations. *Exploitation* of labor is not a part of Varshney's class mapping. Production for *market* is (see Das, 2001a).

Inspired by Patnaik and Bernstein, Pattenden (2006) divides the rural society in India into two main groups in terms of class: net buyers of labor power,
who include the dominant (capitalist) class, and net-sellers of labor power (or
'classes of labor').[13]

While much of class analysis has been about rural areas, Pranab Bardhan
(1999) talks about the India's class system at the national scale. On his class
map are three proprietary classes (urban bourgeoisie; large-scale landowners;
and state elites appropriating scarce rent from their education).

Recently, there has been much talk about the middle class or middle classes
(Fernandes, 2016). Their consumption and income potential are stressed, in
part thanks to economic growth in new sectors of the post-1991 economy (e.g.
Information Technology; financial services). It is said that while a Brahmin will
remain a Brahmin, a poor person can join the middle class (Jodhka et al., 2017).

2.5   Dispossession Studies Approach to Class

A large amount of literature which looks like class analysis and/or which has
something to do with class, has become a study of dispossession. Dispossession, more or less, refers to, the coercive processes in which small-scale producers and those engaged in natural economy are losing access to their means
of production (mainly, land); it can also refer to the privatization of state-
owned companies.[14] Dispossession happens because businesses need the land
held by the small-scale producers, individually or in common, for both production of goods and services, mining, and real estate (including, speculation), or
because big dams, often constructed in the agrarian and urban capitalist class
interests, inundate the land, forcing the inhabitants to leave. Dispossession,
much of which happens in areas of indigenous communities, is seen by some
as internal colonization of the poor (Walker, 2008; see Das, 2019c). In so far as
dispossession has come to be associated with neoliberalism, Chakrabarti
(2009) says that neoliberalism is a tool to obtain the (post) colonial hegemony

---

13   Net buyers include: the dominant class (a proxy for the capitalist class which has eco-
       nomic and political power) consisting of all those who produce a surplus and who culti-
       vate their land solely or mainly by hired labor. Net buyers also include petty capitalists
       and petty commodity producers, who produce some surplus; they are primarily
       self-employed but they also hire some labor. Then there are pure petty commodity pro-
       ducers who produce no surplus, and use only family labor. Finally, the net sellers of labor
       power include: all those who are mainly self-employed but they also sell labor power;
       those who sell labor power to a greater extent than they are self-employed, and those who
       live only by selling their labor power (p. 24).
14   There are simply too many of these studies to cite here (see, for example, Doshi and
       Ranganathan, 2017; Fernandez, 2018; Levien, 2018; Sugden and Punch, 2014; Whitehead,
       2010). Most of the literature is critical, except for a few which argue that the effects are
       good or can be good (see Ghertner, 2014; Moberg, 2015; Paul and Sarma, 2017).

of capital over the small-scale sector. The literature on dispossession has shed light, even if it is very repetitive now, on an important aspect of capitalist class society: the fact of dispossession and struggles against dispossession.

3   A Critique of Existing Approaches to Class in India

3.1   *Is Class Just One among Many 'Things'?*

It is absolutely important to emphasize oppression based on caste,[15] gender, indigeneity, and other relations. But the idea that class is one that just intersects with these relations of oppression, and that one person may therefore experience all these relations, does not advance analysis much.[16] The question that is not posed is this: what is precisely the logic of interaction/intersection? Why do the class relations, and why do the different non-class relations exist, and why do they (have to) interact?[17] Besides, as Gimenez (2017) says: 'Intersectionality, by stressing identity divisions, unwittingly undermines the possibility of workers uniting across gender, race and other differences, thus strengthening the status quo' (p. 451). At the level of Indian capitalism, capitalists of different castes will all behave as capitalists prioritizing profit-making. Of course, in any given concrete situation the ways in which class relations and class processes affect a person's life are mediated by discrimination and oppression based on caste, gender, religion, etc. and corresponding ideologies and politics. Of course, 'a concrete organization of class is impossible minus historical, cultural, sexual and political relations' (Bannerji, 1995: 31). But all these facts do not mean that class mechanisms do not have any primacy.

It *is absolutely* useful and necessary to highlight that many women, low caste people, Muslims and indigenous groups are not benefitting from

---

15   On atrocities against Dalits, see Teltumbde (2010). He talks about the need for 'trans-caste unity of all the lower-classes of society' (p. 186).

16   This is the case, even if it appears to emphasize an important principle of dialectics: what a process is, it is because of its relation to many other processes.

17   It is not enough to say that X and Y interact; one must say why do X and Y exist in the first place, and why does the reality appear to be divided into X and Y? Why does a Brahmin oppress a Dalit (an ex-untouchable person/group in India's caste hierarchy) or why does a Hindu hate a Muslim? Are there social-material conditions underlying social oppression at the level of *society as a whole*, the logic of which then trickles down to the level of individuals and groups, in order to shape their behavior? And why is it that incidence of certain kinds of oppression (e.g. discrimination against Muslims) increase at a certain point in time (say, early 1990s and especially in the last 5 years or so) and why does the incidence of oppression (against Dalits) tend to be concentrated in specific areas? To what extent might the explanation lie in the historical and geographical character of capitalist class relation?

economic development and social policy and that they are subjected to deplorable levels of discrimination with their democratic rights disrespected routinely. But such an emphasis on social oppression *outside* of class relations fails to seriously consider the following idea: the unequal and oppressive relation between men and women, or between castes and religions, is not the fundamental reason why women, low castes, and religious minorities are experiencing an attack on their lives as workers, although such relationship may explain why some workers (e.g. upper caste male workers) live better than other workers (e.g. female Dalit workers). The fundamental reason why their basic needs remain unfulfilled lies in what the toiling masses of different castes and religions and what both men and women workers have in common: class relations.

Many can agree that class is important, but class is said to be one among many social forces. One can have different entry points in social analysis, so one may start with class, or with caste, or gender, etc. There is no necessary reason for any given entry point, and there is no necessary reason for the primacy of class. However, to refuse to assign primacy to class is to refuse to agree that productive activity is crucial to life, and that productive activity is a social activity that happens in class-structured ways, which means that a tiny minority own and control the use of productive resources, while the majority do not do so, and are, therefore, economically forced to surrender a large part of what they produce to the minority-class supported by the class state. Therefore, it is un-dialectical to reject, or ignore, the following idea: in the lives of a working class person (or of a small-scale producer), class mechanisms relate to non-class mechanisms in a system within which class mechanisms have a degree of causal primacy. It is mistaken to think that class is just one of several categories such as caste, gender, indigeneity, etc. Class is *the* social relation that fundamentally structures the lives of men, women and children, even though it is not the only relationship that counts.

3.2   Is the Two-Class Model, Including the Thesis of Class Polarization, Irrelevant?

It is true that the two-class model of class analysis does not necessarily reflect the concrete empirical reality: there are many more classes than capitalists and workers in India which is experiencing 'belated' capitalist development in a post-colonial context, and this is especially so given that the majority of the population lives in rural areas. Closely associated with the two-class model is the idea of polarization and proletarianization, as indicated earlier.

The two-class model represents class mechanisms at a more abstract level. The model's aim is not to map out – count – what are the different classes on the ground or indeed how quickly a class of commodity producers is being class-differentiated. Its aim is to supply the mechanisms of a class society, including class differentiation among commodity producers, and to show how these mechanisms can be modified by counter-tendencies (as explained later). The tendency towards class polarization and proletarianization can be countered by many processes (e.g. self-exploitation, use of remittance from wage-work in the city, welfare from the capitalist state, etc.). But then all these counter-mechanisms are not unrelated to class (as explained below). So, how is class analysis invalid if polarization is slower than expected in class analysis? Even then, as Basu shows: the relative size of the middle class is shrinking (see Table 2.1), and this implies that, since the size of the ruling class has remained more or less constant, some sections of what is called the middle class are being pushed down into the working class. Arguably, this is consistent with the polarization thesis.

It is true that a person who is an agricultural labor in the village can also be a seasonal migrant in the city. But this fact poses problems for Marxist class analysis and class-based action (Sinha, 2009: 167–168), *only if* the main or sole concern of class analysis, including the two-class model, is to figure out which individual belongs to which class. But such a fact does not pose any problem for class analysis if the latter is about uncovering class processes and relations, which give rise to classes as large groups of people. Neither is class analysis invalidated by the fact that some people who must depend on the sale of their labor power, called middle class people (e.g. professors, journalists, etc.), are much more educated and earn much more than an average worker, and have a degree of control over their conditions of work. After all, they also operate within the logics of commodity economy and profit-seeking capitalism, and they are also being subjected to proletarianization.

In part responding to the inadequacy of the two-class model, some scholars talk about how a given class has a different experience from another class. To examine this matter is useful but it is still inadequate. Once again, to talk about class should be more about class relation giving rise to large groups of people than about figuring out how many of these large groups exist, which individuals belong to which class, and how they behave.

TABLE 2.1   Class structure in India (percentage share in population)

	1993–94	2004–05
Ruling class	11.89	11.71
Middle class	24.26	21.08
Working class	63.85	67.21

SOURCE: BASU (2009)

As we have seen, many say that there is only partial proletarianization. Not only does that criticism ignore the polarization idea as a class-based tendency. It fails to note that proletarianization is a concept that concerns class, and not a concept that concerns sectors or sub-sectors. Just because a person having lost her/his productive assets in market processes does not work in, say, agriculture but works part-time in the city (as a waitress in a restaurant or as a lightboy in Bollywood), that does not mean that she/he is *partially* proletarianized.

Given all this, it is therefore mistaken to say as many do (e.g. Herring and Agarwala, or Beteille, etc.) that classes are important, but not in the way Marx, or even, Lenin, thought them to be. In other words, what they are saying is that class analysis is not that important because polarization is not happening at the pace predicted or that it is not happening in a given sector (e.g. farming). The criticism that class polarization does not (quite) happen is an age-old criticism against class analysis. During Lenin's time, 'the revisionists were systematically painting a rose-colored picture of modern small-scale production' (Lenin, 1908), and this trend of revisionist thinking, including within some version of Marxism, unfortunately, continues. The criticism against class polarization appears to be from the standpoint of small-scale owners in a class society. Lenin (1908) writes about those who critique the class polarization idea:

> From the political point of view, they sinned by the fact that they inevitably, whether they wanted to or not, invited or urged the peasant to adopt the attitude of a small proprietor (i.e., the attitude of the bourgeoisie) instead of urging him to adopt the point of view of the revolutionary proletarian.

To reiterate a point made above, it is true that the two-class model cannot reflect an empirical reality and that in India, there are peasants of different classes, and there are workers, rent-appropriating landowners, and capitalists. It is also true that while the dominant form of exchange involved in surplus-producing activities is based on equal exchange in the market, there are also coercive unequal exchanges. But none of this invalidates class analysis at all because all those things are parts of class analysis.

3.3   Is Class Mainly about Dispossession?

As I have said, a large amount of literature which has something to do with class has focused on dispossession. Much of this literature has been influenced by the highly problematic approach of David Harvey to capitalism and dispossession (Das, 2017b for a theoretical critique). Many of the underlying ideas in this literature are simply flawed. One of them is that: the emphasis on the exploitative relation between property owners and the property-less has been, more or less, replaced by the emphasis on the coercive relations between the dispossessor and the dispossessed.[18] And consequently, analysis of class struggle has more or less become one of anti-dispossession struggles. Some even mistakenly claim that Indian workers are not the most important anti-capitalist agent; it is the farmers fighting against dispossession who are (Levien, 2012). For this claim to be true something else must be true: that capital-labor contradiction is not the main contradiction in India. And *that* is not true.

The literature on dispossession (implicitly) recognizes that class is about differential control over property. This is useful. But what is generally forgotten is that there is a world of difference not only between property for personal use and property for accumulation purpose (Subramanian, 2008) but also between property based on family labor and property based on the exploitation of wage-labor. As well, in this literature, it is as if the main class process is one where the capitalist class is forcing the masses to surrender their physical property (e.g. land).

One must ask: if small-scale producers are allowed to keep their property in a society dominated by capitalist market relations, how long will they be able to hold on to their property, given the class-based differentiation? Much class analysis as dispossession analysis also assumes that there is a capitalism that is imperfect and that needs to be perfected through restrictions on dispossession (see Brass, 2011; and Das, 2017b). A focus on primitive accumulation (along with unfree labor) as coercive aspects of capitalism means that: 'what is on the political agenda is a transition not to socialism but – still – to a "fully-functioning" capitalism' (Brass, 2011: 2).

Just like the class analysis that critiques the polarization thesis, the class-analysis-as-dispossession is, objectively speaking, mounted from the standpoint of small-scale property owners, and not the proletariat. To the extent that the literature on dispossession does raise the issue of class, it does this by ignoring crucial issues concerning class: exploitative production relations.

So: as in the West, so in India, class analysis (and attendant political economy) has really become the analysis of dispossession and anti-dispossession

---

18   In a book that seeks to connect caste to capitalism and globalization, Tumbde (2010) says: globalization is 'the intensified extension of the capitalist project' and that it is 'a phase of capitalism seeking to extend capitalist relations across the world economy' (p. 174). And what is capitalism? It is a process of 'accumulation by dispossession' (p. 32). This mistaken claim reduces capitalism as a class relation to a part of what it is about (dispossession) (Das, 2017b).

struggles at the expense of other aspects of class. The dispossession literature really dispossesses the theory of class of some of its analytical power.

3.4   Is Class Merely about Economic Inequality?

Amartya Sen (2006) says 'interest in class as a source of disparity has to be placed within a bigger picture that includes other divisive influences: gender, caste, region, community and so on' (p. 205). The question is: how should we *conceptualize*, and what should we *call*, that 'bigger picture'? If it is inequality (or injustice), or some such thing, there is a real danger of stripping class of its explanatory specificity and power. Class is not just an abstract form of inequality or injustice. What *is* the logic explaining why class is only a part of that bigger picture rather than class being *that* bigger picture? What is it that connects the two groups, or many groups, among whom inequality is said to exist? It is also interesting that Amartya Sen, who insists that the capitalist market relation must unavoidably continue to exist,[19] talks about inequality, as if inequality is not the logical outcome of the capitalist market relation and the processes it is associated with?

3.5   Is Class Analysis Merely about This or That Issue in
the Economic Sphere?

Ignoring class as a context – class character of state and society – leads many scholars to take not only a quantitative approach to class (identifying multiple classes) but also a 'sectoral' approach to class, which explores a class approach to this or that issue, outside of an overall class-theoretical approach to society as such. For example, Amartya Sen's (2006) idea is that public programs can fight against 'class-based inequality' and can even succeed in 'overcoming class divisions in the economic, social and political progress' (p. 218). Sen assumes that it is only society, or economy, that is class-divided but that the class-neutral state can overcome class divisions in society. Therefore, Sen's view effectively amounts to a rejection of two fundamental principles of class

---

19   Sen (2002) asks: 'can those less-well-off groups get a better deal from globalized economic and social relations without dispensing with the market economy itself?' His answer: 'They certainly can'.
The Nobel laureate then goes on to produce more strident defense of capitalism, which he euphemistically calls the market: 'The central question is not whether to use the market economy. That shallow question is easy to answer, because it is hard to achieve economic prosperity without making extensive use of the opportunities of exchange and specialization that market relations offer. Even though the operation of a given market economy can be significantly defective, there is no way of dispensing with the institution of markets in general as a powerful engine of economic progress' (ibid.).

theory: (a) there cannot be *class equality*,[20] (b) that the lack of effective control over state's coercive and powers is an aspect of classness of the toilers, and (c) that the capitalist state cannot overcome class divisions because its own class nature will, more or less, preordain it to maintain the class divisions. Herring and Agarwala (2006) have useful things to say about class and yet they also believe that old class theory's stress on the material forms of property deflects attention from 'the developmental state in distributing life chances' (p. 348). It is not, of course, outside of class analysis to examine welfare schemes. But they need to be seen in terms of their *class* character: the logic of their origin, implementation and effects is all dominantly shaped by the overall logic of capitalist class relations. Heller's (2000) highly optimistic claims (e.g. pp. 115, 140) about the favourable relation between the state/bureaucracy in Kerala and lower-class struggles, often come close to the view that the capitalist state could operate as an instrument of the lower classes. All these claims are far removed from much of the Marxist debate about class and the state, which has shown among other things, how the structure of the capitalist state and bourgeois democracy, in fact, weaken working class struggle (Das, 1996; Das, 2017a: Chapter 9; Clarke, 1991). If the reification of constraints is theoretically and politically unacceptable, an idealist approach to the enabling conditions is no less so.

Class analysis is about the overall context in which all the different classes operate in their mutual political-economic relation. While Sen sees the ability of the state to help the lower classes in significant ways, others talk about the capitalist class constraining the state (Chibber, 2003). This view is also problematic from the standpoint of class theory: even if the capitalist class does not act, there is the court, there is the army, and there are bourgeois ideas, to keep the class order going. To say that the capitalist class constrains the state is to miss the fundamental fact that the capitalist class and the state are two sides of the same coin, two arms of the same body, which is the class context or the class relation. Class analysis is much more than about how two or more classes behave in their economic interests. Class analysis is about the entire class society, including the class state.

---

20   'As long as there is exploitation there cannot be equality' (Lenin, 1919). More specifically, the capitalist or 'the landowner cannot be the equal of the worker, or the hungry man the equal of the full man' (ibid.). Therefore, class inequality, as a term, cannot have an antonym, which would be class equality.

3.6   *Is Class Not about Property?*

Post-modernists (e.g. Chakrabarti and Cullenberg) think about class only in terms of transfer of fruits of surplus labor (including between family members), and for them, ownership of property or anything else does not count. Their concept of exploitation is deeply a-historical as is their tendency to avoid the question of who owns property in the means of production. Underlying their view of class, is a social-democratic consciousness: the emphasis on surplus extraction means that property ownership of the capitalist class should not be a matter of challenge, and that class struggle is about putting pressure on capitalists so they can share the surplus a bit more with workers (i.e. reduce the rate of surplus appropriation) (for detailed discussion and critique of the postmodernist-Marxist theory of class at a general level, and not in an Indian context, see Das, 2017a: Chapters 3–4).

3.7   *Does the State of Class Politics Suggest a Weakness in Class Analysis?*

Some say that class conflict is only one of many different types of conflict (gender-based conflict, caste conflict, etc.) and therefore has no special significance. Others say that class politics is missing or is not very developed (as indicated by the fact that a small percentage of workers is unionized and that communist parties have only a few Members of the Parliament). So class is not a useful category. Some (e.g. post-modernists) say that there can be no such thing as a class actor as a given class can have multiple identities: in other words, there is no a priori class interest as an objective reality and that one cannot expect workers and other classes to act in their class interests. It is also said that the traditional class analysis is too much focused on work-place politics and that Marx himself had this idea (Herring and Agarwala, 2006).

First of all, it is a profound misinterpretation of Marx when Herring and Aggarwal (2016) say this: 'Marx himself was convinced that the point of production was decisive as a determinant of class formation and collective action' (pp. 347–348). Marx – and Marxist class analysis – has always been for class struggle in different spheres. Marx says that while struggle in a given workplace over wages and working day is more economic in character, the struggle for a legislation that forces all capitalists to reduce the working day, is of a political character, and he encouraged this. Similarly, in an article called 'Political indifferentism', Marx (2010) argued against anyone ('apostles of political indifferentism') who would think that workers should not fight for state spending 'to give primary education' to their children on the ground that 'primary education is not complete education' (p. 327). He was always for workers to fight for reforms, but he also argued that there are significant limits to what is possible to achieve within capitalism (Das, 2019). In India, workers have engaged in struggles in the workplace and struggles outside.

Secondly, it is mistaken to deny any connection between political activity and class: political activity *is* prompted by class interests and class relations (including trade union struggle) and this always happens. India regularly experiences trade union struggles (see Chapter 7). And in India, a Maoism-influenced movement of small-scale producers and aboriginal peoples is going on for decades (see Chapters 8–9). So, workers and peasants *do* oppose the system, however inadequately. So class analysis does matter from that angle. Class politics is not missing.

Thirdly, to the extent that class politics is not seen more recurrently and more powerfully, it is once again class (class relations and class processes) that explains it. These mechanisms include the influence of bourgeois class and its state on the ideas that circulate in society, and all the coercive and other reactions to lower-class struggle from the capitalists class and its state (explained in the next section). So class analysis matters here as well. When some say that class politics is not happening, they have a narrow view of class and class politics. Indeed, everything that the capitalist class and its state do to respond to lower-class struggle and/or to pre-empt it, is indeed class struggle – it is class struggle from above. Lower classes in India struggle, but they struggle under conditions which they do not always choose.

There is, generally, an inverse relation between the power of lower classes and that of exploiting/dominant classes. When class struggle from below does not seem to happen, it means that the dominant class is winning in the class battle (however, temporarily), in its struggle from above. Class struggle is always in the form of struggle from below and struggle from above. It is important to re-emphasize this: to say that class is not important, because class struggle does not happen much or it does not happen in the way theory 'predicts', is to forget that class is the reason for that!

3.8 *Is Class Analysis Really about the Local Scale and Everyday Life?*

Some say that old class analysis has a deductivist and macro-view. This not only means that class analysis must focus on agency. It is also to prioritize the need to understand how class works at the local and regional level (e.g. Gujarat). It is important that we understand how class mechanisms are played out at the local level. But an emphasis on the local scale can potentially ignore the fact that the regional/national scale is not given, that it is not a class-neutral thing: it is created and reproduced by the capitalist class relation. Capitalism produces uneven development whereby some areas are more developed than others, and it is the context in which multiple scales (national, regional, etc.) exist, and this production of scales and unevenness is a precondition for different class mechanisms operating differently in different ways. So the fact that different mechanisms operate in different areas is not indicative of the autonomy of processes at the local scale vis-à-vis the capitalist class relation. So uncovering how class mechanisms work at the local/regional scale presupposes uncovering how that scale is produced via tendencies towards capitalist uneven development.

4   Constructing a Class-Based Framework

In the light of my criticisms against the criticisms of class analysis and my criticisms against certain ways in which class analysis has been conducted, what is attempted below is a very basic outline of what class analysis should be. It, of course, partially, builds on existing ideas about class that are defensible.

4.1   *Class as a Relation/Process Producing Large Groups of People*
In class analysis, it *is* important to talk about individual classes and their mutual differences. I have indicated the existence of much existing research on this topic. I might mention here the excellent work done by Basu (2009). Building on Vakulabharanam et al. (2009), Basu (2009) comes up with the following class-map. Ruling classes are the owners or managers of the formal and informal sector enterprises and the rich farmers. The working class is composed of the unskilled workers in manufacturing and services, the small and marginal peasants and the landless laborers. And finally, what Basu calls the middle class consists of two main segments: '(a) the petty bourgeoisie, who largely own their means of production: middle peasants in agriculture, the merchants, the traders, and the owner-operators of small enterprises, and (b) the professionals: the technical experts, the managers, and the skilled workers in large-scale private enterprises, and the large majority of the employees of the State sector'. Basically, according to Basu, the middle class consists of professionals and skilled workers in manufacturing and services, middle peasants, rural professionals, and moneylenders.[21] Whether one agrees that everyone in

---

21   Conceptually, the 'middle class' is defined by Basu (2014) by the following two characteristics: '(1) this class is the recipient of a part of the economic surplus, i.e., the total compensation earned by the middle-class is higher than the value of its labour power (i.e., the cost of producing and reproducing the labour power); and (2) the middle class is crucial for the reproduction of the existing social relations in India which is what fetches it the extra income', i.e., the income above the value of its labour power, in the form of rent from the ruling classes. There are two main segments of the middle class: (a) the petty bourgeoisie, who largely own their means of production: middle peasants in agriculture, the merchants, the traders, and the owner-operators of small enterprises, and (b) the professionals: the technical experts, the managers, and the skilled workers in large-scale private enterprises, and the large majority of the employees of the State sector.

the middle class position receives more than the value of their labor power, one can get at least a rough overview of the class structure of India from Basu's class analysis.

However, the examination of how many classes exist, what their relative size is, how different groups within the working class (or another class) experience life differently, or how workers live in poorer conditions than rich property owners, must be a part of a larger consideration in which the emphasis should be given to the fact that there is class as a relationship and as a complex set of processes operating at multiple levels of society (see below), that affects politics, economy and culture and how we relate to nature and to one another. It is *that* relationship that underlies how classes, class-fractions and individuals of specific classes of different modes of production including capitalism, as well as state agencies and state elites, function or do not function and how they exercise their agency or how they do not or how they seem not to.

To repeat: class *is* a *relationship* and a *process*. Or, it is a structure of – sum total of – relationships among classes, and processes connecting them. What one class is, it is because of its relations to other classes.[22] Class analysis is about the overall context in which all the different classes operate in their mutual relation. It is about:

> *the sum total* of the relations between absolutely all the classes in a given society, and consequently a consideration of the objective stage of development reached by that society and of the relations between it and other societies.
>
> LENIN, 1914; italics added

Class as a relationship and as a process are materialized – expressed in the form of – large groups of men, women and children called classes. As Lenin (1919) famously said:

> Classes are large groups of people differing from each other by the place they occupy in a historically determined system of social production, by their relation (in most cases fixed and formulated in law) to the means of production, by their role in the social organisation of labor, and, consequently, by the dimensions of the share of social wealth of which they dispose and the mode of acquiring it. Classes are groups of people one of

---

22   A given class, and a system of classes, stands for, and is, a relationship, in the same way that not only is capital related to labor, but also is capital a relationship itself. In one meaning of relationship, X and Y are related, and in another meaning of relationship, X itself and Y itself is a relationship (see Ollman, 2003).

which can appropriate the labor of another owing to the different places they occupy in a definite system of social economy.

The relations between classes, as large groups of people, sets up certain mechanisms (e.g. competition, technological change, exploitation, etc.) which produce certain effects (e.g. unemployment, massive accumulation of wealth, etc.) which are experienced by an entire class, its fractions and individuals of given classes.

To say that class has effects is to say, for example, that class relations enable and constrain the condition for economic development and redistribution of the social product, with implications for poverty. As Marx himself maintained, and as many Marxists have argued since, class relations can fetter or further the development of productive forces: class shapes both incentive and ability to accumulate.

4.2 Class Exists at Multiple Levels and Operates in Both Abstract and Concrete Ways

If class is a set of relationships, these relationships are necessary or contingent, and they exist at multiple levels of generality (e.g. all class society vs capitalism), and can have multiple forms. In other words, class – the system of classes – is very *complex*, and its various elements are inter-connected, so we should examine it by employing various methods of abstraction.[23] One method is to abstract necessary from contingent relations, within an overall perspective of internal relation.[24] In understanding how a given class, or a system of classes, functions, certain things/processes are seen as (more or less) necessary and others as (more or less) contingent: it is necessary that a capitalist will hire and exploit a worker but whether that worker is a male or a female or a Dalit or Brahmin is contingent. That means that: hiring a worker is an essential part of what being a capitalist is about, but hiring a Dalit worker or a female worker is not so. It is possible that a worker hired is a Dalit women, but it is not necessary that a capitalist, to be a capitalist, must hire a Dalit woman. This is the case even if hiring Dalit women can make an enormous difference, at a concrete level, to the way a capitalist makes money.

---

23   While concentrating on a particular aspect, we need to abstract from other aspects, making sure that the abstraction is not chaotic (that we do not separate – abstract – X from Y while they cannot be separated, or we do not put together X and Y where there is no necessary reason to).

24   Such an abstraction must indeed happen within the overall perspective of internal relation which says that X is what it is because of its relations to Y, Z, etc. and that therefore one must start with the social totality (e.g. totality of class society) constituted by relationships.

Embedded in the distinction between the necessary and the contingent is another distinction: between the abstract and the concrete. Something that is more concrete is a form of development – or a form of existence – of something that is more abstract. As a category, the worker is more abstract relative to the category of male worker or industrial worker.[25] Of course, this does not mean that an abstract thing (e.g. worker) is less real than something that is more concrete (a worker in a capitalist banks), or even that an abstract thing (worker) does not exist relative to an informally employed worker or an indigenous female worker or an industrial worker.[26] It is mistaken to believe that an abstract thing (worker) does not exist but an informally employed worker or an indigenous female worker does.[27] In *theorizing* class, i.e. in saying what the conditions of class are (e.g. how its development is associated with the development productive forces and the accumulation of surplus product), how the class system works (its mechanisms) and what effects it produces, more or less, irrespective of a time or a place, it is the *necessary* relations involving classes that matter. But in understanding a concrete situation in which classes function, in a given time and place, both necessary and contingent relations need to be combined – that is, the concrete situation must be seen in the light of the abstract relations. A fundamental implication for class analysis is this: understanding social oppression based on relations such as caste and gender is crucial to the understanding of how class works concretely, but class is *not* constituted by social oppression.[28] Another implication is that: in what sectors

---

25   The distinctions between the abstract and the concrete, and between the necessary and the contingent are to be understood in a relative sense, and not in an absolute sense (for example, a category is more or less abstract; what is necessary now can be contingent later in part due to changes in human practice).

26   Much misconception in class analysis is based on a mis-construal of the distinctions of the type mentioned above: if workers are not employed in industry (as in advanced countries), then, some think, the worker does not exist, and class analysis is not important, while others think that unless one talks about informally employed workers or female workers, one cannot legitimately talk about class analysis.

27   In the mode of abstraction in which the necessary is abstracted from the concrete, there are two sub-methods. One is more 'theoretical' in nature, which reflects real historical development: abstracting direct producer from the worker as a direct producer. The second one is the more empirical type of abstraction: one abstracts a worker from a female worker, and the latter from a female worker in capitalist mining. Both types of abstraction are necessary (while I consider the first type to be analytically superior), but we need to bear in mind their differences (cf. Cox, 2013). The theoretical sub-method of abstraction connects to the abstraction of the level of generality (see below).

28   One can, of course, make general statements about how class – or, capitalism – is affected by caste and argue that Indian capitalism is casteist capitalism, but then here, one is no longer theorizing capitalism-as-such, but a more concrete form of capitalism. The question of what is *capitalism itself* is different from the question of what is *capitalism as it*

workers work or what kind of use-values workers produce, does not define workers' *class* status.

In another method of abstraction, and as already alluded to, class must be analyzed at multiple levels: history of class society, capitalism-as-class-society, capitalism at a specific stage of capitalist development, and capitalism in India (see Das, 2017a: Chapter 5). At this level, some class processes (e.g. those that are talked about in a two-class model) are more abstract than other class processes (those that are talked about when one arrives at a concrete map of all the classes). We should also examine capitalism (or capitalism in India) in terms of its specific forms: neoliberalism or state-directed; domestic market oriented or export-oriented, agrarian capitalism and capitalism outside of agriculture, urban and rural capitalism (urbanization of capital and ruralization of capital, in the sense of spatial concentration of capital in cities and transplantation of capital in villages, respectively), and so on. Capitalism-as-class (content) and its specific forms need to be combined.

4.3   *Capitalism as Class*

At the level of capitalism as a level of class analysis, it is important to examine class relation between capital and labor in the two-class model. The two-class model represents class mechanisms at a more abstract level, and it points to the relations that define capitalism (Das, 2017a: Chapter 7). These relations between workers and capitalists are not only the relations of exchange: the capitalist has a lot more command over exchange relations than the working class does, and has the ability to buy labor power which is sold by the working class only when the capitalist class needs it to make money off the labor power. The relations between workers and capitalists are also relations of property (one class controls means of production, and expands their control through on-going dispossession of small-scale producers, and another class does not), and relations of production, value and surplus value, that underlie the exploitation of the people who have no property or very insignificant amounts of property relative to their reproductive needs. These relations create positions in the structure of capitalism-as-class, the positions which are filled by human practices and individuals.[29] Class analysis at this level must

---

works in a concrete situation by deploying relations such as caste, etc. Once again, the more abstract aspects of capitalism are no less real than the more concrete aspects.

29   It is important to emphasize how these positions are filled by practices signified by class relation and class process: a *given person* may mainly rely on performing wage-labor as a *process,* in a *relationship* to the capitalist, but may also engage in the process of small-scale production, in a relationship to large-scale property owners (e.g. bankers; landlords; merchants, etc.), to supplement her income. If class is seen as a relation and a process,

figure out how different classes experience benefits of economic development, or respond to fascistic movement, differently. But a prior question to address is: what is the class logic of capitalist economic development, or what is the class logic of the fascistic movement, as such? Focusing on the class relation – the relation between interests of property owners and property-less toilers (workers and small-scale self-employed producers) – makes sure that we remain focused on this fact: wealth in its capitalist form (that we see and read about in newspapers and government documents and watch on TV), is, ultimately, a product of the labor of these toilers. This issue is prior to the issue of how the wealth/income is concentrated in the hands of a few (e.g. monopoly capitalists) and how wealth/income can be distributed more equally through (less neoliberal) government intervention, etc. The capitalist wealth is, fundamentally, the form that appropriation of surplus value from wage-labor takes, and it is also partly the wealth that has been taken away from small-scale producers through coercive and market-based mechanisms and converted into the capitalist form of wealth. Capitalist wealth exists because a tiny minority of people have control over productive resources (i.e. over property based in exploitation of labor), and because of the dispossession of small-scale producers by capitalists and their state. This is the case, more or less.[30] The majority of people lack control over means of production and how they are used; they lack control over the fruits of their labor; they lack effective control over their property based in their family labor, i.e. their own private property, because they can lose it through market-based class differentiation (see below). All these class

_____

then the class position of a worker is to be seen as being filled, primarily, by the content of the relation/process that is an essential part of being worker-class, and secondarily by certain individuals. Such a distinction is necessary as long as a part of the labor that workers perform is not wage-labor, and this happens in part because given certain *class* processes – increasing precarity and the on-going tendency for wages to fall below the value of labor power – those with no property or with insignificant amount of property are forced to engage in some form of non-wage-labor; and some of them even may not perform any kind of labor. Once again, figuring out which individual belongs to the class of worker must be seen as only a part of the larger analytical process of determining the nature of the class position defined as a relationship and as a process.

30 I say 'more or less' because a part of the capitalist wealth is because of the contribution of capitalists as workers: many capitalists (e.g. Mukesh Ambani; Narayana Murthy, etc.) are highly educated (in engineering, management, etc.) and they do perform certain useful functions as highly educated people would in any society, but their personal contribution to their wealth seen as imputed wages is an extremely small part of the total amount of wealth each of them possesses. Nearly all of their wealth exists because it is a form of surplus value, and because they have taken away non-capitalist forms of property (peasants' property and the commons).

mechanisms are enforced by the political arm of the capitalist class, the class state, the state of the capitalist class, irrespective of the parties in power.

Whether capitalism is in its lower, and more general form, or in its higher and more developed form (Chapter 3), whether in its neoliberal or state-directed form (Chapter 4), whether it is based on technological change or not (Chapter 5), whether it is export-oriented or not (Chapter 6), and so on, the fundamental aim of capitalism as a class relation (or the fundamental aim of the capitalist class) is to make profit by exploiting ordinary people (and, where necessary, by dispossessing small-scale owners), and not to satisfy the needs of the masses who lack effective control over society's property and how it is used. This is partly why the interests of capital protected by the state and interests of workers who have little effective control over the state, are incompatible. This fact underlies, in however mediated a manner, major political conflicts and struggles.

4.4   The Two-Class Model, the Tendency for the Class Polarization to Happen, and Counter-tendencies in the Capitalist Society

Mapping out the different classes belongs to a different level of abstraction than the two class model. In a society dominated by private property and relations of commodity production and the logic of value, existing independent commodity producers will be over time differentiated into different kinds of classes. There is a tendency for the class polarization to happen: I will call this TCPH. In rural or urban areas, a very small percentage of all commodity producers will have the ability to exploit the labor power of others, and others will have to, more or less, sell their labor power. In a capitalist society, generally speaking, given the need for commodity owners to sell commodities competitively, if one cannot produce at a cost that is more or less the social average, one is liable to go into debt, and in clearing the debt, one may have to sell off some of the assets that one owns. Consider how many millions of farmers in India, most of them are small-scale producers, are leaving cultivation (on their own property or rented property) to join the class of part-time or full-time workers either in farming or outside of farming: 2035 are leaving farming every day since 1991, as they cannot pay their bills. That's 15 million since 1991 (when neoliberalism formally began). *This* is in line with the class theory including TCPH.

One should hear what Lenin (1899) has to say about class differentiation: 'Undoubtedly, the emergence of property inequality is the starting-point of the whole process [of differentiation], but the process is not at all confined to property "differentiation."' (Lenin, 1899: para 5). The class of property owners does not only differentiate; it also gets dissolved; it ceases to exist (ibid.). This class is ousted by absolutely new types of property owners, 'types that are the basis of a society in which commodity economy and capitalist production prevail'. These types are: a class of property owners, with varying amount of property, who employ wage-laborers, and a class of wage-laborers. In the process, a class of proletarians is produced from the 'class' of independent producers (Lenin, 1899).

Perhaps, Lenin was overzealous to attack those (the populists of his time) who were saying that capitalism was not developing in Russia? Consider then these lines from Lenin written in 1908.

> The technical and commercial superiority of large-scale *production* over small-scale production not only in industry, but also in agriculture, is proved by irrefutable facts. ...Small-scale production maintains itself on the ruins of natural economy by constant worsening of diet, by chronic starvation, by lengthening of the working day, by deterioration in the quality and the care of cattle, in a word, by the very methods whereby handicraft production maintained itself against capitalist manufacture. Every advance in science and technology inevitably and relentlessly undermines the foundations of small-scale production in capitalist society; and it is the task of socialist political economy to investigate this process in all its forms, often complicated and intricate, and to demonstrate to the small producer the impossibility of his holding his own under capitalism, the hopelessness of peasant farming under capitalism, and the necessity for the peasant to adopt the standpoint of the proletarian.

Lenin wrote these lines almost 10 years *after* he completed his *Development of Capitalism in Russia*, which means that he continued to take the class polarization/differentiation idea very seriously.

However, like all tendencies such as the tendency of the rate of profit to fall (TRPF), the TCPH can not only be hastened by certain mechanisms (e.g. globalization of capitalism) but also countered by many mechanisms: self-exploitation (not paying oneself the imputed full value of the labor power per hour), use of remittance money from a family member working as a wage-earner in the city, part-time work in the city or the village (as proletarians or semi-proletarians), and welfare benefits from the capitalist state which seeks to, among other things, calm the anger of the lower classes. But then all these counter-mechanisms, including government welfare, are also *class-based* mechanisms as they primarily concern the totality of all class relations. The mechanisms of TCPH are always modified in their working 'by many circumstances, the analysis of which does not concern us here', i.e. theory cannot do justice to these circumstances (Marx, 1977: 798).

There are two implications of the fact of 'incomplete class differentiation'. One is that all members of a subordinate class do not have to be completely property-less for the capitalist class relation to exist: the capitalist class relation needs only a sufficient amount of wage-labor for the production of surplus value. The other implication is political: 'it would be a profound mistake to think that the "complete" proletarianisation of the majority of the population is essential for bringing about ...a [proletarian] revolution' (Lenin, 1977a: 56). This view is in direct contrast to all those (e.g. Utsa Patnaik, Henry Bernstein, etc.) who think that incomplete polarization is a barrier to class politics. The barrier, much rather, lies in the specific strategy that the communist movement and allied left intellectuals deploy, to organize subordinate classes (see Chapter 3).

4.5 Capitalism as a System of Relations of Accumulation by Class Differentiation, Accumulation by Dispossession, and Accumulation by Exploitation

Capitalist class relations are about property relations (monopolization over property by a few) and not just about exploitative relation between capital and labor, so the dispossession of small-scale producers as a class mechanism must be a crucial aspect of class analysis of India. The surplus value appropriated from wage-earners is converted into capitalist wealth that they see but do not enjoy, and that the capitalists and governments brag about as being a product of their hard work and good policies respectively. And, direct producers (e.g. small-scale producers) are coercively separated from means of production and are then converted into the capitalist form of wealth. Besides: when the capitalist state neglects areas where small-scale producers and wage workers live, by not investing in the physical infrastructure because it needs to meet the financial needs of big business, the value of property in those areas declines and income-earning ability of direct producers is also reduced. This contributes to the low price at which small-scale property owners may – and may have to – sell their property.[31] To understand capitalism as a specific form of class in our times is therefore to see capitalism in terms of a dialectical articulation of: 'accumulation by dispossession' (in the specific sense of dispossession of small scale producers and privatization of society's commons including common

---

31   Vijayabaskar and Menon (2018) say, rightly, that land grabs occur less due to coercive action by the state and more due to the state underinvesting in agriculture, resulting in dispossession by neglect of those who are economically vulnerable (people with tiny amount of asset), and this process means that the boundary between the coercive and voluntary land grabs could be fluid in certain cases.

land and state-owned wealth), accumulation by class differentiation, and accumulation by class exploitation (which is expressed as multiple forms of subsumption, as discussed in Chapter 3). The last is the predominant form of the triad.

4.6   *Classes and Class-Fractions Have Common and Different Interests*

A class can have *some* common interests, at a point in time, with another class. For example, both workers and capitalists benefit from anti-feudal struggles and both, generally speaking, and within limits, may benefit more from a high rate of economic development than from a very low rate or from recession, and both benefit from a better environment or from a social atmosphere where there is respect for democratic rights and for civility, than not. But the two classes are more different from one another than they are similar in terms of material interest: their interests are antagonistic much more than they are harmonious. Capitalists appropriate the fruit of labor from workers, and capitalists can abandon their support for democratic rights and even resort to – or support – fascistic tendencies when it is in their economic-political interests *as capitalists*, as they do in India now. This means that not only does class analysis say that workers and capitalists are the two main classes in a society where wealth is in the form of capitalist commodities, and that class is the most important cause of the problems that the toiling masses, the majority-class, experience because their life is subordinated to the exploiting class. Class analysis also says that the interest of the majority-class (the exploited) and the minority class (exploiters) are, ultimately, incompatible, and therefore, class relations must be abolished.

Those whom capital exploits belong to different classes (classes of peasants; workers, etc.). But there are also important intra-class differences. These are not only social-cultural differences as just mentioned (e.g. Dalit worker vs Brahmin worker) but also economic differences in terms of income, job security, working conditions, etc. Recently, many scholars have stressed the difference between workers in the informal sector and those in the formal sector. This *is* a crucial difference to make,[32] but one should see this difference, as all differences, dialectically, i.e. in relation to their common ground. There are

---

32   In fact, the discussion on the difference between formal sector and informal sector workers can be enriched by pointing to the difference in terms of labor freedom, and this is not generally done. Consider the excellent point made by Brass (2000: 134) in his critique of Jan Breman's approach: 'the most common production relation encountered in the informal sector of India must be unfree labour which, when combined with the additional process of formal sector contraction coupled with informal sector expansion, permits only one conclusion: ... work in the formal sector, and with it free labour, is being

differences *and* common grounds between the two types of workers, at the level of (a) relations of property, production and value (they are all, more or less, property-less and are subjected to the appropriation of surplus value in commodity production, although some are exploited more than others, and they engage in production of different kinds of use-values) and (b) relations of exchange (while all workers rely on the sale of labor power, their wages vary). [33]

4.7   *Changes over Time and over Space, in the System of Classes*
The system – the totality – of classes, and the dynamics of each class, are not static. They undergo changes over time:

> all classes ... are regarded, not statistically, but dynamically – i.e., not in a state of immobility – but in motion (whose laws are determined by the economic conditions of existence of each class).
>> Ibid.

Some workers who used to be formally employed could be in the informal sector, and this fact should pose no problems for class analysis. A class that began as a mercantile class can become an industrial class. A peasant can become a proletarian. And the effects of class relations also change over space. The rate of exploitation – and indeed, conditions of existence of each class – may vary from one place to another, within limits, in part because of the ways in which the general mechanisms of capitalism as a class society interact with place-specific mechanisms. And the historical and geographical changes may not be linear: a peasant who has gone to the city to work as a laborer may return to the village to cultivate her land. Or a peasant who has lost her land and has become a laborer may gain some of it. [34] Changes in the class system can be gradual: a situation of passivity may change to one where there is some trade union consciousness at least. It can be more drastic: big political movements can happen when there is a widely prevalent consciousness that interests of capitalists and interests of workers are fundamentally incompatible.

---

  replaced with employment in the informal sector, where unfree working relations prevail. In other words, a process of 'deproletarianization'.

33   The average daily wage in the informal sector is approximately $2 while that in the formal sector is approximately $3.5, so there is a difference, but the wages of both types of workers are poverty-level wages – they fall below the value of labor power. Besides, increasingly, even those who are in the formal sector are subjected to fixed term contracts which we will talk about in a later chapter.

34   She can do this by using her remittance from a relative in the city or from dowry received for her son, or from a government scheme of land redistribution.

4.8   *Non-class Relations within Class Relations*

At a general level, class is about the relations between classes, and that capital does not worry about whether a worker is a male or a low-caste person. To say that the life of a low-caste female worker in Delhi is shaped more by class rela- tions than by caste and gender relations, does not, however, mean any moral evaluation of non-class identities.[35] Primacy of class does not mean that wom- en's issues are subordinated to issues that concern men, that a man's life and words are more important than a women. *Not at all.* Indeed, class analysis says that a society which does not treat its women (and children), and one should add, all the hitherto-oppressed groups such as Dalits and indigenous groups, with respect, and which does not meet their material needs, is a society with which there is something terribly wrong.

At a more concrete level, the reality is a little different, because here the effects of class relations, and capitalist class relations, deeply impact, and are impacted by relations of caste and gender, and so on.[36] And how a given class actually functions (reproduction of its conditions of existence) in a given time and a place depends on its relation to non-class relations (e.g. caste and gen- der): a Dalit worker is class-exploited by land owners/capitalists and caste- oppressed by non-Dalit higher castes. A Brahmin worker may live better than a low-caste worker.

At the level of Indian capitalism, low caste, female Muslim capitalists will not generally behave differently, in any fundamental sense, from their upper caste and Hindu and male counterparts, given the logic of capitalism. Capital- ists are and will be capitalists. What an individual capitalist or a group of capi- talists does, as a part of the class of capitalists and as a part of the totality of capitalist society, reflects the logic of the functioning of that class as a whole, and it must reflect that totality of the capitalist society as a whole, more or less. They have to be capitalists, given the logic of competition and given the law of value, operating at multiple geographical scales, including the global.

---

35   'To assert the priority of a class analysis is not to claim that a worker is more important
        than a homemaker, or even that the worker primarily thinks of herself as a worker' (Foley,
        2018: 273).

36   Mohanty (2004) makes these useful remarks: 'In studying the interface of class, caste and
        gender we recognize the centrality of class, especially in the context of the modern his-
        tory of capitalism where *it is the most powerful force* with a worldwide drive shaping hu-
        man relationships *in all sectors of society*. This, however, does not in any way reduce the
        centrality of caste and gender *in particular contexts and spheres of action.* ...In my view,
        capitalism as a class system is such a powerful, all-encompassing process in the contem-
        porary world that all other categories despite their autonomy and specificity are forced to
        reckon with it.... This is not to say that caste and gender are not autonomous categories'
        (pp. 24–25).

Caste and gender relations define some individuals and groups belonging to the class of workers as second-class citizens (as oppressed groups). These groups do not enjoy the full democratic rights that, say, upper-caste, male workers ordinarily enjoy. As a result, these oppressed groups of workers can be exploited more than others by the property-owning class: the value of their labor power could be driven below the value of labor power in society as a whole, and/or their wages could fall below the social average, leading to their *super*-exploitation (i.e. above-average magnitude of exploitation). The oppressed groups' control over their family-based property could be much more tenuous than others'.[37] Their power to resist exploitation and curtailment of democratic rights is restricted. And, the ability of the *entire* class of workers to resist exploitation and curtailment of democratic rights is adversely impacted because they are divided on the basis of gender or caste or religion.[38] Indeed, the anger of some workers (or small-scale producers) is channeled along the lines of caste or gender or religion, and when this happens, some people come to believe that the chief cause of their problems is the caste structure or gender or religious difference, so they politically conduct themselves accordingly – i.e. they engage in what is merely politics of recognition (politics of respect and solidarity with some, and politics of hatred against others).[39]

---

37   Consider the fate of residential property and small-scale business-property of Muslims in certain areas (see Mitra and Ray, 2014). The dispossession of property of people from socially oppressed categories (e.g. Muslims) is not un-connected to the property interests of capitalists of non-oppressed groups.

38   One might say that when a Hindu hates a Muslim or when a Brahmin oppresses a Dalit, the former may enjoy some symbolic value from such oppression, by 'othering' the Dalit or the Muslim, by making the latter look inferior, that such oppression brings a sense of cultural and political superiority to the oppressor. But the question is: what social-material conditions have put value on such symbolic value on social oppression and allow one group to be powerful by curtailing the democratic rights of another group, which is what oppression is about? It is important to uncover what people think and how that thinking shapes their cultural and political behavior. But it is also important to explain the social-material mechanisms behind that thinking. Why is oppression necessary and why is it possible is the question?.

39   Habib (2014), one of India's most well-known historians, rightly says: 'while "class" is a category based on the mode of surplus extraction, ...its reality is obscured....by modes of social gradations' of various kinds ....[which originate in pre-capitalist societies and which] could also survive changes in modes of production...'. Habib continues: 'caste [as a kind of social gradation] has to be seen historically, as not only a divisive social force, but also a mechanism of class exploitation that, by denying status and mobility to the lowest elements of society, reduces labour costs, and facilitates and increases extraction of surplus. The main beneficiary of the caste system must then be not so much the Brahmins, as the ruling classes – whatever be their religion and the prevailing mode of surplus extraction' (pp. 205–206).

Of course, none of what is said above means the following: if a Brahmin landlord makes a Dalit worker drink cow urine because the latter dared to chal-lenge the landlord or if a Hindu fanatic lynches a Muslim for exercising his choice of eating beef, then the immediate – proximate – material cause is necessarily some material class interest at the site of oppression. The same goes for a non-Dalit worker oppressing a Dalit worker. There is a reason for this. Firstly, the logic of social oppression is rooted in class mechanisms at the soci-etal level, and not at the individual level.[40] Secondly, the *material practice* of the deployment of social oppression by class relations creates certain *ideas* about the socially oppressed in relation to the oppressor. These ideas travel in space and time. While certain ideas about social oppression may be reflective of caste or gender or religious oppression at the time when such oppression began to emerge, these ideas still stay on, even if the exact social-material con-ditions which gave rise to those ideas do not exist. The ideas about social op-pression also travel beyond the site – or even logic – of class exploitation, and appears to be detached from any class basis, in a concrete situation, so such ideas enter into the common-sense of people, both exploited and exploiting. This partly explains why Dalit workers are oppressed by non-Dalit workers.[41]

The existence of women and low-castes, especially, Dalits, as under-privileged sections within the proletariat (and semi-proletarian masses), is a matter of interest to the proletariat as a whole: it can never emancipate itself from exploitation and domination by capital and capitalist state, while parts of it (i.e. the male part, the high-caste part, the majority-religion part) continue to

---

40   This is akin to the fact that: the main logic of exploitation of a worker (Dalit or not) by a capitalist (Brahmin or not) is not rooted in the workplace owned by that capitalist. That logic only works itself out at the workplace in concrete ways. What the capitalist does must be, more or less, within the limits of the law of value: there is a logic according to which all commodity producers must produce at least at the social value. The value of a commodity produced in a given workplace is not determined by the conditions of pro-duction in *that* workplace (by the time needed to produce the commodity in that work-place). The value of the commodity from a given workplace is still the social value. But a capitalist can make use of social oppression either to bridge the gap between the overly high individual value and the social value of the commoddities produced, or even to pro-duce her commodity at below the social value, in which case an extra amount of surplus value is made by that person.

41   It is also the case that an illusory notion of belonginess works among the people who are both exploited and oppressed: non-Dalit workers who are exploited by the Brahmin or middle-caste property owners might identify themselves with their exploiters against Dalit workers/peasants, and such a feeling of belonginess could function as an illusory – ideological – compensation – to offset the effect of their own exploitation by high-caste exploiters. The above does not deny the importance of the fact that upper-caste property owners make a concerted attempt to divide the exploited class on the basis of caste.

oppress other parts (i.e. women workers, low-caste workers, minority-religion workers).[42]

4.9   *Ideas, Class Politics, and Objective Conditions in Class Society*

Within a system of classes, different classes have different kinds of ideas about themselves and about other classes and about the system of classes, and these ideas/concepts interact with objective conditions (e.g. employment, economic development, rate of profit declining/increasing). But ultimately the objective conditions have a primacy over the ideas. Ultimately, ideas of the exploiting propertied classes have more power vis-à-vis the ideas of subordinate classes as long as the former classes control the means of production.

Class is not just an economic but also a political concept. Class relations, as social relations as such, are relations of contradiction. This is expressed in the fact that class relations are relations of exploitation and relations involving differential control over property and production, which is why the reproduction (or dissolution) occurs as a result of class struggle, which may happen covertly or overtly, whose intensity and expression vary over time and space. Class struggle takes multiple forms (as discussed in Chapter 7). Class struggle depends on class formation (formation of collectivity of groups as a class) and class consciousness (consciousness of the fact that different classes have different interests, at the level of exchange relations, and production and property relations). The latter process is in turn enabled/constrained by the structure of class relations, along with the labor process on which the class structure is based. Consider, for example, how changes in class structure or class differentiation – which is partly enabled by state policies – can affect class struggle.[43] Class mechanisms – exploitation and dispossession, etc. – and their effects prompt class struggle. But there are also class mechanisms that can impede class struggle.

It has been shown that class relations influence how well – and how differently – women, men and children from different classes live. However, 'It is much more demanding to expect class – or any notion of social structure – to predict or explain politics that drive policy' as Herring and Agarwala (2006: 331) rightly note. And that is because there is an objective situation on the

---

42   These lines are based on my paraphrase of a few lines from Sathyamurthy (1999: 39) (and on Marx's statement that 'Labor in the white skin can never free itself as long as labor in the black skin is branded').

43   When property-less people receive some means of production through a government program as a product of prior struggle, they can become petty bourgeois and find more in common with the capitalist class than with labor.

ground that is demanding (difficult), which explains why, for example, the sub-ordinate classes face various difficulties in their struggle. For a start, while winning over the hearts and minds is important in any struggle, class-based organizations receive little 'media attention relative to the exploding array of "grassroots organizations"' (ibid.: 329). The dominant class strata in India control media and other means of modes of dissemination of ideas, as they control means of material production as well as the state. And there is also ideological coercion (censorship) against the practice of progressive ideas, and especially, against Marxism itself (see Das, 2012b, 2013a), which *is* a body of scholarly work and which seeks to both understand class relations and class consciousness and contribute towards the further development of class consciousness.[44]

Class politics of subordinate classes is hindered because class formation in the face of the fragmentation of workers and small-scale producers is difficult: as noted earlier, the ruling class and its agencies make use of discourses around caste, etc. to fragment class consciousness, so the masses start engaging in caste-based or religious-sectarian conflicts, instead of fighting as a class against class exploitation, dispossession, as well as social oppression of various forms. Besides, resources are lacking to establish and support class-organizations. The business class and the state are not going to support these, given their own class character. As well, when established, many workers' organizations are influenced by the capitalist context in which they operate: ideas reflecting bourgeois politics of workers and various reformist ideas as well as bureaucratic practices of working class leaders influence the effectivity of workers' organizations. One such organization is a party. As Herring (2013) rightly says: whether a worker or a poor peasant votes for a communist party depends on the presence of such a party and how freely it can operate, but if the political system operates in such a way that political mobilization aimed at significant redistribution is not possible, which is increasingly the case under neoliberalism, then common voters vote on the basis of non-class criteria such as caste, religion, region, etc. Besides, class-based mobilization invites the ruling class repression. A communist party seeks to mobilize votes partly on the basis of extra-electoral resistance against property owners and state. But: 'The obstacles to mobilization along class lines involve serious risk of detention and

---

44   In an article originally written in 1981, Beteille (2000), one of the most progressive liberal-minded non-Marxist scholars of India, laments the attacks on Marxism: 'the current attacks are ...an indication of ...a large and as yet unexplored reservoir of intolerance in India of any serious critique of society'. And attacks on Marxism/Marxists have reached unprecedented level in the recent times with the rise of the fascistic movement.

death: under these circumstances it is not surprising that a class project faces daunting odds' (Herring, 2013: 134).

When the capitalist state sends police and paramilitary forces to repress progressive movements or when it implements economic policies on behalf of the ruling class or when it protects private property rights of capital while taking away such rights from small-scale producers in villages and cities, or when it allows the capitalist class to take away much of what the workers produce (appropriation of surplus value), all this *is* class struggle, pure and simple. This is class struggle from above. What the association/institutions of capitalists (e.g. FICCI, CII) do to lobby the governments, including for labor reforms (to allow capitalists to hire and fire at will), or when they threaten not to invest because they wish to see a more favorable business climate,[45] or when they provide election funding to bourgeois parties while doing everything possible to stop workers' unions from operating, that *is* class struggle. When the ruling class and its political agents (right-wing movements and governments) engage in fascistic politics aiming to destroy democratic rights and progressive organizations of workers and peasants, that *is* class struggle from above. Just as mechanisms and counter-mechanisms in the proletarianization thesis (TCPH) are both class mechanisms, the mechanisms that promote class politics and the mechanisms that impede class politics, are both *class* mechanisms.

Class analysis is about the context in which different classes exist, a context in which the state of the dominant class (the main exploiting class) manages the commons affairs of this class. Alienation from state's coercive power is a fundamental attribute of classness of the exploited classes. Whatever else the state is, its primary job is to protect class relations, including capitalist property relations and the right of capitalists to hire and fire and to exploit and to dispossess, at the cost of satisfying the needs of the masses and by crushing their hard-fought democratic rights. If there is so much inequality and if there is so much dispossession, and if the vast majority cannot meet their basic needs, why is it that the state cannot dispossess the small minority (top 0.1–1%, or at best top 10%) and put the resources under the democratic control of the masses who can then use these resources to produce the things that they need in order to satisfy their material and cultural needs? This fundamental question is asked and answered only in the Marxist class analysis.

Class – class relations and processes – explains class politics, in ways that are more or less mediated, whether it is the politics of the right or of the left, and it also explains why politics takes non-class forms (e.g. clientelism,

---

45   On the functioning of business associations in India, see Bandyopadhyay (2000).

populism, etc.).[46] Herring correctly notes that class explains why non-class forms of politics happens.[47] Class relations govern, and set limit within which, non-class politics works (see Chapters 8–9 and 10–13).

5   Conclusion

Class analysis identifies classes, their relations, and the implications of the latter for a wide variety of processes (e.g. economic development, political power, etc.). Class analysis is doubly important: not only does it tell us what society is like at a given moment (class as a structure of relations among multiple classes and class-fractions), but it also sheds light on how society is changing (class as a contradictory process).

Scholars have raised various objections to Marxist class analysis of India. For example, they say that class analysis is mistaken to assign primacy to class as a social relation over other relations, and to assume that class polarization leading to proletarianization will happen. I have tried to theoretically counter these objections. In spite of these objections, there is a tradition of class analysis of India. It deals with a set of inter-related themes: it explores how the Indian society is differentiated into not two classes but a multiplicity of classes, how, for example, the informally employed workers engage in struggle outside of production, how the effects of class 'intersect' with the non-class relations of caste and gender, etc. There has been also much discussion on the dispossession of the small-scale producers class. While appreciating the merits of some of the existing literature on class in India, I have also made a series of criticisms of this literature. Class cannot be treated as one of several social relations; it has analytical primacy. But, once again, that does not imply any moral valuation of social groups: i.e. that does not mean that a woman (or a Dalit) is inferior to a worker. I critically consider the skepticism about the two-class model and

---

46   In many areas, the existence of a substantial self-employed peasantry and a mass of small agrarian capitalists makes the ideological gulf separating workers and exploiters less apparent. For this reason, this is potentially a fertile ground for the emergence of populism ('we are basically all the same') which frequently blunts the edges of class struggle (see Brass, 1999: 266).

47   Herring says that 'The effects of class on politics that are not readily observable as proximate causes, but enable and limit conditions for other forms of political behavior, are difficult to access and account for' and these other forms of political behavior include: quiescence, clientelism, populism, a social movement (Herring, 2013: 129). He says that 'class analysis is compatible with forms of theorizing politics that take for granted structural inequalities' (p. 135).

about the class polarization thesis. Class analysis should be much more than about inequality or injustice and about dispossession. Class analysis is not to be seen as merely figuring out how many classes there are and which individual is in which class. Nor is class analysis anything if it is not about the class character of society *as a whole* and of the state's fundamental class-role: examination of class nature of this or that topic must be situated within the overall class context of society and of the state. It is also mistaken to think that class politics is not happening and therefore class analysis is not relevant. If class politics is not happening in the way it should, the reasons lie in class itself. I then go on to briefly outline some of the aspects of class analysis as I see it.

Class should be seen in its material conditions, in terms of relations between classes, and at a concrete level, in terms of the relations between classes and non-class relations such as caste, gender and religion. We need to have a conception of the structure of class relations (system of classes), and of the contradictions between classes and within a given class, and in terms of how the system is changing, sometimes slowly and sometimes not so slowly, on the basis of various forms of class struggle which coexist with non-class struggles.

Class relations, including specific forms of capitalism as a class relation, and a given level of economic development are combined, and this combination has an effect on political (and cultural) matters which in turn shape class relations and economic development. But ultimately, it is class relations with their impact on the development of productive forces, that have the primacy, over, for example, matters concerning the political (e.g. state actions; political struggles, etc.).

Class analysis must be about the overall context in which all the different classes operate, first at the level of capitalism and then at the level of Indian society as a whole, in their mutual relation. It is about *the sum total* of the relations between all the classes. It is at a more concrete level, where class relations and capitalist class relations deeply impact caste and gender, etc. relations which, in turn, impact the effects of how class relations work.

It *is* important to talk about individual classes. However, the examination of how many classes exist and how different groups within the working class experience life differently must be a part of a larger consideration in which the emphasis should be given to the fact that there is class as a relationship (with its contradictions), that affects politics, economic development and culture and how we relate to nature and to one another. It is *that* relationship that underlies how classes and class-fractions and individuals of specific classes, as well as state agencies and state elites, function or do not function, and how they exercise their agency or how they do not. The class analysis concerns the *entire* society, including the state. The class perspective on India (and other

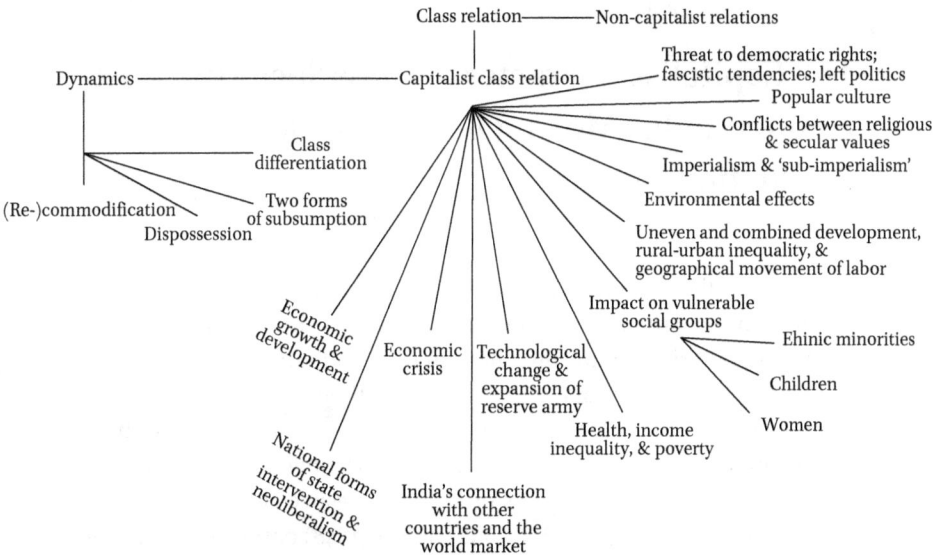

FIGURE 2.1   A partial map of what to study in India from a class perspective
SOURCE: AUTHOR

countries) can prompt theoretically rigorous and empirically-corroborated research on a wide variety of topics. Figure 2.1 is a map of some of these.

Only some of the topics that appear on the map are dealt with in this book:
nature of India's capitalism as a form of class society; nature of neoliberalism
with Indian traits; technological change in relation to direct producers; production for the world market and a dual metabolic rift and implications for
workers of different oppressed categories; the social character the capitalist
state in relation to dominant and subordinate classes; lower-class struggles,
and fascistic tendencies as a ruling class response to capitalist crisis, in relation
to Left politics.

The Capitalist Character of Class Society in Post-colonial India: Moving Beyond the Mode of Production Debate

As in many other countries in the global periphery, overall labor productivity per hour in India remains very low (see Figure 3.1).[1] It was approximately one-tenth of that of the USA in 2015.[2] Both in rural and urban areas, producers/entrepreneurs, generally, work with relatively rudimentary technologies. In rural India, where most people live, millions of people still cultivate land with wooden ploughs or with their improvised versions. The nature of the economic development process in most parts of India, and especially, in the countryside, does not appear to support Marx and Engels's (1848) optimism in *The Communist Manifesto* that the bourgeoisie (or the capitalist mode of production led by this class) constantly revolutionizes the mode of production.[3] Perhaps, his comments were relevant to the place and the time in which they lived, but not to the India (and similar other countries) of today?

If capitalism revolutionizes the development of productive forces, and yet if labor productivity per hour is still so low, then could it be that India is not (dominantly) a capitalist country? Conversely, if India *is* a capitalist country, why does it have such a low level of labor productivity? Indeed, the question of whether or not India is a capitalist country proper and the question of what the barriers are to its further development, if capitalism does exist, are not yet settled. This fact potentially supports Ellen Wood's point that 'there is no general agreement about the meaning of capitalism or its basic dynamics' (Wood, 2007: 145, 159).

The remainder of the chapter, which is a continuation of the previous chapter, is divided into nine sections. Beginning the chapter with the famous Indian

---

1 An earlier version of this chapter appeared as Das (2012c).
2 Labor productivity (GDP per person employed per hour, PPP dollars in 2015) was 6.46 in India and was 59.77 in the USA, according to World Competitiveness Yearbook, 2015 (quoted in GOI, 2015).
3 'The bourgeoisie cannot exist without constantly revolutionising the instruments of production, and thereby the relations of production, and with them the whole relations of society. ...Constant revolutionising of production, uninterrupted disturbance of all social conditions, everlasting uncertainty and agitation distinguish the bourgeois epoch from all earlier ones' (Marx and Engels, 1948).

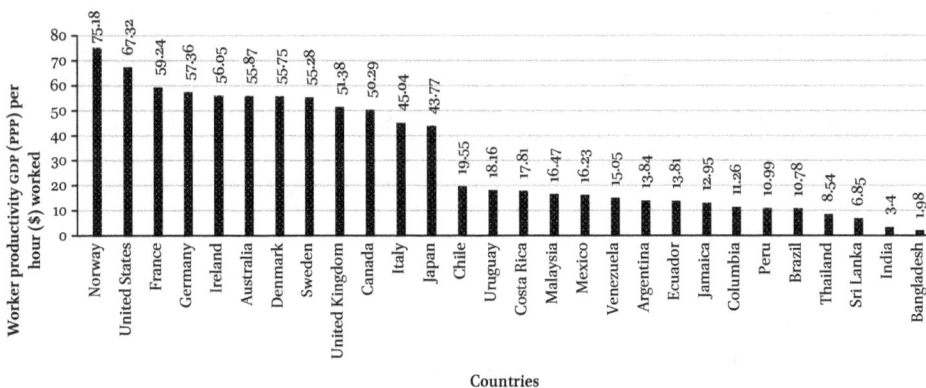

FIGURE 3.1   Worker Productivity GDP (PPP) per hour ($) worked (2013): Selected rich and poor countries
SOURCE: HTTPS://EN.WIKIPEDIA.ORG/WIKI/LIST_OF_COUNTRIES_BY_GDP _(PPP)_PER_HOUR_WORKED

mode of production debate (henceforward, Indian MOP debate), I discuss, in Section 1, how certain scholars working on India define capitalism in general and in the Indian context (including in Indian agriculture). In Section 2, I critique some of the most influential ideas in the debate. In Section 3, I present an alternative framework for understanding capitalism in general and capitalism in the context of the less developed countries such as India. In doing so I build on Marx's discussion in *Capital* volume 1 on formal, hybrid and real subsumptions of labor, a discussion that is often neglected or misinterpreted. I argue that capitalism can exist when formal subsumption prevails. I also argue that the transition to real subsumption, with attendant technological change, can be a very long process, and, that *notwithstanding* Marx's optimistic view about 'spontaneous' transition to real subsumption, it is anything but spontaneous. That transition is mediated by the changing balance of power of capital and labor (class struggle), which occurs in a context of a whole host of geographically-specific factors such as capitalist state interventions. In the next two sections (Sections 4–5), I provide some empirical discussion to corroborate my argument about the relation between class struggle and the transition from formal subsumption. Thus, in Section 4, I discuss how class struggle can prompt real subsumption though not in any unilinear, straightforward, way, and in Section 5, I show how property owners can respond to class struggle against formal subsumption by way of *reinforcing* formal subsumption and/or introducing hybrid subsumption (exploitation based on mercantile-usury-rental extraction). In Section 6, I discuss why there are technical reasons for a transition to real subsumption (for example, in the industrial sector) but why there are limits to such a transition, within the context of peripheral capitalism. In the following section, I critically reflect on Jairus Banaji's (and others') view of subsumption, which was an important part of the mode of production debate, and argue that his views are mistaken. I contrast his views to what I think are Marx's views which I defend and deploy. In the conclusion I summarize the discussion and draw its implications for understanding uneven and combined development, and for political practice.

1   **The Development of Capitalist Relations, and the Barriers to This: A Brief Discussion on the Indian Mode of Production Debate**

In the 1960s and 1970s, the Indian MOP debate took place, which is now known internationally. This debate discussed, among other things, the extent of development of capitalist relations and the barriers to this.[4] I do not want to review this debate in any great detail, as it has been reviewed earlier (see Bidwai, 2015: 353–365; Nadkarni, 1991; Thorner, 1982). Rather, my aim is to develop a critique of some selective parts of this debate, and based on my critique, to address the question of the nature of capitalism in India.[5]

A mode of production is an articulated combination of forces of production (technological development; organization of the labor process) and relations of production (class relations). One mode of production (e.g. capitalism) is different from another (e.g. slavery or feudalism) in terms of the nature of class relations – the actual ways in which surplus labor/product is pumped out of direct producers – and also in terms of the logic and the extent of the development of productive forces based on the deployment of the surplus.

---

4   The Indian debate that mainly took place in the pages of *Economic and Political Weekly* and *Social Scientist*, 'built on' and is a part of, a global debate on the nature of, and the transition to, capitalism. The first of these took place in the 1950s in *Science & Society*, published since 1936 (this is, incidentally, the longest continuously published journal of Marxist scholarship in the world). In this debate stalwarts such as Maurice Dobb, Christopher Hill, Rodney Hilton, Eric Hobsbawm, Paul Sweezy, Kohachiro Takahshi, and others participated. Their work was later reprinted in Hilton (1978). It should be noted that Sweezy (1986) revisited the debate in a *Science & Society* article. The *Science & Society* debate was followed by another debate, known as the Brenner debate, on the issue of the transition. Originally published in 1976 in the influential and progressive British journal, *Past and Present*, the set of articles that constituted the Brenner debate was published in Aston and Philipin (1985). Examining the nature of capitalism – capitalism in general or capitalism in the specific historical-geographical context – constitutes an on-going intellectual task at the international scale, one to which scholars from India as well as those from Europe, North America and other regions of the world continue to contribute. Some of this work will be referenced in this chapter.
5   In this chapter, the term 'development' means development of productive forces (technological change and attendant increase in productivity of land and labor).

Of several issues discussed in the MOP debate in India, the following were important from the standpoint of this chapter: how to identify the capitalist mode of production, how widespread it was and what were the barriers to the development of capitalist relations. These questions were important not only to the period when the debate took place but also to the current period, and not only for India but also for other parts of the (less developed) world.

While it is widely held that nominally free wage labor is necessary for capitalism to exist, according to Patnaik (1990a: 41), many freely hired laborers in India, however, are not actually free. This is in the sense that the employer of these laborers 'does not appropriate surplus value from free laborers; he [or she] maximizes the returns from exploiting the destitute labor tied to agriculture and with no other employment opportunities' (1972a: 22). And, for her, being tied to agriculture because of lack of alternative employment opportunities is analogous to serfs being tied to feudal lords.[6] This system of exploitation cannot be called feudal, but by default, it cannot be called capitalist either, she says. *Even* if wage laborers are free, she argues, free wage labor by itself, though a necessary, is not a sufficient condition for capitalism, because labor employers must also produce for the market. This is her second criterion for identifying capitalism. Yet, capitalism needs more than this for its existence. She says that 'Production for the market must not ... be confused with capitalist production: the former antedates the latter and though necessary, is not sufficient for its development' (1990a: 44).[7] Thus neither production for the market, nor wage labor, is a sufficient condition for capitalism. She identifies the third necessary criterion of capitalism in India: 'accumulation and reinvestment of surplus value [in modern equipment] in order to generate more surplus value' (1990a: 44). Elsewhere she says 'If the holding [i.e. a landowner] employing

---

6   This is similar to Chandra's (1974) argument that enormous rural unemployment or rural labor surplus is perpetuating the semi-feudal set-up.

7   Patnaik clarifies that: unlike Western Europe: 'India was forced to enter the network of world capitalist exchange relations; its pre-capitalist economy was broken up and a fair section of the peasantry was pauperized into landlessness' (1990c: 93–94). Unlike in Western Europe, this landless labor force was not absorbed in industry as there was none. If the surplus could have been reinvested in Indian industry the latter could have absorbed the rural labor force and provided impetus for capitalist agriculture by expanding markets for agricultural products. But the surplus was transferred to Britain instead. As a result, commodity production 'led to an inordinate development of capital in the sphere of exchange, to a prolonged disintegration of pre-capitalist mode without its reconstitution on a capitalist basis' (ibid.). Exploitation took the forms of rack-renting (leasing out land at very high rents) and usury rather than appropriation of surplus value from wage laborers. This continues till today although to a less extent than before. Because employment of wage labor does not necessarily encourage productive investment in equipment, etc., that has to be added to the definition of capitalism in countries such as India.

wage labor does not reinvest and expand, lower production costs and try to move up on the scale of competitive efficiency, then where is the element of dynamism which marks off this so-called 'capitalist' enterprise ... from other exploitative relations such as the landlord-tenant one?' (ibid.: 91). For Patnaik, because employment of wage labor does not necessarily encourage productive investment in modern equipment, etc. to increase efficiency, as in Western Europe, that has to be added to the definition of capitalism as a separate criterion, in countries such as India. In other words, as Chattopadhyay (1990b) said: she has two different definitions of capitalism for two different geographical contexts. The question is: does she distinguish between capitalism in general and capitalism in its Indian form? It is not clear that she does.

As if to 'echo' Patnaik, Rudra (Rudra et al., 1990) says that: a capitalist has to, among other things, simultaneously: produce things for the *market* for a *profit* by *employing wage labor*, and make wage-payments *in cash*; and invest in *modern equipment*. Unless a property owner satisfies all these criteria, they are not capitalist. Patnaik and Rudra disagree with each other *empirically* on whether and the extent to which capitalism existed in the 1960s,[8] but their *conceptual* views of capitalism are actually more similar than different.[9]

For Bhaduri (1983), capitalism requires free labor in Marx's senses. However, to the extent that labor owns some means of production and that people cannot freely sell their labor power, capitalism does not exist. Banaji does not think that free wage-labor is a defining attribute of capitalism. He (more or less) accepts a definition of capitalism in terms of 'the laws of motion of capitalist production' which include: 'the production and accumulation of surplus-value,

---

8   Patnaik says that capitalism does not appear in a pure form and that it coexists with pre-capitalist relations and that Rudra was ignoring this.

9   In his study of the Punjab in 1969, Rudra (Rudra et al., 1990) did not find much capitalism there that satisfies his three criteria: 'there was not yet the emergence of any class, how-ever small, of full-fledged capitalist farmers', as he recalled later (Rudra, 1983: 421). Neither did he say that there was feudalism or semi-feudalism. He subscribed to a 'Neither capitalist nor feudal (or semi-feudal) ... position' (ibid.).

In his later (mid-1970s) study of West Bengal, he said this: 'If generation of surplus through the employment of wage labor, appropriation of that surplus by the owners of capital and reinvestment of that surplus for the purpose of expansion of that capital be a characteristic feature of capitalism, then there are indeed increasing manifestations of such capitalist feature in West Bengal agriculture' (Rudra, 1974; also 1978). Describing this research of his, he said: 'my rejection of the emergence of a full-fledged capitalist class was not in any way in contradiction with my later argument that 'there are increasing manifestations of characteristic features of capitalism', which...co-exist with continuing manifestations of characteristic features of pre- capitalist relations' (Rudra, 1983: 421).

the revolutionisation of the labor-process, the production of relative surplus-value on the basis of a capitalistically-constituted labor-process, the compulsion to increase the productivity of labor, etc. The 'relations of capitalist production' are the relations which 'express and realise these laws of motion at different levels of the social process of production' (Banaji, 2013: 60; italics added). Capitalism is whatever form of social relation of production allows these laws of motion to exist, for him. It is sufficient to note that revolutionization of productive forces is a part of the definition of capitalism for Banaji, so his definition is close to Patnaik's and Rudra's, to some extent. We will return to Banaji to see how his views are also different from Patnaik's and Rudra's and are problematic.

We might briefly add here the view of the so-called post-modernist Marxists who have commented on the mode of production debate in more recent times. These scholars reject the concept of mode of production altogether. For them, the question of whether a country is capitalist or not is a wrong question. They say that the criteria of commodity production and wage labor, let alone property relations, do not define capitalism. Capitalism – like any society – has to be defined in terms of relations of exploitation understood as performance, appropriation, distribution and receipt of surplus labor and that 'relations of exploitation [are] ... the constitutive factor in the definition of capitalism' (Chakrabarti and Cullenberg, 2003: 60–61, 65). They also argue that: 'households are sites of surplus generation', that 'most of the household enterprises are noncapitalist' and that 'The characterization of the Indian mode of production as "capitalist" immediately collapses with the inclusion of household class processes' and that Indian mode of production cannot be called semi-feudal either because 'the household class process could be independent or communal' (Chakrabarti and Cullenberg, 2003: 75–76).

Returning to the original debate, if capitalism does not exist – or if it exists in a limited manner, in a few areas – *why* is this the case? Two sets of barriers have been highlighted by scholars. Amit Bhaduri says that the semi-feudal social relations act as a fetter on the development of productive forces under capitalism, and therefore, by implication, on the development of capitalism itself. Semi-feudalism that characterizes Indian social formation has more in common with classic feudalism of the master-serf type than with industrial capitalism (1973: 120; also Prasad, 1990). It has four characteristics in the agrarian context: share-cropping; the perpetual indebtedness of small tenants; existence of two modes of exploitation, namely usury and land-ownership in the hands of the same class (land owners lending money to their tenants at very high interest rates), and lack of accessibility to the market for the poor tenants (the latter 'surrender' their product to the landlord-creditors) (Bhaduri, 1973:

120–121). The last criterion refers to forced commerce as a form of primitive accumulation: because of their poverty, peasants are forced to sell their produce just after harvest when the foodgrain price is lower, and buy back foodgrains at a higher cost at a later time when the foodgrain price is higher. This purchase and sale of products is forced because peasants cannot enter the market when they wish to and cannot freely buy and sell at the market price. This has implication for the development of productive forces. The practice of usury and the appropriation of the surplus product through rent will require that the available balance of paddy with the tenant must always fall short of her family's consumption requirements. So investment in land by landlords might increase the income of tenants, and with increased income, they will not have to borrow from the landlords. As a result, landlords' usury business will be adversely affected. So they have no incentive to invest in land to improve productivity – or more generally, landlords do not have an incentive to cultivate their land by hiring laborers and investing in land to increase productivity.

While for Bhaduri, it is mainly usury – the unequal relation between debtors and creditors – that is the barrier to development of capitalism, for Patnaik (1983; 1972a) and others, it is mainly tenancy or rental extraction – the unequal relation of production between landlords and tenants – that acts as a barrier. Her argument on this topic begins with nature of capitalist rent, which is the rent that represents a surplus of produce (surplus product) *after* all cultivation cost and a normal rate of profit to the cultivator (or the entrepreneur) have been met. We can express her view like this: $R_c = T - C - P$. Where: R_c = capitalist rent, T = total product, C = cost of production, including imputed wage for family labor, and P = profit.

She says that those who lease in property in Indian countryside (tenants) are not paying capitalist ground rent. Instead, they are paying *pre-capitalist* ground rent. This is simply because after paying the high level of rent, tenants do not enjoy the profit part (P) of the total product (P = 0). So: $R_p = T - C$, where R_p is the pre-capitalist ground rent.

The level of this rent (R_p) is very high – 50% of the gross produce for most of the tenants. Tenants can pay such a high level of rent because they can depress consumption per family labor unit for the sake of the minimum secure income ensured by the possession of land through lease (Patnaik, 1972a: 21). In other words, the imputed wage part of the cost of production tends to be extremely low.

Given that the level of rent is very high, tenants do not have any capacity to invest because little is left with them after they pay their rent. In fact, this is a point that Daniel Thorner also made (Thorner, 1969: 332). According to

Thorner,[10] there is a built-in depressor in the form of legal, economic and so-cial relations in a context characterized by unequal landownership, the reli-ance of the common villagers on usurious loans, landlord domination over direct producers as tenants, and landowners appropriating high profit through trading. All this depresses the tendency towards technological change: land-owners can make money through usury, rent and trade so they have little in-centive to invest in increasing productivity, and peasants, deprived of any surplus, have little ability to invest either.[11]

Building on Daniel Thorner's work, Patnaik (1986) further explains how the rent-barrier allows only a limited development of capitalist relations. If the members of the property-owning class are to switch to capitalist production from merely buying up assets (e.g. land) and leasing it out, they will have to invest a certain amount of money which already gets them a return any way (in the form of usurious interest, and in the form of rent from the land that some-one with money can buy up and lease out). So the person renting out her land to peasants will switch to what Patnaik calls *capitalist* production if the rate of profit becomes at least equal to the sum of: (a) the rate of return from leasing out (i.e. the rental income as a percentage of expenditures in cultivation by the tenant) and (b) the rate of return on money-capital invested in non-agricultural activities (e.g. usury). Such a rate of profit is very high. This is impossible to get unless the investment embodies productivity-raising new techniques, or better ways of organizing production, which raise surplus per unit area by the re-quired quantum. 'A *quantum-jump* is required for the rent barrier to be over-come, so that investible funds are directed into capitalist agriculture' (Patnaik, 1986: 782; stress added). Unlike in the case of peasant capitalism (the American or French path to capitalism), a *small or gradual improvement* in productivity is not sufficient to make landlords invest money to make more money (p. 786; stress added) and become capitalists proper.

Bhaduri and Patnaik thus show that the development of capitalism in India is constrained, at least in the vast rural areas where most people live. Thus it is the social relations of usury or rental extraction from direct producers that fet-ter the development of productive forces under capitalism. Although from the surface their arguments appear to be different, I will argue, and *pace* Patnaik (1995: 91), that their theories of fetters on productive forces – usury or the rent-barrier – presuppose one common factor, that is, unequal distribution of means of production (land). It is the unequal distribution of land which allows the landowners to (a) engage in usury, because landless and land-poor people

---

10   According to Rudra (1983), the MOP debate was inspired by Thorner's work.
11   On 'the depressor theory', see Harriss (1992, 2013).

need loans (the semi-feudalism thesis of Bhaduri) and (b) rack-rent these people, for they need and compete for land-on-lease (the rent-barrier thesis of
Patnaik).[12]

2   A Critique of Some Influential Ideas in the Indian Mode of Production Debate

My critique revolves around the economic and extra-economic coercion in
economic transaction, and the nature of the relationship between capitalism
and technological change. I accept Patnaik's point that market relations *per se*
are not to be conflated with capitalist mode of production – indeed this point
has been made in the discussion on the European transition to capitalism by
Robert Brenner (1977) and by Ellen Wood (1997). Patnaik goes on to claim,
problematically in my view, that the landowner-employer does not appropriate surplus value from free laborers but maximizes the returns from exploiting
the destitute labor tied to agriculture. For her, being tied to agriculture owing
to the lack of alternative employment opportunities is analogous to serfs being
tied to feudal lords. Clearly, Patnaik fails to maintain the distinction between
economic and extra-economic (un)freedom of direct producers. If laborers
can freely choose their capitalist employers, they are said to have freedom (i.e.
there is no extra-economic coercion/unfreedom), although they are not free
not to choose any employer because they are dispossessed of their own means
of production. Laborers are free in 'the double sense that they neither form
part of the means of production themselves, as would be the case with slaves,
serfs, etc., nor do they own the means of production, as would be the case with
self-employed peasant proprietors' (Marx, 1977: 874). It is difficult to accept
Patnaik's logic that if people, who are dispossessed of their means of production, cannot find alternative employment outside of a given sector, then these
people would never constitute a 'proletariat' in that sector (1995: 82).

I find problematic Patnaik's concept of free labor, a concept (and its opposite, unfree-labor), which has been a subject of much discussion.[13] I will make
two arguments briefly. Firstly, the conceptual definition of wage labor concerns her *causal powers* (e.g. she can choose his/her employer) and *causal
liabilities* (e.g. she has to depend mainly on wage-work for her subsistence)

---

12   Interestingly, unequal land distribution is considered a given, without it being considered
      in relation to capitalist development in the country, including the penetration of market
      relations (i.e. Leninist class differentiation).

13   See: Banaji, 2003; Bhandari, 2008; Brass, 1999, 2011, 2012; 2017; Breman, 2010; Lerche 2013;
      and Rao, 1999. See Das, 2013c for a comradely discussion of Brass's excellent work, that is
      in fundamental agreement with Brass.

arising out of her structural (= class) conditions (i.e. she has been stripped of the means of production). So, an essential aspect of capitalist production relation is free labor in the sense Marx defines it: it does not have access to any/ sufficient means of production which is why it is economically forced to seek wage-work (so it is freed from means of production),[14] and it is free to sell its labor power to whichever employer it wants to, although it is (generally speaking) not free not to sell labor power at all.

Secondly, and with respect to the second aspect of freedom (being able to freely enter and exit a labor contract), in certain conditions, employers transform what is hitherto free labor into unfree labor, as Brass has been forcefully arguing for decades. Employers employ various strategies (e.g. locking up workers in a place) to stop them from running away. It should be added that while Patnaik fails to distinguish between economic and extra-economic forms of unfree labor, Banaji thinks that the free and unfree labor distinction is fictional: that whether labor is economically free is not an essential aspect of capitalism. Although Marx stipulated free labor as a necessary characteristic of capita*lism*, as mentioned earlier, the history of actual capitalist societies does indicate that specific capit*als* do make use of various forms of unfree labor – where labor's right to freely enter and exit the labor market has been taken away by capital, making it difficult for labor to exercise the right to negotiate wages.

Just as Patnaik fails to adequately distinguish between economic and extra-economic forms of labor, Bhaduri fails to distinguish between economic and extra-economic coercion that small-scale direct producers – peasants – experience. He conflates forced commerce with extra-economic coercion: he abstracts from the fact that no extra-economic coercion is imposed on peasants to freely enter and exit the market. What he calls forced commerce is an economic transaction, and any element of coercion is economic in character. It is also not clear why it is that: a property owner leasing their property to a (small-scale) direct producer for a rent is not compatible with capitalism, and more specifically, why it indicates *extra*-economic coercion. How is this different from a property owner leasing in or out a building in the city? (While Patnaik does not view the rental payments by peasants as extra-economic, she sees this as *pre*-capitalist, so for both Patnaik and Bhaduri, the rental payments by peasants are pre-capitalist). As well, Bhaduri fails to explain why property owners

---

14 It is interesting to note what Gerald Cohen (1978) argued: in some cases, unless proletarians own some instruments, (e.g. a spade), they may not be hired, so ownership/possession of some means of production becomes a defining aspect of – a necessary condition for – proletarian-hood. In my view, it is possible that: asking workers to bring their own tools is a way of a) reducing the necessary investment on constant capital and thus the cost of production, and b) recruiting suitable workers (if one has a spade, it is more likely than not that one knows how to use it).

cannot do the following: promote investment in technological change, increase the total net product, and increase the rent, and thus benefit from technological change (Bardhan, 1983).[15]

Let me now deal with the second part of my critique to set the context for my alternative view. This concerns the question of whether generalized commodity production is the necessary and sufficient condition for capitalism or whether an additional criterion of surplus reinvestment *in productivity-raising techniques* has to be specified, which is what Patnaik thinks should be the case.[16]

The idea that technological change in production can raise the rate of profit, attract capital and thus promote capitalism implies that the development of productive forces in itself can result in a change in production relations or class relations. It is as if whether or not capitalism exists is a matter of what individuals are able to choose do (i.e. choose to obtain higher profit in production rather than from another way of making money such as renting out means of production or money lending). Mere opportunities to make money whether by using a new technology or by producing a large volume of a commodity for an external market in itself will not result in a change in class relations to capitalism. The essence of capitalism is not a higher level of development of productive forces. That is generally, but not always or everywhere, a consequence of its essence. Capitalism is fundamentally a class relation.

Chattopadhyay, one of Patnaik's main protagonists, rightly argues that commodity production and wage-labor are necessary and sufficient conditions for capitalism. He correctly says that 'Accumulation and reinvestment of surplus value fall within this definition and need not be stated separately as far as the definition of capitalism is concerned' (1990a: 82). But he mistakenly seems to assume that the *production* of surplus value *necessarily* generates its productive *reinvestment* in technological change: 'The very process of commodity production with the sale of labor power as its ultimate form generates the process of surplus value and its reinvestment...' in technological change (1990a: 82). He argues that the use of sophisticated technical equipment indicates only a higher level of capitalist development, not the capitalist development itself (1990a:

---

15   From an empirical angle, Rudra found no significant differences in the input – output patterns of owner-operated farms and tenant-operated farms, especially when one examines medium and large-sized farms (Chakravarty and Rudra, 1973).

16   For her, if a property owner employing labor does not reinvest profit and expand the enterprise and lower production, then the element of dynamism that characterizes capitalism vis-à-vis pre-capitalism is absent, so there is no capitalism. In other words, she implies that there is nothing in between landlord-tenant relations and relations of a dynamic capitalism. Her view also implies that in the conceptualization of capitalism, productive forces have primacy over production relations or class relations.

82; see also Ram, 1972: 54). This is true, and this is in line with Lenin's point that 'Hired labour is the chief sign and indicator capitalism' (cf. Bukharin, 1933) but the question, not resolved by Chattopadhyay, is this: under what condition will reinvestment of surplus value in technology happen? Why indeed may the surplus value be produced in agriculture under capital-labor relations not necessarily be invested in agriculture to raise productivity of labor? Chattopadhyay's assumption – as Lenin's – appears to be that relations between capital and labor will automatically give rise to technological change. While the Patnaik-Bhaduri type argument seems to deal with the distinction *between* capitalism and its 'other' (pre- or non-capitalism), the Chattopadhyay type argument seems not to bother with any distinction *within* capitalism itself (i.e. between different forms of capitalism itself). On the other hand, post-modernist Marxists think that the very question of whether a country is capitalist or not is a wrong question, a position that is based on a problematic theory of class itself (for a longer critical discussion of their approach, see Das, 2017a: Chapter 4).

A problematic corollary of the conception of capitalism employed by the likes of Patnaik and Bhaduri is this: to the extent that capitalism exists, in whatever sense and to whatever extent, the development of productive forces is retarded mainly/solely by factors (e.g. unequal distribution of land) that are *external* to the logic of capitalism. It is true that the rental extraction combined with usurious 'exploitation' may dominate the labor process in *specific places* within a social formation (and can act as a barrier to capitalist development in the sense that Patnaik and Bhaduri, etc. have discussed). This will not be surprising in the context of a large and geographically diverse country such as India. But the fact of local conditions cannot be used to determine the mode of production and associated *dynamics* (= rules of the game; causal powers and liabilities of property owners and direct producers) at the *national* scale, which is where the concept of mode of production properly belongs, given the connection between class relations and power of the state that is concentrated at the national scale.[17] I will have more to say about the so-called semi-feudal processes later. While the rent and usury barriers may be important at the local scale (in specific localities), it is mistaken to think that these are the main barriers at the national scale. Can the barrier to capitalist development not inhere *capitalist* class relation: can the specific nature of capitalist class relation that exists not be a barrier to the further development of productive forces under

---

17   More adequately, given the tendency of the logic of capitalism to operate at the global scale, the concept of the capitalist mode of production belongs to both the national scale and the international scale but one cannot lose sight of how, in a country that is dominantly capitalist, non-capitalist relations can exist, and articulate with, capitalism at the sub-national scales.

capitalism, in the absence of strong counter-vailing forces (e.g. state policies)? Related to all this is the question of class struggle: what significance does actual/potential struggle of direct producers have for the logic of the capitalist mode of production?

3   Examining India's Capitalist Character on the Basis of Marx's
        Distinction between Formal and Real Subsumptions of Labor

I suggest that one solution to the problem surrounding characterization of capitalism and the examination of the fetters on the development of productive forces under capitalism, could be achieved by the deployment of Marx's concepts of formal and real subsumption (subordination) of labor under capital, the concepts that signify the importance Marx himself attached to the forms of integration of labor into capitalist production process at the different stages *within* the history of capitalist class relation (Das, 2011, 2017a: Chapter 8).[18] Marx, the historical-materialist, says that capitalist production is differentiated into two forms/stages: the formal subsumption of labor under capital and the real subsumption of labor under capital. Marx also introduces a third form of subsumption as we will see.

Capitalism is based on wage-labor on a large-scale (not sporadically). No wage-labor, no capitalism. In the initial stage of capitalism, wage-labor is only formally subsumed under capital: capital takes over a pre-existing labor process (e.g. a farm/factory existing under pre-capitalist relations) without 'revolutionizing' the labor process (Marx, 1977: 1021). In this stage, capital 'subordinates [subsumes] labor on the basis of the technical conditions within which labor has been carried on up to that point in history' (Marx, 1977: 425). It does not change the socio-technical conditions of production. The necessary part of the working day (necessary labor) – the labor time that the worker expends for producing the equivalent of her own means of subsistence – cannot be generally decreased during the early stage of capitalism, so the only way more surplus value can be produced within a capitalist country is by increasing the other part of the working day (i.e. surplus labor time). This is done by making workers work longer and/or intensifying the pace of labor process (this is also done by depressing wages below the value of labor power, although Marx generally abstracted from the fact that wages fall below the value of labor

---

18   These concepts are present in the middle of *Capital* volume 1 and in the Appendix to it, called 'Results of the Immediate Process of Production' written between 1863 and 1866. This discussion suffered from its delayed publication and relative neglect as a consequence.

power).[19] During the stage of formal subsumption of labor under capital, absolute surplus value is produced.

Based on Marx's own discussion (1977: 1025–1029), it is possible to identify four main features of formal subsumption of labor in a more systematic way than he did.

1. the absence of extra-economic coercion in the sphere of production: that is, wage-laborers, who do not own (sufficient amount of) means of production and are therefore economically forced to work for a wage, are generally free to choose their employers;

2. no more labor time is consumed in production than is socially necessary (i.e. there is competition to reduce the cost of production of commodities for sale, and this means that the law of value has started operating);

3. the means of production and consumption confront the worker as capital in the sense that they have to be bought in the market;

4. an *economic* relation of supremacy and subordination exists as the worker is supervised and directed by the capitalist.

Formal subsumption of labor is the most general form of capitalism. It need not be associated with pre-modern or non-modern: it 'was no less effective in the old-fashioned bakeries than in the modern cotton factories' (Marx, 1977: 425). Formal subsumption:

> it is at the same time directly a process of the exploitation of the labor of others. [...] It is the general form of any capitalist production process [i.e. production process under the rule of capitalist social relation]; and at the same time, however, it is a *particular* form alongside the *specifically capitalist* mode of production in its developed form [i.e. the real subsumption], because although the latter entails the former, the converse does not necessarily obtain.
>
> MARX, 1977: 1019; parenthesis added

Real subsumption has all the four characteristics of formal subsumption mentioned above. In addition, it involves the reduction of necessary labor time through an increase in labor productivity, through the use of technology, per unit of time and therefore the appropriation of surplus value in its relative form. This happens under what Marx called in his 'Results' the specifically capitalist mode of production. And when this happens, the ratio of constant capital to variable capital tends to increase (Marx, 1977: 762). Of course,

---

19   Marx assumes the wage to cover the means of subsistence. Let's say that the daily wage that covers the cost of maintenance is $10 for 8 hours. If the wage is reduced to $5, this effectively means a working day of 16 hours, other things constant.

technological change has to be such that the time taken to produce workers' means of subsistence is reduced. So, for example, technological change in food production and in the production of means of production of food (e.g. tractors) matters with respect to the production of relative surplus value. Technological change in a systemic manner in various branches of production contributes to technological change that ultimately helps capital appropriate surplus value in its relative form at a societal level.

In addition to the two forms of subsumption, Marx (1977: 645) also mentions in the middle of *Capital* volume 1, what he might call 'hybrid subsumption':

> It will be sufficient if we merely refer to certain *hybrid forms*, in which although surplus-labor is not extorted by direct compulsion from the producer [that is, there is no feudalism or pre-capitalist relation], the producer *has not yet become formally subordinate* to capital. In these forms, capital has not yet acquired a direct control of the labor process. Alongside the independent producers, who carry on their handicrafts or their agriculture in the inherited, traditional way, there steps the usurer or merchant, with his usurer's capital or merchant's capital, which feeds on them like a parasite. (parenthesis added)

Marx adds: 'The predominance of this form of exploitation in a society excludes the capitalist mode of production' which means that *sporadic* existence of these forms does *not* exclude the capitalist mode of production, 'although it may form the transition [to capitalism], as in later Middle Ages'. So, one may treat such things as merchant capital making an advance to petty producers who sell their products to merchants as a transitional process between feudal production relation and capitalist production relation. It should be stressed that hybrid subsumption is *not* the subsumption of wage labor: it is much rather a transitional process between pre-capitalist relations of production and formal subsumption of labor under capital. Banaji is mistaken to conflate hybrid subsumption with subsumption of wage labor (more on this later).

Having developed a historically-inflected (dialectical) view of capitalism, Marx says that real subsumption of labor comes into being spontaneously on the basis of formal subsumption of labor: 'a specifically capitalist mode of production (his code word for technologically dynamic advanced capitalism) ... arises and develops *spontaneously* on the basis of the formal subsumption of labor under capital' (Marx, 1977: 645; italics and parenthesis added).

There are potentially two problems with Marx in my view. *To the extent that* Marx means that the transition to real subsumption is *spontaneous* and thus merely an economic process, not mediated by struggle, this view is mistaken. One cannot assume that the transition to real subsumption is automatic. It was not spontaneous in English capitalism that Marx wrote about in his empirical work. In England, formal subsumption lasted for almost more than two centuries (i.e. until the last third of the 1700s). Here successful working class resistance against appropriation of absolute surplus value (where workers work long hours during the period of formal subsumption of labor under capital) was very much responsible for the introduction of machinery. The transition cannot be spontaneous especially in the global capitalist periphery, given a large reserve army of labor (created partly during colonial times) allowing capital to appropriate absolute surplus value through lower wages and through overwork.[20] The 'spontaneity argument' contradicts Marx's more general view about the proximate role of class struggle in social change – social change both within a mode of production (as in *Capital* – see below) and between one to another (as in the opening lines of the *Manifesto*). In fact, Marx himself said that 'It would be possible to write a whole history of the inventions made since 1830 for the sole purpose of providing capital with weapons against working class revolt' (1977: 563).

It is not just Marx who seems to neglect, or to *under-stress*, class struggle in examining the history of changes in the forms of capitalist class relation. As mentioned earlier, it is surprising that most authors in the Indian mode of production debate talk about class relations as if they can be separated from class struggle. And when class struggle is discussed (see the works of Mencher discussed in Thorner, 1982), the relation between it and capitalist accumulation is not dealt with. They, more or less, ignore this fact: while capitalism is characterized by competing capitalists seeking to cut costs and increase surplus value, it is the case that the rate of surplus (and thus the level of real wages) as well as methods of appropriation of surplus value (e.g. whether labor-displacing technology will be used) depend partly on class struggle (or, on the balance of power between capital and labor).[21] This means that given that capitalists act in pursuit of surplus value and given the logic of competition, whether or not the productivity-improving labor-saving methods are used, and thus the transition

---

20 Both of these processes Marx specifically mentions as products of the existence of a reserve army in Chapter 25 of *Capital*, vol. 1.

21 In this chapter, the changing balance of power between capital and labor (or employers/owners and direct producers) is used interchangeably with class struggle, which is seen as occurring in covert and overt ways. If, for a variety of reasons, the labor market is tight allowing labor to put pressure on employers to increase wages without having to go on a strike, that is included under the changing balance of power between capital and labor. Of course, there are more overt actions signifying class struggle. And class struggle is seen as happening both from above (employers' strategies to undermine direct producer's power) and from below (struggle and strategies by direct producers).

to real subsumption of labor made, will, to some extent, depend on the changing balance of power between capital and labor, as expressed in the working class struggles *against* capitalism *under* capitalism.

Class struggle is important not just to the transition *to* capitalism (as has been highlighted in the debates on the nature of capitalism and on the transition to capitalism in Europe) but also to the transition *within* capitalism. It is also interesting that in these discussions (Aston and Philipin, 1985; Hilton, 1978), there has been little if any discussion on the forms of subsumption, while the entire stress is on the transition *between* pre-capitalism to capitalism as such.

The second problem with Marx is this. *Whether or not* Marx believed that class struggle intervened in the transition to real subsumption, he *generally* assumed that *given* capital – labor relations, capitalism will develop into a dynamic, developed capitalism (except during the moments of economic crisis) at all times and in all places. Even if Marx could be interpreted as not ignoring the role of class struggle in the transition to real subsumption, there could still be a potential problem: he could be seen as assuming that class struggle against formal subsumption happens but that the transition to real subsumption also happens because of successful class struggle. In other words, given formal subsumption of labor, real subsumption will follow everywhere, class struggle or no class struggle. Generally ignored is the possibility that *within* the global system of capitalism which as a whole is dynamic (labor productivity tends to rise) relative to pre-capitalism and within which the long-term *tendency* is towards the real subsumption of labor but that within a dominantly capitalist nation or a set of nations, there may be strong obstacles to capitalism systemically developing productive forces (in vast sectors and areas). There is a tendency towards the transition to real subsumption, but whether or not the transition occurs in a specific context must be seen as contingent, and specifically in the context of peripheral capitalism. It does not arise spontaneously as Marx had probably assumed.

I will argue that where/when production has the four characteristics of formal subsumption Marx discusses, production is capitalist in terms of social relations of production and exploitation, even if, and *pace* Patnaik (1990a: 49; 1990b: 68–69) reinvestment in machinery does not exist. In such a case, labor is only formally subsumed under capital. In India, the constitution (e.g. Article 23) guarantees the right to choose one's employer, and the laboring class – most of which owns no or little means of production, and whose numbers are increasing relative to those who are considered employers – works for employers for a wage. This is especially true in agriculture (Figure 3.2).

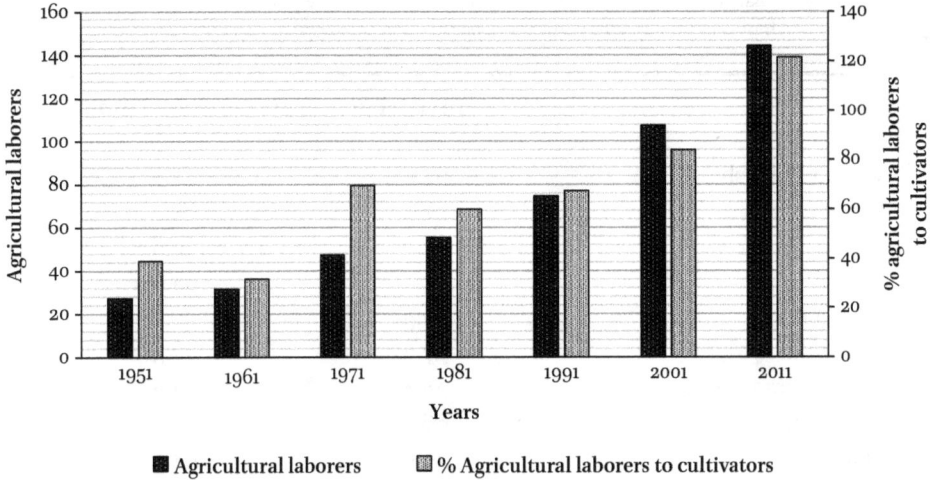

FIGURE 3.2   Agricultural laborers population (in millions) and as a percentage of the
cultivators population.
Notes: 2001 numbers include both main workers and marginal workers. Note that
cultivators include millions of those who do not hire laborers (they belong to
poor and middle peasantry).
SOURCE: DATA IN THE FIRST COLUMNS ARE TAKEN FROM SINGH (2002). THE
DATA FOR 2011 ARE FROM: HTTP://LABOURBUREAU.NIC.IN/ILYB_2011_2012
.PDF

If we consider, once again the agricultural sector, which contains a near majority of the labor force, a large part of the work is done by hired labor. This is the
case, even if, and as expected, the share of hired labor to total human labor
varies from province to province. Clearly, a lot of work is still done by family
labor (Figure 3.2). As well, in terms of investment in agriculture (as in industry), it is dominantly a *private* affair (Table 3.1), and purchased inputs comprise
the majority part of the cost of production in most provinces, meaning that
means of production tend to confront labor as capital in agriculture (Table 3.1
and Figure 3.3).

All these methods of exploitation may not increase the surplus value extracted in its relative form but would increase the mass of absolute surplus
value appropriated by the capitalist. We cannot expect specifically capitalist
production to emerge 'out of the blue'. Given that there is a vast pool of laborers, some of which is historically created under colonialism including through
primitive accumulation (and this Patnaik herself recognizes), there is ample
scope for the appropriation of absolute surplus value. However, in certain
areas (e.g. the Green Revolution areas of the Punjab, and indeed in other parts

TABLE 3.1   Share of hired labor in total human labor, and share of purchased
             inputs in total cost of cultivation, per hectare, 1994–97

	% Hired labor	% Purchased inputs
Andhra Pradesh	61.6	70.8
Assam	31.1	30.1
Bihar	37.2	60.9
Gujarat	44.4	64.6
Haryana	17.3	52.7
Karnataka	57.2	67.3
Madhya Pradesh	38.4	54.2
Maharashtra	66.4	73.8
Orissa	39.9	54.2
Punjab	57.7	80.5
Rajasthan	13.4	44.5
Tamil Nadu	72.4	78.9
Uttar Pradesh	33.8	53.7
West Bengal	55.4	58.1

Note: Figures are (unweighted) average for the different crops grown in particular provinces.
The relatively low figures in some of the advanced provinces such as Haryana may imply that
rich peasants use machines to get the work done instead of hiring labor.
SOURCE: GILL AND GHUMAN (2001)

of the Third World) the specifically capitalist mode of production – the process
of relative surplus value appropriation – has emerged with the aid of the state
that subsidizes the use of the (Green Revolution) technology, which allow
capitalists to increase their profits.[22] In advanced countries, capital was confronted with barriers (e.g. barriers in the form of successful class struggle) to
absolute surplus value being appropriated through workers working long
working days and through intensified labor process. Capital, however, turned
worker's struggle to its own use, in a sense: successful struggle against long working days led to the use of new methods of production, to the conscious use of

---

22   That the use of this technology was promoted by imperialism is another matter. As Harry
      Cleaver (1972) says, the sale of modern farm inputs including tractors by the US in India –
      as a strategy to counter the crisis of overproduction in the US – was indeed a reason why
      the US was keen on the introduction of the Green Revolution.

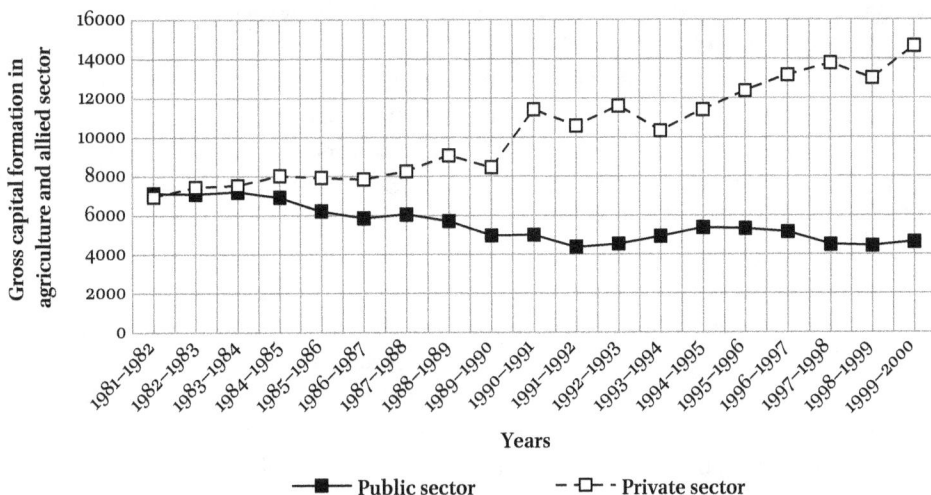

FIGURE 3.3   Gross capital formation in agriculture and allied sector (at 1993–94 prices)
(in million rupees)
SOURCE: DATA FROM SINGH (2003)

science and technology, and thus to an increase in the relative surplus value. Such a process countered the loss of surplus value in its absolute form. Class struggle against formal subsumption of labor – along with vast resources flowing from the colonies which, given the presence of capital – labor relations *already*, were turned into capital – contributed to the transition to real subsumption, and in the resultant dynamism we associate capitalism with. But such class struggle against formal subsumption as has been observed in the center of global capitalism is not as easy to conduct in the periphery, and especially given the presence of a vast reserve army. Globally, capitalism is a progressive force – at least in the sense of promoting the development of productive forces. But this does not mean that in every part of the world this will be so always. The 'absence dynamism' is as much a part of it as the presence of dynamism. To say that where capitalism is not playing its 'assigned'/traditional progressive role it must be because of some pre-capitalist relations,[23] or that capitalism as a social relation does not exist, is being blind to capitalism's

---

23   This is not to deny, once again, that there are localities where pre-capitalist relations exist. It is just that these relations do not define the dynamics of the social system, the social formation, although they may affect the specific ways in which the law of value may work and has its actual impacts in specific places.

socio-spatial dialectics (presence and absence of technological backwardness within a single global system of capitalism).

It is important to stress again that: like the transition from pre-capitalism *to* capitalism, the transition *within* capitalism is mediated by class struggle. Class struggle, however, always occurs amidst specific factors, which provide the context for it, and thus makes the transition to real subsumption non-automatic.[24] These include: availability of affordable technology; ecological conditions (for nature-dependent production); concentration of property in the hands of a few; market demand from a given sector; and state interventions (see Appendix 1). The processes within which class struggle happens, including ecological conditions,[25] vary geographically. So the effect of class struggle on the transition from formal subsumption will vary, producing uneven transition to real subsumption of labor and therefore uneven development of productive forces.[26]

In their geographically uneven struggle against capital, laborers can succeed and have succeeded on at least three fronts to varying degrees: increasing real wages, reduction in the working day and in emancipating themselves, to some extent, from unfree labor relations whereby their right to enter into and exit

---

24   Not to acknowledge the existence of the material (= political-economic) context within which labor struggles happen is to fall in the trap of voluntarism [see Anderson's (1980) discussion of E.P. Thompson, in his Chapter 2, and especially, 32–33].

25   'Uneven development is the concrete process and pattern of the production of nature under capitalism' (Smith, 1992: xiv).

26   For capitalist development to happen, it is important that there is a significant amount of concentration of the means of production (e.g. land) in the hands of a few. Now, the degree of inequality in distribution of the means of production (land) is a function of such processes as: market-driven class differentiation referred to in Chapter 2; and demographic change (population growth) and inheritance laws that lead to the break-up of family-owned holdings, and primitive accumulation (which has been an on-going process).

      Class struggle against primitive accumulation – which happened during colonial times and continue after 1947 (see Dhanagare, 1991; Gough, 1974; Guha, 1983; Surjeet, 1986, 1992) – can sometimes slow down primitive accumulation to some extent (the recent case of Posco, the South Korean company, not being able to acquire land in Odisha partly due to struggle from below is a case in point). Also, such struggle will be more successful in one place (say West Bengal) than in the Punjab (see Bandopadhyaya, 1989: 59–60; Webster, 1990). And the degree of market penetration underlying agrarian class differentiation will also vary from place to place. Thus both these processes (geography of class struggle and geography of market penetration) will create a differentiated terrain on which not only capitalist relations themselves – and labor struggle against formal subsumption within capitalism – emerge/develop but also as Bharadwaj (1982: 606–607) noted, technologies (e.g. the Green Revolution technology) are introduced.

from a labor contract does not exist because of various forms of bondage. In Andhra Pradesh villages, studied by da Corta and Venkateshwarlu (1999), struggle by laborers led to a decline in traditional/permanent bonded labor relations and to increases in real wages for men and women. Even if no overt collective action exists or if the overt collective action fails, the implicit 'go-slow' by laborers at lower-than-reservation-wage may still lead to many employers having to raise wages, as in several UP villages (Srivastava, 1999). It has been pointed out that non-agricultural wages put pressure on property owners to pay higher wages, either through strike actions or simply to be able to *attract* sufficient laborers, who are free to reject any request from employer for work (Lerche, 1999: 205). In villages in the Uttar Pradesh province also, government program of land redistribution and other pro-poor programs (e.g. employment generation program), however limited they may be, have led to a decline in land- and asset-lessness. This has caused an upward pressure on the supply price of labor power and increased labor's bargaining power to some extent. Further, creation of rural infrastructure has enhanced mobility of rural laborers who are able to access extra-local, alternative (often non-farm) employment, and this has enhanced their bargaining power as well vis-à-vis their local employers.

The question then is: how does capital respond to this sort of successful struggle or even to the very possibility of labor resistance. Capital's response has been many-fold. I will try to address these different responses to class struggle against formal subsumption by using findings from research on rural labor struggle as well as my own on-going work on agrarian transition in the eastern Indian province of Odisha (Orissa). Whether or not the discussion convincingly supports my case – that the transition from formal to real subsumption is not automatic and is impacted by the balance of power between the two basic classes – it at least demonstrates the ways/areas in which more research can be conducted. It is important stress that only some responses from property owners to the changing balance of power between the two basic classes are connected to the transition to real subsumption (employers using labor-saving techniques), especially, in a peripheral-capitalist economy.

When wages rise, working periods shorten and unfree labor relations decline due to class struggle, capitalists may use technology to reduce costs and discipline labor (real subsumption of labor). In the light of my conceptual discussion above, this is to be expected. But employers may also continue to use hired labor but try to reduce costs by various traditional means (deepening formal subsumption), and they may resort to 'hybrid subsumption'-cum-rental extraction. I will discuss the first response (slow and uneven transition to real subsumption) in Section 4, and the other two responses in Section 5. In this section and the next section, then, I will discuss the *different* (and sometimes contradictory) ways in which the balance of power between classes can affect accumulation strategies by capital. The main question is this: when laborers launch struggle – at individual and collective levels, and in formal/overt and informal/covert ways – against capital, how do capitalists who are already formally subsuming labor respond and with what implications for the transition to real subsumption of labor?

4   Class Struggle and the (Slow and Uneven) Transition to
       Real Subsumption of Labor

Indian employers are sensitive to costs and to market forces. As wages increase due to political action of laborers and other factors, in many villages in Andhra Pradesh in South India and in Uttar Pradesh in North India, and so on, property owners resort to labor-displacing mechanization to reduce the wage bill (da Corta and Venkateshwarlu, 1999: 91). In some places and at given points in time, if the balance of power is effectively in favor of labor, capital's attempt at using technology – and thus the transition to real subsumption of labor – can be resisted/slowed, at least temporarily. I will spend some time to discuss this process in the context of Kerala, located on the south western coast of the country. Kerala is known for the first communist government elected within a bourgeois democratic system anywhere in the world, and here laborers are more strongly organized than in other parts of India. The transition to real subsumption appears to have passed through three stages. First, laborers strike or bargain for higher wages. Second, following their success capital tries to use mechanization to reduce dependence on labor. Laborers then fight against mechanization thus slowing down the transition to real subsumption. Finally, labor's resistance to capital's introduction of technology softens.

In the 1960s and the 1970s, rice fields owned by capitalist farmers were the hotbed of class tension in Kerala.[27] Laborers launched political action demanding higher wages and better working conditions including an eight-hour day, supported by multiple unions, including those organized by communist parties. Capitalists responded by retrenching workers many of whom had worked for them on a long-term basis. They resorted to casualization of employment, and to the use of tractors to reduce dependence on laborers. In many places, workers reacted by forcibly harvesting rice. They were supported

---

27   The Kerala discussion mainly draws from Kannan (1999).

by pro-labor governments in power which would not interfere in labor disputes. In the rice bowl of Kerala, Kuttanad (in Allepey district), some tractors were broken up by laborers – this was reminiscent of the Luddite movement that Marx talks about in *Capital*. Framers gradually lost control over the process of recruiting laborers. Unions themselves would send in a large number of laborers to farms for harvests which would be completed in a few hours.

Because rice cultivation was profitable in the 1970s, farmers persisted in their attempt to introduce tractors, however, in order to increase labor productivity. Unions did not relent either in their protest. Ultimately, landowners agreed to pay wages to the traditional ploughmen for ploughing the fields. In return, the unions agreed to let the farmers use tractors. This meant that farmers would be free to use the tractors for ploughing after they have paid wages to the ploughmen. So the ploughmen would come and plough the field, take their wage and go away. Farmers would then prepare the land with tractors in whatever way they wanted. Over time ploughing by ploughmen became a ritual. Gradually they stopped ploughing, but yet they would come and collect their wages! Writing about one specific district, Oommen says this:

> When the rich farmers in Allepey district introduced tractors, the labor unions of agricultural workers successfully led their struggle against it so that the farmers had to agree that whether or not they used tractors, the land should be ploughed through bullocks/buffaloes at least for two rounds instead of the traditional three rounds in order that the laborers did not face further unemployment or suffer loss of wages.
>
> OOMMEN, 1990: 234

This system was acceptable in the 1970s when rice price was high. But with the decline in rice price afterwards, farmers complained about it, because they were paying more than their counterparts in other parts of the country. They responded by reducing employment in rice cultivation and also through crop substitution (replacing rice with other less labor-intensive crops). This meant the loss of employment for labor. In the late 1980s and afterwards, there developed a new situation – one of labor shortage – in place of labor surplus. There was an expansion of the non-agricultural economy, especially the service sector, due to the flow of remittance money from the Middle East. Younger people preferred to work outside of agriculture. Also, through years of struggle, laborers had earned a high social wage (see Heller, 1989) in the form of poor relief from the government: the social wage was almost equal to the consumption requirement of one adult in a family. This meant that unemployed people could wait for the right employment without starving. Both these factors caused labor shortage and had positive implication for their bargaining power over wages and working conditions. And this prompted landowners to use mechanization as a counter-response. This time unions no longer protested against the use of machines. But they did stick to their earlier strategy of demanding payment of wages to the same number of workers at the prevailing rate when machines were to be introduced. This actually meant the payment of double wages to an operation.[28] This did put a brake on introducing mechanization in post-harvest operations. But eventually, the introduction of tractors and other machines has now been widely accepted.[29]

As Oommen (1990: 234) has said, in Kerala 'mobilization of the agrarian proletariat is moderating, if not halting, capitalist development in Indian agriculture'. This may not happen everywhere. This slowing down of the transition to real subsumption will happen where laborers' organization has reached a sufficiently high level and where there are other favorable factors including a certain degree of support from local state apparatuses to laborers.[30] As the left organization in the industrial sector shows, workers' ability to slow down capitalist mechanization where it occurs is only, can only be, transient, as long as capitalist relations exist.[31]

---

28   When in the 1990s mechanical threshers were sought to be introduced, laborers demanded the same rate of payment 'even when the job is done with the aid of the threshing machine.... The farmers aver that when the machine is introduced, the manual labor involved would be considerably reduced and then there is no justification for paying the labor at the old rates' (Venugopal in Kannan, 1999).

29   More recently, in the harvesting season, farmers brought harvesting machines from the neighbouring Tamil Nadu State on rent and workers resisted it in Kuttanad. However, the Communist Party of India (Marxist) intervened and settled the issue in favour of farmers and allowed them to harvest with the machine. I am grateful to Dr. Mohanakumar, a political economist from Kerala, for this point (personal communication).

30   Kerala has had leftist governments quite frequently which have implemented pro-labor welfare policies better than many other provinces, thus increasing the reservation price of labor power.

31   The West Bengal experience is the most significant example. In this State there had been a Left-Front government in power since 1977 until 2011, and it had shared power for a few years in the 1960s (Mallick, 1994). In the early years of the government, it was supporting workers' strikes enthusiastically, which contributed to capital flight to other States. In consequence, the workers were exhorted by the party leaders to behave in a disciplined manner! Capital is capital, whether it is in agriculture or in industry. As in industry, in agriculture too, workers' ability to even moderate the effects of capitalism on workers (including such effects as technological change) is very transient.

5   Class Struggle and the 'Blocked' Transition to
        Real Subsumption of Labor

In less developed countries such as India, the dominant responses of capitalists
may be those which are other than real subsumption, resulting in a capitalism
that can remain relatively backward (in the sense of per-hour labor productivity) for a long time. The first of these responses is just 'business-as-usual': reinforcement of formal subsumption. The second type of response includes a
combination of Marx's 'hybrid subsumption' (mercantile-usury based exploitation) and rental extraction.[32]

5.1   *Reinforcement of Formal Subsumption*
In response to actual/potential struggle from below by men over low wages,
long working days and unfree labor relations, capital may intensify/reinforce
formal subsumption by increasing the use of women labor. For example, in
response to successful male labor struggles against bondage relations and low
wages in parts of Andhra Pradesh, capital hired women laborers who accepted
relatively unfree labor contracts (more on this below) and lower wages, which
their husbands refused, in order to support their families (da Corta and Venkateshwarlu, 1999). Thus capital resorts to a 'gender fix' in response to class
struggle: it reinforces formal subsumption of labor through the substitution of
male laborers' freedom for the unfreedom for female laborers. It should also be
noted that by taking up work refused by men, women enable men to prolong
men's strike against capital.[33]

    In other areas, when local laborers go on a strike, capital may take advantage
of geographical differentiation in wages and in working class organization:
capital can use laborers *elsewhere* ready to work with lower wages and less satisfactory working conditions that local laborers are rejecting. Thus capital uses
a 'spatial fix' as a response to class struggle. This is exactly what happened in
Gujarat on the west coast of India where landowners 'imported' non-local docile aboriginal laborers in order to undermine the bargaining power of local

32   Still another response is what I will call political accumulation. Landowners formally sub-
     suming labor use local state apparatuses including police (through bribing, etc.) to beat
     up laborers on strike, or to have them jailed on false charges or to file court cases. Surplus
     from agriculture is used to support political parties and to bribe the state bureaucracy
     which in turn helps capital use state's rural development resources illegally, in a form of
     primitive accumulation (Wilson, 1999).
33   Studies in future may reveal what the long-term impact of such prolongation of strikes on
     technological change will be.

laborers who demanded higher wages (Breman, 1985). This is actually a country-wide process. To the extent that property owners can make use of the spatial differentiation in wages and in proletarian solidarity, this differentiation is a barrier to the transition to real subsumption, although the strategy may enhance profits for specific capitalists locally.

A most important response in this category – reinforcement of formal subsumption of labor – is the tied labor use. In response to struggles for higher wages and against permanent bonded relations (permanent laborers work for given landowners almost throughout their lives), landowning capital uses non-permanent attached labor arrangements. Under these arrangements, debtor-laborers are obliged to report to the lender's farm first before other employers and to work off the loan based on a pre-arranged tied wage. Capitalists resort to these arrangements not only to secure labor supply – especially during peak seasons (Bhalla, 1999: 50) – but also to secure it at a lower than the market rate (da Corta and Venkateshwarlu, 1999: 92). The use of attached labor relations must be seen as a mechanism of labor control. This can be seen as a form of class struggle from above (p. 113), which is a response to class struggle from below. More specifically, it segments the labor market by dividing laborers into two fractions: permanent laborers who tend to possess land, and casual or daily laborers who tend to be landless and who belong to the lowest positions in the caste hierarchy (ex-untouchables). The use of attached labor reduces the bargaining power of casual laborers as casual labor days are reduced (Lerche, 1990: 199) which happens as more work is done by attached laborers, and indeed reduces wages of casual workers (Bhalla, 1999: 50). Even in villages in Haryana, a State which is a bastion of capitalism based on the use of the Green Revolution technology, but which is not traditionally known for class struggle from below, many landowners reportedly seek to exercise greater control over labor process by using permanent labor contracts in order to prevent possible struggle.

5.2   *Reversion to Hybrid Subsumption and Rental Extraction*
In many localities as those in Andhra Pradesh, with a rise in real wages, landowners respond partly by moving into commission trading: buying up farm produce at harvest, and reselling them at higher prices to urban merchants. Sometimes merchants advance cash loan to small landholders, and/or lease out some land, and borrowers promise to pay in kind at harvest at a price determined by the lender. This is called tied harvest (da Corta and Venkateshwarlu, 1999: 88). Thus, as wage costs rise, landowners seek to appropriate surpluses indirectly through exchange relations rather than through production relations based on hiring in labor (p. 89). Elsewhere as in many Uttar Pradesh

villages also, when wages increase, labor-intensive non-mechanized paddy cultivation is leased out for a rent; the lessee does not provide any means of production (Lerche, 1999; Srivastava, 1999).[34]

I will deal with the hybrid subsumption and rental extraction response of landowners in some more detail by using empirical materials based on my on-going field-work in north-eastern Orissa. The main point to note here is this: even if because of successful wage-bargaining (in a condition where government-provided non-farm wage-work puts upward pressure on wages) local employers are forced to pay higher wages, the transition from formal to real subsumption can be counter-acted by locally existing conditions such as the nature of class-(re)composition of direct producers and their consequent lack of solidarity, and degree of land concentration (i.e. the contextual factors mentioned in the last section). This is an area where I first conducted a study in two villages located in Jajpur District (less than 400 kms south of Calcutta) in 1988 and have returned frequently till now. Let me first discuss the situation existing up till the late 1980s. I will then briefly discuss the more recent changes.

The area has fertile soils. But it is completely dependent on the monsoon. Landowners are small owners. The average size of operational holdings (owned land plus land leased in minus land leased out) was less than three acres in the late 1980s.[35] There were half a dozen landowners, among a sample of 70 families, with 10 acres and more land. Instruments of production were (and still are) very rudimentary: bullocks were being used as draught animals; wooden ploughs, wooden yokes and iron sickles were some of the instruments of production. Laborers were mainly of two types. There were those who worked on daily wages. And others were attached laborers on annual contracts, whose wages had two components. They received wages on a monthly basis in cash and/or in kind (paddy). They were also given a piece of land during the annual tenure of the contract by the employer the product of which the laborer kept. The attached laborers did not have any fixed working day: they worked as long as they were needed to by their employer. There was generally no extra-economic coercive relation between laborers and employers. But being an attached labor carried low social status.

Employers in my study-area were and are small capitalists, and they were formally subordinating labor. They did not invest in machines. Rather, the

---

34 It should be noted that rental extraction as a method of exploitation, stressed in the semi-feudal thesis (in the 1960s/1970s), has considerably decreased in importance, nationally, although in certain areas it can be widely prevalent.

35 The all-India figure for the average area operated per holding was 3.31 acres in 1991–92 and 2.62 acres in 2002–03 (Government of India, 2007).

surplus, which was produced on the basis of the methods of formal subsumption of labor (long working day, low wages), found its way into many non-farming avenues including Marx's 'hybrid forms' of subsumption. Usury was very attractive, the annual rate of interest being 36% to as high as 120%. Many landowners did invest in local politics (election campaigning): being a part of local state apparatuses helps one to get government loans (for farming and also for non-farming purposes such as daughter's marriage for which a dowry has to be paid). Also becoming a local politician is a source of earning bribes from the locals in return for official favors. Many invested in children's education: this could fetch money in future in the form of urban remittances and in the form of a dowry for male educated children with good jobs at the time of their marriage. Going into mercantile business also helped many landowner-traders to have some control over the supply of laborers: two biggest landowners in the area were also shopkeepers. Such control is very important because getting farm work done at the right time is crucial to productivity, especially when farming depends entirely on the rainwater. The laborer, who is usually very poor, can get means of subsistence such as flour and rice on credit from the landowner-trader, and this obliges him/her to work for the landowner when he/she wants them and in a relatively 'disciplined' manner. Investing the farm-generated surplus in trading also allows the landowner-trader to sell his/her stock to customers (i.e. laborers whom he/she usually hires) over whose earnings he/she has some control.

It must be stressed here that the landowners in the study area, like landowners elsewhere, are involved in a cycle of expanded reproduction, though this may not show up in investment in productivity-raising techniques *within* the farm sector. This also means that, as Gunder Frank, a participant in the MOP debate, and Brass (1995a: 96; Mies, 2012: 173) have noted, surplus does not have to be reinvested in the individual capitalist enterprise that generates it or even locally, for there to be the capitalist mode of production. More generally, and *pace* Patnaik, the farmers employing legally free wage labor but *not* investing in productivity-raising techniques *in* agriculture *are* capitalists, just as those employing free wage labor and making such investments (as in the Green Revolution areas) are. While in the case of (e.g.) the Green Revolution farmers the tendency for expanded reproduction is expressed in terms of investment in machines enhancing productivity, in the case of other farmers that may not be the case. Expanded reproduction can happen when a property owner can buy a lot of land which she/he cultivates by employing a lot of workers for long hours and low wages.

I notice three stages through which class relations have evolved in the study area. This is an area where strikes for higher wages occurred very frequently between the 1970s and mid-1980s. Nominal wages for farm work increased from Rupees 2.5 in 1974 to Rupees 15 in 1995. In 2008, it was Rupees 50–60 (which would fetch 3.5 kilos of rice now in the local market).[36] Locally, 'real wages' – as measured by the amount of paddy that can be bought at these nominal wages – increased by 200% between the 1970s and the 1990s. The working day has also shrunk by at least two hours relative to the earlier period (i.e. prior to the 1970s). The attached labor arrangement, which was profitable for landowners, has *completely* disappeared as laborers did not like being on call for 24 hours at low wages. Laborers have also become much less 'docile' and 'disciplined' from landowners' standpoint. Landowners complain that unless laborers are supervised directly, the work assigned may not get done, and this is a problem especially for upper caste landowners who will not work on their land themselves. As a result of these changes, however limited they be from laborers' standpoint, landowners who were earlier hiring low-caste laborers to cultivate their land started renting out their lands and often to these same laborers, leading to a process of deproletarianization or re-peasantization. This has been happening in the last 25 years or so.[37] This process – landowners switching from direct cultivation of land with hired labor to the cultivation of land by using tenants – is the second stage in the evolution of relations in the area.[38] The possibility of exploiting these poor peasants (small landholders who rely on wage labor as well as self-employment on their own land or on land leased in) enables the local landowners to shift the negative impact of wage-strikes (e.g. higher wages) on to these laborers who are now poor peasants.[39] If

---

36   In 1999–2000, one rural person needed 19 rupees a day to be able to buy enough food to give her the minimum calories needed (i.e. 2400) (Patnaik, 2007: 141). If the daily wage was 50–60 rupees, one can imagine how far the wage was below the cost of reproduction of a family of five members.

37   It must also be said that with the neoliberal economic policy in force since 1991, the prices of inputs such as fertilizers have been increasing much faster than the price of paddy, the dominant crop in the area, and thus cultivation based on directly hiring wage labor has been unviable for many (smaller) landowners.

38   It can be asked why landowners in the study area, confronted with increasing wage-hikes, did not go in for mechanical innovations, whereas many farmers in Punjab and Haryana would have done so. One important reason is the fact that landowners in the study area are very small owners: less than 10% of them own more than 5 acres, whereas in Punjab and Haryana, 25.3% of owners own more than 5 acres (Sharma, 1992). This means that and as explained earlier, the effect of class struggle on accumulation/development in a place will depend on local contextual factors, including land concentration.

39   It is necessary to consider whether the labor process involved in the leasing of land to poor peasants is to be viewed as (disguised) piece-wage work, and sharecroppers as piece-rated workers, as Srivastava (1999) suggests.

the strikes were organized jointly by poor peasants (i.e. tenants) for lower rents and by laborers for higher wages, landowners would not have been able to rent out land at high rent. This did not happen. For one thing, there was a conflict between their class interests: as more land is leased out to tenants, the availability of wage-work on employers' farm for daily laborers is reduced, and this is what I mean by class-recomposition of direct producers. For another, the local communist organization, many members of which were labor employers, lacked better organizational ability. To the extent that tenants have limited economic resources to invest in land because of high level of rental as well as usurious exploitation, and have less incentive also to make productivity-raising investments (because land does not belong to them), the productivity of land suffered. I have heard many landowners who were hiring labor earlier and have rented out their land now complaining about this.

In more recent times (since 1990s), and this is the beginning of the third stage, some landowners are a bit alarmed at the fact that not far from their villages, poor peasants are getting organized (more informally than formally) to demand a higher crop-share (presently, tenants pay half of the gross produce to landowners who do not contribute anything towards costs of production). In some cases, tenants have stopped cultivating the land they have rented on the basis of a verbal contract, allow the land to remain fallow. It remains to be seen what the response of landowners will be to the growing resistance of tenants to high rent. Development of productive forces will be furthered if in response to increase in both wages and in the crop-share demanded by tenants, landowners individually and/or collectively make productivity-raising investments so that cultivation with hired labor will be profitable. In the last few years, a new development has happened: there has been a sporadic use of tractors and power tillers. Tractors are bought by large owners, many of whom tend to belong to middle castes for whom performing manual labor is not a taboo. They use tractors on their own land cultivated with hired labor, and also lease out tractors to the tenants who have leased in land from higher caste landowners (and in some cases, to the landowners whose land lies fallow because their tenants would not cultivate it). These poor tenants use tractors to plough their own land and land leased-in; note that most of the work is still done by hand, and only ploughing is done by tractors. They do this because there is a pressure on them to cut costs of cultivation as the rental payment they have to make to landowners is high, indeed higher than the legal limit, and this is high because tenants as poor peasants have not been able to be organized to strike against landowners for lower rent. So in this sense the ability of landowners to extract a high level of rent – which reflects their power vis-à-vis poor peasants/laborers-as-tenants, or in other words, class struggle from the top – has started to prompt resorting to tractorization from below, but given the financial situation of poor peasants their turn to mechanization will be limited. And the wage increase to which changing balance of power between workers and property owners in favor of workers has contributed has prompted the (middle caste) landowners to use tractors and power tillers as well. It remains to be seen how far this latter tendency – a form of incipient transition to real subsumption of labor – develops.

6   Possibilities of, and Limits to, Real Subsumption of Labor

Wherever productive activity satisfies the four criteria for formal subsumption of labor, we have capitalism as a class relation. This could be in manufacturing, tourism, mining, etc. And given class struggle against formal subsumption, employers may further reinforce formal subsumption or may resort to real subsumption.

Whether the argument is about agriculture or industry, we need to be mindful of the fact that it is not true that real subsumption is not at all happening. To the extent that it is happening, one can argue that there are islands of real subsumption in an ocean of formal subsumption (and hybrid subsumption in rural areas). Ultimately, the transition to real subsumption is a matter of relative cost: whether an employer will use a machine to make workers process a large amount of raw material and to thus produce more at less cost or they will hire many people for long hours and low wages, depends on what is more profitable. A balance of power between the classes in favour of the direct producers imposes a cost (it can increase wages and reduce the length of the working day, without a corresponding reduction in real wage).

Under certain conditions, real subsumption can indeed happen even if there is no evident class struggle against formal subsumption. One condition is the technical character of labor process. Oil drilling requires machines, and one cannot get the work done by hiring many people for long hours. Nationally operating capitalists are increasingly competing at a global level, so they must cut costs and may be forced to use technology – often borrowed from developed – imperialist – countries – to do so: if machines can lower costs more than the strategy of hiring people for lower wages, the people who can resist low wages in future, real subsumption of labor will be resorted to, even in the absence of class struggle now. Imperialist capital (multinational companies) may sell a given technology as a commodity, which is then used in production. All this means that India – like many other backward countries – does not exactly have to follow the stages that, for example, England followed. As Trotsky (2008) says: 'The privilege of historic backwardness [...] permits, or rather compels, the adoption of whatever is ready in advance of any specified date, skipping a whole series of intermediate stages' (p. 4).

However, there are limits, and obstacles, to the extent to which a late developing country can adopt advanced technology, especially in agriculture and industry, and thus skip the stages of development that already-advanced countries had to travel by having to development the technologies themselves. Some of these obstacles, Trotsky (2008) himself describes:

> The possibility of skipping over intermediate steps is of course by no means absolute. Its degree is determined in the long run by the economic and cultural capacities of the country. The backward nation, moreover, not infrequently debases the achievements borrowed from outside in the process of adapting them to its own more primitive culture. In this the very process of assimilation acquires a self-contradictory character. Thus the introduction of certain elements of Western technique and training... [could lead] to a strengthening of serfdom as the fundamental form of labor organisation. (pp. 4–5)

There are obstacles not only to the transition from pre-capitalist to capitalist development that Trotsky talks about. There are also obstacles to a higher form of development from a lower form of development, within capitalism. Trotsky, unfortunately, abstracts from this.[40] That is, there are obstacles to the transition from one form of capitalist class relation (formal subsumption) to another form (real subsumption). Real subsumption requires investment of capital in machinery and the built environment, but in part owing to the transfer of surplus from peripheral countries such as India to imperialist countries, there is a problem of the relative lack of investible surplus.[41] Then there are opportunities for capitalists to make money outside of production that weaken the pressure to make profit-in-production in a competitive environment. These opportunities include buying up property at cheap prices and speculating on it; getting access to society's resources (commons) at a cheaper-than-market rate; and being able to sell things (e.g. arms) to the state or provide welfare-services to the public on behalf of the state, at the above-the-market rate. Besides, given globalization, the power of unions operating mainly within a sector, within a city or region, is rather weak (in a relative sense), so the struggle against formal subsumption does not succeed (much). This allows the capitalists to continue to exploit workers by making them work long hours for low wages. Capitalism

---

40   One can say that some of the obstacles (e.g. cultural obstacles) that Trotsky talks about are relevant to the transition from formal to real subsumption in India.
41   On the topic of the surplus transfer in the imperialist system, see Ding (2015); and Smith (2016).

is simply not developing productive forces, whether in farming or industry, in a *systemic* way that it was, for example, during Marx's time in England, or indeed, in the US in the 20th century.

To the extent that real subsumption and associated technological change is happening, it is not systemic: there is not a very strong economic compulsion and pressure on those with money to invest in creating and using technology to use labor productivity per hour. To the extent that technology is used, it is often adaptive: borrowed technology being used (sporadically). So Beams's statement about China might apply to India even better:

> The assembly-line system of production, which spread to other major capitalist economies after World War II, lifted the productivity of labor, thereby providing the foundation for capitalist expansion.
>
> Unlike the US, however, Chinese economic expansion has not been associated with a similar development of the productive forces. Its growth has been rooted in an adaptation of assembly line methods, not in the development of the new system of production. While it has provided a boost to profits, this has been obtained not through an increase in the productivity of labour, as was previously accomplished by American capitalism, but through the employment of ultra-cheap labour.
>
> BEAMS, 2012

7   Jairus Banaji's (and Others') Mistaken Subsumption of Labor Perspective

As I have argued, the subsumption perspective is an important one when it comes to understanding the nature of class relations. There is one scholar, Banaji, who was an important participant in the Indian MOP debate and who does talk about subsumption, in his theoretical work and in his historical discussion (of the small-scale producers). My approach to subsumption is different from his and that of some other scholars.

It is true that capital in its usury form can exploit labor (e.g. family labor) without what Marx calls specifically capitalist mode of production (mode of production in the technical sense). But that does not mean that one cannot distinguish between exploitation of wage labor by productive capital and exploitation of labor in the hands anti-diluvean capital (usury).

Banaji sees formal subsumption of labor mainly in terms of 'The subjugation of the *simple commodity form of production* to capital' (2013: 96; stress added). For him: 'The relations of production which tie the enterprise of small commodity producers to capital are already relations of *capitalist* production' (ibid.: 97; italics added). What he calls *capitalist relations of production* are compatible with a variety of forms *of deployment labor*: using share-croppers, bonded labor and labor tenants (who may be given some land by the land-owner to use) are different ways in which *'wage labor* is recruited, exploited and controlled' (2013: 145; italics added). He says: 'The argument is not that *all* share croppers, labor tenants and bonded laborers are wage-workers, but that these 'forms' [of labor] may reflect the subsumption of labor into capital in ways where the 'sale' of labor power for wages is mediated and possibly disguised in more complex arrangements' (ibid.).

Banaji thinks, rightly, that formal subsumption of labor 'presupposes a process of labor that is 'technologically' continuous with earlier modes of labor'. But then he wrongly concludes that: *before* the advent of advanced capitalism (real subsumption), whatever forms of exploitation (e.g. exploitation of small producers selling their products to landlords-usurers) that exist in a commodity producing society, constitute formal subsumption of labor. Banaji says: formal subsumption of labor 'crystalizes when capital confronts the small producer, invades his process of production and 'takes over' without subjecting it to technical transformation' (2013: 280). In formal subsumption of labor, 'the labor process remains *external* to the movement of capital' and it 'is technically fragmented, or decentralised'. There is 'no centralisation of social means of production and labor power', and there is no 'objective social interconnection', among individual capitals.

Banaji argues that: 'Behind the superficial 'surface' sale of products' small-scale producers formally subsumed under capital 'sell their labor power' and not their products, to 'the monied bourgeoisie of moneylenders and merchants through whom the small producer was brought into relation with the market' (2013: 98) by way of the latter receiving advances towards the cost of reproduction and means of production. The 'price' which small-scale producers receive signifies a relation, not of exchange, but of production; it is 'a concealed wage' (ibid.). So they are 'disguised laborers'.[42] Banaji says: 'a monied capitalist

---

42   More broadly: Banaji, who, as mentioned before, rejects the equation of the capitalist mode of production with juridically free wage-labor as a particular form of exploitation, conceptualizes that mode of production, in terms of its laws of motion (i.e. continuous accumulation of capital). Such a mode of production is not about any specific relations of exploitation, and can be based on a variety of forms of exploitation based on free wage-labor, sharecropping, labor tenancy, bonded labor. These forms of exploitation may just be ways in which paid labor is recruited, exploited and controlled by employers. Share-croppers, tenants working on landowners' lands, and bonded laborers are not necessarily wage-workers, but the forms of exploitation these categories represent may reflect the subsumption of labor into capital in ways where the 'sale' of labor power for wages is

(for example, a merchant, moneylender) may dominate the small producer on a *capitalist* basis, he may, in other words, extort surplus value from him, without standing out as the 'immediate owner of means of production' (2013: 281–282). Thus 'the labor of small producers... can be seen as formally subsumed under capital'.[43]

'When the process of production of small-peasant household depends from one cycle to the next on the advances of the usurer – i.e. when, without such 'advances', the process of production would come to a halt – then in this case the 'usurer', i.e. the monied capitalist, exerts a definite *command* over the process of production' (2013: 308). And this command over the process of production involves appropriation of surplus value, as happened in the Deccan of the 19th century (p. 308, 329). 'All that is necessary to the constitution of this command is that a relationship of pure economic dependence prevail between the producer and himself, and that on this basis he compels the production of surplus-labour' (2013: 329). When direct producers in villages or towns are unable to engage in production without loans, then the capitalist advances 'them their wages and means of production as 'loans', and recovers his surplus value as 'interest' (Banaji, 2013: 330). This, once again, for him, is formal subsumption of labor. Banaji says: 'forms of bondage [i.e. tying of labor to this or that property owners] are precisely a characteristic of the *formal* subordination of labour to capital' (2013: 328). Associated with Banaji's concept of formal subsumption are his problematic views concerning labor and value, as I show below.[44]

---

mediated and possibly disguised in more complex arrangements. Sharecroppers, etc. are disguised wage-workers (see also Post, 2013; also Srivastava, 1999).

43   In at least one place, Banaji admits that what he describes is in fact 'pre-formal' subsumption. The latter 'would tend *to lead* in the vast majority of cases to the system of formal subordination' (italics added). He says that, for Marx, 'pre-formal' subsumption can be 'assimilated' into formal subsumption, and that is how he (i.e. Banaji) treats the matter (2013: 282).

44   Banaji says that 'free labour, so-called, *cannot* be an essential moment of capital', and it 'is not a precondition for the accumulation of capital or even whole forms of capitalist economy' because 'the self-expansion of value is intrinsically indifferent to the forms in which it dominates labour' (2013: 11, 13) and because free labor is 'the contingent outcome of struggles to shape the law and the social relations behind it' (p. 13). Banaji says, for Marx, free labor means labor without means of production (p. 13). He is against what he calls the vulgar notion of wage-labor in which a wage-laborer is one who is divorced from means of subsistence and means of production and is forced to sell her labor power (p. 53). For him, wage labor does not have to be commodity labor power or free labor: wage-labor is value-creating (p. 55). But what is value for him? He does not define it. In my view, to say that free wage-labor is not the essence – general attribute – of capitalism is to accept the following: when one walks, 'steps may be long or short' and therefore walking cannot be defined (that is, one cannot identify the 'general attribute' of walking) as

Banaji's subsumption perspective is mistaken in many ways. Marx, in fact, clearly distinguishes between formal and hybrid subsumptions, and Banaji does not. Banaji loses sight of the specificity of capitalism as a class relation rooted in the relation of *production*, which is generally based in nominally free wage-labor, although it may make use of unfree labor as a strategy of class struggle from above as mentioned earlier.[45]

Let me return to *Capital* volume 1 again. Formal subsumption is characterized by a relation of *control* between capital and labor.

> The labour process is subsumed under capital (it is capital's *own* process) and the capitalist enters the process *as its director, manager.* For him it also represents the *direct* exploitation of the labour of others. It is this that I refer to as the formal subsumption of labour under capital
>
> MARX, 1977: 1019; italics added

Further:

> A merely formal subsumption of labour under capital suffices for the production of absolute surplus-value. It is enough, for example, that handicraftsmen who previously worked on their own account, or as apprentices of a master, should become wage labourers under the *direct control of a capitalist.*
>
> Ibid.: 645; italics added

This relation of control is manifested in the fact that: 'the capitalist *takes good care* that the labor adheres to normal standards of quality and intensity level of quality and intensity, and he extends its duration as far as possible...' (p. 1020). But Banaji's formally subsumed workers are *not* 'under the direct control of a capitalist' as their director/manager. And it is not important to examine what happens 'within the process of production'.[46]

'a rhythmical motion [of the body] from one place to another' (Dietzgen, 2011: 25). The labor that Marx talks about as being the essence of capitalism is different from the worker in pre-capitalist societies (i.e. the worker as a slave or a serf, etc.) and it is also different from the *sporadically* existing wage-labor in pre-capitalist societies. The worker under capitalism is a unique category and has a unique historical-political role.

45   Besides, it is class struggle, among other things, over formal subsumption of labor, that partly explains the transition to real subsumption, but there is little role of class struggle in Banaji's conception of subsumption.

46   'Before the production process they all [capitalists, and the slaves or peasants turned into wage-laborers] confront each other as commodity owners and their relations involve nothing but *money*; [and] *within* [italics in original] the process of production they meet as its components personified' (Marx, 1977: 1020).

The formal subsumption is characterized by an inversion in the relation be-tween the direct producer and the means of production: 'It is no longer the worker who employs the means of production, but the means of production which employ the worker' (Marx, 1977: 425). Concomitantly, when formal sub-sumption happens, there is also a deepening of material-economic depen-dence of one class (direct producer) on another (the exploiting class). 'A man who was formerly an independent peasant now finds himself a factor *in the production process* and *dependent* on *the capitalist directing it* [i.e. the produc-tion process]' (p. 1020; italics added). Not only does the way in which the direct producer is integrated into labor process (i.e. the way in which the direct pro-ducer as the worker performs the work of production) depend on the capitalist *as the director* of the labor process. It is also the case that 'his [her] own *liveli-hood* depends on a *contract* which he [she] as *commodity owner* (viz. the owner of labor power) has previously concluded with the capitalist as the *owner of money*' (ibid.; italics added). There is a relation between the market relation between direct producers and capital on the one hand, and the nature of labor process under capitalism on the other. As Marx says: 'The *continuity* of labour increases when producers dependent on individual customers are supplanted by producers who, *bereft of wares to sell*, have a constant paymaster in the shape of the capitalist' (p. 1020). All this simply means that there is a direct, unequal, economically coercive market relation between two commodity owners (la-borers and capitalists), a relation which is exploitative. But these consider-ations, including those about the labor market, are not important for Banaji.

Historically, formal subsumption comes after a stage when capital appeared in a subordinate position. Formal subsumption coincides with the dominance of capital as a relation of production:

> The distinctive character of the *formal* subsumption of labour under cap-ital appears at its sharpest if we compare it [i.e. the formal subsumption] to situations in which capital is to be found in certain specific, subordi-nate functions, but where it has not emerged as the *immediate owner of the process of production* [italics added], and where in consequence it has not yet succeeded in becoming the dominant force, capable of determin-ing the form of society as a whole.
>
> MARX, 1977: 1023

While Marx contrasts formal subsumption to those situations 'in which capital is to be found in certain specific, subordinate functions', Banaji treats these situations themselves as constituting formal subsumption. Interestingly, Marx gives an example from the India of his time, which is worth considering:

In India, for example, the capital of the usurer advances raw materials or tools or even both to the immediate producer in the form of money. The exorbitant interest which it extracts ... is just another name for surplus-value.[47] It transforms its money into capital by extorting unpaid labour, surplus labour, from the immediate producer. But it does not intervene in the process of production itself.... *But here we have not yet reached the stage of the formal subsumption of labour under capital.*

> Ibid.; italics added

Marx goes on to add:

A further example is merchant's capital, which commissions a number of immediate producers, then collects their produce and sells it, perhaps making them advances in the form of raw materials, etc. or even money. *It is this form that provides the soil from which modern capitalism has grown* [and which means that this form is not yet capitalism in the form of formal subsumption] and here and there it still forms the transition to capitalism proper. Here too we find no formal subsumption of labour under capital. The immediate producer still performs the functions of selling his wares and making use of his own labour.

> Ibid.; italics and parenthesis added

It is very clear that Banaji's views on subsumption is different from Marx's use of it, which I defend, deploy and retheorize here. The inadequacy of Banaji's thinking is not necessarily because it differs from Marx's: one's view does not have to coincide with Marx's to be correct or adequate, and one's view can coincide with Marx's and can be incorrect and inadequate. The problem is that Banaji's conceptualization of capitalist production, its historical specificity, is inadequate as he conflates it with forms of commodity production which are not based on nominally free wage-labor. To the extent that the term he uses (formal subsumption) refers to a concept, this concept is a chaotic concept because it includes under it the processes which are not necessarily connected.

It should be added that Banaji is not alone in mis-conceptualizing formal subsumption of labor (in the Indian context). Consider D'Mello (2018: 135), a great scholar, with sympathy for the Maoist view of society, who says the following about formal subsumption in contemporary India:

---

47   Technically speaking, Marx is not accurate in his use of 'surplus value' (what he means is 'surplus labor'), just as he sometimes uses sale of 'labor' when he means sale of 'labor power'. Banaji however makes much of Marx's use of the term 'surplus value'.

there has been mostly a formal subsumption of agricultural labour to capital; the extent of real subsumption of labour to capital, where capital directly takes over the process of cultivation, hires wage labour, reinvests the surplus and adopts new production techniques has been very limited.

Needless to say that D'Mello is wrong on the same ground as Banaji is.[48] In North America, David Harvey also has a mistaken view of subsumption.[49]

8   Conclusion

There are empirical, theoretical and political implications of my argument in this chapter. Using the subsumption perspective on capitalism as a class relation, I have critiqued in this chapter the view of many radicals who doubt that India (especially, rural India), as a place is capitalist. In India, there *are* the necessary conditions for capitalist relations (e.g. a class of legally 'free' laborers; commodity production; investment of money in production and exchange to make more money). Therefore, as capitalists elsewhere, property owners in India hiring these nominally free laborers possess the same sorts of causal powers (e.g. they can earn profits) and suffer from the same sorts of causal liabilities (e.g. they can lose their means of production if they do not produce commodities efficiently, i.e. at the value). They are capitalists whether or not they use, for example, the Green Revolution type technology or biotechnology or any other form of technology.[50] In some areas, property owners may be formally subsuming labor, and in other areas there may exist real subsumption. The ways in which capitalists' powers and liabilities are expressed in actual patterns of investment, and the effects of the exercise of these powers and liabilities on the development of productive forces (i.e. whether the transition from formal to real subsumption of labor under capital happens) are contingent

---

48   Alavi (1981) also sees interaction between capital and peasants as formal subsumption of labor.

49   Harvey (1982: 373) has got the class character of capitalism wrong when he says that: 'Monetary relations have penetrated into every nook and cranny of the world and into almost every aspect of social, even private life. This formal subordination of human activity [or labour], exercised through the market, has been increasingly complemented by that real subordination which requires the conversion of labour into the commodity labour power through primitive accumulation'. One can see how different Harvey's conceptualization of formal and real subordination/subsumption is from Marx's.

50   In a later chapter, we will discuss the class character of the use of technology.

on the balance of power, or struggle, between property owners and workers. The forms and outcomes of the struggle – which are affected by the overall capitalist development and developmental activities of the capitalist state at the national and provincial scales – condition the extent to which capitalists who are competing with one another cut costs of production through the use of technology aimed at increasing labor productivity or through the formal subsumption of labor (e.g. the use of highly vulnerable and low-cost labor, including labor that is reproduced outside of capitalism as in indigenous communities) or indeed through a locally and sectorally varying combination of these two methods.[51]

In the light of what has been said above, the mode of production in India is decidedly and near-exclusively capitalist.[52] This is capitalist at least in the sense of formal subsumption of labor under capital. And it is decidedly not semi-feudal.[53] Of course, the semi-feudal thesis continues to be subscribed to by many (implicitly or explicitly).[54] The view of capitalism and capitalist

---

51 Capital also makes use of labor whose reproduction is only partly borne by the capitalist
      wage system (e.g. laboring households working seasonally for capital as migrant laborers
      may collect means of subsistence such as fuel, etc. from common property for free, and/
      or laboring households who may own some land). Capital also relies on the fact that those
      responsible for reproduction of the laboring households, and they are generally women
      and girl children, spend many hours of unpaid labor at home and are often denied access
      to a normal amount of necessaries to consume, and all these processes in the realm of the
      private sphere of necessary labor (Vogel, 2014) reduces the social value of labor power
      that is bought and sold.

52 In some specific localities, land and labor may not have attained the status of full com-
      modities, and extra-economic coercion may be exercised in the sphere of production.

53 Banaji (2010) says that categories such as semi-feudalism 'are all slavishly copied from
      Mao's theorisations for China that will soon be almost a century old!', indicating that for
      him the category of semi-feudalism is problematic (at least in part) because it is histori-
      cally old. On that ground many of Marx's categories developed that predate Mao's would
      be inadequate. In fact, many mainstream scholars critique Marxism because it was 'so
      19th century'. My opposition to semi-feudalism is not on the basis of it being an old cate-
      gory but rather on the ground that it does not help us interpret the reality of class society
      that India is and that its political implication is reformist (as explained later).

54 For example, Sugden (2017) says that the Mithilanchal area spanning the Nepal – Bihar
      border is semi-feudal as it is dominated by landlordism and usury, even if the area serves
      as a surplus labor pool for urban areas in India. Sugden says: 'The concept of a "semi-
      colonial" social formation remains relevant in the post-liberalization context, even if the
      term is not always used. In spite of the growth of capitalism in India's (and Nepal's) urban
      centers and rising rural–urban migration, labor is mostly casual, low paid, and unskilled,
      being dominated by work in low-value industries such as agro-processing where wages
      and conditions of employment are poor' (p. 134). So, according to Sugden, if employers
      use casual wage-labor, they are not capitalist employers. This is a mistaken view.
          Similarly, Kar (2018) says that: in a feudal system there are generally big landlords, the
      serf system, rent collection, and natural economy, while in a semi-feudal economy, due to

(uneven) development offered here is different from that of many (Indian) Marxists. This is the case even if they, with their inadequate *concept* of capitalism might think that there is 'more' capitalism now than there was earlier. For them, the development of productive forces, to the extent that it has taken place, has taken place only due to capitalist reinvestment of surplus in specific areas. Patnaik, like Bhaduri, thinks that only those property owners who invest in technological change are capitalists.

There are other theoretical implications of the subsumption perspective as well. By deploying Marx's notion of subsumption of labor, I have critiqued a restrictive concept of capitalism that many Indian Marxist political economists subscribe to. This is a concept in which the development of capitalist class relations is conflated with the development of productive forces *under* such relations. In the restrictive concept, capitalism as such is equated with advanced capitalism, rather than the latter being seen as a higher *form* of capitalism-as-class. Therefore, in this restrictive concept, where there is a lower level of economic development, capitalism is assumed not to exist or to exist partly.

In advancing a subsumption of labor perspective, I claim, in line with Marx (1977), that formal subsumption of labor, which is based on the appropriation of surplus value in its absolute form, is the most abstract – general – form of capitalism: it 'is at the same time directly a process of the exploitation of the labour of others. ...It is the general form of any capitalist production process' (i.e. production process under the rule of capitalist social relation) (p. 1019). In other words, the formal subsumption, as the more general form of capitalist production, 'can be found in the absence of the specifically capitalist mode of production', which Marx calls the real subsumption of labor (p. 1019). For Marx, real subsumption of labor entails the formal subsumption, but 'the converse does not necessarily obtain' (p. 1019). Contrary to what Marx might (sometimes) have believed, the transition to real subsumption is not automatic, though. I accept that there *is* a long-term tendency towards the real subsumption of labor, associated with a rise in the ratio of constant to variable capital, that follows formal subsumption in which lots of workers are hired to work for long hours on an enormous amount of raw materials with little labor-shedding

---

the penetration of capital and the operation of markets in the context of the international capitalist system, the feudal traits are somewhat weakened, giving the *appearance* that the system is capitalist. In a semi-feudal economy, *essentially* feudal categories remain operational through the functioning of various capitalist traits relating to capital investment, commercialization, wage labor, and market operation. For Kar, the domination of small-scale production based on family labor, along with various noneconomic forms of exploitation, neither corresponds to capitalist development, nor is a transitional phase moving toward capitalism. This is, once again, a very strong variant of semi-feudalism thesis. I return to the political implication of this sort of problematic views below.

technological change used.[55] This long-term tendency, under certain conditions, is countered by the possibilities for a prolonged process of formal subsumption. The transition to real subsumption is mediated by the balance of power between capital and labor, including more overt struggle against formal subsumption of labor.

The formal subsumption may benefit specific capitals in specific places but opportunities for formal subsumption may counter the long-term tendency towards the development of productive forces at the society-wide scale that Marx associates with real subsumption of labor. This shows that social relations of production in the form of formal subsumption of labor, under certain conditions, can fetter the development of productive forces. From the perspective of many participants in the Indian MOP debate, it is the social relations of usury or rental extraction from direct producers – that is, relations other than those of capitalist production – that fetter the development of productive forces under capitalism.[56] Incidentally, this view is the Marxist counter-part of the non-Marxist modernization theory which says that pre-modern ideas/practices are the main cause of lack of development. While the importance of the relations other than those of capitalist production in specific cases cannot be denied (see below), a larger nation-wide obstacle is formal subsumption of labor itself: being able to appropriate surplus value in its absolute form on the basis of formal subsumption alleviates – or to some extent, counters – the pressure to have to resort to real subsumption in a systemic way.

Even if some might think that relations other than those of capitalist production are less of a barrier to the development of productive forces now than before, the barrier to capitalist development is generally not conceived as the totality of capitalism as a class relation: much rather, the barrier is seen as emanating from such things as inadequate policy influenced by monopolies. For Marx (1991: Chapter 47), the *specific economic form in which unpaid surplus*

---

55   But it is also true that ultimately, there is a limit to the mass of surplus value that can be appropriated in its absolute form, given that there are only 24 hours a day and there are bodily limits to how much a person can perform in an hour and in a working day, which is why there is class struggle over formal subsumption. (Note that both of these limits apply to all forms of society, but they acquire a special significance in capitalism because of its tendency of accumulation for accumulation sake, which means almost limitless tendency towards the exploitation of labor). This is not to say that the rate of technological change (as indicated by c/v) will not rise faster than that of exploitation of labor (s/v), over a reasonably long period of time.

56   This is the Marxist counter-part of the non-Marxist modernization theory which says that pre-modern ideas and pre-modern practices are the main cause of the lack of development (see Bordoloi and Das, 2017).

labor is pumped out of direct producers plays a key explanatory role in understanding society. And, in my view, appropriation of surplus labor in the form of absolute surplus value via formal subsumption of labor *is* key, and especially in the vast rural areas as well as in the massive urban informal sector where most workers work (of course, the dominance of the formal subsumption has to be seen in relation to the appropriation of relative surplus value through the real subsumption, as well as class differentiation, dispossession of small-scale producers, and hybrid subsumption). Marx himself would point to the significance of formal subsumption of labor more than he did, if he had a chance to observe the functioning of capitalism outside of advanced capitalism. *Even in* the more developed countries, the formal subsumption of labor – appropriation of absolute surplus value – is increasingly becoming an important fact of life, given increasing precarity of the proletariat allowing capitalists to appropriate surplus value in its absolute form. This could be a potential *counter-tendency* to the tendency of the rate of profit to fall (TRPF) (see Grossman, 1929; Marx, 1991): this is a topic that is definitely worth exploring. In fact, at the level of the world market, the prevalence of the significant extent of the formal subsumption of labor in the South could be seen within the framework of the TRPF as a counter-tendency to the profitability crisis in advanced countries; examining this is also beyond the scope of the chapter and the book.

There are theoretical implications of the subsumption perspective for understanding capitalist uneven development as well. The view that only those property owners who invest in technological change are capitalists and therefore capitalist relation must necessarily involve reinvestment of surplus in technological change mean that: uneven *development of productive forces* is a function of spatially limited amount of *development of capitalist social relations* as represented by technological change. I disagree. Capitalist property owners must cut costs to remain competitive. But in what ways they do so (for example, whether they use labor-saving technology) is, within limits, a different matter. In large countries such as India, there is much geographical unevenness, ecologically and in terms of other factors such as the degree of concentration of means of production, the balance of power between capital and labor. So one will expect that property owners in some areas are unable to rely mainly on the use of labor that works for low wages and for long hours, and are therefore economically compelled to use productivity-raising technological change, thus manifesting capitalism's long-term tendency towards real subsumption. This causes productive forces to be developed in some areas to a greater extent and more systematically than in others, causing uneven development *under* capitalism. In other words, there is a more general tendency under the capitalist mode of production (i.e. the pressure on competing capitalists to make a profit, i.e. the pressure coming from the capitalist class relations) and that this general tendency interacts with locally existing contingent conditions (e.g. government policies) to produce geographically uneven development, the concrete forms of which must be subjected to empirical analysis.[57]

All political economists agree that there is uneven development in India, but many of them think that uneven development exists because 'non-capitalist' relations (e.g. pre-capitalist type relations) exist in some areas, associated with low level of economic development, and capitalist relations exist in other areas, associated with higher level of economic development. My argument, however, is that, uneven development is mainly taking place because of, and in the framework of, social relations that are predominantly *capitalist in terms* of class relations. Uneven development is partly a product of uneven transition to the real subsumption of labor under capital. Uneven development is a *capitalist* matter.

There is a further implication of the class perspective in this chapter. To the extent that uneven development is happening within the framework of varied class relations in a backward country such as India, one where technological change is partly happening under the influence of the world market and with some support from the state, uneven development is uneven and combined development. But what is the combined character of uneven development? As we have seen: according to Trotsky (2008: 4), backward countries can adopt technology from already-advanced countries, and this means that:

> The development of historically backward nations leads necessarily to a peculiar combination of different stages in the historic process. Their development as a whole acquires a planless, complex, combined character.

Trotsky, who is sadly an untouchable among Marxists in India, and who is the original theorist of uneven and combined development, explains:[58]

---

57   This cannot be fully captured through data at the provincial scale but must be investigated at smaller scales (villages, clusters of villages, etc.).

58   There is a growing amount of attention to uneven and combined development: see Ashman, A. (2010); Allinson and Anievas (2009); Bond and Desai (2006); Lowy (2010); O'Brien (2007); and van der Linden (2007). It is interesting that David Harvey, one of the most influential theorists of uneven development (see Das, 2017c for a critical analysis of his work), pays no attention to this important concept in his work. It is entirely possible that Harvey, like many other Marxists, does not wish to have any intellectual connection to Trotsky and his intellectual legacy, suggesting the existence of sectarianism within Marxism.

Unevenness, the most general law of the historic process, reveals itself most sharply and complexly in the destiny of the backward countries. Under the whip of external necessity their backward culture is compelled to make leaps. From the universal law of unevenness thus derives another law which, for the lack of a better name, we may call the law of *combined development* – by which we mean a drawing together of the different stages of the journey, a combining of the separate steps, an amalgam of archaic with more contemporary forms.

Ibid.: 5

This means that in a less developed country, technologically backward 'peasant land-cultivation' can co-exist with an industry which 'in its technique and capitalist structure' is 'at the level of the advanced countries', and in certain respects it can even surpass industry in advanced countries (ibid.: 8).

For Trotsky, it is not just that capitalist development is *uneven* but also that capitalist relations are *combined* with pre-capitalist relations (e.g. serfdom). This is an advance over the perspective that focusses only on the unevenness of capitalist development. Trotsky's perspective, however, homogenizes the capitalist class relation (by treating its different forms as one). It thus abstracts from the ways in which class struggle intervenes in the transition from one form of capitalist class relation (formal subsumption) to another form (real subsumption) and from the obstacles to the transition within capitalism. His perspective needs to be broadened a little bit in the light of the subsumption theory presented here. In India and similar other backward countries, it is not just that capitalism is combined with remnants of pre-capitalist or non-capitalist relations existing in specific areas. The matter is more complex than that. What is happening is this: capitalist class relations of formal subsumption of labor co-exist not only with, hybrid subsumption, pre-capitalist relations, including relations of commons (as in aboriginal areas), and small-scale commodity production subjected to market-based class differentiation and extra-economically coercive dispossession (primitive accumulation), but also with capitalist class relations of real subsumption, which is, in part, driven by the external influence (the operation of the imperialist world market).

And there is further complexity when we recognize the fact that there are limits to the extent to which India and other similar countries, operating under the impact of the world market can move quickly to the stage of real subsumption of labor in agriculture and industry, exhibiting a systemic tendency towards a rise in productivity of labor per hour. Trotsky (2008: 4–5) himself says:

The possibility of skipping over intermediate steps is of course by no means absolute. Its degree is determined in the long run by the economic and cultural capacities of the country. The backward nation, moreover, not infrequently debases the achievements borrowed from outside in the process of adapting them to its own more primitive culture. In this the very process of assimilation acquires a self-contradictory character. Thus the introduction of certain elements of Western technique and training... [could lead] ... to a strengthening of serfdom as the fundamental form of labour organisation.

I would say that the introduction of advanced techniques could strengthen not only the use of forms of extra-economic relations, but also relations of formal subsumption of labor. We may recall that: formal subsumption of labor can exist 'alongside the *specifically capitalist* mode of production in its developed form' i.e. the real subsumption (Marx, 1977: 1019). In other words, enterprises using advanced technology can – and do – resort to a regime of long hours and low wages (just as they can use unfree labor).[59]

The MOP debate and my alternative views presented here shed light on not only uneven (and combined) development of capitalism but also on the related topic of capital switch. Once we assume that there is a class with money (property owners, more generally) intending to make money by investing it in production and exchange, the concept of switching capital comes to be an important one. There are three forms of capital switch within the landscape of uneven and combined development of capitalist social formation: (1) switch of capital within the real subsumption of labour (the advanced form of capitalism); (2) switch of capital from rental and money-lending business ('anti-diluvean' capital) to productive investment; and (3) switch of capital from formal to real subsumption of labor. Let me explain this briefly.

---

59   If a lot of capital has been sunk in machinery, the latter must be in contact with labor for as long as possible in a day. This is because without such contact, no surplus value will be produced. What Marx calls moral depreciation of machinery is also a permanent threat: when new and better machines are introduced, the existing machines face the threat of being replaced even if they are physically functional, and such replacement prior to the full amortization of the value embedded in the existing machinery, is a potential loss of value: 'in addition to the material wear and tear, a machine also undergoes what we might call a moral depreciation. It loses exchange-value, either because machines of the same sort are being produced more cheaply than it was, or because better machines are entering into competition with it. In both cases, however young and full of life the machine may be, its value is no longer determined by the necessary labour time actually objectified in it, but by the labour-time necessary to reproduce either it or the better machine. It has therefore been devalued to a greater or less extent. The shorter the period taken to reproduce its total value, the less is the danger of moral depreciation; and the longer the working-day, the shorter that period in fact is. ... It is therefore in the early days of a machine's life that this special incentive to the prolongation of the working day makes itself felt most acutely' (Marx, 1977: 528).

Within advanced capitalism, the capitalism which is dominantly character-ized by real subsumption of labor, there are at least two forms of capital switch. When the rate of profit is low in the production sphere, capital switches to financial, etc. services (Smith, 2010). And, according to Harvey, when there is what he calls overaccumulation in the sector that produces commodities that are produced and consumed within a given time period (primary circuit), capi-tal is switched to the sectors that specialize in the built environment for produc-tion and for consumption (e.g. durables) and into science and education as well as social welfare and repressive and consent-generating activities (Harvey, 1978).

Within economically less developed capitalist social formations, capital switch takes different forms. Firstly, as Patnaik (1986) and others have argued, when property owners can make more money by investing it in production, they will switch capital from rental and usurious activities to production. Pat-naik says: a person renting out her land to peasants will switch to what Patnaik calls *capitalist* production if she can make more profit in production than by leasing out land (i.e. the rental income) and by lending money-capital at a higher rate of interest (usury). But a rate of profit that can prompt switching capital to production is very high (because rental income and usurious interest are very high), and is difficult to obtain, unless there is a quantum jump in pro-ductivity caused by technological change. In other words, the obstacle to the switch to capitalist production comes from *outside* of capitalist production. Secondly, there is the switch of capital from formal subsumption (or indeed from hybrid subsumption) to real subsumption, as I have discussed. This switch is not yet complete. This leads us to the topic of the specificity of capitalism in India, as the final theoretical implication of the argument in the chapter.

How different is Indian capitalism from that of the European core which is characterized by capitalism or mature capitalism? What Sinha (2017: 540) calls capitalism, or mature capitalism, exists with 'capitalists and workers respond-ing to "the dull compulsion of economic force"'. This 'implies the completion of a transition to something resembling mature capitalism: a condition of gener-alized commodity production, in which the imperative of accumulation drives capitalists' behaviour, and where labour [sic] becomes a commodity'. All this is quite reasonable.

Sinha, however, goes on to say that 'In places like India today not only is this process [of emergence of capitalism] not 'complete', but as Sanyal (2007) sug-gests, it is never likely to be' (ibid.). This means that: 'in India the annihilation of non-capitalist ways of life ... is necessarily incomplete'. From this, Sinha con-cludes: 'That deferral of completeness of the transition', or the incomplete character of the transition to capitalism, is what 'is the central point of differ-ence between capitalism in India and in the original trajectories of the Euro-pean core' (ibid.). And, this incompleteness, the fact that non-capitalist ways of life have not been annihilated, has a political reason: 'these ways of life are kept alive by development interventions [of the state] to benefit those who are excluded from capitalist relations but have some political power in the form of laws and justice and solidarity discourses that firm up non-capitalist forms of subjectivity and put limits to the violence of the universalization process on extra-economic grounds' (p. 541). So just as non-capitalist or pre-capitalist relations act as a fetter on the development of capitalist class relations in the work of Patnaik and others, so according to Sinha and Sanyal, 'non-capitalist forms of subjectivity ... put limits' on the universalization of capitalism. So, what limits capitalism is not an agent within capitalism (i.e. the working class) but an agent that is outside of capitalism ('non-capitalist forms of subjectivity'). One can clearly see how close this sort of thinking is to some of the discourse that informs class struggle in India (e.g. Naxalism, discussed in Chapters 8–9).

Sinha and Sanyal are right to say that in India, wage-labor co-exists with other forms of labor. But to the extent that this is the case, India's capitalism cannot be credited with any uniqueness relative to advanced countries. In all capitalist countries, wage-labor exists along with other forms of labor, to varying degrees, with wage-labor as the dominant form of labor. Consider Lenin, the best class-analyst after Marx:

> Capitalism would not be capitalism if the proletariat *pur sang* were not surrounded by a large number of exceedingly motley types intermediate between the proletarian and the semi-proletarian (who earns his livelihood in part by the sale of his labour-power), between the semi-proletarian and the small peasant (and petty artisan, handicraft worker and small master in general), between the small peasant and the middle peasant, and so on
>
> LENIN, 1968: 59

But that does not mean that the imperative of *capitalist* accumulation, does not exist where wage-labor as the dominant form of labor coexists with other forms of labor, as in India. Capitalism does not require that *all* labor power become a commodity. As long as a sufficient amount of labor power is in the commodity-form, capitalism's fundamental mechanisms (e.g. competition, appropriation of surplus value, etc.) can be in full force. In fact, the existence of a semi-commodified labor power is no barrier to capital's pursuit of surplus. Capital can benefit at the expense of petty producers in multiple ways.[60]

---

60   Petty producers are adversely impacted by the capitalist class in at least three different but connected ways. 1) They work as wage-laborers for a part of the year, so they are

The *main* difference between India and the European core is *not* what Sinha and Sanyal say (i.e. the co-existence of non-capitalist forms of labor with wage-labor). The main difference is that India (like similar other countries in the Global South) is characterized by the dominance of formal subsumption of wage-labor under capital, which co-exists, or is unevenly combined, with real subsumption of labor under capital (as well as relations of hybrid subsumption and remnants of pre-capitalist exploitation based on extra-economic coercion, and natural economy), in a context of the operation of the world market and imperialist subjugation. In other words, it is the specific form of uneven and combined development and imperialist subjugation, that define the specificity of India (and countries such as India within the global periphery), relative to advanced regions such as Western Europe and its offshoots (North America). Conversely, the processes that could hasten the transition from formal to real subsumption in Western Europe (e.g. massive out-migration of surplus labor reducing the size of the reserve army, and the resources plundered from the subjugated countries that were then converted into capital) are missing in India and other similar countries.[61] There *is, no doubt,* an incompleteness, indicative of combined development. But this is not in the sense of the incomplete transition *to* capitalism, for India is decidedly a capitalist country already. Much rather, the incompleteness exists in the sense that there is an incomplete – on-going – transition to real subsumption of labor, within the landscape of uneven and combined development of *capitalist* social formation.

Whether capitalism exists or not and if it exists, then in what form it does, is not a matter of academic squabbling. Theoretical ideas about capitalism, like all theoretical ideas, have implications for political practice.[62] To say that a social formation in India (or indeed in other country) is decidedly capitalist has a different political implication than the contrary view. This contrary view is that (a) the social formation is not dominantly capitalist or it is capitalist in limited ways, and (b) obstacles to capitalist development are in pre- or non-capitalist relations of production. There are two implications of this view. One

---

exploited as full-time wage-laborers are. 2) They are dispossessed of their property by the capitalist class and its state. 3) They do not receive the full price of the products of their labor from the capitalist class and its state, so they are exploited in the commodity market. Note that apart from being impacted by the capitalist class, the petty producers are also exploited by the landlords (on the basis of appropriation of ground rent) and by the state (on the basis of the payment of indirect taxes).

61   Patnaik (2016) also points to these two processes (plunder and out-migration), but her theoretical interpretation of these processes, as well as the political conclusions that follow, are different from mine.

62   Lerche et al. (2013) draw implications for Left politics of their and others' political-economic analysis of capitalism in rural areas.

is that capitalist class relations are everywhere and all times associated with higher level of the development of productive forces.[63] Another is that: the obstacles to capitalist development are not in capitalism-as a class relation as such[64] and can be removed by forces other than those that seek to abolish capitalism. That is, a government that is more democratic than the current form of bourgeois government but that still operates within the logic of capitalist relations can remove these barriers and promote a nicer form of capitalism, thus creating conditions for socialism in the distant future.[65] More generally, for many, inadequate government policies constitute an obstacle to economic development.

If a country such as India is dominantly semi-feudal or if it is not capitalist enough, then the radical strategy is one that is to be directed against semi-feudal landlords or at the creation of advanced capitalism somehow. This is the strategy pursued by India's communist parties.[66] This strategy licenses a long

---

63   Those who have this view are likely to also believe that capitalism is everywhere and al-
       ways associated with nominally free labor.

64   Sometimes, it is implied that the monopoly section of capital is the problem. This view is
       also problematic in that it fails to consider that within capitalist class relation, competi-
       tive relations between capitals, all of which control capitalist private property and exploit
       labor, do lead to monopolies, and that a less monopolistic capitalism presided over by, say,
       a workers' government, would not necessarily be a better capitalism, over the long run.
       Monopolies and other companies are deeply inter-connected through sub-contracting
       and other networks, within the structure of capitalism as a relation of social power any-
       way. What is seen as problematic by many is the idea that monopoly capital makes use of
       state power in its own interest. This implies that its political power is the problem, and
       not the matter of its exploitative relation as such, or, not the fact that monopoly capital-
       ists, like other capitalists, are bearers of capital as a class relation. Therefore, almost out of
       view is the idea of the totality of capitalist relations being incompatible with the interests
       of the workers and poor peasants.

65   Recall that for Patnaik and many others, whose views shape and/or influence the main-
       stream communist movement, the rate of profit that can prompt switching capital to pro-
       duction is very high and is difficult to obtain. Why is it high: because property owners can
       earn a lot of rental income and usurious interest in a backward society. Only when a quan-
       tum jump in productivity caused by technological change occurs can the rate of profit
       from production can be enhanced, an only this can cause a transition from pre- or
       non-capitalism to capitalism as they see it. In other words, the obstacle to the switch to
       capitalist production comes from *outside* of capitalist production. So what need to be
       transcended are relations that are not of capitalism.

66   According to CPI(M-L) Liberation (2018): 'Agriculture [is] ...weighed down by the prepon-
       derance of a semi-feudal small peasant economy and caught in a perennial crisis of capi-
       talist transition via landlord path....'. It further says that: 'Indian society is driven by four
       main contradictions – the contradiction between imperialism and the Indian people,
       that between feudal fetters and remnants and the broad masses of the people, between
       big capital and the Indian people, the working class and the peasantry in particular, and
       the contradiction among various sections of the ruling classes. ...The antagonism between

and indefinite wait for the fight for socialism (= abolition of class relations) to start and requires collaboration with some good (progressive) capitalists.[67] But if what is present is already capitalism, albeit one that is not very progressive,[68] and one that is not going to be very progressive for a long period of time because of all the constraints on the transition to real subsumption of labor within the contemporary imperialist world market which severely constrains economic development in India and other low-income countries, and if there are forces that make the appropriation of absolute surplus value salient, then the nature of class politics must be seen in an entirely different manner: this means that revolution as the highest point of class struggle against capitalism in India must be on the agenda right now.

But does this mean that one cannot fight for reforms within capitalism? Or, more specifically, does this mean that small-scale producers' demand for access to means of production (land and credit) can be ignored?[69] The answer is no: within limits, the fight for land and for other such concessions is a means of political mobilization of the masses, and under the pressure of mass mobilization, *some* land redistribution and some restriction on primitive accumulation might even happen under a bourgeois government. What the anti-semi-feudalism claim made in this Chapter suggests is this: it is only a state under the control

---

this nexus and the broad Indian masses thus constitutes the principal contradiction of present Indian society...These main contradictions determine the stage of our revolution – the stage of people's democratic revolution with agrarian revolution as its axis. ... The main force of the democratic revolution led by the working class is the peasantry'.

One of the major communist parties in India, CPI (Maoist) (2014), says that: 'The contemporary Indian society is semi-colonial and semi-feudal under neo-colonial form of indirect rule, exploitation, and control'.

According to the CPI(M) (2017), India's largest communist party: 'The three main contradictions that exist in Indian society are: (i) the contradiction between landlordism and the mass of the peasantry; (ii) the contradiction between imperialism and the Indian people; and (iii) the contradiction between the working class and the bourgeoisie'. It says that 'the contradiction between big landlordism and the mass of the peasantry is the principal contradiction'.

In other words, as one can see, the capital – labor contradiction is not the main contradiction, and the labor is not the main revolutionary agent in contemporary times and the socialist movement is a distant goal, for any of these organizations and their organic intellectuals.

67   Basole (2016: 297) says that such a view signifies 'the stagism of historical materialism'. More correctly, to me, such a view characterizes the *Stalinist* version of historical materialism, rather than historical materialism *as such*.

68   Progressive (non-monopoly capitalists) capitalists will develop productive forces and remove pre-capitalist or non-capitalist barriers to capitalist development.

69   It has been argued (for example, by Kar, 2018) from the semi-feudal perspective that: the claim that a country such as India is a dominantly capitalist economy (and not a small peasant economy) means that land redistribution is off the agenda.

of the proletariat, following a *socialist* revolution, that can successfully carry out land redistribution *and* stop the beneficiaries from losing their land through extra-economic dispossession or market-based class differentiation. No government that still respects the rules of the capitalist market, whether or not there are capitalist monopolies, can protect the small-scale producers against the loss of their property that is based on family labor. And it is only a socialist government that can create a situation where small-scale producers will voluntarily opt out of family-based production and join large-scale democratically-organized workers-controlled production units, in part because only such a government can *drastically* expand the remuneration of workers by dispossessing the capitalist class and by cutting down on wasteful and unproductive expenditures that are the hallmarks of capitalist society.

If India is dominantly capitalist, then the core of the political agenda must be the anti-capitalist struggle of the working class (both proletarian and semi-proletarian elements) against the totality of capitalist class relation, including in its most general form (i.e. formal subsumption of labor). This class must be politically allied with small-scale producers which are adversely impacted, in so many ways, by the capitalist class (and by its class partner, i.e. rent-receiving landlords). The combined and common goal of these two toiling classes must be a socialist state, a state of workers, allied with self-employed small-scale producers. By driving all propertied classes (pre-capitalist or capitalist) from their ruling positions, such a state can create conditions for a higher level of development of productive forces and for a society without exploitation and oppression as a part of a South-Asia-wide and global revolutionary process.

CHAPTER 4

Neoliberal Capitalism with Indian Characteristics

Like everything else in the world, capitalism comes in multiple forms (and many stages) (see Figure 4.1 below).[1] We have seen in the previous chapter that capitalist class relation, in India or elsewhere, exists in different forms: formal and real subsumption of labor, for example. The formal subsumption is the most general form of capitalism. It has four traits including, commodification of labor power and of the means of production and subsistence, and exploitation of labor in the workplace (on the basis of the appropriation of absolute surplus value). From another angle, the stages (or the chronological forms) through which capitalism has developed can be expressed as: laissez faire; monopolistic; Keyenesian/developmentalist; and neoliberal (Fine and Saad-Filho, 2017: 695).[2] The focus of this chapter is on the neoliberal form/stage of capitalism.

The remainder of this chapter is divided into four sections. In the first section, it makes some brief conceptual observations on the neoliberal phase of capitalism in general. In the second section, it sets the context for a discussion on neoliberalism as it is expressed in India. The third section presents nine theses on how neoliberal capitalism operates, and impacts people's lives, in India. The fourth, and the final section summarizes the discussion and then addresses the following question: how should we think about various forms of struggle – struggle around the agrarian question, national question (anti-imperialism), and the democratic question, and the struggle against capitalism – in a *neoliberal*-capitalist world?

1 Neoliberalism: Its General Traits

Neoliberalism is a historical *form* of capitalism *itself.* The neoliberal form of capitalism is a capitalism where the business activity is relatively less 'state-directed' in the interest of national development and welfare of the masses, and where the *nation*-state responds to *global* market forces relative to national-level market forces (Steger and Roy, 2010).

---

1 Sections 3–4 of this chapter draw on: Das (2012d) and Das (2015).
2 Of course, no stage is a pure stage: a given stage will have traits from a preceding stage and the succeeding stage, and yet a given stage will have a trait which distinguishes it from other stages.

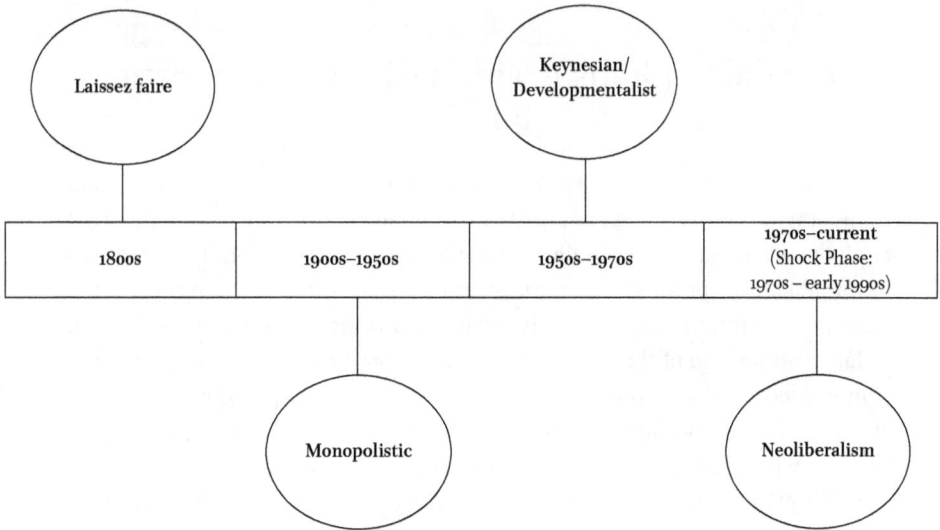

FIGURE 4.1   The evolution of capitalism
SOURCE: AUTHOR (BASED ON FINE AND SAAD-FILHO, 2017)

Neoliberalism is above all 'a theory of political economic practices that proposes that human well-being can best be advanced by liberating individual entrepreneurial freedoms and skills' by reducing governmental regulation and by promoting 'strong private property rights, free markets, and free trade' (Harvey, 2005: 2). The state's role is usually restricted, at least in theory, to the following: money supply, private property rights and the creation and maintenance of the markets, all of which are essential elements of capitalism as such but which cannot be created by individual capitalists.

Neoliberalism is a capitalist class project 'on steroids' as reflected in governmental policy. Marx's (1977) general formula in *Capital 1* to describe capitalism – i.e. to describe capital's circuit – is: M–C (MP + LP) –P–C'–M'.[3] At each of the points in capital's circuit (e.g. supply of credit/money; conditions of profitable production with a relatively pliant labor force; ensuring import and export of new commodities produced), capital wants – 'uses' – the state to help it make money, and quickly, through pro-business policies (this is explained in the next section in the discussion on Indian neoliberalism). The

---

3   This formula says that money (M) is invested to buy commodities (MP = means of production including machines/tools and raw materials; LP = labor power) to use them to produce (P) new commodities (C') which is sold for more money (M') than invested.

capitalist state intervenes at each moment of the circuit, more or less, in all the different phases of capitalism, but the capitalist state in its neoliberal form behaves in a much more pro-capitalist way than before. The turnover-time – including the transition from M' to M and from M to C, and so on – has to be quickened, and any obstacles to that must be annihilated by the state itself, directly or indirectly.

In spite of the state helping capital at each point in the circuit and in spite of relaxation of state control over capital, there has not necessarily been fast economy-wide growth in most countries going neoliberal over a sustained period of time. Harvey (2005) has said that neoliberalism has been less successful in generating growth and more successful in redistributing wealth between and among fractions of the capitalist class. This has led to increasing level of financialization: 'the immediate realization of profits based on the anticipated creation of surplus value' (O'Connor, 2010: 702). In other words, 'This new form of neoliberal appropriation manifests itself in short-term speculative gains, foreign exchange arbitrage, and various forms of financial trading' (ibid.). As the rate of profit has dropped in the actual production of commodities, thanks to the rising organic composition of capital, a section of the capitalist class has been in pursuit of 'financial returns at the expense of production' under neo-liberalism.[4] As Fine and Saad-Filho (2016: 691) say, 'The creation and circulation of these financial assets is an intrinsically speculative activity that tends to become unmoored from the constraints of production, even though this autonomy can never be complete'.[5] This is why the long circuit of capital mentioned before is shortened to M–M'. Even while certain parts of the economy (e.g. IT-related industries) have grown,[6] the financial sector under neoliberalism has failed to address the major problems of the world. Neoliberalism has

---

4 'In this sense, a mortgage, for example, remains a simple (transhistoric) credit relation between borrower and lender. However, it becomes embroiled in financialization once that mortgage obligation is sold on as part of some other asset, which becomes routinized only under neoliberalism' (O'Connor, 2010: 691).

5 The fact of 'financial sector control of economic resources and the main sources of capital allows it to drain capital from production; at the same time, neoliberalism systematically, if unevenly, favours large capital at the expense of small capital and the workers, belying its claims to foster competition and 'level the playing field'. As a result, accumulation in neoliberal economies tends to take the form of bubbles which eventually collapse with destructive implications and requiring expensive state-sponsored bailouts. These cycles include the international debt crisis [and regional debt crises]' (p. 698).

6 How the IT industry promoted under neoliberalism has benefitted some and excluded many, see D'Costa (2011).

not produced much employment, while it has produced enormous inequality in income and wealth.[7]

The essential feature of the capitalist society is in the relation between capital and labor, which is based in relations of exchange, property, and value/surplus-value (Das, 2017a: Chapter 7). In capitalist society which is dominated by the commodity-form or value-form (generalized commodity production), workers must sell their commodity (labor power) to capital. They must depend on capital for a given amount of exchange value, with which to buy the commodities they need in order to meet their needs.[8] Capitalism is not only dominated by the value-form or commodity-form (of things and of labor power). It is also dominated by a specific property-form (capitalist form of property). It is 'that kind of property which exploits wage-labour' and which 'is based on the antagonism of capital and wage labour' (Marx and Engels, 1848: Chapter 2). One special characteristic of capitalist property (as opposed to property based in family labor) is that only a tiny minority can possess it and that the vast majority must have none of it or very little of it.[9] Without any property or with a very limited amount of property, labor is not only compelled to rely on capital for living. Because labor has been, more or less, separated from property, a process of separation that must be maintained, capital can also economically force labor – that is, impose market relations on labor whereby, at best, wages cover the average cost of reproduction of the commodity labor power – to surrender to it a large part of the net product that labor produces. The latter – the surrendered/alienated product (which takes the form of surplus value) – is then transformed into fresh capital, which, in turn, controls and exploits labor in an incessant movement. Marx and Engels say in the *Communist Manifesto*: 'To be a capitalist, is to have not only a purely personal, but a social *status* in production. ... Capital is therefore not only personal; it is a social power' (ibid.).[10]

---

7   'So-called global cities of finance and command functions have become spectacular islands of wealth and privilege, with towering skyscrapers and millions upon millions of square feet of office space to house these operations. Within these towers, trading between floors creates a vast amount of fictitious wealth. Speculative urban property markets, furthermore, have become prime engines of capital accumulation. The rapidly evolving skylines of Manhattan, Tokyo, London, Paris, Frankfurt, Hong Kong, and now Shanghai are marvels to behold' (Harvey, 2005: 157).

8   If capital cannot make money out of such an exchange (purchase and sale of labor power), labor will not be able to sell its commodity.

9   The distribution of property is an aspect of class relation. If everyone, or if most men and women, have capitalist property, that property cannot be capitalist property, and there will be no capitalism. The fact that most of the productive resources (property) is in the hands of the capitalists class explains why capital has the social control over labor.

10   Because of the nature of the relations between labor and capital, capital is a *social* power: its power lies in the totality of relations between capital and labor. A capitalist, or a group of capitalists, personifies that social power.

There is a distinction between power and its effects. More specifically, power (social power of capital) is one thing, and effects that are produced when that power is exercised (by capital) are another. Capital has the power to exploit labor, but the actual effects of the exercise of that power can vary a bit. This is the case when the ratio of wages to surplus value can change to some extent, depending on political bargaining by labor, the level/pace of accumulation, etc., or when the reliance of labor on capital to provide wage-work can be a little less strong with the availability of alternative sources of income (e.g. state benefits), or when the amount of exchange value in the hands of the capitalist class is reduced through taxation, and so on.[11] There are indeed times when, as Marx says in *Capital* volume 1, 'the length and weight of the golden chain the wage-labourer has already forged for himself allow it to be loosened somewhat' (1977: 769). But 'the exploitation of the wage-labourer, and his [or her] situation of dependence' on capital remain intact (ibid.). That is because the social power of capital remains intact, whose *effects* are the varying 'length and weight of the golden chain'.

In any fundamental sense, in capitalist societies, there is not a time when the capitalist class does not have its social power to control and exploit labor (and indeed to dispossess small-scale producers). But the effects of the exercise of that power can change, within limits. So the neoliberal phase of capitalism, strictly speaking, cannot represent the *restoration* of class power, as Harvey and others mistakenly think. As long as there is capitalism, there cannot be any question of *restoration* of the power of capital. The capitalist class must have had to lose that power in the past for that power to be restored in the present.[12] Neoliberalism must be seen as enhancing the *effects* of the exercise of power that the capitalist class always has by virtue of it being that class. Under neoliberalism, that power is the power that large owners of business have over the working masses in a situation where markets are less and less regulated by the state in their interests or indeed on behalf of weaker/smaller capitalists. Neoliberalism represents an increase in the *effects* of capitalists' political power over the economy, as a response to the crisis of capitalism itself (crisis of profitability).

---

11   Even then one has to distinguish between different forms of such restriction: restrictions as a purported solution to the problems of capitalism (e.g. socializing some companies in trouble; putting some exchange values in the hands of workers in order to create a market for capitalists) are not the same as restrictions that are fundamentally caused by class struggle from below in the interest of toiling masses.

12   The thesis about the restoration of capitalist power does apply to countries such as Russia where capital's social power was overthrown, but not to the countries which have remained capitalist throughout the 20th century. It is a great mistake to club the two types of social formation in one category of countries that are neoliberal.

Neoliberalism is not a product of certain ideas, any more than capitalism is. But like all class projects, neoliberalism's existence and continuation is supported by certain ideas. As a class project, the neoliberal discourse *must* represent the interests of the capitalist class (including certain hegemonic fractions within it, and especially, those which do business globally), and the interests of all those sections of the 'middle class' (e.g. top officials; editors of journals, etc.) that are allied with, and serve, the capitalist class.[13] That is not enough. Any project of an exploiting class must have a dual ideological/discursive project of universalization and temporalization. The exploiting class, which is always the minority, must represent, through a discourse (a certain set of ideas informing certain practices), the material interests of its own (and a narrow section of the population that serves it) *as the interests of society as a whole.* Such false discursive universalization of parochial-class interest (where, for example, the capitalist class is seen as the wealth- and job-creator, and capitalist growth at any cost is said to be good for the country) is necessary if neoliberalism has to make people (the toiling masses) tolerate its intensely contradictory and adverse consequences. What is also necessary is a false discursive temporalization: to make the majority-class believe that any sacrifices (e.g. cuts in wages and welfare) they are made to experience are only temporary, and that those sacrifices are good for them over the long-term. The reality is that those sacrifices are in the interest of the minority class, and are not in the short-term or long-term interests of the toiling masses. In all phases of capitalism, false universalization and false temporalization are necessary, but their need is stronger under neoliberalism because now the adverse effects of capitalism on the majority are worse.

In the discourse of capitalism, growth/development is a very important idea. Growth/development indicates that total investment (sum of constant and variable capital) rises and that with it rises the income from such investment for the investing class. The stress on growth/development has become much more important under neoliberalism. National governments and international institutions such as the World Bank always talk about this, justifying neoliberalism in the name of growth/development. Neoliberalism is indeed associated with the fetishism of growth: the endless and unmindful pursuit of growth at any cost is everywhere to see. An important indicator of growth is taken to be increase in GDP:

---

13   On the topic of how neoliberalism has benefitted the middle class, see D'Costa (2013); Mukherji (2008); and McCartney (2013). Murphy (2011) discusses how neoliberalism is causing an emergence of transnational middle class values, especially, in the IT-related industries.

> The GDP statistic has become a potent force in the globalization of a particular way of economic thinking that we term neoliberalism. The hegemony and spread of this way of understanding our world and the way forward are powerfully underlain by the GDP and the meanings imputed to its trajectory.
>
> KRISHNA, 2015: 869[14]

Such an obsession with growth (as a rise in GDP) is in spite of the fact that neoliberalism has not been particularly associated with long-term high rate of growth in the majority of countries of the world.

Connected to the idea of growth/development in the neoliberal discourse is the idea of nationalism. There is a reciprocal relation between neoliberalism and nationalism. The neoliberal state works to promote globalization. Yet, 'Forced to operate as a competitive agent in the world market and seeking to establish the best possible business climate, it mobilizes nationalism in its effort to succeed' (Harvey, 2005: 85). Although Harvey does not quite explain this, it is not difficult to see why this is the case: when all capitalist states are competing to attract (the mobile) global capital to the areas under their jurisdictions, they will have to create an idea of national uniqueness. That is: they have to say that what their nation has – in terms of helping global capital make higher profit – is superior to what exists in other nations. This discourse of national uniqueness is a potentially cheap fodder for national*ism*. Nationalism is used by capital and its politicians to implement a neoliberal project including austerity that demands self-sacrifice on the part of the masses. Nationalism can also be a product of neoliberalism. When capital's mobility (and especially that of money-capital) has increased tremendously, all the nations, competing with another, may not succeed in attracting much foreign capital. Some may succeed. Others may not. This can produce pride for some nations and pain for others, and thus antagonism between nations. Harvey correctly says: 'Competition produces ephemeral winners and losers in the global struggle for position, and this in itself can be a source of national pride or of national soul-searching' (Harvey, 2005: 85). Nationalism can also serve as a psychological compensation for the adverse effects of neoliberalism or neoliberal globalization, that threatens a nation's economy, culture and sovereignty. All this is the "inter-state aspect" of the nationalist discourse of neoliberalism.

There is an intra-state aspect as well. Neoliberalism produces massive suffering for the people, thus creating a potential for antagonism towards

---

14   Therefore, 'The fascination with number and the fetishization of a highly misleading index should be evaluated in terms of the illocutionary force of this economic concept' (ibid.). In fact, 'A progressive politics that can think outside the thrall of neoliberal globalization would do well to begin by demystifying the GDP' (ibid).

it, from the toiling masses (and also from small-scale business-men and business-women). To pre-empt this and to cope with struggle against neoliberalism when it happens, the capitalist state has to mobilize all sections of the people. It does so, in part, on the basis of national unity created by appeal to culture, language, history, etc. The purpose is to produce people's loyalty to the nation and to the state, a state of the nation that, however, fundamentally works for a tiny minority of the nation, the capitalist class.

Appeals to national unity do not have to be based on extra-economic traits (language, history, etc.). Such appeals can indeed be made to the need for growth/development. This is where two sets of ideas within the neoliberal discourse come together: nationalism (a trait of a territorially-bounded people), and growth/development (which is basically an international process – thanks to the global law of value and international character of capitalism – which is manifested differently in different national territories). Socially-created belief in growth/development binds all the people in a nation, and this economic basis for nationalism adds to the extra-economic basis (culture, etc.). Anyone against growth/development runs the risk of being constructed as anti-national. Besides, neoliberalism causes suffering for people – and this is expressed in the form of the absence of development for the masses, including loss of employment, lack of good infrastructure, etc. – and yet they are told that what is necessary is growth/development and that neoliberalism is the way to achieve it. Quietly, development/growth is equated to the (state-promoted) production of the conditions necessary for an increase in profit for the capitalist class, such as roads, so development is not about reduced unemployment or increased income for the common people. What is hidden is that development/growth really means capitalist growth/development. And, national unity – non-antagonism towards the agenda of development/growth and towards the capitalist class driving the neoliberal project – makes the pursuit of that agenda easier.

Belief in the necessity of growth/development as capitalist growth/development has a dual ideological effect: it not only produces consent to capitalist relations (that growth/development can only occur within a capitalist framework unleashing the entrepreneurial spirit, etc.), but also reproduces nationalism (uniting masses with the capitalist class) that serves the capitalist class. Growth and development – i.e. neoliberal capitalist growth and development – are justified in the interest of the nation as a whole, even if it is the case that the discourse of nationalism represents the interests of the capitalist class (domestic and foreign) as the interests of the nation as a whole.[15]

---

15   Of course, as a method of securing citizens' loyalty, nationalism might not work always. This is because, Harvey says, nationalism 'is profoundly antagonistic to the neoliberal agenda', as 'the nationalism required for the state to function effectively as a corporate and competitive entity in the world market gets in the way of market freedoms more

Then there is a series of other neoliberal ideas: the ideas of competition; citizens-as-clients/consumers; naturalization of buying and selling (the idea that to satisfy a need, one must buy and sell things); obsession with market-governed actions; privatization-as-all-good; meritocracy; the idea that government deficits and debts are inherently bad while corporates bloat with unpayable debts; and so on (Monbiot, 2016). Because neoliberalism produces massive suffering and inequalities, it must operate on the basis of myths, false promises and false explanations of what is happening in the world. There are myths about state failure, and myths produce more myths. State failure is explained in terms of the state not freeing the markets enough. So the underlying myth is that the neoliberal state, a state that frees the market and is market-conforming, can hardly fail. Another myth is that inequality produces innovation, and if people's living standards do not rise, that is because of their *personal* failures, and not because of the increased effects of the social power of capital.

It is not enough to have neoliberal ideas. These ideas have to have bearers and propagators. As Harvey (2005: 3) says, its advocates 'occupy positions of considerable influence' not only in the education sector (the universities and many 'think tanks'), and in the media but also 'in corporate boardrooms and financial institutions, in key state institutions' and 'in those international institutions ... that regulate global finance and trade'.

It is also not enough that a few powerful people have neoliberal ideas and propagate them. A large number of common people must accept neoliberalism as their common-sense. This seems to have happened. 'Neoliberalism has, in short, become hegemonic as a mode of discourse', says Harvey. Indeed, 'it has become incorporated into the common-sense way many of us interpret, live in, and understand the world' (Harvey, 2005: 3). Once people live under neoliberalism, independently of their will, they – the rich and the poor – begin to accept the ideas that, in turn, support the practice of neoliberalism, a process that also applies to capitalism as such. Given the hegemony of neoliberalism-as-common-sense, people – both within academia and outside – talk more and more of neoliberalism and less and less of capitalism explicitly.

2   Neoliberalism in India: The Context

Neoliberalism is called by different names in different contexts. In India, neoliberalism goes by the name of 'economic reforms' and the New Economic Policy (NEP). The views of proponents of neoliberalism have been widely published in India, including in its influential (and slightly progressive) *Economic*

---

generally' (Harvey, 2005: 79). But as with neoliberalism so with nationalism: when it fails, demand is made for a higher dosage of it.

Political Weekly, and the more radical, *Social Scientist*.[16] Bhagwati (2001: 843), a Columbia University economics professor, and an intellectual proponent of neoliberalism, conceptualizes reforms *qua* neoliberalism as representing 'a reversal of the anti-globalisation, anti-market, pro-public-enterprise attitudes and policies that produced our dismal growth performance [during the pre-1991 period]'. He says that these reforms are the most important factor in reducing poverty by increasing growth. His argument is that growth creates employment: it puts money in the hands of the government, which can provide health and other facilities for the poor, and it also provides incentive to the poor to invest in human capital. It is also said that 'the higher post-reform growth rates are delivering a steeper decline in poverty' (Datt and Ravallion, 2010: 57). By raising living standards in urban areas, economic growth has had a positive effect on rural incomes (ibid.).

A former Finance Minister, Mr. Chidambaram, like many others (e.g. Khatkhate, 2006), thinks that 'growth is the best antidote to poverty'; so, he says, 'what is needed is not less, but more reforms' (quoted in the *Hindu* on November 8, 2006). Such views are held by large segments of the Congress party, the traditional party of the big business, and by the BJP, the other national-party of the big business, which has now overshadowed the Congress party.

The former prime minister of India, who is himself an economist, talks about the need to encourage and revive the 'animal spirit' of the investors,[17] which will, in turn, promote welfare; the NEP is about this. The mantra of the current Prime Minister (Mr. Modi) of the BJP, 'minimum government and maximum governance', is a part of the same neoliberal agenda.

While proponents of neoliberalism – in other words, economic reform – say that it benefits everyone, it is interesting that in one survey, 'three-fourths of respondents who had any opinion on the subject say that the reforms benefit only the rich' (Bardhan, 2005). This chapter seeks to discuss neoliberalism in the Indian context in terms of its multi-dimensionality and its contradictions.

---

16   There is a massive amount of literature on the nature of the NEP (or neoliberalism in India), including about its positive and negative effects. Apart from the authors already referred to in the text, the literature includes: Ahluwalia (2002); Bhattacharya (2013); Byres (1997, 2013); Chandrasekhar and Ghosh (2004); Nayar (2001); Sengupta (2008); Subramanian (2008); Sackley (2015) and Tiwana and Singh (2015). This chapter does not aim to review this literature.

17   The *Hindu* (2012) reports: 'Reverse the climate of pessimism ... revive the animal spirit in the country's economy ... Millions of our countrymen look up to the government to throw open channels for their progress, prosperity and welfare', Dr. [Manmohan] Singh told Finance Ministry officials.

The neoliberal form of capitalism with its several general traits mentioned above (liberalization, privatization, globalization, marketization, selective state withdrawal from welfare provision, etc.) in practice will take different forms, depending on peculiarities of a country, thus producing what Harvey calls the 'uneven geographical development of neoliberalism on the world stage'. In considering neoliberalism in India, one has to examine the ways in which what are regarded as the 'general traits' of neoliberalism (which are deployed to increase the exploitation of workers and dispossess small-scale producers) work in India. India shares certain traits with other countries and the global economy, but it has also its own socio-historical specificities. It is important that our views of neoliberalism are not unduly based on the conditions in advanced capitalism of the US, UK, etc. For example, in the context of advanced capitalism, there may be some truth that 'The main substantive achievement of neoliberalization ... has been to redistribute, rather than to generate, wealth and income' (Harvey, 2005: 159), but in the context of less developed countries such as India or China, neoliberalism is very much about neoliberal accumulation in production on the basis of super-exploitation of workers and small-scale producers. According to some, the neoliberal period followed a period of post-war growth which entered into crisis of over-accumulation, a period which coincided with a capital-labor pact and some redistribution in favor of labor. But this was not quite true about India: in fact, the pre-neoliberal period was called the period of sluggish growth (Hindu rate of growth), although economic inequality was less than in neoliberal times. Harvey (2006: 42), following Dumenil, says that 'It [neoliberalism] has either restored class power to ruling elites (as in the US and to some extent in Britain...) or created conditions for capitalist class formation (as in China, India, Russia, and elsewhere)'. This description only partly fits Indian neoliberalism, because pre-neoliberal India did not represent a golden age for Indian private capital or indeed for the masses which experienced massive level of absolute poverty, nor can one say that neoliberalism 'created conditions for capitalist class formation' in India, for pre-neoliberal India did have a capitalist class, however weak, and however dependent on the state.

There are several specificities of India one might consider.

1.   India has maintained a liberal-democratic system, even though it has been under pressure. Over the decades the voter turnout has been rather high (greater than 60% or so),[18] and there are more than 3 million elected representatives. The poor people of the country and rural people

---

18   At the general election held in 2014, 551 million people voted, and the voter turnout was 66.38%.

enthusiastically exercise their democratic right, and thus the electoral system is a big source of legitimacy for the socio-economic system. A part of the democratic system is federalism: the 29 States have a degree of autonomy relative to the central government (especially, in relation to agriculture, public order, health, and some aspects of industrial development), although this autonomy is under attack now.

2.   While the democratic system gives a semblance of political equality, there is a massive amount of social inequality and oppression, on the basis of gender, caste, ethnicity, religion, language, etc. as well as inequality on the basis of income and wealth/property ownership (capitalists vs workers and petty producers).

3.   There is a history of post-colonial state-led capitalist development since 1950s until late 1980s.[19]

4.   India is characterized by massive absolute poverty, comparatively low labor productivity per hour, low per capita income and the numerical dominance of the rural population, most of which is in economic distress. These are all associated with the fundamental character of India's peripheral capitalism (including formal subsumption of labor under capital, which we have discussed in the last chapter) and imperialism (in the form of imperialist institutions such as World Bank, and imperialist governments). As well, colonial-era laws continue to exist, and impacts of colonialism continue to be experienced. While there is massive poverty of people, there is also a massive 'poverty' in the way poverty is measured by bourgeois intellectuals and the pliant bureaucrats, which officially underestimates poverty. Free market economics can produce some growth. As a result a person can earn a little more than the absolutely minimal

---

19   Unequal distribution of assets and income, which India partly inherited from its colonial past, meant limited purchasing power in the hands of the majority and therefore limited market for indigenously produced goods and services. Limited market was/is not conducive to growth of productive investment, employment and income, so the state stepped in: to generate demand for indigenous capital through its own investment, and to make resources (e.g. credit) available to the private sector at a subsidized rate. For all this the state needed resources, which it was short of, given its limited abilities to discipline the propertied class (taxation, etc.), so its debt level increased which forced it to look for loans on the condition that it frees up the market. The state also protected domestic market through tariffs, etc. to generate demand for indigenous capital, but such a policy went against the demand of international capital to have access to the Indian market. Protection of domestic markets also went against the appetite of higher-income groups that wanted foreign consumer goods. All of these contributed to the production of a context in which neoliberalism had an appeal.

cut-off point for the definition of poverty,[20] and this allows the state, international financial institutions, and organic intellectuals of the ruling class to declare that there has been a massive reduction in poverty because of neoliberalism, and thus to manufacture support for neoliberalism. This massiveness in poverty reduction, as a legitimizing device for neoliberalism, is therefore actually a gimmick: it is a product of extremely low cut-off point for the poverty definition (which means that a slight increase in income means moving above the poverty line).

5. India's geopolitical location is useful to the imperialist powers such as the US which seeks to counter the China threat by using India. India is also rich in natural resources and has a large pool of relatively cheap skilled and unskilled labor, which satisfies the pursuit of profit by domestic and imperialist capital.

6. India has a 'strong' presence of a communist movement relative to most other countries, prompting the editor of *International Socialism* to suggest that 'India is by far the most important country in the world where Communism remains a powerful political force' (Callinicos, 2010). Millions of people (20–40 million) vote for the parliamentary communist parties, and in large areas there is a presence of a militant Maoist movement. The communist parties as well as mainstream parties have their own labor unions and peasant associations. It is useful to note that labor strikes and farmers' marches happen regularly.

The combination of the general traits of neoliberalism (deregulation, privatization, liberalization, etc.) with India's specificities produces 'neoliberal capitalism with Indian characteristics'. Neoliberalism with Indian traits is thus located at the intersection between the logics of capitalism itself, in India and those in the world. Keeping this in mind, a number of observations are made on the multiple, internally-related aspects of Indian neoliberalism as a class project. No attempt is made to offer extensive empirical evidence for the statements made, nor are there exhaustive references to the existing literature on the topic.

3   Neoliberalism with Indian Characteristics: Eight Theses

3.1   *Neoliberalism as a Form of Capitalist Class Relation: More Than a Matter of Government Policy*

Neoliberalism in India, as elsewhere, is fundamentally a capitalist accumulation project under changed global and national conditions. It is a mistake to

---

20   The per capita monthly cut-off is Rs. 816 in rural areas and Rs. 1,000 in urban areas. This is as per a 2013 Planning Commission report.

see neoliberalism in India or elsewhere as a mere policy. Begun (semi-stealthily) in the 1980s, and formally introduced in 1991, the New Economic Policy (NEP) is not just a government *policy*. NEP – or Indian neoliberalism – is not merely a way of running India's capitalist economy on the basis of a particular set of policy interventions and associated mind-sets that could change (for example, the economy could delink itself from global economy) with support from sections of the capitalist class. Neoliberalism is, more than anything else, something that is *intrinsic* to the present phase of capitalist development in India, as a part of the global capitalist-economy.

While a greater role for the state was tolerated, and indeed, needed, by the Indian capitalist class immediately after independence when that class was economically weak, after almost three decades of state-assisted capitalism, the class became powerful enough to let go of the crutch that was the state, which was now considered a barrier to a higher rate and mass of profit. Indian neoliberalism is partly a specific response to the contradictions of India's post-colonial state-led capitalist development ('Indian Keynesianism' or Nehruvianism) within the global economy, where a state-regulated redistributionist capitalism ran into problems in the 1970s, much earlier than in India.

NEP is neither entirely *new* nor merely *economic*. It basically represents the demands of the capitalist class, and more specifically, the demands of *hegemonic* fractions of the domestic and foreign-diasporic capitalist class, including those capitalists who did not heavily depend on state-support, at a particular stage in the development of Indian and global capitalism.[21] The neoliberal policy signifies the fact that these economic demands get transformed into specific policies, even if in a manner that is state-mediated.[22] This class now

---

21 One of the demands was to open the foreign market for Indian capitalists, and this was to counter the stagnation in the domestic market (Patnaik et al., 2004: 90). The state intervention occurred in the interest of global capital and its Indian allies (ibid.). That the NEP agenda hurts the weaker sections of the capitalist class is a different matter.

22 Note that the demands for liberalization were made a long time ago. 'The opposition (the first force that openly proposed this idea was the Swatantra Party, created in 1959) offered the opinion that the authorities should undertake destatization in their approaches to economic problems, trust more "the forces of supply and demand", liberate prices from the state's control, and, finally, gradually dismantle the state sector. Such was the extreme point of view concerning means of struggling against inflation, which the upper layer of the private corporate sector feared to declare openly. However, the reality did not confirm the justness of the market alternative to the compromising policy of the Congress. At the parliamentary election of 1971, the Swatantra Party and its closest allies fell into political oblivion' (Volodin, 2018: 102). The Swatantra Party was a right-wing secular party while the BJP established in 1980, like its predecessor, Bharatiya Jana Sangh (1951–1977), is a right-wing communal party. Some sections of the Indian bourgeoisie want to see a variant of the Swatantra Party now.

wants to – and with modern technological changes in transportation and communication, is *able* to – do business in a different manner than in the past. It wants the state to clear the way for this new way of doing things. India's annual national budget now, more or less, represents a wish-list of capitalist fractions represented by chambers of commerce and corporate lobbyists in a way not quite possible earlier.[23] The NEP outlines the specific demands of the capitalist class for the state to create conditions where domestic and foreign capital can invest money to make a lot of money.[24] Their wish-list gets a sympathetic hearing from the pro-market state managers, who are the political CEOs occupying important positions within the state.[25]

Much-needed support is provided by the opinion makers in the media and intellectuals (including its television intellectuals and professors from imperialist countries). No social – material practice can continue to operate without a corresponding discursive practice that justifies it.

The idea of neoliberalism is to make money not only by using natural resources like land, water, forests, and minerals that are made available to capital by the state at a cheap rate, and that India has plenty of, but also by using speculation and other non-productive means and by exploiting cheap skilled and unskilled labor. An important goal is to attract foreign capital and strengthen the position of Indian business in the fight for export markets and to obtain

---

23   'The first policy initiatives taken under the banner of liberalisation, lifting many of the restrictions of the licence-control raj, benefitted industrial capitalists disproportionately.... Removing restrictions was definitely easier as policy than implementing new programmes. The consequence was that industrial capitalists were able to secure huge surpluses from expansion through international trade and from catering to the pent-up demands of a growing domestic middle class' (Gupta and Sivaramakrishnan, 2011: 8). The second phase of liberalisation saw the decision to allow the States [provinces] more freedom to promote their own economic strategies, especially to seek out their own sources of foreign direct investment (FDI). This led to the consolidation of industrial capitalists' power and undermined the dominance of agricultural interests at the State level without displacing them entirely. States favour industries by giving them special economic zones (SEZs), tax holidays and other sops; they appeal to farmers by giving free electricity and subsidised canal water (ibid.: 9).

24   Lockwood (2014: 2) says that NEP did not happen because of demand of the bourgeoisie, but because of autonomous state action.

25   The most enthusiastic of the listeners in the government was Dr. Manmohan Singh, the former prime minister who, incidentally, had declared his respect for Thatcher, the co-architect of global neoliberalism with Reagan. The new Prime Minister, Modi, who, some believe, is India's Reagan, is in the same league as Dr. Singh whom he replaced in 2014, as far as economic policy is concerned, except that he is more strident, vocal and unabashed than the quiet, polite and erudite Dr. Singh.

foreign technology and capital. The NEP model pursues the goal of transform-ing India into a world power by making it an office (e.g. call centers; software companies), a laboratory (for pharmaceutical and biotech companies, for example), a factory and a raw-material source of agri-produce, for internation-al capital, based on (relatively) cheap labor in a labor market characterized by state-promoted flexibility and precarity.[26]

In the NEP model, existing barriers to money-making, such as government regulations of business or small-scale producers' control over property (e.g. land), should be removed and new facilitative conditions (e.g. pro-business policies) for money-making should be created. Indeed, some of the specific demands of business, as expressed politically by the NEP, include: the deregu-lation of private businesses; the privatization of government businesses;[27] trade liberalization; the granting of permission to foreign capital to own busi-nesses in India; the enactment of tax cuts and other incentives for businesses; regressive taxation (e.g. GST or similar types); and the reduction or complete withdrawal of government benefits for the poor, with extreme targeting as opposed to universal benefits; and complete freedom for private capital to hire and fire labor. The NEP, therefore, is the neoliberal program of the bourgeois class first, and a government policy second.[28]

The specific demands that the NEP articulates emanate from the ways in which capital seeks to connect to each term in Marx's (1977) general formula in *Capital 1* referred to earlier: M–C–P–C'–M'. This is to be seen as integrated into the world market. Through various policies (e.g. low-interest loans; loan waivers to the business class euphemistically called non-performing assets; various bailout packages), the neoliberal state in India makes liquid investible

---

26   Dasgupta (2017) talks about how capitalist accumulation is happening through a flexible labor regime aimed at making labor as cheap as possible. Such flexibilization is creating a reserve army and repressing the organized voice of workers (ibid.; 57; also Tiwana, 2015).

27   In spite of their capitalist and bureaucratic character in terms of functioning, they had a degree of pro-worker orientation as seen in the fact that these units had provided subsi-dized housing and other facilities to workers (Subramanian, 2015).

28   This does not mean that the NEP can be *entirely* reduced to capital's interests. These inter-ests are mediated by the state (or by the political sphere of society), so the autonomy of the state (including electoral compulsions in India) must be borne in mind. This is one reason why welfare policies are not entirely off the agenda of the neoliberal state, espe-cially in a liberal-democracy existing in a country of massive absolute poverty, a combina-tion that can be a serious threat to the ruling class. Harriss (2011b) says: 'the neoliberal project in India is tempered by India's constitutional design and state tradition as well as by social movements... and popular democracy' (p. 128). This is true, as I have shown elsewhere (Das, 2007). But the point to emphasize is this: to function as a neoliberal state, it does not have to spend nothing for the poor.

resources (M) available to big business, often at below-market rates. Liberaliza-tion of financial markets allows domestic businesses access foreign capital, which a relatively under-developed economy is said to rely on. The state makes commodities available in the form of cheap raw materials and cheap land (C), which have been obtained from people via primitive accumulation, including in areas inhabited by indigenous communities. In a developing society such as India's, the state plays an important role in converting what are non-commodities into commodities. Through the liberalization of trade, the state makes foreign commodities available as intermediate goods.

An important part of the C in the capital circuit is labor power that capital buys. The non-implementation of a living wage by the state – in a context where there is a massive and growing reserve army to which primitive accumu-lation under neoliberalism contributes – drives wages below the cost of main-tenance (i.e. the value of labor power). Further, the state, including the courts, often suppresses the right to strike, including in the name of inviting foreign capital. Factory Acts that seek to ensure workers' safety remain unimplement-ed, in part because of the nefarious nexus of state officials/politicians and the business world and the overall climate of free market ideology. Capital's despotic rule in the labor process becomes even more despotic than before, a despotic rule that is strengthened by the ease with which capital can hire and fire labor. The existing rules protecting nature and workers from the harmful effects of capitalist production are being gutted. All this makes for a height-ened level of accumulation by exploitation.

The capitalist class character of neoliberalism can be gauged partly from the following fact: while neoliberalism has put enormous amount of wealth in the hands of the capitalist class (especially top 0.1% to top 1% of the nation), the share of labor in the national income has fallen from an already low level of 40% in 1991 (when neoliberalism was officially launched) to 35% in 2013. If capitalists have subjected labor to super-exploitation (with the average wage for most workers being $2 a day), one would 'expect' a 'liberal-democratic' state to spend more for labor. However, government spending to alleviate labor's problems has also declined: for example, the funding for the biggest employ-ment generation program for rural workers has come down from 0.42% of GDP in 2010–2011 to 0.42% in 2017–2018, while tax cuts for the capitalist class have been massive.

Following the production process, the state helps capital access foreign markets (C'). Sometimes, the state creates markets (e.g. state-promoted insur-ance to farmers, which is sold by the private sector; state-promoted building of physical infrastructure which is actually built by private companies for enor-mous profits). Privatization of state services (e.g. education and health-care, etc.) also creates and expands markets for production of goods and services in the private sector. And finally, the state makes sure that the business world gets to keep much of the surplus value it appropriates from workers and small-scale producers, and that this happens in the form of tax exemptions, tax reduction, write-off of tax arrears, and so on.[29]

The NEP is certainly new, as its name suggests, but it is not as new as is commonly thought. All major interventions, including major anti-poverty policies since de-colonization, have been more or less about propping up a national capitalist regime (with some support from erstwhile 'socialist' countries), a regime that is a little protected from imperialism and a little free from the fetters of feudal remnants. Even in terms of actual spending, the Indian state *has been* a welfare state of the rich elite. Many of the resources in the hands of the state have been used for the propertied classes (in the form of various subsidies and cheap loans) and for wealthier, higher-income, more educated people.[30] According to the government's own estimates, in the mid-1990s (when the NEP was only a few years old), the central and state governments together gave out more than 10 per cent of the GDP in the form of explicit or implicit budgetary subsidies for 'nonmerit' goods and services (the latter largely accrue to the relatively rich) (Bardhan, 2005).[31] The pre-1991 age, including the so-called Nehruvian age, was not exactly a golden age for the masses, although the degree of economic inequality was much less. Mass poverty and (petty) bureaucratic heavy-handedness were rampant. It is not that there is no absolute difference between the NEP and the pre-1991 regime. But the similarity between the two is not to be un-dialectically under-stressed. The neoliberal Indian state is a *capitalist* state like the pre-neoliberal Indian state.

---

29   To the extent that M–C–P–C′–M′ can be shortened to M–M′ (meaning money can simply be made from money), the state helps capitalists increase their profit in the form of interest and profit from speculation, etc. in the sphere of financialization.

30   See the early work of Bardhan (1990) as well as Bardhan (2005). While I agree that state resources have been used to benefit the proprietary classes, I do not endorse Bardhan's analytical Marxist sympathies for the market economy, nor his viewing of state actors as a class (see Chapter 7 of this book).

31   Advocates of neoliberalism 'do not dither when it comes to condemning any sign of the government using tax revenues to provide transfers or subsidies to the poor or undertake expenditures that are expressly meant to favour the poor, in the form of livelihood protection, poverty alleviation or free and universal provision of basic health and educational facilities. Their justification for this is twofold: that expenditure to support growth must be favoured over spending to directly improve welfare; and that fiscal prudence must be privileged over all else when deciding the use of the exchequer's resources. So, if spending has to be tailored to correspond to revenues, expenditure on "populist" measures must be limited or abjured' (Chandrasekhar, 2018). 'There is a twist in the arithmetic underlying such reasoning. It assumes that the difference between tax and non-tax revenues on the one hand, and total expenditures on the other can be reduced only by reducing expenditures and not by increasing revenues' (i.e. not by increases in taxes on the rich) (ibid.).

That neoliberalism is a capitalist project, that it is a project of capitalists, by capitalists and for capitalists, is very clear from what the following top captains of Indian industry and enterprise themselves say about what is euphemistically called new economic policy or economic reforms (or just reforms).

> Post reforms, businesses are much more in control of their own destiny than before.
>
> MURTHY, 2018: 609

> The 1991 economic liberalization was truly an extraordinary leap of faith that not just swept aside the decades-old legacy of socialism and state control but scripted a new landscape carved around fee market and globalization ... The story of Indian liberalization has truly been the story of Indian entrepreneurship.
>
> MITTAL, 2018: 567–568, 574

> Reliance (Reliance Industries Limited) ambitiously seized the opportunities created by the post-1991 reforms, expanding the competencies of our group. This happened because we realized the strong synergies between wealth generation for the nation and value creation for the company.
>
> AMBANI, 2018: 557–558

These words are echoed by T. Das, a capitalist and a former CEO of a national business association (the Confederation of Indian Industry):

> Government and business need each other to strengthen the national economy and the economic growth process in the country. They are two sides of the same coin. Both need each other. To remember this fact of life...is the real need.
>
> DAS, T., 2018: 235

He is not saying what *should* be the case. He is describing what the state of affairs *is*.

3.2   *Agrarian Neoliberalism*
In poor countries such as India, there is a specific form of neoliberalism known as agrarian neoliberalism.[32] This requires a special treatment, given that the

---

32   Just as it is important to think about neoliberalism in terms of agrarian neoliberalism (see Oya, 2005; Vakulabharanam and Motiram, 2011; Walker, 2008; see also Appendix 2), it is also important to think about neoliberalism in terms of industrialization and what can be

vast majority of the workforce still depends on farming in most parts of the country. Agrarian neoliberalism represents an internally contradictory logic: on the one hand, rural areas are *emphasized* as being attractive venues for big business activities because of rural markets and cheap land and labor in rural and semi-rural areas; on the other hand, from the standpoint of state investment, rural areas are not a priority. Rural areas have indeed an interesting relation to the business class. They have become an arena for new forms of private accumulation: buying peasants' land dirt cheap; agribusiness selling seeds and other inputs to peasants at a high price; and patenting of peasants' knowledge; industrial and financial capital selling consumer goods including cell phones, and insurance, etc. Rural areas have attracted investment from agribusiness which is in search of cheap labor and land and new markets (for seeds, etc.). An important form of capitalist investment in rural areas is on the basis of contract farming.[33] This has at least two aspects from the standpoint of the neoliberal state. On the one hand, operating in a context where the neoliberal state is not guaranteeing a remunerative price in spite of rising input prices, farmers enter into contracts with big business on unequal terms. On the other hand, encouraged by the state, contract farming allows coordination of mercantile, financial and productive forms of capital when domestic and foreign businesses are able to procure agro-raw materials, without experiencing any risk involved in the actual production process (which might involve capital-labor conflict and which also involve the risk that nature might create).[34]

In terms of the relation between the state and rural areas, they have been subjected to neglect: rural development expenditure as a percentage of the net national product has been decreasing. Government subsidies for fertilizers, electricity, and other farm inputs, as well as investment in irrigation, have all been slashed. Access to cheap loans for farmers has been limited. Price supports to farmers have been reduced, and the Public Distribution System has been drastically curtailed. It should be noted that the extent of the cuts has been debated, and some say that such cuts have not happened because of India's democratic system in which the poor have some voice and because

---

called extractive neoliberalism, i.e. neoliberalism in the mining sector. On the latter, see Adduci (2017).

33   On contract farming, see Shrimali (forthcoming) and Vicol (2019).

34   The coordination among three forms of capital refer to the fact that contract farming allows capitalist production (productive capital) of an agro-product (e.g. potato chips) by commercial farmers who receive inputs (mercantile capital) and financial assistance (financial capital) from the big business, including the MNCs.

therefore there is a fear of class war owing to the adverse impacts of neoliberalism itself.[35]

Peasants are losing land to capitalist industrialization and land-speculation. Land ceiling laws are reversed because they are considered to be constraints on capital flows into farming. Peasants are being forced to leave their land because farming is not viable: the costs of cultivation are going up due to shrinking government support. These people are also adversely affected by the import of subsidized foreign farm goods. Highly indebted, many are driven to distress sales.

As Utsa Patnaik (2007) has admirably documented, there is a decline in food production and availability per capita. This is in part because land is converted to non-food crops both by big companies and by smaller owners who do not have many alternative ways of earning money and who are therefore attracted to the prospect of making a little cash. This is a grave threat to food security (Patnaik, 2013). Also, in the areas where high-value farm products are produced (e.g. shrimps, flowers), intense exploitation of labor, land, and water happens in order to make the sector competitive in the global market. Declining investment in rural infrastructure (especially flood and irrigation control) is increasing vulnerability to such natural calamities as drought and floods. The role of the government in buying farm produce at a favorable rate from peasants is less and less important. With trade liberalization, changes in international prices make farmers, especially those with less land and limited investible

---

35   'In the standard narrative of neoliberalism, the emphasis has always been on the slashing of public expenditure by cost-conscious governments and not on increasing public outlays to enable people to meet their basic needs. In India, however, the reverse may appear to be true. One could argue that this is a peculiar outcome of Indian democracy because the participation of poor, subaltern, and rural populations in the electoral process is often higher than that of urban, middle-class people; numerically, poor and rural groups form a preponderant part of the electorate'. Therefore, the state resorts to increased public expenditures to enable people to meet their basic needs. This is what explains, according to the editors, ambitious social programmes such as the National Rural Employment Guarantee Scheme (Gupta and Sivaramakrishnan, 2011: 5). Partha Chatterjee has argued 'the paradoxical growth of state welfare programmes after liberalisation can be explained by the political compulsions of a pattern of growth that is immiserising a vast majority of people in the country'. He emphasises the real fear of class war. 'If the effects of liberalisation on the poor and those displaced from their land and deprived of livelihoods by primary accumulation are not reversed by government policies, they might turn into "dangerous" classes' (Gupta and Sivaramakrishnan, 2011: 6). Of course, 'Inclusive growth has not meant including the poor in growth. What it has meant is taking the higher government revenues obtained from rapid growth in sectors of the economy tied to the global market and redistributing them to indigent sections of the population. Growth of the rural economy has not been a central concern of government policy' (ibid.: 6).

surplus, more vulnerable when prices fall; they become dependent on exploitative private traders (as in the pre-1991 times). Agrarian distress (crisis of income and livelihood of the farm-dependent classes) is creating a huge reserve army, a part of which is forced to migrate to cities (permanently or periodically). This, along with shrinking government support for workers reducing the already-meagre social wage, allows capital to raise the level of exploitation (one person does the work of two, which cuts demand for labor from rural areas, from the latent reserve army). That the NEP is producing increasing numbers of wealthy people, on the one hand, and hundreds of millions of (rural) people whose basic needs (e.g. for food) remain singularly unsatisfied, on the other, speaks to the fact that neoliberalism is *a* class project with severe implications for the rural periphery.

Agrarian neoliberalism is often associated with what I will call New Agricultural Production (NAP), i.e. production of high-value farm products such as shrimps (and flowers) for exports (this is discussed in details in a later chapter) with the support of the state. The 'lean' neoliberal state exists in a selectively hollowed out manner (Jessop, 2002) and institutionalizes within its form the tensions of civil society. It encourages, for example, flori- and shrimp production, but, as mentioned before, withdraws, or reduces, food subsidizes for the poorer laborers and peasants who produce fish and flowers neither of which they can afford to consume. Indeed, the drastic reduction of public investment and public provisions of food can be compared in terms of its effect on people to the enclosures of the commons. This trend exists in other countries producing high-value agri-commodities for export (Newly Agricultural Countries), but India has a certain degree of specificity. On the one hand, and more akin to the countries of the Global North, it is a liberal parliamentary democracy; indeed, the world's largest. On the other hand, unlike in these countries a vast majority of India's population of 1.3 billion depend on farming and other rural activities and are adversely affected by neoliberalism (Dasgupta, 1998). This unique context in which neoliberalism is practiced, and the way rural areas are affected, demands comprehensive investigation. Understanding the relation between neoliberal capitalism and rural areas is very important not least because most people live in rural areas but also because the rural areas suffer from more adverse impacts of neoliberalism than urban areas, which happen to be the major seat of capital, including in its neoliberal form, and of the segments of the population that capital absolutely needs (e.g. highly educated people with technical and managerial skills). A fuller consideration of the relation between neoliberalism and rural areas must include: (1) the shift in agricultural production to new and luxury crops for export; (2) emergence of differential rates of development at multiple scales; (3) intensification of pressures emanating from changing agricultural production upon labor and environmental resources; (4) geographically uneven consolidation and centralization in new agriculture; (5) cultural changes that help legitimize neoliberal reforms in rural areas; (6) the state's political and economic role in securing a neoliberal agrarian-development path (see Appendix 2 for details).

3.3 Unspectacular Economic Growth and Rising Economic Inequality

On its own terms, the NEP is not a big success. It has unleashed some entrepreneurial energy. The rate of growth has increased relative to the pre-liberalization period but it has not been spectacular over a long period of time. India still accounts for barely 5 per cent of the global economy. Even in the IT sector, India remains a relatively minor player dependent on the technology and markets of the West. There is little sign that the average level of labor productivity per hour in key sectors has improved much relative to that in richer countries. As we have discussed earlier, India's capitalism remains one that is more based on the formal subsumption of labor – a regime of exploitation based on long hours and low wages – than real subsumption of labor, which is based on the systemic tendency towards technological changes and increasing labor productivity. Of course, if labor productivity is not rising, how are the rich making money? One answer is from the recently published Oxfam report:

> the richest in India have made their money through crony capitalism rather than through innovation or the fair rules of the market...Specific policy choices which favoured capital rather than labour, and favoured skilled rather than unskilled labour, are part of the structure of the growth trajectory in India.
>
> as quoted in INDIAN EXPRESS, 2018

Not only in terms of its underlying driving forces, but also in terms of its necessary consequences, the NEP is a class project. Not only is it driven by the capitalist class in terms of why and how it happened: it has also produced an enormous amount of economic inequality. According to Chancel and Piketty (2017), inequality has been intensifying, especially since the introduction of neoliberal policies (Figure 4.2). The growth of income in India's post-independence period (from 1951 to 1980) went overwhelmingly to the toiling masses: while national income grew by 67%, the incomes of the bottom half of the population grew by 87% and that of the middle 40% of the population grew by 74%. But, during these three decades, the income of the top 1% of the population grew only by 5%, and the incomes of the top 0.001% of the population have seen a negative growth rate of –42%. The share of top 1% which was

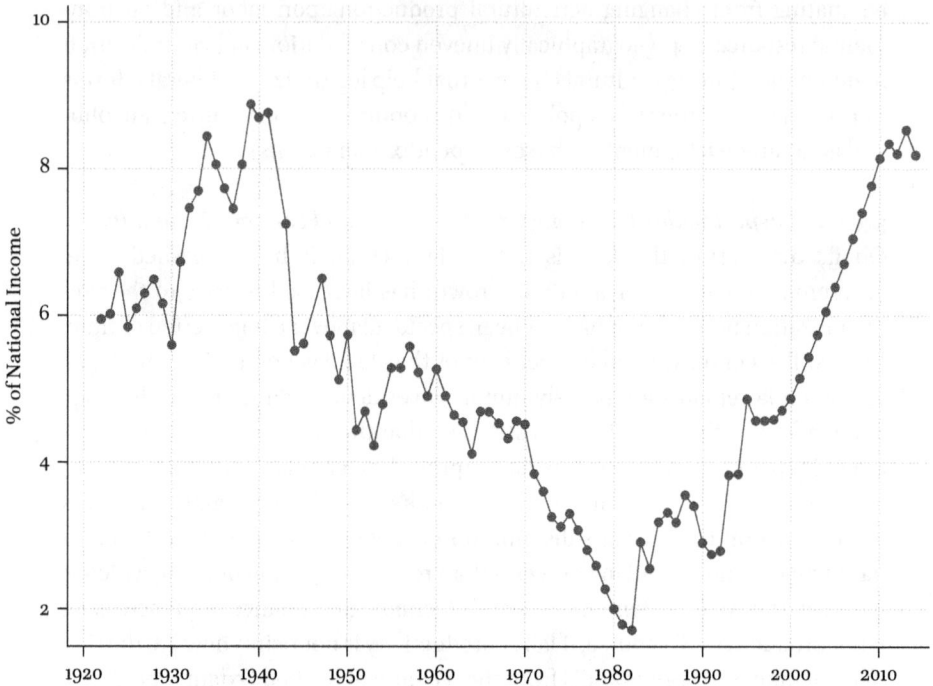

FIGURE 4.2 Top 0.1% national income share in India, 1922–2015
SOURCE: CHANCEL AND PIKETTY, 2017

as high as 21% of the total national income during the British colonial rule (in 1939), declined to 6% by 1983 (ibid.). The decline in inequalities was reversed. From 1983 onwards, the share of top 1% started increasing. From 6% in 1983, their share increased to 22% in 2014, higher than even the British times.

While the 34 years from 1980 to 2014 saw a much higher growth than did previous three decades (67% vs 187%), this growth mainly went to the rich. The income of the bottom 50% only grew by 89% in these 34 years. Compare this to the growth rate of 87% for this group from 1951 to 1980.[36] The fact that this growth entirely benefited the super-rich is evident, as the incomes of the top 0.001% of the population, among whom we can list the likes of Ambanis and the Adanis, grew by 2726% (Srujana, 2017). The share of top 1% of the

---

36   'In fact, the growth of effective incomes of the bottom 50% would be even lower, considering the gradual withdraw of the welfare state. With privatisation of public transport and withdrawal of various subsidies to the poor including the universal public distribution system – the real cost of living has gone up much more in the post-liberalisation era' (Srujana, 2017).

population in India's income has increased from about 6% in 1983 to 22% in 2014. The share of bottom 50% of the country's income fell from about 24% in 1983 to 15% in 2014 (ibid.). This is in terms of *income*, and not *capital* as such.

Inequalities were reduced sharply in India in the post-independence period from 1951 to 1980, *because* of various progressive economic policies that were adopted by the Indian governments after independence (ibid.) in a context where the bourgeois class power was expressed in relatively less extreme and blatant form.[37]

Consider these two facts: 1983–84 was the year of the lowest income-share for the top 1 per cent, after which this share started rising, and that neoliberalism first made its appearance around that very time. 'The association between growth in inequality and the pursuit of neoliberalism is thus strikingly close' (Patnaik, 2017a; see also Jaydev et al., 2011).

As in many other countries, both rich and poor, so in India, neoliberalism is causally associated with wealth inequality. According to Credit Suisse's data on wealth distribution, the top 1 per cent of households in India currently owns more than half (57 per cent) of the total wealth of all households (up from 17 per cent in 1991), and wealth inequality in India has been rising extremely rapidly, indeed more rapidly than even in the United States.[38] There are several reasons for rising wealth inequality. In a brilliant, though, short article, Prabhat Patnaik (2018), the most well-known Marxist economist from India, explains the mechanisms in his characteristically lucid manner. There are five

---

37   'Indian government nationalised railways in 1951 and air transport in 1953.... Subsequently, in the 1960s and 1970s, almost all of the banking sector and the oil industry were nationalised, along with many others. These reforms have allowed the government to redistribute income into the hands of the working class and the peasantry, that would have otherwise gone into the coffers of the rich industrialists' (Srujana, 2017).

38   'Wealth distribution is invariably more unequal than income distribution, because the working class which has no wealth has nonetheless an income. Two separate reports released this year capture the tragedy of modern India. One says that in 2017, the number of dollar millionaires increased by 20%, as did their wealth. 'Dollar millionaires' are those individuals who own wealth of more than one million dollars. The other report, released earlier this year says that 73% of the wealth generated in 2016–17 went to the richest one percent, while 67 crore Indians making up half of the country's population saw a meagre one percent increase in their wealth' (Varma, 2018a). According to a report from a French firm Capgemini, which calculates the dollar millionaires by prices of equities and real estate owned, 'In 2016, there were 219,000 such millionaires in India which increased to 263,000 in 2017, thanks to a rise in the market value of owned shares and in realty prices. The total wealth owned by these millionaires crossed $1 trillion in 2017' (ibid.). 'Another report by Credit Suisse, a Swiss investment bank, for 2017 had revealed that about 73% of wealth in India is owned by the richest 10% of the population. Within this bracket, the top 1% of Indians owned a staggering 45% of the country's wealth' (ibid.).

mechanisms: the increase in income inequality; the privatization of essential services like education and healthcare; the intensive process of primitive accumulation of capital; tax concessions and tax breaks to the rich, and the formation of asset price bubbles. These may be explained briefly.

a)   There is increasing concentration of income in fewer hands resulting in their savings which are converted to an asset base (Patnaik, 2018):

> The tendency under neo-liberalism is to keep worsening income distribution. This is because the number of jobs created under it falls woefully short of the number of job-seekers, which increases the relative size of the reserve army of labour, so that wages remain tied to a subsistence level even as labour productivity increases. The share of surplus accruing to the rich therefore keeps increasing over time under neo-liberal capitalism, entailing an increase in income, and hence wealth, inequality.

b)   Privatization of essential services under neoliberalism leads to many people selling their assets to be able to access the services such as education and health-care.[39] Note also that those who have access to education and health care etc. generally earn more than those who do not.

c)   The on-going primitive accumulation puts assets in the hands of big capitalists:

> Through a variety of means, ranging from an outright takeover of petty property, including peasant property, (or its purchase "for a song"); to encroachment on common property; to appropriation of State property (which is built up through taxes imposed on ordinary people); to the sheer filching of bank credit from the public sector banks (what is commonly referred to as a build-up of their "Non-Performing Assets"), the big capitalists increase their share in the total wealth of the economy.
>
> PATNAIK, 2018

> Primitive accumulation increases wealth inequality as wealth is transferred from many to a few. It also causes a vast reserve army of labor, keeping wages low and allows entrepreneurs to make a lot of money: primitive accumulation squeezes peasants and petty producers and forces 'them out of their traditional occupations to migrate to cities where they join the ranks of the job seekers and hence swell the relative size

---

39   On an excellent discussion on marketisation of health and educational facilities characterizing the shift from an interventionist state to a neoliberal state, see Tiwana and Singh (2015).

of the reserve army of labor' (Patnaik, 2018); this reduces wages and increases profit' and thus accentuates income inequality, and with it wealth inequality.

d) Concessions (tax breaks etc.) from the governments promote asset concentration.

There has been a decline in the tax payment by the rich and this means they have more income in their hands which is converted into their savings/wealth: the highest marginal income tax rate got reduced from 98 per cent to 30 per cent. Such concessions increase wealth inequality because the resources that the wealthy should share with society/state remain in their hands, while they continue to use public services whose full cost they do not pay.[40]

In addition since they are balanced by reducing government expenditure on education and healthcare, and thereby directly or indirectly privatising these essential services, they contribute to the impoverishment of large segments of the ordinary people, which as we saw earlier, also increases wealth inequality.

PATNAIK, 2018

e) The formation of asset price bubbles also promotes wealth inequality under neoliberalism.

---

40 'The unwillingness or "inability" of the state to tax the rich reveals that it is not a neutral agency standing above all classes. It is partisan: it represents the interests of a few. But such partisanship also serves the specific interests of the party in government. Resources are needed to fight elections or consolidate a political position, leading to a financial nexus between those wielding political power and those with access to the nation's surpluses' (Chandrasekhar, 2014). One should add that: capitalists also need money for luxury consumption and for the accumulation fund, and they need to pay money to obedient politicians to fight elections who in turn introduce pro-business policies, and they need corruption money (money to be paid to specific politicians and officials in order have a competitive advantage vis-à-vis competitors and be able to avoid certain labor and other regulations).

'Under neoliberalism, which is based on an anti-statist and pro-market rhetoric, this nexus is strengthened. Since the neoliberal state is openly committed to favouring private capital, handouts to the rich in the form of tax reductions or direct transfers are seen as normal, and higher taxes on surplus incomes as abnormal. In such a system, state functionaries who have a role in deciding the magnitude of such transfers and determining the favoured recipients often see nothing wrong in claiming a share in the spoils. The space for corruption is considerably enlarged. The result is that expenditure reduction has to be focussed even more on curtailing so-called "populist" expenditures favouring the poor, to release the resources needed to finance the handouts provided to the rich and the payouts made to state functionaries' (Chandrasekhar, 2014).

Speculative booms on the stock market or on other asset markets give a
boost to the value of assets, because of which the top percentiles which
figure prominently among the asset-holders find the absolute value of
their wealth, and hence their share in total wealth, increasing quite
sharply within a very short period.[41]

   Ibid.

It should be borne in mind that whether or not there is neoliberalism, there
will be concentration and centralization of wealth so we should not reduce the
fact of wealth inequality to the fact that we have capitalism that is less state-
regulated. The fundamental reason for wealth inequality remains irrespective
of neoliberalism, and this tends to be under-stressed by Patnaik and others:
surplus labor appropriated from workers – including when technological
change expands the reserve army and depresses wages and increases profits –
is converted into capitalist wealth, or into what Marx calls property based on
exploitation of others, as opposed to property based on own labor. Arguably,
wealth inequality of the type we see in neoliberal India as elsewhere, is a more
extreme form of the 'normal' wealth inequality associated with capitalism as
such. In considering wealth inequality it is not adequate to see this only in
terms of what the government does or does not do.

India's neoliberalism has indeed led to a small minority of winners and a
very large majority of losers. It has vastly benefited the capitalist class, including those fractions that specialize in finances, IT, real estate, and natural resources, producing more than 130 dollar billionaires in 2018. It has placed a
colossal amount of wealth – wealth produced by the sweat of the property-less
masses – in the hands of a few.[42] A part of this wealth has been hidden away in
overseas banks or invested abroad. A not-inconsiderable part is publicly dis-
played via pretentious lifestyles, which constitute one way in which the elite
ideologically reinforces its class position by differentiating it from the majority,
and this fact is geographically manifested as two *Indias*: one where the elite
lives and one where the 'commoners' do. A wide variety of consumer items is
indeed now available for those with money (approximately 200–300 million

---

41   Under 'a neo-liberal regime, governments try to prevent a collapse of the bubble (which
      would have seriously adverse repercussions on the economy) by sustaining it through
      various means. These range from fiscal support ... to the commoditisation of elements of
      nature like water and air (so that new profitable assets are introduced to keep the boom
      going), to the privatisation of government assets such as "spectrum" (with the same objec-
      tive)' (Patnaik, 2018).

42   As Patnaik (2010a) says: 'The State under neoliberalism ... actively promotes an increase
      in the share of surplus value in the hands of domestic and foreign corporates as an es-
      sential component of its so-called "development strategy"'.

people in a country of 1300 million). The NEP has certainly brought with it some foreign technology and cheaper intermediate goods. It has also benefited some educated people employed in IT and related industries, including tech-coolies. Many of these people tend to easily acquiesce to their own exploitation, despite the huge difference in remuneration between India and imperialist countries, and between their own remuneration and the earnings of ordinary souls. In spite of them being exploited by global capital, this stratum does enjoy a certain level of economic success, which has promoted a habit of conspicuous consumption among them and which is mobilized as an ideological prop for neoliberalism and market fetishism.

On the other hand, the NEP has heaped unspeakable miseries on the bottom 800–1000 million people in India, who include urban proletarians and semi-proletarians, a large number of urban small-scale business owners, and peasants. Neoliberalism has produced a massive amount of insecurity, unemployment and under-employment, casualization, informalization, greater labor exploitation, and lax or nonexistent implementation of protective factory acts. It has produced what Utsa Patnaik calls 'a republic of hunger' and what Jean Dreze calls 'a nutritional emergency'. It has produced a graveyard of people in villages who have committed suicide (at a rate of two per hour) (Sainath, 2013), because of their economic insecurity and inability to pay the bills. This is also happening in formerly booming cities like Tirupur in South India.

3.4   *Intensifying Geographical Inequality*
The NEP as a capitalist class agenda has definite geographical effects. It is implemented through accumulation projects that involve massive restructuring of space relations, which produces spatial unevenness at multiple scales. It also involves institutions and actors at multiple scales: international, national, regional, and local.

The restructuring of space relations has two aspects. First of all, a new built environment is being produced in order to accelerate the movement of commodities at a cheaper cost between places in India and between India and the rest of the world, and to increase the pace of elite consumption (see D'Costa, 2005; Jenkins, 2011). And such production of the built environment itself is a means of profit-making.[43] What Harvey says about real-estate development in

---

43   Bear (2018) points to 'a triple predation of the private sector on Indian public infrastructures. Firstly, the private sector would benefit from investing and trading in infrastructure bonds making profits from the ruins generated by fiscal austerity. Secondly, it would benefit from the outsourcing of public work and selling of public assets. Thirdly, companies running or constructing infrastructure would gain guarantees of profits from taxpayers' revenues [just like railways companies did during the British times]. These accumulations from PPPs would be invisible to citizens because contracts were private, concealed from

China applies to real-estate development and other forms of the production of the built environment in India: 'Real-estate development, particularly in and around the large cities and in the export development zones, appears to be another privileged path towards amassing immense wealth in a few hands' (Harvey, 2005: 146). The transformation of space relations is revealed not only in the form of special economic zones (Levien, 2011) and urban shopping malls, but also in the form of new roads, highways, railway lines (including dedicated railway lines), airports, seaports, etc.[44]

The production of the built environment can create some employment.[45] But given its unplanned and profit-driven character, it can have adverse consequences as well. For example, the production of the built environment, to the extent that it is occurring on the basis of debt-financing, has its own risk, especially, given the tendency towards 'over-production' of some elements of the built environment (e.g. houses; shopping malls).

Besides, in order to produce the built environment and set up enterprises (e.g. hotels; manufacturing units) as well as construct housing for sale, low-income working class areas or slums are being cleared, and peasants and aboriginal people are being dispossessed of their land. Their land is required not only for residence but also for its natural resources, which are subjected to intense exploitation. Indeed, 'displacement has been an integral constitutive component of the process of development in India' (Vasudevan, 2008: 41). Between the big bosses' right and the little people's right to be in a given place, between these two equal rights, it is usually force that decides the matter. This force is often the brute force wielded by the legal agents of the state (police, paramilitary forces, courts, etc.). This force is also that of the private coercive personnel hired by big business and the illegally-operating goons, including fascistic elements operating inside and outside legal political parties or outfits.[46]

The production of space facilitates accumulation and money-making in the ways just noted. It should be emphasized again that the production of space is

---

public scrutiny.... This vision is being relentlessly pursued by the current BJP government in India. A full-scale 'reform' of the railways is underway and freight corridors are being constructed' (p. 6; parenthesis added).

44   The class bias in the space transformation (road building, etc.) is evident from the fact that while millions of rupees are spent on high-speed roads, the vast majority of villages with a population of 1000 or less are not connected by a road. Obviously, people in these places do not have enough market power.

45   When new cities develop, some employment is created for people in the surrounding villages. Construction work in rural and urban areas does create some jobs.

46   In India, where increasingly the pursuit of money is above most things in life, murdering anyone who is an obstacle to that pursuit can be delivered on a cheap platter to whoever can afford to spend a little.

also an opportunity *in itself* to make money. This is because space – the economic landscape – is a commodity. What is called infrastructure is big business indeed. The production of space has an ideological/discursive moment to it as well. By constantly asserting that the country needs a large amount of money for infrastructure, the state justifies cuts in welfare expenditure as well as measures to court private capital through various incentives.

While today this State or region and tomorrow that State or region is in trouble, it is also the case that there is always a successful State or a region or a city, where things *are* going right in some sense. Because some regions are always doing well, relative to others, people feel that all is well with the system, and all will be well if all regions do what the successful regions do (Harvey, 2014: 154). And, when specific places have problems, it is said, they have to get it right. Capital gets off scot-free. The blame is often on the greedy unions or on political mismanagement (e.g. corruption) or merely on the crony character of capitalism (i.e. some capitalists with nepotistic nexus with selected and powerful politicians and/or officials). The rural and urban landscapes hide the fact that it is capital that is behind them. These landscapes hide the power of capital to create uneven geographical development. 'The landscape of capitalism [both mansions and deprived areas] exists as a diversionary image of another world closer to some transcendental sense of human longing and desire' (ibid.: 160). As well, given that financialization is an important aspect of neoliberal capitalism, even if banks are under nominal state control,[47] there is much speculative activity which is partly expressed in the form of spectacular production of built environment (skyscrapers and shopping malls in big cities such as Mumbai and Delhi), which give the false view of neoliberalism's dynamism.

The NEP has also resulted in an enormous amount of unevenness between areas. This is because neoliberal investment (including in infrastructure), the main motive of which is profit-making, tends to be geographically concentrated, although the actual patterns of unevenness are not written in stone: a region that is backward today can thrive tomorrow. The fact that investment happens in a few cities or States, producing impressive glass buildings, gorgeous shopping malls, and islands of 'high-tech' firms, does not mean that all places in India can experience this: the process through which some places in the country become developed *includes* the process of most places not developing. Yet geographical differences are being put to ideological purpose – that is, to further the neoliberal agenda: a few places have achieved some economic development through neoliberal policies, and people are being told that *all* places can achieve this *in that way*. Neoliberalism *is* a process of production of spatial

---

47   This effectively means satisfying the collective financial needs of capital, and increasingly, of politically-neglected capitalists.

inequalities and spatial displacements – indeed, of 'uneven and combined development'.[48] A highly important manifestation of this unevenness is between rural and urban areas, with urban areas growing five times faster than rural areas.[49] Agriculture has more or less stagnated as public expenditure has dwindled and public resources are being diverted from it to infrastructure projects in the interest of big business. The socio-geographical face of the villages drained of skilled labor and investible surplus is dismal; this is not to deny the enormous unevenness between areas within cities (e.g. between gated communities and slums).[50] It should be borne in mind that: rural India has on average a lower income than urban India, so if rural areas do not do as well as urban areas which is where capital is invested and where middle class workers on whom capital crucially depends work and live, this fact, other things being equal, can widen overall income inequality. Another pattern of uneven development is within the rural hinterland: i.e. between the rural areas which are closer to the cities and those that are in more remote areas (see Das and Mishra, 2019; Pattenden, 2018; Singh, 2017).

The patterns of uneven development both between cities and between States have interesting political dynamics. With regards to pro-business reforms, regional elites (in States and cities) have some power vis-à-vis the central government. These regionally based elites – comprised of alliances between politicians and local-regional businesses – compete with each other for external loans and domestic as well as foreign capital. Some States and cities get more investment than others.[51] And this process creates a new layer of uneven economic development on top of an already existing layer. When all places are equally neoliberal in their courting of capital, small differences in policy and other factors necessary for profitmaking become metamorphosed into large differences. And competition between States and cities becomes a means

---

48   Consider newly constructed good roads and tall buildings in cities in the minerally-rich areas (e.g. Raipur) that are alongside, and are combined with, the poverty of the Adivasis in the surrounding areas and the archaic social relationships within which they live their lives.

49   On urban development under neoliberalism, see Cowan (2018). On the idea that NEP prioritizes urban areas, see Walker (2008).

50   The cities have experienced neoliberalization in specific ways. As Banerjee-Guha (2009: 105) writes, 'The consequences [of neoliberalization for cities] can be seen in the increasing focus on hyper forms and mega construction activities, increased speculation and expanded investment in land and real estate ..., service sector, signature projects, mega cultural events and a reduced focus on the employment generating production process, affordable housing, and collective sharing of urban space and resources'.

51   Sud (2014: 241): 'states can compete directly with each other and other international subnational regions to attract investment and forge neo-liberal development'. See also Murali, 2017.

of discipline and punish by which neoliberalism is imposed/implemented: if a State/city fails to provide enough concessions (i.e. bribe) to big business, it fails to attract (much) investment. Geography of capitalist development is a geography of bribing capital, or sections of capital.

3.5   Neoliberalism and Imperialism

From one angle, in neoliberalism, the market forces are expected to play a more important role than the state in economic development. From another angle, neoliberalism is about the shifting balance between globalization and nationalism (Nayar, 2001): business activities must respond to price signals in the global market places and not (or, not just) within the national boundaries. It is from the latter angle that one can see neoliberalism implemented in a peripheral country such as India as a part of the imperialist project. After all, imperialism is capitalist accumulation (including profit making, inter-capitalist competition, production process) at the international scale, assisted by the coercive and ideological power of the states of advanced capitalist countries.

Neoliberalism in peripheral countries is a part of global neoliberalism, the history of which is connected to working-class struggle in the West and anti-colonial struggles in the periphery. More specifically, since the 1970s, capitalism has been seeking to withdraw many of the concessions (e.g. welfare benefits) it previously conceded to the working class of the advanced countries due to its struggles. Global big business is also no more willing to concede some autonomy to the peripheral states and the national bourgeoisie of poor countries, the bourgeoisie that it tolerated in the aftermath of anti-colonial struggles. From the perspective of global big business, the natural resources, markets, space (including the space to dump waste), and laboring bodies of these poorer countries cannot be entirely left in the hands of the national bourgeoisie to exploit: international capital must have relatively free (i.e. less constrained) and direct access to them. As it plays itself out in India, the NEP, which is both a medium for, and an outcome of, global neoliberalism, establishes a direct exploitative connection between the bourgeoisie (including its financial segments) of rich countries and India's poor masses to a degree that did not quite exist previously. An important aspect of neoliberalism is indeed 'the new determination to drain the resources of the periphery toward the center' (Duménil and Lévy, 2005: 10) via the activities of international financial capital and other segments of international big business. India's debt payment is 65% of its annual GDP, and India's interest payment is a quarter of its budget spending.[52] India has to simply borrow money to pay the interest due on its old loans. Tax concessions to big business, which constitute an important

---

52   Borrowing at a rate of 1–3%, much lower than India's borrowing rate, the US spends 6%.

neoliberal agenda, worsen the situation with respect to the proportion of government budget that goes towards servicing debts.

Interest payments represent a transfer of resources from the country. This is not the only form of transfer. It also occurs when imperialist capital exploits the workers and peasants of India, a process that the NEP furthers. This imperialist exploitation is abetted by the states of imperialist countries as well as by India's pliant compradore[53] state, an exploitation that is epitomized by 'sultans' (monarchs) of reform like the Manmohan Singhs and the Narendra Modis.[54] Not only this. Some of the Indian States are run under budgetary guidelines formulated by the American 'knowledge' firm McKinsey, and by the IMF, the World Bank, the international development agencies of the governments of advanced countries (the DFID of the UK), and 'compradore' intellectuals and advisors bought off by these institutions. In many ways, and as is widely known, neoliberalism (embodied in privatization, cuts in government spending, etc.) was imposed by international institutions under the name of conditionalities for loans. In particular, the World Bank has been instrumental in pushing for the privatization of water-supply and electricity services, as well as other crucial public services, all in the name of efficiency and development. The same sorts of measures (e.g. austerity measures) have been undertaken in the imperialist countries themselves in the interest of their top '1–10%' and to the detriment of their direct producers, who are the vast majority. Neoliberalism, signifying a new onslaught of capital on the toiling masses, is the thread that links the toiling masses of the world, although the masses in poorer countries are affected a lot more than those in richer countries.[55]

---

53   The word *compradore* here it refers to the state managers and businesses in a peripheral country that enter into an alliance with the state and businesses of imperialist countries, an alliance which may promote the development of productive forces under capitalism in the periphery in an uneven manner; it is an alliance in which those class forces of the periphery are subordinate allies. So 'compradore' is used here in a sense which is somewhat different from the way it is used in the dependency literature or by Mao. For Mao (1926): 'the comprador class' is wholly an appendage 'of the international bourgeoisie, depending upon imperialism for its survival and growth, and hinders economic development'.

54   In fact, the state apparatus is increasingly occupied by pro-market ideologues and neoliberal technocrats and indeed by businesspeople themselves. This signifies the neoliberalization and technocratization of the state apparatus, a distinct colonization of the state by neoliberals. Kohli (2012) says that a distinct marker of the current epoch is the increasing and deepening alliance between state managers and the business class in India, an alliance that is responsible for growth with inequality.

55   I am abstracting from the discussion on the idea that Indian neoliberal capitalism potentially is showing signs of what is called sub-imperialism (see Bond, 2014).

3.6   *Neoliberalism and Class Struggle from Below and from Above*

No economic process is purely economic. Neoliberalism is not merely economic. It is deeply political. It has been an arena of, and an object of, class struggle, both from below and from above.

Given the NEP's devastating impacts, it is not surprising that broad sections of the toiling class have risen up against it.[56] Since the 1990s, millions of people have gone on numerous strikes over wages, freedom to form new unions independent of the management, contractualization of work, anti-people government policies, and so on. Some of the resistance has been against crony capitalism: atrociously corrupt ways in which the partnership between specific segments of capital and the state has undemocratically milked the resources of the society as a whole. Much of the resistance has been directly against privatization, liberalization, globalization, and reduction in state support for the poor and farmers. Because of the struggle from below (both real and potential),[57] the state has sometimes slowed the pace of reforms slightly. Reforms have been slowed especially when a given reform will adversely affect the weaker members of the bourgeoisie, who cannot compete in the global market. The state has also tried to provide some palliatives as a part of the neoliberal policy to ensure that reforms are not derailed by social unrest in a liberal-democratic set-up. So-called employment guarantee schemes, like loan waivers for farmers and legislation guaranteeing access to food, are one such palliative measure. Relative to the amount of damage caused by neoliberalism, there is too little actual support for the poor.[58]

The bourgeoisie needs 'growth' (that is, a massive increase in the money in its pocket in the shortest possible time). The political parties and the neoliberal state, both at the central and the provincial levels, promise to deliver this growth.[59] This is the limit to how much and in what way the workers and peasants can benefit from the palliatives. The idea that there is such a thing as

---

56   On the trade union and political forms of struggles of the masses against neoliberalism, see Meyer (2016).

57   The on-going struggle from below is partly a struggle between laws, as people seek to defend rights enshrined in earlier laws against new legislation that seeks to diminish these as privileges or deny them altogether and people are also struggling for fresh laws to reflect the democratic aspirations of a post-colonial age (Sundar, 2011).

58   The rural poor, and particularly, Adivasis and Dalits have seen little benefit from the country's economic growth over the last three decades (Roy, 2018).

59   For this service, politicians are compensated by businesses. Politicians use some of the money they get from businesses that benefit from neoliberal policies in order to produce trickery and deception (via, e.g. television air time, and bought news) and for bribery, all of which are necessary for obtaining votes and reproducing the political legitimacy of the neoliberal state.

neoliberalism with a human face – and the fact that neoliberalism has had to be *sold* to people – means that neoliberalism itself is inhumane and does not exist in the interest of the masses. Such an idea is essentially based on this lie: basic interests of capital are compatible with basic interests of toiling masses, in a sustainable manner and on a national scale.

In fact, neoliberalism *itself* is a form of class struggle from the top, the class struggle launched by the ruling class with the help of the state to ensure conditions for accumulation. As a form of class struggle from above, several elements of neoliberalism need to be considered. One is the withdrawal of benefits for the poorer sections, which is an attack on their living standards. Making it difficult for labor to launch trade union struggles is another. A major capitalist association says this:

> Industrial Relations paradigm in India had dramatically changed following the adaptation of free market policy in the early nineties. With the dawn of liberalization, privatization and globalization (LPG), the country is, by and large, able to preserve *a sound and positive industrial relations climate*. This is apparent from the statistical figures of Union Government's Labor Bureau, which exhibits drastic decline of industrial disputes from 3049 in 1979 to 391 (P) in 2009.
>
> AIOE/FICCI, n.d.: 1; italics added

India's labor minister said this in 2015 while appealing to trade unions not to strike: 'We in government do not believe in confrontation...We are in favour of industries and workers working towards mutual benefits' (Nanda, 2015). Such a view, not surprisingly echoes the view of employers' organizations such as FICCI which says: 'Strikes can never be hoped to yield any satisfactory solution to pressing labor problems'. Strikes lead to loss of production and also affects investors' confidence and thus foreign investment on which a poor country depends, it is said (ibid.).

Where the numbing of consciousness through the official and academic–market-oriented propaganda, including the propaganda doled out by finance ministers and other spokespersons of capital, fails, where the intoxication wof the masses by the fetishism of seasonal festivals called 'elections' eases off,[60] where official bribing in the form of limited welfare is ineffective, and where, as a result, the masses *do* rise in revolt, the state has been using repression. This is class struggle from above as well. The state's aim is to clear away the barriers to the twin methods of wealth accumulation, whether in agriculture or industry:

---

60   Note that the majority of the masses think that reforms are pro-rich.

dispossession (of small-scale producers) and exploitation. The dispossession, exploitation, and oppression of aboriginal people, all of which have been exacerbated by neoliberalism, have contributed to Maoist resistance in several hundred districts (Das, 2010), although this resistance goes back to the pre-NEP days. The Maoist threat is elevated to be the biggest threat to the nation. It is then conveniently used as an excuse to suppress any democratically organized protest against neoliberalism, as seen in the recent arrest of 6 activists who are labelled 'urban Naxals'. If the Maoist threat did not exist, a similar other threat would be invented. In fact, under the BJP's version of neoliberalism, apart from the Maoist threat (and indeed the general threat from people in the form of resistance against neoliberal government policies), there is the Muslim threat to the nation. Perceiving resistance and dissent against neoliberal capitalist policies that serve the capitalist interests and their political backers, *as a threat to the nation as a whole*, and falsely constructing religious minorities (especially, Muslims) as a threat to the nation as a whole simply because their religious beliefs are not those of Hindus, constitute a convenient way of diverting the minds of common people, Hindus and non-Hindus, from the failure of neoliberal capitalist policies of the government to meet the needs of the masses.

The capitalist class has also directly engaged in struggle from above by undermining the power of workers who strike against capital. Repression of striking Maruti workers is a case in point. Capital has repressed workers by hiring goons to hurt or kill them, by bribing union leaders, and by locking employees out. A major employers' organization justifies the curtailment of the right to strike on the grounds of neoliberal globalization:

> Today, most of the countries, especially the developing countries like India, are dependent on foreign investment and under these circumstances, it is necessary that countries who seek foreign investment must keep some safeguard in their respective industrial laws so that there will be no misuse of right to strike. In India, right to protest is a fundamental right under Article 19 of the Constitution of India but, right to strike is not a fundamental right rather, a legal right with statutory restriction attached in the Industrial Dispute Act, 1947... [A]dequate arrangement should be done including amending section 16 of the Trade Union Act, 1926 to insulate trade unionism from politics.
>
> AIOE/FICCI, n.d.: p. 9

Between investors' right to not invest, and workers' right to not sell their labor power, between these two equal rights, once again, it is force that decides. And force is used more freely under neoliberalism. Employers, backed by the force of the state and by its pro-business laws, want that trade unionism be insulated from politics (read: the efforts of the left political parties to mobilize the workers). The courts also have ruled against the right to strike. To support the private property rights of big businesses whose accumulation strategies are destroying the livelihoods of millions and to protect the increasing inequality between the consuming-and-possessing class and the rest, the state is turning increasingly authoritarian.[61] It even deploys or threatens to deploy, draconian anti-terror laws against anyone opposing neoliberalism.

3.7 'Neoliberalization' of the Left

It is undeniably true that parties on the Left in India have put pressure on governments to implement certain pro-poor measures (e.g. public works to generate employment for the rural poor) and to slow the pace of certain reforms.[62] It is partly because of the pressure from the left that public sector banks were not privatized and therefore they were able to withstand the effects of the 2008 financial crisis. But the *objective* effect of the practice of the Left forces has, overall, been this: they have been converted into a conduit for the implementation of the NEP through ideological and political-administrative means.

The parliamentary Left (as well as much of the 'unorganized Left')[63] has not provided a serious ideological critique of the NEP. Whatever critique the Left has is rather muted. The effect of the Left is limited because, philosophically speaking, it has focused on the two 'upper layers' of the reality of capitalism (i.e. the *effects* of the operation of the capitalist system, and especially, the effects of the form in which capitalism comes to exist, i.e. neoliberal capitalism

---

61   Under neoliberalism, 'Governance by majority rule is seen as a potential threat to individual rights and constitutional liberties. Democracy is viewed as a luxury, only possible under conditions of relative affluence coupled with a strong middle-class presence to guarantee political stability. Neoliberals therefore tend to favour governance by experts and elites. A strong preference exists for government by executive order and by judicial decision rather than democratic and parliamentary decision-making. Neoliberals prefer to insulate key institutions, such as the central bank, from democratic pressures. Given that neoliberal theory centres on the rule of law and a strict interpretation of constitutionality, it follows that conflict and opposition must be mediated through the courts' (Harvey, 2005: 66).

62   It should be noted that a section of the capitalist class which was reliant on the government support, and which was not ready for foreign competition, did not wholeheartedly accept the reforms agenda, and this also partly explains why reforms have not been as fast as they could have been (and as they were, in other countries).

63   This Left – like much of the academic Left – is informed by the spirit of civil society activism and micro-political resistance. The specter of 'post-isms' (e.g. post-Marxism) haunts this Left.

as opposed to 'state-directed' capitalism). By doing this, the Left has, more or less, abstracted from, and done little with regard to, the third, underlying, layer (i.e. the sphere of capitalist class *relations* and the associated *mechanisms* of marketization/commodification, competition, appropriation of surplus value, private control over production and production process, production for profit being more important than production to meet human needs, and so on). More concretely, the effect of the Left is limited because it takes place, more or less, from the standpoint of less economically competitive sections of the so-called progressive national bourgeoisie (and a very small segment of the 'relatively well-paid' salaried working class, mainly unionized public sector workers). Not only that, but the critique is 'regulationist': it suggests that the solutions to the problems with the NEP (or with neoliberalism) lie in greater government regulation by the bourgeois governments (i.e. less neoliberalism). The Left critique has not, generally speaking, looked at the NEP as being essentially a *capitalist* project, a project of and by the capitalist class; the Left sees it as merely a new government policy that can be changed by more 'pro-poor' government. The Left critique has not been conducted from the vantage point of the working class and poor peasants as comprising a bloc of anti-capitalist classes, and from the standpoint of the need to intellectually and politically act on all the three layers of the capitalist reality mentioned above. The Left critique has therefore not been from the vantage point of the *transcendence* of capitalism. In terms of strategy, the Left is at the *pre*-democratic-revolution stage – that is, at *least* two stages removed from posing anti-capitalist, proletarian, revolutionary socialism as the goal. Indeed, it is this political vision that directly influences the Left's view of everything, including neoliberalism. Without revolutionary theory, it lacks revolutionary practice.

Politically, in terms of practice, the Left, which has been suffering from the 'parliamentary diseases',[64] and whose framework of operation has, in effect, little to do with the fight for socialism, has propped up and supported various bourgeois parties (e.g. Janata, which included political characters which now constitute the BJP; Congress) from time to time, the parties that have implemented neoliberalism. The Left has justified its support for certain bourgeois parties on two grounds: anti-imperialism (and anti-feudalism), and to keep the Hindu fundamentalists out of power. For the sake of an argument, its support for more-secular bourgeois neoliberal parties, for the purpose of keeping the communal-right-wing BJP out could be considered somehow un-problematic *if* and only if the Left did this tactically/conjuncturally, i.e. just to win a breathing

---

64   A disproportionate amount of its energy is spent on elections rather than on the extra-electoral mobilization of the masses and on raising the level of their class consciousness.

space so it could launch an ideological and political offensive against the capitalist class and landlords, *in the extra-parliamentary sphere,* which should be its main sphere of action on the basis of which it should engage in electoral politics. But that has *generally* not been the case, and especially, at the national and provincial scales.[65] Besides, such a policy of alignment with bourgeois forces has failed as indicated by the 2014 electoral success of BJP which is promoting a naked form of neoliberal capitalism. In fact, in a sense, Left's support for neoliberal parties that are relatively secular such as Congress *in a context* where the Left has not adequately mobilized its constituents (workers and poor peasants) *independently* of bourgeois forces in the extra-parliamentary sphere and where it is pursuing the project of a more democratic and a more egalitarian capitalism, has objectively meant the following. The relatively-secular parties' neoliberal policies have caused the disenchantment of the masses with them as well as with the Left, and this has led the masses to the lap of communal-Hindu-nationalist-neoliberal BJP which has now captured power and which rules on the basis of populist authoritarianism (more on this below). Absence of independent class-based extra-electoral mobilization by the Left and the attendant absence of a real threat to the capitalist class[66] from the Left mean this: the political-electoral subordination of the masses to the politics of bourgeois parties.

The Left, on whose radar anti-capitalist, proletarian socialism does not yet exist because it is more interested in democratic changes *within* the capitalist class system, has lent a pro-poor cover to various bourgeois governments that it has supported. This has allowed the governments of the day to administer the bitter pill of neoliberalism with a little sweetener – that is to say, to give the NEP a human face – and in a more consensual manner. The objective effect of this is that *in practice, if not in theory,* the Left has effectively turned itself into a radical-nationalist fraction of the political bloc of the bourgeoisie.

At the provincial scale, where the organized parliamentary Left was and is in power, it has itself pursued the NEP and pro-big business measures.[67] One prominent State-level Left politician said to me once that 'we [i.e. the Left

---

65   At the sub-national scales, matters can be a bit different as indicated by various on-the-ground-struggles organized by the Left.

66   The Left has, more or less, sought to limit the struggles of the working class to trade union struggles (i.e. bourgeois consciousness/politics in Lenin's words) and to electoral fights.

67   Sumanta Banerjee (2008b: 12–13) says: 'It was under ... [Jyoti Basu's] leadership that the West Bengal Left Front government opened up the state's economy to private investors from outside...Following this, in 1994 the CPI(M)-led Left Front government ... adopted a new industrial policy which offered concessions to the magnates of the private sector and multinationals to set up industries in the state. ... [in the process of pursuing neoliberal policies], the party ended up ... grabbing agricultural land (without paying adequate compensation to the farmers) and subsidising the investor industrialists by huge tax relief and other concessions that eat into the state exchequer'.

when it is in power in the States] need to establish industries at any cost and create a working class and make available consumer items before we think about other things'. Underlying this kind of Left politics is its commitment to the reproduction of capitalist social relations. When the Left was in power in Bengal, it embraced neoliberalism, arguing that it was following the model of 'socialist' China.[68] The Left attacked 'the trade unions, saying that workers must learn discipline and forego strikes if West Bengal is to be able to secure investment' (Wickremasinghe and Jones, 2004). Left-in-power has more or less pursued neoliberalism at the provincial scale while sounding critical of it at the national scale. It has done this in a ruthless fashion, using both its control over trade unions and the misperception that the Left is pro-working class. Revealingly, when asked how his government would respond if a labor dispute arose against a foreign company operating in his State, the last Left Front Chief Minister of West Bengal said this:

> Our involvement in trade unions is an advantage. The majority of work-
> ers are in support of this government. And we are trying to change their
> mindset. I tell them, look this is a new situation. We need FDI [foreign
> direct investments], we need infrastructure.
>
> DIAS, 2005

This, to me, is the twenty-first century version of the Stalinist theory of social-ism, as expressed in one country. The slogan of the Left at the provincial scale should really be: 'neoliberal socialism' in one province. In part because of its neoliberal policies, the Left has also lost some of its traditional legitimacy and electoral support, and this serves the capitalist class as a whole, politically. Apart from Left's own neoliberal policies, there is another reason for its loss of electoral support. The pre-neoliberal state used to be a source of some conces-sions (e.g. pro-poor policies), so the Left could politically organize people for various benefits, including, in the form of workers' benefits from the state-owned sector. With the neoliberal turn, the material basis for this kind of Left politics has been weakened.

Let us turn to the non-parliamentary Left in neoliberal times. This includes the Naxalite Left (which is influenced by versions of Maoism), the emer-gence of which was partly sparked by the weakness of the parliamentary Left and the aborted democratic revolution. It is no less responsible, however, for the current rot of the entire Left. Since their emergence in the late 1960s, the

---

68   On neoliberalization of the Left in Bengal, see Das, Ritanjan (2018); Das and Mahmood (2015); Chakrabarty (2008). See Sreeraj and Vakulabharanam (2016) on the neoliberaliza-tion of the Left in Kerala.

Naxalites have focused their activities on the oppressed peasantry and in more recent decades on the aboriginal people living in the most remote parts of India; they have also won some localized concessions (Das, 2010). This orientation is in keeping with the Maoists' nationalist and Stalinist perspective which declares the peasantry the principal revolutionary force (in contemporary India) and the coming Indian revolution to be a type of 'democratic', and not a socialist, revolution. From this perspective, the system of capitalist relations as such is not the enemy of the Naxalite Left. On occasion the Maoists make ritualistic references to the working class, but in practice they are, hitherto, more or less, disconnected from that class, which is the only class that has the potential to radically challenge neoliberalism and capitalism itself. The Naxalite Left is not necessarily against capitalist accumulation as such; it does not even recognize that India is a dominantly capitalist social formation.[69] Ironically, the politics of the state's fight against Maoism is being used to remove all barriers to capitalist accumulation. And the non-Naxalite Left outside of the fold of the electoral-mainstream Left is as good as non-existent: it is thoroughly fragmented into little groups, busy criticizing one another and criticizing the mainstream Left, and without engaging in constructive theoretical developments or immersion in day-to-day struggles.[70]

3.8 Neoliberalism as the Indian Capitalist Class's Political-Ideological Project, Including Communalism

NEP is a political-ideological project of the capitalist class because it must ensure political and ideological conditions for various accumulation strategies. 'Political conditions' in this case means state repression and judicial coercion (including the suppression of democratic rights, to be discussed later).[71] 'Ideological conditions' here includes the fetishism of economic growth at any

---

69   See Chapter 3 for the argument about how to conceptualize capitalism and why social formations such as India are dominantly capitalist.

70   Outside of India as well, this is the situation of much of the revolutionary Marxist Left, which is outside of the mainstream communist movement.

71   The leaders of workers at Maruti Suzuki factory have been targeted for exemplary punishment because they led a struggle at the Japanese-owned car assembly plant, during which a company manager died a mysterious death that was blamed on workers.
      'Prosecutors and judges involved in legal proceedings concerning the victimized Maruti Suzuki workers have stated repeatedly and bluntly that an example must be made of them so as to reassure investors. In arguing for the 13 to be sentenced to death by hanging at their March 2017 sentence hearing, special prosecutor Anurag Hooda declared, "Our industrial growth has dipped, FDI [Foreign Direct Investment] has dried up. Prime Minister Narendra Modi is calling for 'Make in India', but such incidents are a stain on our image"' (in Jones, 2018).

cost (often conflated with development) and indeed promotion of market fe-tishism in all spheres of everyday life, including social consciousness, and this began happening in a society where the market relations have *relatively* less impact relative to advanced capitalist countries. Associated with market fe-tishism is the idea of getting rich quickly by any means.[72] Associated with mar-ket fetishism is also the idea that market is the dominant method of helping the poor (hence the popularity of such things as self-help groups and micro-credit in the discourse of development, happily promoted by the state and civil society groups).[73] The concept of animal spirits (entrepreneurialism) and un-leashing the sleeping tiger, (perceived) prestige associated with working for MNCs, all these are a part of the neoliberal capitalist culture. Neoliberal cul-ture is especially manifested in a craze for technical education in a relatively backward society like India. India's focus apolitical promotion of engineering disciplines has fed into hegemonic discourses on apolitical good governance and meritocracy, propagated more or less by all political parties with an adverse social and political implication: the educated and professionally-oriented mid-dle classes in India and (other developing countries), unlike their Western counterparts, tend to be socially illiberal and politically authoritarian (Krish-nan, 2017: 364).

The dominant neoliberal view is one of market idolatry: the poor should be sacrificed at the altar of the god of the market, the god of reforms, the god of growth. This god has more power than the numerous gods in India's holy land. This god will, in the long run, benefit 'the poor' and less well-off people, the ordinary people. In the short term, while the poor are prostrating themselves before the market god, they get bruised laying on the hard surface, so they need some kind of band-aid.

There has been also a change in the culture of state-society relations broadly in the interest of the business class. A former civil servant of the Indian Administrative Service (IAS), Mr. Harsh Mander (2016), who has been a vocal supporter of pro-poor interventions upon leaving office, writes:

---

72   It is thought that 'because the "nation" needs "development", some people are going to lose land, subsistence livelihoods, [and] living space.... The strategy in class terms is to obscure differential rewards of aggressive capitalist development in favour of universal valents summarized by a growing gross domestic product (GDP)' (Herring, 2013: 131).

73   Interestingly, the obsession with growth is such that a party can engage in sectarian vio-lence of religious and other types (e.g. the BJP in Gujarat), but still be more or less 'con-doned' if it promotes economic growth through pro-business policies. Neoliberalism and communalism are not unrelated (see Chapters 11–12).

I think economic reforms have done many things but one of them is that they have entirely transformed the culture, the functioning, and the moral yardsticks of a good government, in ways that could not have been imagined in 1991.

...What worries me is our collective indifference to inequality. The middle-class feels that this inequality is not only tolerable but justified and legitimate. So the sense of moral outrage against suffering and injustice around us has sharply declined and that is what worries me even more than the material aspects of inequality.

There is still another way in which NEP is political-ideological. This concerns the connection between NEP and what is called communalism in India (i.e. politics based on religious division or Indian version of fascistic tendencies). In the 1980s, as mentioned before, two things happened: increase in inequality and the introduction of neoliberal economics. Something else joined them: rise of communalism. The fact that these three things happened almost at the same time could not have been coincidental. Neoliberal capitalism that has been immiserizing has hastened capitalism's tendency to promote communalism in part as a deflection from the real problems confronting the masses. The right-wing forces, appearing to be pro-poor in the most demagogic-populist manner, and championing the economic interests of the capitalist class, endorse and implement the most virulent form of neoliberalism. And these right-wing forces propagate ideas (e.g. individual initiative and entrepreneurial-ism; nationalism, etc.) that are the legitimizing ideology of such extreme neoliberalism. *In a context* where the Left has not extra-electorally mobilized its constituents (workers and poor peasants) *independently* of bourgeois forces, its parliamentary support for neoliberal parties such as Congress and its regional offshoots has objectively meant this: these parties have been in power and they have formulated and implemented' neoliberal policies which in turn have led the masses to accept communal-neoliberal BJP's demagogic appeal as their friend. It has, of course, and naturally, become the darling of vast sections of the capitalist class, which has secretively funded it and provided public support in some cases. The communal project has been helped by the national and global business class (including in the diasporic elements) who benefit from a national-level conservative and authoritarian government which makes common people gulp bitter pills (read: labor reforms, further privatization of state-owned companies, and the like). These pills are said to be necessary to cure the illness of declining economic growth in the bourgeois economy.[74]

---

74   On the link between neoliberalism and Hindu nationalism, see Ruparelia (2011; Desai, 2011). This theme is discussed in more details in Chapters 10–13 of this book.

4 Concluding Comments: What Is to Be Done?

Neoliberalism and capitalism do not inhabit different worlds. Neoliberalism, in word or deed, is not a 'substitute' for capitalism. Neoliberalism is a specific form of capitalism, whether in advanced countries or in countries such as India. It is not to be seen primarily as a set of government policies which can be replaced by another. Murray Smith reminds us (2018: 21):

> ...most would-be progressives cling desperately to the notion that 'neo-liberal capitalism' is but the ugly mutation of a set of short-sighted policies that the capitalist ruling class may prefer but might also be pressured to abandon in favour of a more humane, just, and equitable species of capitalism. For this reason, the established, 'reform'-oriented left is loath to characterise neoliberalism for what it is: a predictable and inevitable strategic response on the part of capital and the state to a deepening crisis of the capitalist profit system – a crisis that has been unfolding now for several decades.

It is mistaken to belief that neoliberalism is facing a crisis, while capitalism is not. Neoliberalism is a form of crisis-ridden capitalism. Capitalism and neoliberal capitalism are both crisis-ridden.

The neoliberal state experiences internal contradictions, like the capitalist form of the state as such. There is clearly a contradiction 'between the declared public aims of neoliberalism—the well-being of all—and its actual consequences' for the people, which are, more or less, negative (Harvey, 2005: 25). Additionally, 'there lies a whole series of more specific contradictions' as Harvey notes: between need for the state to let markets function freely and the need to intervene in order to deliberately create a business climate; need to enforce market rules in an authoritarian way and the ideas of individual freedom; the integrity of the financial system and its volatile character; between competition and monopolistic tendencies; and between individual market freedom and loss of solidarity, and so on.

As a new stage in the development of capitalism emerging in the wake of the post-war boom, neoliberalism has several general traits (deregulation, privatization, liberalization, financialization, etc.) that are affecting all spheres of life, including culture and everyday life.

This chapter seeks to provide a dialectical conceptualization of India's NEP and neoliberalism, on the basis of some general ideas about neoliberalism as outlined in part 1. Such a conceptualization must be sensitive to both the differences and similarities between the pre-1991 and post-1991 regimes, and to both the economic and the non-economic character of the NEP. Such a conceptualization must also see the governmental or policy aspect of the NEP as rooted in the class character of Indian society.

As in many other countries, so in India, neoliberal capitalism has meant a series of *reduction*:

1. reduction in corporate contributions to society/state (= reduction in taxes);
2. reduction in the power of unions;
3. reduction in state control over pricing of services and over business activities;
4. reduction in restrictions on trade (lowering tariffs) (companies can go to a cheaper location, get things made and export them);
5. reduction in state's support for the less-well off (e.g. farmers);
6. reduction in the sphere of state ownership of productive enterprises and facilities (schools, prisons, etc.) and commons, and so on.

As a result, there has been the opposite of this reduction: an *expansion* of the effect of class power of ruling class and expansion of the misery for the masses. So the neoliberal project is a perfect example of the inter-penetration of opposites.

In any fundamental sense, there was not a time before or since independence when the Indian capitalist class did not have its power to exploit labor and dispossess small-scale producers. So neoliberalism, strictly speaking, is not the restoration of class power, as Harvey and others think. Yet, to the extent that there was *some* restriction on its power within the political sphere (e.g. what it could produce and what it could not), neoliberalism is an *effect* of the changing balance of political power between the capitalist class and the masses. On the basis of its growing economic strength, supported in many ways by the state, between the 1950s and the mid-1980s, and with support from imperialist capital and its institutions, Indian capitalist class was able to impose its economic will in a much more strident manner than before. NEP is a political expression of the capitalist class's need to 'bridge' the gap between its economic power (in terms of its control over property) and its political power. NEP is a policy, but it is not just that. It is the political articulation of the interests of the Indian capitalist class in the context of a globalizing world-capitalism. Neoliberalism is 'capitalism without Leftist illusions' (e.g. illusions that there can be such a thing as humane capitalism on a long-term basis). If this is true of rich countries, it is no less true of poor countries such as India. India's NEP is a policy *on behalf* of capital. It is therefore a policy *of* capital, *tout court*, mediated and implemented by the state, at central and provincial scales.[75] This chapter has shown that India's NEP is more than a governmental

---

75   This error is not too dissimilar to the error of thinking about imperialism merely as a government policy, an error that Lenin pointed out in Kautsky.

policy. It is a program of the bourgeoisie that promotes economic growth and bestows benefits to certain privileged sections of the population, but has devastating impacts on the toiling masses, the majority. Indeed, this is what neoliberal capitalism generally does in the less developed world as a whole (Naruzzaman, 2005).

Neoliberalism in rural areas – agrarian neoliberalism – is particularly ruthless in its impacts. Neoliberalism has also produced enormous spatial unevenness. Neoliberalism in India, like in the periphery as such, is also a part of the imperialist project, being implemented via burgeoning 'new compradore' elements both in the bourgeois class and outside. Given the adverse impacts of neoliberalism, it has inspired massive resistance from below, which has been countered by the state via a combination of meagre concession, heavy repression, and unfathomable deception (i.e. the idea that neoliberal growth is good for all). Interestingly, in spite of offering some opposition, the Left has ended up becoming, more or less, a conduit through which neoliberalism has been delivered, even against its own intention.

To conclude, I will consider neoliberalism in terms of the 'What is to be done' question? The less developed countries such as India are often seen as countries that have less income and more absolute poverty. Instead, they must be fundamentally seen in class terms: as countries that have suffered from aborted – or incomplete – revolutions against the propertied class. They have suffered from: aborted democratic (bourgeois) revolutions, including agrarian revolutions against feudal(-type) relations, aborted national (or anti-imperialist) revolutions, and aborted/untried anti-capitalist revolutions.[76] A dialectical view of neoliberalism and the NEP connects them both to the democratic and agrarian questions, the national question, and the question of socialism itself.

Consider the democratic question. There has been massive resistance to the NEP, as mentioned earlier, to which the state is responding in a most undemocratic (= repressive) manner. The state is also promoting *venal* capitalism; massive corruption in the public offices has been endemic since the 1990s, a time during which markets have been less regulated, thus refuting the argument that de-regulation reduces corruption. Corruption means undemocratic use of public offices for private gains ('private' meaning the nexus of the business world and the state managers).[77] Given that all the parties – including the Left

---

76   Indeed, with respect to the socialist revolution, the fertilization has not even happened in many contexts. On India's bourgeois revolution, see Stern, 2011, and Davey, 1974.

77   State actors (government officials and politicians) use the power of the state to illegitimately satisfy their private interests often at the expense of the lower classes (proletarian and semi-proletarian classes). In so far as corruption adversely affects these classes, it is a class issue. Corruption is also a class issue in terms of its origin. The structure of the capitalist state is such that its day-to-day activities at different geographical scales are

parties – are forced to follow neoliberalism, the room for democratic dissent is shrunk, and this is more so now, with the election of a new government led by a Hindu-fundamentalist party with fascistic tendencies. This has a more specific implication: by making all political parties/groups equal as far as their adherence to neoliberalism is concerned, the NEP has created a situation where casteism and religious fundamentalism are used to divide the poor electorate and to garner votes.[78] This creates conditions for the perpetuation of undemocratic relations based on religious and caste identity.[79] This also creates a condition where capitalists can subject workers – including those who belong to vulnerable social groups – to super-exploitation and weaken any potential resistance by dividing the masses along the lines of religion, caste, gender, etc. Given that various petty-bourgeois or regionalist parties (some of which call themselves, bizarrely, socialist) thriving by playing identity politics, it is not unusual for a party or a coalition of parties in power to buy their support for neoliberal policies by giving some material concession to identity politics (e.g. reservation in promotion for scheduled castes). Identity politics becomes a vehicle of capitalist and landlord class politics, that is to say, politics in the service of neoliberalism. The NEP, under which small-scale producers are subjected by the capitalist class and its state to primitive accumulation, is also creating new aspects of the agrarian question. The agrarian question now is the question about peasants' property and about their miseries caused by national and international agribusiness (*not* feudal or semi-feudal landlords) and by the neoliberal state acting on behalf of agribusiness. So the democratic question broadly understood – including democratic governance, equal rights of

---

generally insulated from the direct lower-class political influence. This structure of the state enables it to reproduce class relations. But it is precisely this structure of the state that allows corruption to happen by enhancing the power of state actors over lower classes. The structure and activities of the state are, however, subject to geographically varying class struggle. Therefore, in those places where politically organized lower classes can democratically influence the (everyday) state, the extent of corruption can be a little less than in other places.

78   How else can a party say 'vote for us and not for them', when both the parties are almost exactly the same in terms of economic policies? Teltumbde (2011) writes: 'The beauty of India's parliamentary system is that there is essential similarity between all ruling class parties on most core policy matters and behaviours, whether it is economic reforms or foreign policy or secularism and communalism. They differ at the most in shade. In class terms it may thus be called political oligopoly'.

79   Of course, why the masses fall for these lies – that caste and religious identities are crucial determinants of their economic miseries – is an interesting question (see Kumar, 2008 for a discussion on this).

citizens irrespective of their castes or religious backgrounds, and the agrarian question – becomes important in new ways in neoliberal times. Neoliberalism has created the need for a heightened battle for democracy.

In light of this need, consider the national question. This question is no longer about fighting formal colonialism. It is rather about fighting 'new imperialism', which is predominantly practiced through economic mechanisms and ultimately backed up by the threat of force.[80] It is the imperialism of the powerful governments of the developed world, of MNCs, and of international institutions (IMF, the World Bank, MNCs, and 'aid' agencies). This is an imperialism that is justified and sold to ordinary people through the discourse of development (as growth). It is also sold using chauvinistic ideas about India's 'superpower status', which is only as a regional subordinate of the supreme guardian of global capitalism, the USA.[81] The post-colonial neoliberal state itself, managed by people with the neoliberal mentality ('neoliberality'), has become a new mechanism of imperialism. So, neoliberalism has heightened the need for anti-imperialist struggle and for the sovereignty of oppressed nations such as India. The national question and the democratic question (i.e. the questions of the new imperialist subordination, the state and society becoming more undemocratic, and of peasants losing land) are rooted in the fact that the NEP represents capitalism in its most naked and ruthless form.[82]

If the above assessment is broadly correct, it indicates a very different sort of solution to the national and democratic question and to the specific problems, such as mass impoverishment, spatially uneven development and agrarian crisis, that neoliberalism is creating than what the traditional Left has been

---

80   No peripheral country is a permanent friend of an imperialist power.

81   The USA 'guards' the subordinate guardians (= subordinate states such as India) of the capitalist property rights in different parts of the world (Wood, 2003: 133).

82   Class analysis of neoliberalism in Indian shows that those with little or no productive asset – various classes of self-employed non-exploiting peasants and laborers – will gain from a unified political struggle against imperialism, with the intent to unfetter the use (and also the development) of the productive forces. Such an attack on the institutions of imperialism will, of course, need to be linked to challenges mounted against forces within India, among whom the most obvious are (a) traders looting food-grains in the government stores meant for the working class and for the poor peasantry (neither of which are able to purchase this resource due to IMF subsidy cuts), (b) rural and urban capitalists benefiting from the opening up of Indian agriculture to imperialist exploitation, and (c) high-level state actors and institutions supporting and facilitating this process of imperialist penetration.

offering. The intellectual and political fight against the NEP cannot be merely about changing the dirty clothes of the state (meaning changing its policy and making it regulate the affairs of capitalism, as in 'olden times'). It cannot be about interrupting, deconstructing, and destabilizing narratives about neoliberalism and wider society a bit here and a bit there, although the struggle for the regulation of business is not entirely unnecessary. The idea that there is such a thing as neoliberalism (or capitalism) with a human face is, once again, based on the lie, the deception, that the basic interests of capital are fundamentally compatible with the basic interests of the toiling masses in a sustainable, contradiction-free, manner. Unregulated growth, control of society's resources by big business, the exploitation of labor, income inequality, and ecological devastation cannot be compatible with socially coordinated wealth creation, equality, solidarity, popular democracy, and satisfaction of human needs. If this critique is right, then the intellectual and political project must have the larger goal of theoretically and practically transcending the very conditions that produce the neoliberalism model itself and going beyond the content of whose form neoliberalism is.[83]

Indicative of the hegemony of neoliberalism, in India (as elsewhere), is the fact that scholars talk about neoliberalism more than about capitalism. So a major discursive, or ideological, success of neoliberalism is that it has hidden capitalism under its *choli* (a short-sleeved blouse worn by many Indian women).[84] Scholars explain society's economic, social and ecological problems in terms of neoliberalism (and its twin, globalization) and not capitalism. Form is prioritized over content. When critical ideas about economy are produced, they are often against neoliberalism as such and not against capitalism per se.

What is problematic about neoliberalism, including neoliberal policy, is not *this or that* aspect of it (e.g. the idea that it increases poverty and inequality or the idea that restriction on short-term capital flows or shrinking government intervention is the problem).[85] Rather, the *whole* 'policy' is the problem. So it

83   And this requires a massive, democratically organized mobilization of workers and poor peasants against profit-making, at multiple scales within India, in South Asia as a whole, and, globally.

84   Interestingly, the Hindi word to describe neoliberalism is mystifying. In Hindi, neoliberalism is नव-उदारतावाद. नव = new. उदारतावाद means such things as generosity (उदार = generous; उदारता = generosity; वाद = ism). One can see that given the massive adverse economic, social and ecological consequences of neoliberalism, there is nothing generous (उदार) about neoliberalism. In English language as well, the liberalism in neoliberalism means such things as tolerance, individual freedom, democratic form of government, equality, etc., all of which are under attack under neoliberalism.

85   Criticisms are now coming from inside the agencies that have promoted neoliberalism: 'there are aspects of the neoliberal agenda that have not delivered as expected', say Ostry

requires a totalizing dialectical critique, one that situates its limited benefits in relation to its enormous costs and sees it from multiple vantage points.

There is nothing wrong in critiquing neoliberalism, and there is nothing wrong in raising anti-neoliberalism demands. But the scope of this anti-neoliberalism is narrow. In explaining society's problems, one needs to include neoliberalism but one must go beyond it to include the content of capitalism itself. And political action that is merely anti-neoliberalism fails to convert the fight against neoliberalism into a fight against the capitalist class relation. It remains merely a partial demand aimed at fighting for a better capitalism.

Indeed much critical discourse and much progressive politics, in India and outside India, are stuck with a critique of neoliberalism as such, in the hope of a world that is less neoliberal, rather than a world that is not capitalist. As we have seen in the last chapter, a restrictive concept of capitalism a concept in which capitalism exists when there is economically advanced capitalism, has licensed a bourgeois politics of the Left that aims to produce a better (= more democratic) and more advanced capitalism. Similarly, a Left critique of capitalism that more or less equates it to neoliberalism is bound to encourage a bourgeois politics of the Left, one that aims for a capitalism that is a little more state-directed than neoliberalism. And underlying this view is not only a profoundly mistaken view of capitalism but also an equally mistaken view of the capitalist state.

---

et al. (2016: 38). These include two policies: 'removing restrictions on the movement of capital across a country's borders (so-called capital account liberalization); and fiscal consolidation, sometimes called "austerity", which is shorthand for policies to reduce fiscal deficits and debt levels' (ibid.). While 'Some capital inflows, such as foreign direct investment – which may include a transfer of technology or human capital – do seem to boost long-term growth. But the impact of other flows – such as portfolio investment and banking and especially hot, or speculative, debt inflows – seem neither to boost growth ·nor allow the country to better share risks with its trading partners' (ibid.). 'The benefits in terms of increased growth seem fairly difficult to establish when looking at a broad group of countries. The costs in terms of increased inequality are prominent. ...Increased inequality in turn hurts the level and sustainability of growth. Even if growth is the sole or main purpose of the neoliberal agenda, advocates of that agenda still need to pay attention to the distributional effects' (ibid.). The authors say that 'Curbing the size of the state is another aspect of the neoliberal agenda. ...Austerity policies not only generate substantial welfare costs due to supply-side channels, they also hurt demand – and thus worsen employment and unemployment'. They add that fiscal consolidation can raise investor confidence and boost investment, but 'in practice, episodes of fiscal consolidation have been followed, on average, by drops rather than by expansions in output' (ibid.: 40). The IMF economists conclude that: openness to short-term capital flows and fiscal austerity have resulted in inequality, and that 'There is now strong evidence that inequality can significantly lower both the level and the durability of growth' (p. 41).

CHAPTER 5

Capitalism and Technological Change: Reflections on the Technology – Poverty Relation

Technology is seen as a sign of modernity.[1] Technological change is expected to be a means of bringing about development. For the less developed world, technological change is a means of catching up with advanced countries as well.

Often technology is associated with information technology (IT), so much so that IT-related companies are referred to as technology companies. This is a narrow conception of what technology is. Technology simply means application of scientific ideas to solve practical problems. A technology can be a set of ideas (e.g. software) or a mechanical thing (e.g. an equipment) or a (bio-)chemical thing (e.g. fertilizer or a hybrid/genetically-modified seed).

Given society's obsession with technology, in both rich and poor countries, we should ask what is the social nature of technology and whether technological change itself can solve social problems such as poverty? This question can be asked in the context of many different forms of human activity (e.g. agriculture, industry, services). We will ask the question in the context of agriculture which has been going through many technological revolutions in the last 10,000 years or so. One might ask: why should we examine technological change *in agriculture*?

Firstly, agriculture is the sphere of activity that produces food. Summarizing Marx's intellectual contribution, Engels (1883) said this:

> Just as Darwin discovered the law of development or organic nature, so Marx discovered the law of development of human history: the simple fact, hitherto concealed by an overgrowth of ideology, that mankind must first of all eat, drink, have shelter and clothing, before it can pursue politics, science, art, religion, etc.

The idea that the humankind 'must first of all eat, drink, have shelter and clothing' not only signifies the importance that Marx attached to the philosophy of materialism. At a more concrete level, that idea is indicative of the (trans-historical) importance of agriculture, from which food and drink come,

---

1 An earlier version of this chapter appeared as Das (2002).

and from which some of the raw materials for shelter and clothing, among other things, also come.

Agriculture is therefore an important area of the humankind's productive activity. The fact that a relatively small percentage of the workforce in richer countries is engaged in agriculture and the fact that the percentage of the workforce in agriculture is slowly decreasing in poorer countries such as India, do not diminish the theoretical and practical importance of agriculture and its social relations. Secondly, agriculture is important because of the *historically-specific form* that its contribution to economic development takes. Agriculture provides raw materials and investible surplus for industrial development in capitalist societies, as agrarian political economy (agrarian transition) literature has highlighted (see Byres, 1996). Importantly, it also produces food, which is an important item consumed by the working class. And when less labor time is needed to produce wage-goods including food, other things constant, more profit can be produced (this is explained later).

If agriculture is an important sector of productive activity as a producer of food (and as a producer of raw materials for industrial development producing means of subsistence), this raises the question of technology that is used in that sector. In particular, how do we understand the class character of technology? There is also a distributional issue, which is connected to the previous question: given that those who depend on agriculture for a living tend to be poor (they cannot satisfy their basic needs), what is the relation between technology and poverty? These issues are discussed in the context of the Green Revolution technology that began to be widely used in the 1960s in India (and elsewhere).

The world has seen four agricultural revolutions, all having resulted in a dramatic acceleration of growth (Lipton, 1989: 316). The Green Revolution (GR), which is more than half a century old now, is the last but one of these (the GR is followed by the genetic – biotechnological – revolution). Its speed, scale and spread have 'far exceeded those of any earlier technical change in food farming' (ibid.: 14–15). It has made possible a 'revolutionary' increase in food production in less developed countries. More than hundred poor countries use the new technology.

There is a large literature on the GR which explores various dimensions of what is clearly a complex topic. There are studies on the GR's impacts on changes in the cropping pattern, on agricultural productivity, economic growth, food self-sufficiency, diversification in investment and employment, and on wages (Alauddin and Tisdell, 1995; Harwood, 2013; Jain, 2010; Jeffrey, 1997; Naher, 1997; Palmerjones, 1993; Rao, 1998). Several authors have highlighted its socially and spatially uneven adoption (Das, 1999b; Patnaik, 1986) while others show that GR is poor-farmer friendly (Eicher, 1995). The GR is said to have influenced, and been influenced by, commoditization, agrarian class differentiation, the structure of class relations, including mercantile and usurious relations, and the investment decisions and productivity of petty commodity producers (Dyer, 1997; Harriss-White and Janakarajan, 1997; Patnaik, 1986; Goldman and Smith, 1995). Indeed, the GR triggered off an extremely important debate in development studies, the celebrated mode of production debate, that focused on the nature and the extent of capitalist development in India, which we have discussed in Chapter 3. There are studies on the politics of the GR which show that: on the one hand, the GR enriches larger, surplus-producing farmers who in turn mobilize themselves and put pressure on the state for better prices and other benefits; and on the other hand, rural laborers (those whose main source of income is wage-work) have been involved in struggle over wages (Breman, 1990, 1989; Gill, 1994; Bentall and Corbridge, 1996; Bhalla, 1999; Oommen, 1971). Studies have also dealt with the impacts of the GR on employment opportunities for women and their freedom, and on the environment (Da Corta and Venkateshwarlu, 1999; Shiva, 1991; Rahul, 1995). A post-structuralist, 'anti-developmentalist' approach to the GR has also emerged arguing that the GR represents a development-induced scarcity (Yapa, 1993).

But the fact that there is an enormous literature on the topic does not mean that our level of knowledge about the GR is necessarily adequate. Jonathan Rigg says, the GR 'suffers from a surfeit of attention which has sometimes obscured the issues being discussed' (Rigg, 1989: 144). Rigg suggests that it is clearly time 'to conduct a reappraisal of the Green Revolution' (p. 149). One area that surely needs this reappraisal is the relation between the GR and poverty/ inequality.

The relation between the GR and poverty/inequality is among the most widely researched topics not only in the GR debate but more generally in geography and development studies (Alauddin and Tisdell, 1991, 1995; Beck, 1995; Dasgupta, 1977; Frankel, 1971; Harriss, 1991, 1992; Lipton, 1989; Pearse, 1980; Sharma and Poleman, 1993; Yapa, 1993, 1979). The literature on the GR–poverty relation has been almost polarized between the 'GR enthusiasts' who see favorable impacts of the GR on poverty/inequality and 'GR sceptics' who take almost an opposite view. Separating the poverty issue from the inequality issue, it can be said that there is a near consensus that the GR has caused an increase in inequality (Lipton, 1989). Freebairn (1995) reviews more than 300 studies on the GR which were published between 1970 and 1989. Freebairn's analysis shows that in 80% of these studies the GR is associated with a rise in inequality. But there does not seem to be any agreement on whether the GR has caused an increase or decrease in absolute poverty.

Indeed, the research on the GR–poverty relation has gone through several phases (see Figure 5.1 below). Some of these are discussed in Lipton (1989: 18–19). The GR started in about 1960 in the Third World, generally (and in the mid-1960s in India). The period 1960–1970, and more specifically, 1967–1970, is considered to be the period of GR euphoria. This phase was characterized by the normal neo-Malthusian enthusiasm about the positive impact of the technology on the poor. In the second phase (the early and mid-1970s), there were growing fears that the GR hurt the poor, that the technology was enriching the richer farmers at the expense of the poorer farmers, and landowners at the expense of laborers. In the third phase, the later part of the 1970s, the GR's impacts on poverty were subjected to reassessment. Smaller farmers (i.e. family farmers) were said to be catching up with larger ones even with some delay. Laborers benefited from increased labor use, so employment opportunities rose, although wages did so rarely. The poor as consumers gained because increased food production restrained food prices. In the GR areas, the poor benefitted absolutely but lost relatively. The poor living outside the GR areas got nothing.

In the 1980s, the fourth phase started: this is the period when the extreme neo-Malthusian optimism began again. There was a revival of the early

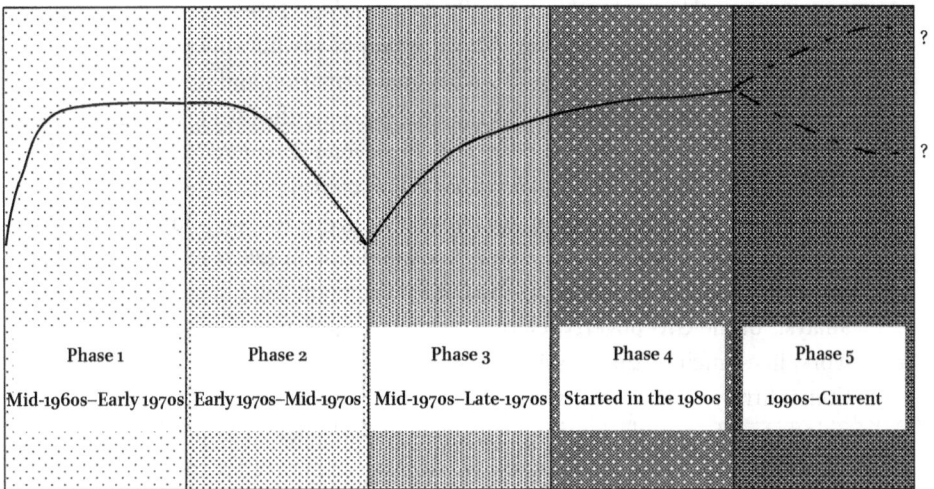

——————— The Green Revolution trend from phase 1–phase 4

— - — - Two predictions for the Green Revolution trend for phase 5

FIGURE 5.1   The phases of the Green Revolution
SOURCE: AUTHOR

euphoria. It was argued that smaller farmers sometimes adopted the technology even earlier and more intensively than larger ones and that the GR raised labor's share in rural income. A technically appropriate and profitable technology, if used everywhere, would benefit the poor everywhere.

I would add a fifth phase (1990s–). This would be the most recent phase whose precise direction of development is not clear. There are two possibilities. One is that recent (post-colonial) critiques of science and technology generally and the GR technology more specifically (Ullrich, 1992; Yapa, 1996) and concerns about the ecological impacts of the GR (Shiva, 1991) might resemble the second phase of pessimism (which was based on a critical scrutiny of the GR on more materialist–economic grounds). Alternatively, the 1980s euphoria might continue with the additional support from biotechnology and related research, with the GR technology is increasingly replaced by, or supplemented with, the technology of GM (genetically-modified) crops.

The GR–poverty relation, the intellectual construction of which has changed over time as seen in the above brief description of swings in research on the topic, is an interesting issue more generally. It can be considered to be a part of the larger literature on the relation between technology and society, including the poor people in society.

Michael Lipton is one of the most widely cited researchers on the GR and poverty topic. He wrote a book in 1989, *New Seeds and Poor People*. Lipton says in this book that the GR signifies 'the interplay of institutions with technology and human actions, as causes of social transformation and hence changes in the lot of the poor' (Lipton, 1989: 17). This book synthesises a vast amount of work on the consequences of the GR on poverty in a most comprehensive manner, and at the same time puts forward his own views on the topic. Lipton's work is characterized by his deep and real concern for the poor in the Third World. Unlike many others, Lipton is careful not to reach easy conclusions about the supposed benefits of the GR for the poor. Yet, I find Lipton's causal analysis of the GR–poverty relation faulty. In this chapter I argue that Lipton's work, like much of the massive amount of research on the GR–poverty relation, is firmly within a paradigm which gives much more causal power to technology and to population than they can possibly bear. I hope that my arguments about the GR as a technology will have relevance for the more general issue of the relation between technology and society. Finally, it may be noted that the chapter is a 'negative' statement. This is in that my main aim is *not* to say what the necessary causes of poverty *are* (although I touch on that issue very briefly). It is rather to say what the necessary causes of poverty (or poverty reduction) are *not* ('necessary' as understood in the critical realist philosophy of science) (Sayer, 1992). More specifically, I argue against Lipton's view that the GR has a *necessary* poverty-reducing property. The poor would be poorer without the technology.

Let me clarify some terminological issues pertaining to poverty and the GR. Poverty, even absolute poverty, has many meanings. In this chapter, people are said to be in absolute poverty when they do not enjoy a level of income that is sufficient to secure the *bare essentials* of food, clothing and shelter (Nafziger, 1990: 100; stress added). A person is said to be poor if her/his income falls below the government-determined poverty-line. In the context of rural India, the latter is defined as the mid-point of the monthly per-capita expenditure class having a daily per capita intake of 2400 calories.[2] Similarly, there are several meanings of the term 'Green Revolution' (Dixon, 1990). In this chapter, I have used the term to refer to the use of modern varieties of seeds (MVs) which are also known as high yield varieties of seeds (HYVs). The GR and the use of MVs are taken to be synonymous.[3]

The chapter has five sections. In Section 1, I present a 'slice' of the GR debate – in particular, Lipton's and others' views on the supposed positive and negative benefits of the GR for the poor. In Section 2, I critique this literature for its underlying neo-Malthusianism. In Section 3, I present an alternative statement on the GR and poverty relation, one that sees the relation as a contingent one, rather than necessary. In the light of my criticisms and my

---

2   Lack of income is, however, not the only indicator of poverty. Infant mortality, illiteracy, low life expectancy, and so on are some of the other indicators. Indeed, Dreze and Sen say, poverty lies not merely in the impoverished state in which the person actually lives, but also in the lack of real opportunity to choose other types of living (Dreze and Sen, 1995). In this chapter I am dealing with 'the impoverished state' in which the poor actually live, as indicated by the most popular income-based poverty measure (the head-count ratio), without implying at all that that is the best measure of poverty.

3   I do not include non-irrigation mechanical inputs in the definition. Although I do not accept many of the ideological underpinnings of his work as made clear later, I follow Lipton in considering that mechanical inputs, generally speaking, are not a necessary aspect of the GR. 'The link between capital-linked inputs such as tractors to MVs is usually artificial' (Lipton, 1989: 122, 126–127). Furthermore, many would equate the GR with agrarian capitalism or would consider capitalist property relations as a part of the GR. This, in my view, is erroneous. Agrarian capitalism can exist without the GR, although the introduction of this technology deepened the development of agrarian capitalist relations (Patnaik, 1986). Besides, *noncapitalist* cultivators such as land-poor peasants using the family labor can also use the GR technology; but whether in fact the latter will use the technology is a function not of the technology as such but of the structure of the property relations within which the technology is used (depending on the context, the technology has to be bought or can be provided communally without the mediation of the market). For me, and I am aware that this might be contentious, property relations provide the *context* in which the technology works, but these relations are not a *necessary part* of it.

alternative view, I provide in Section 4 a brief empirical analysis of the GR–poverty relation in India, which is one of the 'model' GR countries in the mid-1990s. Section 5 summarizes the discussion and briefly relates it back to the literature. It also very briefly reflects on the genetic (biotechnological) revolution in terms of its proponents' claim about its pro-poor benefits, the claims that are similar to the claims made about the GR's pro-poor effects.

1   The Literature on the Green Revolution and Poverty: The Thesis and the Anti-thesis

Smaller farmers and laborers are the two most important constituents of the poor in India and many other less developed countries. Lipton (and others) argue that the GR can benefit and has benefited these groups. Without MVs, most poor people would be poorer (Lipton, 1989: 160; hence forward, all references to Lipton are those to his 1989 book). As MVs are designed to make better use of nutrients from all sources, including fertilizer and water, than traditional seeds, it has land-augmenting effects that benefit small farmers (Lipton, 1989: Chapter 3; Sharma, 1992).[4]

As Lipton rightly says, world-wide, the poor are increasingly laborers, rather than smaller farmers. Yet, as he points out, the effects on laborers have been relatively neglected until very recently as most of the research has focused on smaller farmers. There are mainly three effects on labor. I will call them employment effects, wage effects, and price effects.[5]

Lipton and others (Bhalla, 1995; Sharma and Poleman, 1993; Vaidyanathan, 1986) argue that the GR has increased employment opportunities for laborers.[6] There are several reasons for this.

(a) Since MVs mature sooner than traditional varieties, they allow multiple cropping.[7] This leads to an increased demand for labor per acre. (b) If MVs are

---

4   This is in the sense that what was being produced on (e.g.) a five-acre land-holding earlier can be produced on less land with the GR technology. So 'the new technology has tended to help the small farms overcome their most restrictive bottleneck, that is, limited land area, to a great extent' (Sharma, 1992: 183).

5   From the standpoint of GR optimists such as Lipton, the effects of the Green Revolution (GR_e) on labor can be represented as thus: $GR_e = (ew) / i$, where e is the employment in person-days and w is the money wage per person-day, and i is the rate of inflation of food price.

6   Labor use per acre could increase by about a fifth at least at the early stage (Barker and Herdt quoted in Lipton).

7   The poorer people are more likely to suffer from seasonal fluctuation in labor demand. Multiple cropping helps them by providing year round employment (Lipton, 1989: 196).

to give economically feasible yield, densities of plants in the fields need to be high. This, in turn, requires increased input of sowing and transplantation labor (and, given the gendered division of labor, women often benefit from this). (c) MVs increase returns to fertilizer. This leads to the need for extra labor input required to place the fertilizer. Also, fertilizer-use might lead to seed growth requiring extra labor for weeding. (d) The increased food production, caused by MV-use, leads to increased demand for harvesting and threshing labor and post-harvest labor (e.g. for food processing) (Lipton: 187, 194). (e) MV-use increases larger landowners' income. This rise in income leads to their preference for leisure which then leads to greater use of hired labor by them (Lipton: 179). Further, the increased expenditure of large landowners also causes growth in non-agricultural employment (e.g. employment in trading activities owing to the increased demand for urban goods from the rich farmers) (Sharma and Poleman, 1993; Vaidyanathan, 1986).[8]

The use of MVs not only increases employment opportunities. It is also said to have caused higher wages (Sharma, 1992: 185). Lipton, however, is less sanguine about the wage effect of the MVs, as we shall see later.

Lipton rightly stresses that the poor people are not just small farmers and laborers, and that they are also net buyers of food. He (and others) argue that MV-induced increased food production contributes to lower food prices which benefit the poor food buyers in MV and non-MV areas (Dantawala, 1987; Parthasarathy, 1987; Rao, 1994: 54). Lower food prices benefit especially laborers as they spend the larger part of their income on buying food. No doubt, food prices have increased in many regions. But these prices would have been much higher without MVs (Singh, 1990: 196). This is consistent with Lipton's idea that the poor would have been poorer without the new technology.

Lower food prices affect the poor in another way, according to Lipton. The state in the less-developed countries would not have felt able to undertake the expansion of anti-poverty programs (e.g. food for work) without its large food reserves to back up such schemes, the reserves that were mainly due to MVs (Lipton: 294). Also, cheaper food means less pressure on the state for wage increases in the public sector. This may make it possible for the state to make investments in health, infrastructure, etc., which may benefit the poor (ibid.).

MVs can then lower rural poverty levels in all these ways. This argument is, in fact, a part of the more general idea that there is a negative association between (rural) poverty and (agricultural) development/growth (Ahluwalia,

---

8   This is an argument that Lipton does not make. He does say that the impacts of MVs on non-farm employment have been neglected (p. 205; cf. p. 8; also see Gill, 1994) on lack of non-farm employment in GR areas.

1978; Chadha, 1984; Chadha, 1994; Misra and Hazell, 1996; Parthasarathy, 1995; Tendulkar and Jain, 1995; Dollar and Kraay, 2000).

This is, however, only one side of the debate. This is the thesis, to which there is an anti-thesis. The latter is also shared by Lipton and many others, that the MV technology is socially discriminatory and that it hurts the poor (Byres, 1989, 1983, 1972; Frankel, 1971; Griffin, 1974; Yapa, 1993, 1979). Lipton himself offers several reservations about the positive benefits of the technology. He says that in spite of the possible favorable effects of the *miracle* seeds, the fact that their poverty reduction impact is minimal in many places is a *mystery* (p. 5, 7–8). At a theoretical level, for Lipton, the GR is *necessarily* pro-poor. But this *theoretical* expectation, which is the main subject of my critique, is not materialized empirically. Why is this so?

1)   First of all, if the poorer farmers cannot use the technology, it cannot benefit them. Although Lipton believes that the smaller farmers eventually catch up with the larger farmers in adopting the new technology (see also Eicher, 1995; Herath and Jayasuriya, 1996: 1200), he does recognize that poverty delays adoption of the technology by smaller farmers (p. 118). Yapa explains this better. He says that the GR technology 'produces higher yields, but it confers these benefits unequally to different classes' (1992: 260). The GR has a 'material-bias' in that the inputs have to be bought in the market (Yapa, 1979: 373). So one would 'expect the techniques to be adopted chiefly by those who have greater access to credit and capital' (ibid.). Finally, given that the GR depends on the use of heavy doses of water and given that the larger farmers have the resources to use underground water much more than the smaller ones, the level of underground water is reduced. This makes it much more expensive for smaller farmers to use the water, without which MVs will not give high yields on a sustainable basis (Shiva, 1991). Thus, if smaller farmers cannot use the technology, it cannot have the impact that Lipton and others say it will.[9] Besides, given that MVs do better in irrigated areas than in rainfed areas, the benefits from MVs for the poorer farmers will be rather limited in these areas.

---

9   However, while Lipton recognizes that poverty delays adoption of the technology, he nonetheless says that market favors smaller farmers. (a) MVs convert a high proportion of nutrients into grain matter, and (b) using fertilizers and water control is labor intensive, (c) smaller farmers have much family labor to employ, if they can get money/credit to buy the physical inputs. Given (a), (b) and (c), small farmers will use more inputs because they will gain more because they can use more labor per acre; so they can pay more (p. 125). Lipton also says that whether small farmers adopt early or catch up depends on initial inequality and institutional inadequacy or bias. There is no universal law (p. 117).

2)   Secondly, even if smaller, poorer farmers can get access to the new tech-
      nology somehow, they may not be able to *continue* using it. This would be
      the case if they started losing their land in the process of adopting the
      new technology which caused them to be indebted. Some scholars point
      out that there are MV-induced mechanisms that cause this. (a) Erstwhile
      landlords have evicted their tenants, as cultivation with the use of hired
      labor and the MVs has become more profitable. Lipton indeed agrees
      that at least at the early stage of MV adoption, MV-induced changes in
      land distribution occur and that GR enhances proletarianization (p. 187).
      This is in the sense that, he explains, those farmers who adopt the tech-
      nology early increase their resources and power and thus are able to push
      poorer farmers off their land (see also Heble, 1979). (b) Larger landown-
      ers lease in land from smaller ones who cannot afford the higher cost of
      the bio-chemical inputs – this is reverse tenancy (Nadkarni, 1976). (c)
      Since the inputs are expensive, smaller owners cannot make appropriate
      investments to increase output and reduce the production cost as larger
      farmers can. So they incur loss, and go into debts. Then, they try to clear
      up the debts by selling their land (see Gill, 1988: 2167). This is the classic
      mechanism of agrarian differentiation from below, as the literature on
      the agrarian question, inspired by Lenin, has shown (Brass, 2016; Byres,
      1991; Lenin, 1899). Thus the GR by causing loss of peasants' access to land
      (either in terms of the right to use or ownership) is said to have worsened
      peasants' economic position. Further, the loss of access to land leads to
      the increased supply of laborers which lowers wages (Lipton: 187). It must
      be stressed, however, that these mechanisms of GR-induced pauperiza-
      tion and proletarianization, generally, do not occupy an *important* place
      in Lipton's framework.[10]

---

10   On the one hand, given that the use of MVs does not involve economies of scale, Lipton
      wonders why should there be eviction or engrossment? Further, large owners cannot buy
      land as it is too expensive. On the other hand, landlords can capture the extra benefits by
      raising rents from tenants rather than by dispossessing them (p. 145). And, if landlords
      rent out from small farmers, the latter should benefit from rents. Besides, even if these
      problems do occur, Lipton says, these may not have to do with the GR. He says that 'most
      Marxist commentators on MVs may err by implicitly assuming that there are great and
      cumulative advantages especially as new techniques increasingly reward (i) the financial
      capacity to innovate, and (ii) the organizational capacity to engage many workers for
      large farmers over smaller ones, and for owners over tenants. If such advantages are also
      operated in adopting, intensifying and getting high incomes from MVs this could indeed
      play a key role in relative, perhaps absolute, immiserization... Marxists... have not always
      appreciated that repossession of tenancies, polarization of size of holdings... largely pre-
      ceded MVs...' (p. 305; cf. Dyer, 1997).

The GR is said to have adverse impacts on the poor *as laborers* as well. There are tendencies toward deceleration in employment opportunities. (a) Increased food output due to MV-use leads to lower food prices. This means that farmers in non-MV areas get lower relative prices for their output and therefore have less incentive to employ labor. (b) MV-associated mechanization – tractors, weedicides, more mechanized irrigation or threshing – has eroded employment opportunities. 'By greatly raising yield, an appropriate MV often renders tractorization and threshers financially feasible' (Lipton: 199). But what, one might ask, makes mechanization necessary, especially in 'labor-surplus' economies?

There are several processes (Rudra et al., 1990: 32). One is that: by allowing multiple cropping in a shorter growing period, the application of biochemical inputs sets up a pressure toward mechanization in order for farmers to cope with the increased time constraint (i.e. farm operations have to be finished on time) (Byres, 1983).[11] That is, farmers resort to mechanization in order deal with sharp seasonal peaks in labor demand (from main crop harvest through second crop weeding time) and the resultant bidding up of wage rates (Lipton: 179). And, as Lipton says, a machine hired or bought for use in the peak season can also be used in other seasons. He agrees that if the use of MVs causes mechanization, this is a direct result of employers' reaction to the labor-using effects mentioned earlier. The post-harvest operation tends to be also mechanized. The high ratio of grain to dry matter of MV grain makes MV husks susceptible to easy shattering, and this gives incentive for mechanical milling, says Lipton.[12]

MV-induced rise in food output has led to low food prices and therefore rises in real wages. But when real wages rise, *given* an over-supply of laborers, employers are able to depress money wages – Lipton's famous 'responsive money-wage deceleration' (214, 219) (I will return to this later). This leads to fall in real wages and thus to the erosion of laborers' consumption gains from extra MV-induced food production. It is not that, Lipton says, GR causes money wages to necessarily fall. It is that the rate of increase of money wages falls.

There is another reason, says Lipton, why wages do not increase much. In many places, due to such factors as subsistence minima, screening and

---

11   Lipton says, however, that the argument that tractorization, etc. causes higher cropping intensity collapses when the inputs of MVs, fertilizers and water are controlled for (pp. 198–199). Besides, incentives for mechanization are buttressed by cheap subsidies.

12   In addition, urbanization of the MV-induced surplus is another problem. '[T]he growing proportion of outputs processed as urban surpluses (the fact that food from villages goes to the city and is processed there for urban consumption) raises the capital/labour ratio in milling, baking, etc.' (Lipton: 187).

nutritional efficiency, pre-MV wages have been kept well above the equilibrium (at the point where the supply of and the demand for labor power intersect) (Lipton: 284). The implication of this is that 'even if MVs induce a considerable increase in demand for labour [sic] ... this need not pull up the equilibrium wage above the actual pre-MV rate' (p. 284). What Lipton is saying is that wages are above the level one would expect from the given supply and demand of labor. So when demand for labor increases, wages do not increase because they have already increased (or been higher)![13]

Consider the negative impact of the GR on the poor as buyers of food. MVs do cause an increase in food production. But the poor may not buy the extra food output because they do not have the necessary purchasing power (Lipton: 13). This is a point others such as Varshney (1994) also make, and rightly so. Besides, and arguably in part because of the lack of purchasing power of the poor, the extra food 'might have displaced food imports and raised stocks, but have not substantially increased food availability per person, especially among the poor' (Lipton: 257; Patnaik, 1991). While prices for crops grown and eaten by the poor are allowed to fall, government stocks and replacement of imports are allowed to prevent a sharp fall in prices of crops grown by larger, surplus – producing farmers, as a fall in prices would undermine the incentive for these richer farmers to deliver food and raw materials to urban areas (Lipton: 217–218, 221).[14]

Thus Lipton (and others) express some reservations about the supposed benefits of the GR for the poor. Despite these major reservations, the balance of advantage to a typical 'poor person' in the Third World, from MVs, appears large, if we 'add up' their various effects on such a person as small farmer, hired worker, and consumer (Lipton: 258).

Overall, the negative effects of the MVs are outweighed by their positive effects, he says. In particular, labor-using effects, normally, outweigh labor-displacing ones. Inequality between smaller and larger farmers increases in MV-areas but 'absolute poverty declines' (p. 319). And, to the extent that MV-technology has not delivered on its promise, it is because of the over-supply of laborers, because of *population factor*, that is. The specter of the population haunts the poor.

---

13   Pre-MV-stickiness downwards explains why wages increase little. Post-MV stickiness downwards explains why laborers will not bargain for increased employment at restricted wage rates in place of labor displacing techniques to meet the extra demand for labor, as wage rates cannot fall below the current level (Lipton: 286).

14   But given that Lipton believes farmers should get rewards for risk-taking, he cannot find anything wrong with this.

2 The Literature on the Green Revolution and Poverty: A Critique of Neo-Malthusianism

Lipton's (and others') idea that the MV-*technology* necessarily has *pro-poor* attributes and can necessarily cause poverty reduction but that if it has not been able to deliver on that promise it is because of *population* problems, is problematic. I want to suggest that underlying this idea is a specific form of neo-Malthusianism. Or, the objective effect of such thinking is resorting to neo-Malthusianism. I define this specific form of neo-Malthusianism as a combination of Malthusianism (the idea that population growth is the prime cause of scarcity and, therefore, of poverty) and technological determinism, which has some amount of pro-poor bias to it. It is true that for Lipton, MV technology interacts with the social aspects such as population and state policy (p. 17). But his framework suffers from inadequate conceptualization of both technology and of social aspects such as population. To the extent that he discusses the non-population aspects of society at all, he always under-stresses and under-conceptualizes them and treats them in an *ad hoc* manner.

There is a large amount of evidence from his book to suggest that his framework smacks of technological determinism (or indeed, technological reification) in the specific sense of giving much more power to technology that it itself can possibly have. Let me explain this.

a)   Lipton says, if MV technology is pro-poor it is because of the nature of the technology itself. MVs' physical properties are pro-poor.

> Certainly [MVs'] physical properties... MVs' use of more labour and management per acre, their production of coarser and cheaper varieties favouring self-consumption rather than marketing... should be more helpful to small farmers than to big ones. (p. 177)
> [W]ithout the extra employment income and food supplies created by the [extra grain] due to MVs, many of the world's poor would today be poorer still, and millions now alive would have died. (p. 9)
> [M]any millions of poor 'small' farmers would be worse off today if MVs did not exist. (p. 12)
> With rapid population growth and scarce land, the position of landless labour is much worse without MVs than with. (p. 186)

All this textual evidence suggests that, for Lipton, there is a relation between GR technology and poverty reduction at a theoretical level, although the actual extent of poverty reduction in different places and in different times might be less or more.

b) Lipton believes, while GR would necessarily cause poverty reduction, if it has not delivered on its promise, it is partly because of technology as well!

> [T]he real poverty problem with MVs arises in the rural areas that they leave out. (p. 147)
> Indeed, the MVs have to some extent failed the poor partly because they have not spread enough to offset mechanization or land-hunger, and especially because they have not spread to areas of insecure water supply [these are mainly rainfed areas]... (p. 9)

So, MVs – *both* when they are present and when they are absent – affect the poor.

c) Lipton recognizes that old, inegalitarian power structures in the village do hurt the poor. But he is also skeptical of the claims made by some Marxists that MVs transform the local power structures and relations of production (p. 324). For, Lipton says, the MV technology is too 'seriable', 'separable' and 'single-unit' for that. It is seriable in that the technology does not have to be used on a farm system as a whole; a piecemeal experiment is feasible. It is separable in that the package can be separated/unpacked. And, it is single-unit in that the adoption does not involve each unit in relationships with neighbors and/or authority structures; how much one gains from the technology does not depend on one's neighbors' or authority structures (p. 316, 318–319).

Thus the MV-technology is an evolutionary one: it does not require the transformation of local power structures (p. 319), which are left intact. This means that the richer people corner more benefit (p. 401), leading to rise in inequality, although absolute poverty can decline.[15] Clearly, for Lipton, to the extent that MVs hurt the poor, that is because *the nature of the technology is such that* it can be used in a context where older power relations do not have to be changed. It is technology that is in the driving seat. It is technology that determines how and whether or not it affects the poor.

---

15   While not changing the local power structures, MVs change *national* power structures, however, and that hurts the rural poor. By increasing production sharply, MVs produced urbanized surplus of food and raw materials and thus adverse internal terms of trade against rural areas. Thus national urban-based power structures got strengthened. Also urban elites do a deal with rural elites who provide the surplus. Because state policy is against the rural areas (farmers and non-farmers), pro-rural poor effects of technology cannot be realized (p. 402). As local power structures are not changed, the impact on strengthening urban, national power structures is larger.

So the technology needs to be and can be more pro-poor (e.g. hand-pump; new seeds for millet for semi-arid areas for subsistence farmers) (Lipton: 126, 325). This means the lack of a sufficiently pro-poor technology is a necessary cause of poverty. So the solution to world poverty lies in poverty-oriented, MV-based food agriculture [which] is the *only chance* to provide the growing poor populations of Asia and Africa with livelihoods during the many decades before their widespread industrialization (p. 425; stress added).

Note that for Lipton, it is not *any* technology that would solve poverty, for to say that would be crude, pure neo-Malthusianism. Rather there is a need for a *particular* type of technology, one that is *necessarily* pro-poor, suggesting that Lipton's neo-Malthusianism, unlike neo-Malthusianism per se, has *some* pro-poor bias. To the list of Sen's entitlements of the poor, Lipton adds one more, one that I would call 'technological entitlement':

> Only MV technology *directly available* to the poor – either because unavoidably labour intensive (*yet profitable*), or because concentrated on crops (or areas or assets) that remain in the control of the poor – is, in our judgement, likely to lastingly overcome the *"population threats"* to the poor people's food entitlements. (p. 215; stress added)

It may be noted that Lipton sees here no possible contradiction between labor-intensiveness of a technology and its profitability. Neither does he recognize the possibility of, and the long term structural tendency towards, the poor losing control over their means of production through pauperization and proletarianization,[16] and therefore, not being able to use the technology, no matter how 'pro-poor' it might be. More significantly, and from the standpoint of this chapter, Lipton's framework sees no need for changes in the way food and other goods and services are produced and distributed and in the power relations underlying this production and distribution. Marxist political economy is banished. Technological entitlement is in. In fact, it is very clear that Lipton's framework takes the current private-property dominated market economy for granted and that he, like Amartya Sen and other pro-poor economists, firmly believes in its underlying principle.[17] Technology can be designed

---

16   These are the processes that Marxist political economy of agrarian change has been drawing attention to.

17   He recognizes that '[B]igger farmers can hang on for higher prices [i.e. they do not have to sell their crops immediately and can wait until price rises happen]'. But such price rises 'seldom reflect more than the cost of storage ... and normal profit to allow for price risks' (p. 128), so that big farmers getting higher prices than smaller, needy farmers is justified. Further, Lipton finds nothing wrong with merchants, who buy from smaller farmers, 'insist[ing] on a lower grain price, in part as a reward for risk-bearing' (p. 129).

that would avert any need for radical social change that is necessary to eliminate poverty. Lipton, in this sense, is not too far from Borlaug, the biological scientist who received Nobel Prize for *Peace* (*not* for science) for inventing the new seeds and making possible GR that would turn the poor away from the danger of *Red Revolution* in the Third World.

Underlying Lipton's stress on technology is his view that there are 'population threats to the poor' (p. 215) and that population is a primary determinant of unemployment and wages. Let us therefore consider the second aspect of Lipton's neo-Malthusianism: his view about population–poverty relation in the context of MV-use. Lipton asks:

> Are poor people's insufficient gains – even losses – traceable to MVs themselves, and their role in the spread of rural capitalism; or to rising person/land ratios and hence weakening in the bargaining power of workers, small tenants and borrowers. The former position is taken by most (not all) Marxists; the latter by neo-Malthusians... (p. 304)

To know whose side Lipton is on, Marxists or neo-Malthusians, consider this.

> Just as population growth has helped to make growing proportions of the poor dependent on labour incomes rather than on MV farms direct, so it has helped to create a "reserve army" of under-employed adults, *Malthusian rather than Marxian*. The former population effect limits poor people's consumption gains from extra income in cultivating MVs even on small farms. The latter effect, the growing reserve army – by permitting "responsive money-wage deceleration" – reduces the prospects that extra MV-based food availability can help the poor by holding food prices in check. (p. 215; stress added)

Population growth has thus been invested with a massive amount of causal power. Population growth, not class differentiation or profit-driven mechanization or extant class relations impeding economic development that creates non-farm high-wage jobs, thus forcing a large number of people to rely on small parcels of land, and ultimately, to become landless, is the major driving force behind proletarianization, an increase in the number of people dependent on labor-income. This means that the poverty-reducing impacts of MVs through their impacts on small farmers is minimized *due to* population growth. Population not only increases the supply of laborers but also reduces their wage-gains. MV-induced increases in food production lead to lower food prices which in turn cause an increase in the real value of money wage in the first instance. The increased real wage then 'enables or induces many more poor and unskilled workers [whose supply is large because of population growth] to come forward and compete for employment' (p. 214); MVs, says Lipton, '*stimulate* poor people to produce even larger populations of potential workers' (Lipton: 404, 415; stress added). This permits employers to reduce money wages in turn (p. 214).

> [*T*]*he main reason* why wage-rates stagnate and why wage shares decline, is that, with work forces growing fast, extra *demand* for labor due to MVs meets increasing *supply* of laborers prepared... to work at rates barely above subsistence.
>
> LIPTON: 185; stress added

The use of MVs leads to more employment and to larger wage bills. But these benefits are to be shared among many people because of natural population growth and migration to MV areas from non-MV areas. So, 'employment and hence wage receipts *per household* rise less, and may even fall' (p. 186). 'This is not usually "because of MVs" but because of population growth' (p. 186; quotes in original). Thus: 'MVs have had to contend with population-linked factors' such as population growth and induced increases in supply of laborers', which weaken the poor (p. 258; parenthesis added).

There is no doubt that Lipton's framework is neo-Malthusian. But he is somewhat different from a pure, crude, neo-Malthusian. 'To say that with to-day's population but 1960s seeds, millions of poor people now alive would now be dead, is not to take a crude neo-Malthusian view [which is] that poverty is caused by an imbalance between food availability and population' (p. 338), and that growing populations can be fed from constant land only through techno-logical innovations (p. 211). The latter view is neo-Malthusianism that was behind the GR, as Lipton rightly points out. Lipton differs from a pure neo-Malthusian in part because he does not believe that the only role of tech-nology is growth of more food at a rate faster than the population growth. Technology has also to generate more *employment* which would increase the poor people's *entitlement* to food. Lipton's therefore is a refined form of neo-Malthusianism.

To cut the long story of Lipton's (and others') theory of the GR–poverty rela-tion short: GR and poverty reduction are necessarily causally related (GR has a necessary causal mechanism whereby poverty reduction will happen) but that if poverty has not been reduced as much as it should have been, it is be-cause the technology has not been sufficiently used or been sufficiently pro-poor and because of the population problem. Both these positions are *con-ceptually* indefensible. The next section will say why.

3   Technology, Population and Poverty: A Contingent Relation

What is revealed in studies on technology development or technology – poverty relation, is a narrow conception of technology: what are deeply social processes are attributed to technology as such. It is forgotten that technology as an aspect of productive force always works within the framework of social relations of production (including relations between property owners and relations between them and workers). It is the social relations of production, class relations expressing the social organization of production, that, ultimately, have the primacy over the productive forces.

In a capitalist economy, production is always a production of a use value (e.g. food) *and* production of value and surplus value (or certain amount of surplus labor) (Marx, 1977). Labor is combined with technology and other means of production, and the product is sold as a commodity, which, in value terms, is the sum of constant and variable capital and surplus value (c + v + s). So, as an input into production, technology bears the same characteristics as production itself. Firstly, it has use value (it contributes to production), and it is bought and sold as a commodity. Secondly, it is also a means of the final product (e.g. grain, computer, or whatever) absorbing more and more surplus labor. It is a means of increasing exploitation, that is.

In the capitalist context of India, the combination of labor and the new technology has meant an increased final product (i.e. grain). But this increased product needs to be looked at both as a use value (grain to be eaten) *and* as a means of soaking up – bearing or embodying – more surplus labor (since in a given time – e.g. a crop season – a given amount of labor input is producing more than before). The level of wages that labor receives does not necessarily reflect the size of the increased product now possible with the use of the technology. In more general terms, the nature of technology and its effects in a class society reflect these two aspects of technology: the use value aspect and the exploitation aspect of technology. The main aim of technology, when adopted by the capitalist, is not to produce more in order to increase wages and to meet human needs. Lipton, like most others, stresses the use value, the production aspect, of technology (how technology increases production), and not its role in exploitation. In the latter role of technology does an important mechanism of poverty lie.

Technological change in agriculture has a special macro-economic significance in terms of understanding the social relations aspect of technology. The agriculture sector produces food, which is an important item consumed by the working class from which capital must appropriate surplus value. And when less labor time is needed to produce wage-goods including food, other things (real wage and the length of the working day) constant, i.e. when labor productivity rises, more surplus value is produced in its relative form. This is 'the surplus-value arising from the curtailment of the necessary labor-time' and thus a fall in the value of labor power (Marx, 1977: 432). This happens when:

> the rise in the productivity of labour ...seize[s] upon those branches of industry whose products determine the value of labour-power, and consequently either belong to the class of normal means of subsistence, or are capable of supplying the place of those means.
>
> Ibid.

The value of labor power is also reduced when:

> those industries which supply the instruments of labour and the material for labour, i.e. the physical elements of constant capital which are required for producing the means of subsistence.
>
> Ibid.

Lipton says, on balance, the MV technology is labor-intensive and can be made more so. But in capitalism, labor intensiveness – ratio of labor input to technological input – depends generally and largely on whether employing a particular technology will increase profits for owners, not on whether that technology will produce employment for laborers. Whether it is an individual capitalist or a collective capitalist, it is not their job to produce jobs. Labor intensiveness of technology also depends partly on class struggle, as the struggle over mechanization in farming (and fisheries) in Kerala shows (see Chapter 3; also Srinivas, 1998).

In Lipton's argument, employers are able to reduce real wages because of an oversupply of laborers (p. 214). But surely the relation between wages and supply of laborers is a contingent affair. I may offer two comments in support of this. (a) Wages are primarily determined by the cost of the production and reproduction of labor power as a commodity; only changes in its price are affected by its supply and demand. (b) The extent of under-/un-employment – the balance between the supply of and the demand for labor – is primarily determined by accumulation and the level of profit. Population growth is not at all immaterial. Indeed, it can, in some circumstances, and for a definite period of time, make the employment situation worse. But it cannot be the fundamental motive force behind that situation. Lipton's money wage deceleration thesis is entirely within the neo-classical framework in which wages are determined by the supply of and the demand for laborers. There is no suggestion in his work that production and wage determination are largely *class* issues: that employers use their class power, the power they have over labor-ers because of their property ownership and control. And to say that population-linked effects destroy the neo-Malthusian optimism about the MV technology (Lipton: 214) is still to be within a populationist paradigm treating population as an independent variable. The capitalist economy, with its law of value, operating historically and at several spatial scales, including the rural/ur-ban, regional, national and global, creates a relative surplus population through replacement of labor by technology, rationalization of work-organization, and class differentiation, etc. This relative surplus population can be used in times of cyclical capitalist expansion and it can be used to undermine the bargaining power of workers during normal times. The relative surplus population – a reserve army of labor – allows capitalists to force a worker to do the work of more than person. The so-called oversupply of labor is largely a class issue: it is class relations between owners and employers that set limit within which population and technology work. Where does this leave us with respect to absolute poverty then?

Absolute poverty means two things: that there are certain absolute needs that one must satisfy (basic minimum food, shelter, clothing, etc.) and that the person lacks the resources to meet those needs. Technology is not the basic determinant of either of these two things. Absolute poverty is a highly con-crete issue. Like any concrete issue, this is a product of multiple determina-tions. It should not be reduced to any one set of mechanisms. Very briefly, absolute poverty can be caused by slow economic growth and by loss of access, or by reduced access, to basic goods and services or to an income. The loss of access to income, or reduced access to income can happen due to unemploy-ment, low wages, low prices of goods produced by smaller property owners, loss of property of smaller owners, and so on.

Reduction in absolute poverty *necessarily presupposes* an increase in the real income of the people living below the poverty-line, however defined. An increase in the real income of the poor will occur when society's income level is increased[18] and when a significant part of that increased income trickles down to the poor through the market process. The real income of the poor can also increase (a) when the poor themselves are involved in growth (e.g. when the *property-owning* poor, i.e. smaller property owners, produce more), and (b) when more employment is created in the economic activities undergoing growth, benefiting the *property-less* poor (i.e. poor laborers).

The poor people can increase their real income as well even *without* an in-crease in the income of the society. Indeed, faster economic growth by itself

---

18   '[S]low economic growth is generally associated with low impact on poverty alleviation' (Vyas and Bhargava, 1995: 2572; Fields, 1995: 80).

does not reduce poverty significantly (Vyas and Bhargava, 1995; Das, 1995). This is because 'economic growth could affect only those at the upper end of the income distribution and thus make no impact on poverty reduction' (Toye and Jackson, 1996: 56). The poor can increase their real income *without* an increase in the income of the society as a whole if there is a significant amount of redistribution by political means (e.g. redistribution by the state), of: (a) existing income-generating *means of production* to the poor and/or (b) the *incomes* of the non-poor people to the poor (e.g. taxing the rich and using the tax to provide subsidized means of subsistence to the poor).

Thus, the real income of the poorer people will necessarily increase owing to three processes. These processes are: (a) the market-based trickle-down of increased income, (b) the involvement of the poorer people themselves in economic activities in which income is undergoing growth, and (c) the state-promoted redistribution of the existing income-generating means of production and/or of the incomes of the rich. However, whether these three processes will occur is *contingent*. It depends on (e.g.) the balance of power between the poor and the non-poor (Wright, 1995). And when these processes work, the extent to which poverty will be reduced is also a contingent matter.

Now, what is the relation of the use of the GR technology to these three processes? The GR farming does not seem to have any link to state-promoted redistribution except that it has circumvented the need for land redistribution, which has a potential to alleviate poverty (Griffin, 1989: 147). So I will focus on the relation of the GR to the market processes [(a) and (b) above].

The GR technology, like any technology, needs to be viewed as having certain causal power (e.g. the power to produce more). The technology has caused a rise in land and labor productivity, thus creating the possibility for increasing the share of the total product allocated to labor (see Das, 1998a: 125). The power of the technology to increase productivity exists by virtue of: (a) the physical *structure* of the technology itself *and* (b) the *structure* of property relations within which the technology is used. I have referred to Lipton's view that the physical structure of MVs themselves is such that they produce more (and are therefore pro-poor) (Lipton: Chapter 2). So, I will focus on the structure of property relations that Lipton under-conceptualizes and under-stresses in order to focus on population. Property relations are interpreted here broadly as the relations mentioned above: (a) between those who own property and those who do not (at least not to such an extent that they will not have to work for wages), and (b) between property owners (e.g. farmers and sellers of seeds).

Consider the first aspect of property relations. As I discussed in the last section, technologies are combined with labor in the labor process. The labor process takes place within the framework of relations between laborers on the one hand and those who own the means of production including technologies on the other. The labor process has certain specific *effects*. These include not only the physical effects – overall development of productive forces (i.e. a rise in productivity of labor) – but also economic-distributional effects – how much income laborers will earn.

Now these effects of the labor process are always mediated by property relations. For an example: it is the case that the use of the GR technology causes higher productivity by virtue of the internal structure of the GR inputs. But farm-*laborers* may not gain if the larger farm *owners* resort to labor-displacing mechanization. Thus the poorer people *may not* be directly involved in the activities where growth occurs and may not benefit from the increased income of the society.[19] But mechanization is not a necessary condition for labor not to get their share of the increased product that the technology of the GR makes possible. There is a limit to the rise in wages, which, irrespective of the reason for it, beyond a point, actually represents a diminution in unpaid labor and decrease in surplus value:

> as soon as this diminution [of unpaid labor] touches the point at which the surplus-labor that nourishes capital is no longer supplied in normal quantity, a reaction sets in: a smaller part of revenue is capitalised, accumulation lags, and the movement of rise in wages receives a check. The rise of wages is therefore confined within limits....
>
> MARX, 1977: 771

And the pressure on the rise in wages to stop is expressed in specific strategies by capitalists. For example, whenever the wage level reaches a point that cuts the average rate of exploitation and profit, employers use their class power to fight back and take necessary steps to reduce wages (investing in labor-saving technologies; suppression of wage-strikes; deproletarianization[20]). The level of wages crucially *depends* on the rate of exploitation and the attendant accumulation,[21] and on class struggle (Das, 1998a). The relation of laborers'

---

19   But, *pace* Byres (1983), and following Lipton, I would say that it is *not necessary* either that the larger landowners using the biochemical technology will also use labor-displacing mechanization. I insist, once again, that the relation between the MV technology and mechanization, including the so-called adverse effects of the latter on labor, is contingent.

20   This means restricting laborers' freedom to sell their labor power as free agents, as Brass has argued. This occurs in GR areas of the less developed world (as in the advanced countries).

21   The two are related: surplus value that is appropriated (exploitation) is reinvested in production (accumulation).

wages to how much they produce and therefore to the technological input into the labor process is not a *necessary* relation. Workers' wages are not primarily a product of how much they produce. Consider here the fact of near-stagnation in wages in the US since the 1970s, while productivity has risen. 'While productivity grew 64.9 percent in the period 1979–2013, hourly pay for production and non-supervisory workers rose by just 8.0 percent' (Jones, 2014).

Now consider the second aspect of the property relations. This refers to the distribution of property itself (land and money). And the distribution of property *affects* what the *effects* of the use of a technology are on (e.g.) smaller property owners. While the use of the GR technology can *necessarily* cause increased productivity, whether particular people will use the GR technology and other needed inputs is *contingent*. For example: if people do not own (much) land on which to use the technology, or if they have some land but do not have the money to buy the inputs, then they may not benefit from the GR technology. Even if they use the GR inputs, they may not use these in *proper* amounts because of lack of money (and knowledge), and therefore may not significantly augment their income on a sustainable basis to remain above the poverty-line.

Combination of technology with labor and other means of production can enhance productivity. But in a class society means of production are unequally distributed, and employers of labor, rather than labor, have the power to make decisions about the labor process, including the decisions about the labor intensiveness of the technology. Under this circumstance, the income benefits from increased production are necessarily unequally distributed. Absolute poverty, the fact of people not being able to meet their basic minimum needs, is a necessary aspect of this unequal distribution of 'income' in a class context, i.e. the income from employment (wage-income) or from property ownership (income in the form of capital), or from a combination of the two. Those people (smaller property owners and especially laborers) who get less than larger, labor employing, property owners *may* remain in absolute poverty. For some of them, the level of benefits from increased production may be relatively high so they may escape absolute poverty.

The point of my discussion is that whether the GR or indeed any technology will enhance or mitigate poverty is a contingent matter. The necessary effects of technology on society are those which are internal to the structure of the technology itself (in the case of the MV technology the necessary effect is greater yield). Technology as a physical (or chemical) thing can have only *physical/chemical* effects. Its *necessary* effects, as opposed to contingent ones, cannot be *social*. This is true about the GR technology just as much as computers. Technology itself does not, and cannot, have any necessary or inherent pro-poor causal property. That is: it is possible that the GR can reduce/increase poverty but not necessary. One cannot deny that some of the causes of poverty and some of 'the effects of the GR' *are* related. It is only that the relation is not *necessary*. Relatedly, my point is also that the so-called negative economic effects of the GR on poverty cannot be *reduced* to the GR itself. For, these effects are mediated by property relations, including how property owners relate to one another (as owners and buyers of commodities) and to workers whose labor power is bought by (larger-scale) property owners. This means and to repeat, the GR – or any technology – *itself* cannot necessarily hurt the poor. I take a theoretically agnostic view of the relation between technology and poverty. The social effects of the technology – effects of technology on society – are socially mediated, and are especially mediated by the class relations (property relations) within which the technology is used.

Similarly, population's relation to poverty or its relation to GR's impacts on poverty is a contingent affair. The over-supply of laborers and therefore un/under-employment may dampen wages. But at a given point in time, the mechanism of under/unemployment is largely *independent* of population growth, even if population growth can exacerbate the already-existing problem of under/unemployment and low wages. It is a function of class power of employers, of accumulation and attendant level of profit. Oversupply of laborers, under some circumstances, can contribute to the lowering of wages. It can make it difficult for laborers in their political struggle over wages by increasing competition among them (Shrestha and Patterson, 1990; Findlay, 1995). But the oversupply of laborers cannot be the fundamental motive force behind the determination of wages. It is not just that wages are never allowed to continue to remain at a high level for a long duration when there is a *shortage* of laborers in a place. More significantly, if/when a rise in wages undercuts the average rate of profit then the capitalist economy can *create* a relative *surplus* population, the so-called oversupply of laborers, through the replacement of labor by technology.[22] This happened when tractors were introduced in the Green Revolution areas, for example. A relative surplus population is created and allowed to continue to exist, one that can be used when it is needed for production of profit by the labor employing class and to undermine the bargaining power of laborers. It is class in the sense of property ownership and the social relations of private accumulation that set limit within which population has its effects. In other words, the effects of the so-called oversupply of labor, of population growth – like the effects of technology – on poverty are contingent and are therefore an empirical question.

---

22   Notice the high capital intensity of India's urban industries and their decreasing ability to absorb labor, for example.

4   The Green Revolution and Poverty in India: An Empirical Analysis

My empirical analysis is at the level of States.[23] I will compare the poverty situation over time and over space, i.e. across 17 major States in India, in the pre-neoliberalism period. From the standpoint of the GR, I have divided the States into two types. (1) I will call the first type, the more advanced GR States. These are the ones where the land under five major MV food crops (rice, wheat, maize, jowar and bajra) as a percentage of the total cultivated land under these crops is more than the median value for all the States. (2) The less advanced GR States are the ones where the percentage is below the median. (The States' ranks remained unchanged between the mid-1970s and mid-1980s.) In addition to this simple comparison across States over time, I will use correlation analysis to look at the relation between the use of the GR technology and the population factor on the one hand and poverty on the other (see Table 5.1).

The poverty level – the percentage of the rural population below the officially defined poverty line – tends to be lower in the more advanced GR States than elsewhere. So, one might expect a negative association between the use of the GR technology and poverty level, as discussed by Lipton and others. The following Table shows (lagged) correlations between poverty level and the use of the GR technology, at different points in time. Poverty levels for the mid-1970s, the mid-1980s and the mid-1990s are correlated with the use of the GR technology both in the mid-1970s (by when the GR had advanced both in terms of its adoption by smaller owners and in terms of spread to areas outside the original GR areas) and in the mid-1980s (by when the GR had advanced even further).

Table 5.2 shows that in the mid-1970s, there was a moderate degree of correlation between the GR and poverty level. But the relation seemed to have weakened afterwards as seen in the correlations between poverty level in the mid-1990s and the use of the GR technology in the mid-1980s. To the extent that there is any correlation between the GR and the poverty level at all, it is largely because of the fact that poverty levels in the States which adopted the technology earlier were lower than in the States which adopted the technology later. Indeed, in the more advanced GR States of the Punjab and Haryana combined, the poverty level throughout the 1960s was never more than 40% (except for 1967–1968) whereas the all-India poverty level was close to 50% at least

---

23   I am aware that using the States, which are huge areas, is problematic on grounds of ecological fallacy, because many of the relations between the new technology, population and poverty work at the intra-State, and especially, the family level.

TABLE 5.1   The Green Revolution and rural poverty, 1970s–1990s

			Rural poverty			
	1973/74	1977/78	1983	1987/88	1993–1994	1973/1994
Advanced GR States						
Andhra	48.4	38.1	26.5	20.9	15.92	67.1
Bihar	63.0	63.3	64.4	52.6	58.21	07.6
Gujarat	46.4	41.8	29.8	28.7	22.18	52.2
Haryana	34.2	27.7	20.6	16.2	28.02	18.07
Himachal	27.4	33.5	17.0	16.3	30.34	−10.73
Jammu & Kashmir	45.5	42.9	26.0	25.7	30.34	33.32
Punjab	28.2	16.4	13.2	12.6	11.95	57.62
Tamil Nadu	57.4	57.7	54.0	45.8	32.48	43.41
Uttar Pradesh	56.4	47.6	46.5	41.1	42.28	25.04
Group average	45.2	41.0	33.1	28.9	30.19	33.21
Less advanced GR States						
Assam	52.7	59.8	42.6	39.4	45.01	14.59
Karnatak	55.1	48.2	36.3	32.8	29.88	45.77
Kerala	59.2	51.5	39.0	29.1	25.76	56.49
Madhya	62.7	62.5	48.9	41.9	40.64	35.18
Maharastra	57.7	64.0	45.2	40.8	37.93	34.26
Orissa	67.3	72.4	67.5	57.6	49.72	26.12
Rajasthan	44.8	35.9	33.5	33.2	26.46	40.93
West Bengal	73.2	68.3	63.1	48.3	40.80	44.26
Group average	59.1	57.8	47.01	40.4	37.03	37.3
All-India	56.4	53.1	45.6	39.1	37.3	33.3

Notes: Expert group on poverty, planning commission (presented in NIRD, 1998). Percent change in poverty levels between 1973 and 1994. A negative sign in the final column means poverty level has increased.
SOURCE: NIRD, 1998; AND HTTP://WWW.SCIENCEDIRECT.COM.EZPROXY.LIBRARY.YORKU
.CA/SCIENCE/ARTICLE/PII/S0016718501000069#TBLFN2

TABLE 5.2   Correlations between the Green Revolution and rural poverty level, 1970s–1990s

	PV77–78	PV83	PV87–88	PV93–94
GR (Early stage)	−0.677	−0.574	−0.610	−0.563
	(0.003)	(0.016)	(0.009)	(0.019)
GR (Late stage)	–	–	−0.554	−0.439
			(0.021)	(0.078)

Note: GR (Early stage) and GR (Late stage) are measured by: the land under five major MV food crops (rice, wheat, maize, jowar and bajra) as a percentage of the total cultivated land under these crops in the 1973–1976 and 1982–1985, respectively. PV77–78 is the percentage of the rural population below the poverty line in 1977–1978; likewise for other years. Figures in parentheses are p values. Correlation between GR (Early stage) and GR (Late stage) are 0.958 (p = 0.000).
SOURCE: CMIE, 1987; AND NIRD, 1998

for most of the 1960s. The unweighted mean poverty level in the 1960s in the Punjab–Haryana region was 35.87% as compared to 55.21% at the all-India level (as per the data from World Bank, 1997).

A better test of the relation between the GR and poverty would be whether the use of the technology is associated with any poverty *reduction*. Poverty reduction signifies the fact that poverty is a process, rather than a thing frozen in time. So, one would expect that the GR would be correlated with the *rate* of poverty reduction over time rather than poverty *levels at a given time*. There seems to have been a weak positive correlation between the GR in its early stage on the one hand and poverty reduction between the early/mid-1970s and the late 1980s on the other, possibly indicating some weak but favorable impacts of the technology on poverty reduction (Das, 2002). But there are no correlations between the GR in its later stage and poverty reduction. The overall message seems to be that there is no statistical correlation between the GR and poverty reduction. Let us probe this a bit further.

Each of the two types of States – more advanced GR States and less advanced GR States – can be divided further into two types based on the poverty reduction rate. These are: (a) States where poverty reduction has been greater than the median for all States (I will call them more pro-poor States), and (b) States where poverty reduction has been less than the median (I will call them less pro-poor States). We have thus four types of States, as shown in Table 5.3: (I) more advanced GR and more pro-poor States; (II) more advanced GR and less pro-poor States; (III) less advanced GR and more pro-poor States; and (IV) less advanced GR and less pro-poor States.

Table 5.3 shows that among the more advanced GR States, there are States where poverty reduction has been very high and also States which have not performed very well in poverty reduction. Similarly, among the less technologically advanced States, poverty reduction has been both more and less. Very significant poverty reduction (56%) has been possible over the 1973–1994 period in (e.g.) Kerala which is not a major GR area but which is known for the re-distributive policies, including land reforms, implemented by various leftist regimes in power there (see Franke and Chasin, 1991; Heller, 1995; Das, 1999c). Whereas, over the same period, a premier GR State, Haryana, has one of the worst records in poverty reduction (only 18%).[24] This is consistent with the fact that the rate of increase in money wage since 1970 in Haryana has been slower than in several less advanced GR States such as Orissa or Madhya Pradesh (Jose, 1988).

From the standpoint of Lipton's theory about GR's necessary pro-poor causal property, categories II and III are problematic, at least on empirical grounds. Why would poverty reduction be so low in spite of the widespread use of the

TABLE 5.3   Poverty reduction (1973–1994) with and without the Green Revolution

Green Revolution	Poverty reduction	
	Greater	*Less*
More advanced	(I) Andhra, Punjab, Gujarat, Tamilnadu	(II) Bihar, Haryana, Himachal;[a] Jammu and Kashmir, Uttar Pradesh
Less advanced	(III) Madhya Pradesh, Karnataka, Rajasthan, Kerala, West Bengal	(IV) Assam, Maharastra, Orissa

a Poverty has increased by 10% in this State (this is the only State where poverty has increased).

SOURCE: DATA FROM NIRD, 1998

24   There is a debate on the impacts on poverty of the new liberalization policy in India which started in 1991 (see Chapter 4). Many scholars argue that it has had an adverse impact (Dev, 2000; Nayyar, 1996; see, Das, 2000b for a brief critical discussion of this literature). So, let us take poverty reduction between 1973 and 1987–88 (the last year for which comparable data for all States is available for the pre-liberalization period). The overall picture does not change, although there are some changes in actual entries in particular boxes. Several of the more advanced GR States have shown relatively low poverty reduction and there are several States where GR is not advanced but which have experienced greater poverty reduction.

TABLE 5.4   Poverty, population growth and population pressure on land

More advanced GR states with greater poverty reduction			More advanced GR states with less poverty reduction		
	Pop. growth	*Pop. pressure*		*Pop. growth*	*Pop. pressure*
Andhra	18.2	3.36	Bihar	22.55	5.94
Punjab	17.36	1.73	Haryana	22.77	1.83
Gujurat	14.89	2.28	Jammu and Kashmir	23.4	4.56
Tamilnadu	13.27	4.58	Himachal	17.5	4.08
			Uttar Pradesh	22.53	3.62
Group average	15.93	2.987	Group average	21.75	4.01
All India	19.71	2.986			

Notes: Population growth: decadal rural population growth – i.e. the percentage rate of rural population growth between 1981 and 1991. Population pressure is defined as no. of persons in rural areas (in 1981) per hectare of gross cropped area (in 1984–1985). All India figures include the 17 States and other smaller States and Territories.
SOURCE: NIRD, 1998; AND BANSIL, 1992

technology (category II) and how can poverty reduction be so large without much use of the technology (category III)?

Is it possible that GR would have caused greater poverty reduction but population growth has been preventing that, an argument which Lipton makes? One way of looking at the population issue would be to look at the population growth rates and population pressure on land in more advanced GR States, including the more pro-poor States and less pro-poor States (type I and II States).

The unweighted average population growth for more advanced GR States with greater poverty reduction is somewhat lower than the average population growth in the more advanced GR States with lower rate of poverty reduction. The pressure of the population on land needs also to be looked at, as Lipton says population pressure in terms of high person/land ratio is a crucial factor that influences unemployment (p. 206). Table 5.4 shows that the unweighted average person/land ratio in more advanced GR States with greater poverty

TABLE 5.5   Correlations between the population factor and poverty reduction, 1970s–1990s

	Poverty reduction over		
	1983–1987	1983–1994	1987–1994
Pop. pressure	0.446	0.067	−0.009
	(0.073)	(0.798)	(0.973)
Pop. growth	−0.214	−0.193	−0.173
	(0.409)	(0.457)	(0.506)

Notes: None of these correlations is statistically significant or significant from the standpoint of Lipton's theory. This result is, however, consistent with a widely held view in population geography/population studies that 'there is no significant correlation, positive or negative, between national population growth rates and various measures of development' in the Third World (Jones, 1990: 168). The 0.446 correlation seems to suggest that there is a mild *positive* association between poverty reduction and population pressure.
SOURCE: AUTHOR'S CALCULATIONS

reduction is a little higher than the corresponding average in the more advanced GR States with lower rate of poverty reduction.

5   Conclusion

The upshot of the foregoing analysis is that while the GR seems to be somewhat associated with the ratio of the rural population below the poverty line *at a point in time,* there seems to be no association between the GR and the important issue of poverty *reduction.* This is the case whether or not the population factor is held constant. The GR technology and the population factor, the twin neo-Malthusian mechanisms in which Lipton and others invest so much causal power, seem to have no statistical relation with poverty reduction (at the State level in India). Poverty reduction has taken place both with and without technological advancement. And persistence of poverty characterizes both technological advancement and the lack of it.[25]

---

25   Here I am abstracting from the real possibility that even if income and assets are equally distributed, there can be still absolute poverty if the level of development of productive forces is very low (i.e. where the total income of all the people in a place is less than the sum of the differences between the poverty line and each person's income). The use of technology can remove this 'natural' condition of scarcity. But it must be noted that whether technology can deliver even on this front and continue to do so depends on

TABLE 5.6   Poverty reduction (1973–1988) with and without GR

Green Revolution	Poverty reduction	
	Greater	*Less*
More advanced	(I) Andhra, Punjab, Gujurat, Haryana, Himachal, Jammu and Kashmir	(II) Bihar, Tamil Nadu, Uttar Pradesh
Less advanced	(III) Karnataka, Rajasthan, Kerala, West Bengal	(IV) Assam, Madhya Pradesh, Maharastra, Orissa, Rajasthan

Notes: Pop. growth: the decadal growth rate of rural population between 1981 and 1991. Pop. pressure: Number of persons in rural areas (in 1981) per hectare of gross cropped area (in 1984–1985).
SOURCE: BASED ON: NIRD, 1998; AND BANSIL, 1992

The statistical results in the chapter are not inconsistent with some similar existing research (at the State level) (Cook, 1996). These results are also not inconsistent with the case studies seen as a whole. For example, case-studies show that the poor have gained from economic development both in GR areas (Harriss, 1991; Alauddin and Tisdell, 1995; Beck, 1995[26]) and in non-GR areas (Vaddiraju, 1999) and that poverty has persisted in both GR areas and non-GR areas (Das, 1995; Datta, 1998; Kamal, 1998; Paul, 1990).

To the extent that there is an association between poverty *levels* and the GR, this should be accepted with caution. In the first place, in the statistical analysis, I have abstracted from the contribution that the various poverty alleviation programs started by the Indian State since the late 1970s may have made to

---

appropriate social relations, for indeed, social relations can be a barrier to development of and the use of productive forces. Where land and other assets are unequally distributed and continue to be so given the failure of the land reforms policy, and where there is mass poverty and lack of non-farm employment opportunities, the land-owning class often finds it profitable to invest their resources in 'non-capitalist' ventures (leasing out land to land-hungry peasants for high rents; usury, etc.), rather than in productivity-raising technology such as the MVs (Das, 1999b; Patnaik, 1986). Lipton does not discuss this class-embeddedness of the GR technology at all.

26   A more recent publication, based in village-studies, show that the Green Revolution has helped the poor, including in their fight against food insecurity (also, Baker and Jewitt, 2007).

poverty reduction (Vyas and Bhargava, 1995; Das, 2000a). In addition, I argue, the very fact that the state could *not* rely on the GR for poverty reduction and thus started a 'direct attack' on poverty through these policies (e.g. loans to the poor to set up small businesses) (Das, 1998b) is an indirect indicator of the limited impact of the GR. I have also abstracted from the ecological impacts of the GR such as salinization, etc. (Shiva, 1991) as well as its impacts on laborers' health (many laborers in the Punjab lose their limbs while operating machines) (Chandan, 1979). If we 'deduct' these costs of the GR from its so-called benefits, we may perhaps find no relation between GR and poverty level or perhaps we will find a negative one! Abstraction from these issues is a limitation of my study and points to a need for incorporating these in an analysis of the GR–poverty connection.

Secondly, the statistical association which I have presented above does not at all suggest any necessary relation between the GR and poverty levels. Any such claims to necessity are, in my view, conceptually indefensible. Besides, the positive association could just mean that the GR started in the States which had lower poverty levels to start with.[27]

The real test of the relation between the GR and poverty lies in its impact on what happens to the poverty process over time (not just at a point in time) and in different States (not just in some particular places), for poverty is not a thing but a *socio-spatial process*. In other words, the more interesting issue to look at is the relation between the GR and poverty reduction. I have shown that the GR has no statistical relation with poverty reduction. Poverty has been, and arguably, can be reduced without the GR (or for that matter, without any other technology or an increase in the economic output as such). And, in some cases, GR can have some favorable impact on the poor (through its impact on non-farm employment and by other means) (Harriss, 1991). But it is not necessary that that will be the case generally. Given the GR, poverty reduction is possible but not necessary. More generally, technology is neither a necessary nor a sufficient condition for poverty reduction. If the lack of technology was a necessary cause of poverty, one in seven people in the United States of America would not have to live below the line of absolute poverty. While the GR technology does not have any necessary poverty reduction impact, it cannot also be said that it has any necessary poverty-increasing impact, *independently* of social relations within which technology operates. There is simply no necessary relation between technology and poverty reduction, positive or negative. Much of what I have said about technology in its Green Revolution form

---

27   This could be because those who are already well-off are able to use the technology more than those who are not.

applies to technology in its biotechnology form. A transition seems to be occurring from the Green Revolution to the gene revolution (biotechnology). The latter is linked to neoliberal capitalism as we have seen in the previous chapter. Biotechnology companies are pushing for the use of GM (genetically modified) seeds to be used on the ground that with these seeds, cultivators will increase their yields and therefore their income. The arguments in favor of the use of GM seeds are almost identical to those for the Green Revolution (HYV seeds) and therefore can be critically assessed in the way that this chapter does. Like the Green Revolution, the gene revolution is controversial, and for similar reasons (Bownas, 2016; Herring and Paarlberg, 2016). Given that the GMO seeds are extremely expensive to buy (Plahe et al., 2017; Shiva et al., 2002) and that they have to be bought every year (a cultivator cannot save the seeds from the current year for use in the next year), and that the use of seeds requires other chemicals which need to be bought, GMO farmers are going into debt, and some of them are committing suicide. The effects of GMO seeds, like those of HYV seeds, will depend on the overall political-economic or class context in which these seeds are accessed and used (Carroll, 2017). If in India's Maharashtra State, the districts using GM cotton seeds are the districts where numerous indebted farmers have committed suicide, this points to the need to examine the GM technology in relation to the context of class relations within which it works.

The analysis of the GR–poverty relation sheds light on the relation between technology and society, or to use the terminology of Marxist political economy, the relation between social relations and productive forces (especially, technology) (Callinicos, 1988; Cohen, 2000; Liodakis, 1997; *Science & Society*, 2006). The analysis supports, and points to, general theoretical ideas about the class character of technology, that 'technological change and its social consequences are shaped by generalised commodity exchange, investment capital, wage labor and other dominant social forms of our epoch' (Smith, 2010: 203).[28] Technology, as a 'thing' exists and operates, in the context of certain social relations, which shape how technology produces its effects. So, technology is not only a 'thing' but also a relationship. Technological change is important as it can help a society produce more in less time and help human beings transcend some of the barriers that nature imposes. Technology itself cannot solve humanity's problems such as poverty, however, as its effects are mediated by capitalist class relations. For Marx:

---

28   On socio-ecological and political aspects of technological change, apart from Smith (2010), see Tisdell and Maitra (2018), Dasgupta (2018) and Herring (2006). On the gender aspect, see Hansda (2017).

capital is defined by a profound ontological inversion of means and ends. Human ends are subordinate to the accumulation of money capital as an end in itself, and human flourishing is subordinate to the flourishing of capital. ...From Marx's standpoint, this inversion fundamentally shapes the nature of technology in capitalism

SMITH, 2010: 206

It is in fact no longer sufficient to define technology solely in terms of use-value as 'the equipment, techniques, and expertise that can be applied to produce a good or service' (ibid.). That definition is not false. But it fails to capture the historically specific nature of technology under *capitalist class relations*. This is 'a social order in which equipment, techniques and expertise are generally developed and employed only if it is anticipated that surplus value will be appropriated as a result of doing so'. Under capitalism, 'technology is not primarily a means to the fulfilment of human ends.... Technology is first and foremost a means to capital's end, valorisation' (Smith, 2010: 206).

Because technology works in the context of social relations, technology can be a window on to the understanding of the structure of social relations itself:

Technology reveals the active relation of [human beings] to nature, the direct process of production of [their] life, and thereby it also lays bare the process of the production of the social relations of [their] life, and of the mental conceptions that flow from those relations.

MARX, 1977: 493

Low-Wage Neoliberal Capitalism, Social-Cultural Difference, and Nature-Dependent Production

Crucial to the neoliberal project have been agricultural exports as a means to earn foreign exchange and to secure fiscal stability.[1] This strategy has led to India becoming a member of a group of nations that Harriet Friedman calls 'New Agricultural Countries' (NACs) (Friedman, 1993: 45). Counterpoised to the Newly Industrialized Countries (NICs) (Brohman, 1996), the emergence of the NACs represent a quintessential strategy of Third World development under neoliberalism, which has occurred, paradoxically, with state support. 'New agriculture' refers to the production of high-value non-traditional crops (e.g. flowers and shrimps) for the world market, as compared to the traditional crops produced under colonialism and during the immediate post-colonial period (Maitra 1997: 247; Watts, 1996: 232–233).

New Agriculture signifies a dialectics of articulation and disarticulation. It *articulates* local social production relations in NACs directly to the global economy – and to its price signals – more closely than achieved during the era of the Green Revolution (the subject of Chapter 5), when national food self-sufficiency was emphasized (Nanda, 1995: 20). So, whilst NACs, such as India, are increasingly specializing in luxury and niche-market crops, fish farming, and animal feeds, developed countries have specialized in the intensive export of heavily subsidized basic wage goods. This trend is indicative of an emergence of a new international division of labor in agriculture (McMichael, 2000). This new division of labor signifies, among other things, the relatively deregulated production of commodities for export, based on a low-paid, unorganized working class that is increasingly deprived of government welfare benefits: in other words, neoliberal capitalism in agrarian/rural contexts. New agriculture practices consequently, and simultaneously, *disarticulate* agricultural production from the requirements of local populations and environments (Teubal, 2000): products of new agriculture are not affordable by the common people, most of whom live under a budget of Rupees 150 or so a day in India.

---

1 An earlier version of this chapter appeared as Das (2014).

The effects of neoliberalism on agriculture are multi-scalar and place-specific. At the national scale, new agricultural production appears to have resulted in less land being used for food crops cultivation, so much so that per capita food availability in India is down to the level experienced during the Bengal famine of 1943 (Patnaik 1999, 2003). This is occurring in the context of WTO-mandated state withdrawal from public food distribution, employment generation, and input subsidies (Chossudovsky, 1999). Other effects of neoliberalism are particularly important at regional and local scales. Export-oriented units in new agriculture employ substantially fewer people per every dollar invested than does traditional cereal farming. Amongst other effects, this depresses the domestic demand for those mass-produced commodities that help promote industrialization. New agriculture has, also, been shown in many countries to lead to the displacement of smaller farmers (Stonich, 1995) and create new social divisions (Jamieson, 2002). Further, new agricultural practices degrade land so significantly that after a single decade of production, fields are in fact no longer suitable for any productive use, including a return to cereal cultivation. Chemical additives in capital-intensive new agriculture not only contaminate land and water (Barbier, 2004; Bhat and Bhatta, 2004; Flaherty, 1999; Ronnback, 2003) but adversely affect the health of (especially female) workers too (see Sass, 2000).

Like many other countries of the South, India is a low-wage platform of global capitalism. Such a platform works in industries, services, mining, as well as in agriculture, of which aquaculture is an important part. Aquaculture is the fastest growing food-producing sector in the world (World Bank, 2007). Shrimp culture is an important part of aquaculture. Shrimp production is a specific form of new agricultural production.

The burgeoning academic literature on export-oriented shrimp culture in the neoliberal world has shed light on ecological as well as selected economic aspects of shrimp culture, including the conditions of small-scale shrimp farmers. What is generally missing in this literature is a theoretically-informed emphasis on the material–social conditions of wage laborers working on shrimp farms. If shrimp-culture is being promoted, we must understand whether it benefits the men, women and children who produce shrimps as wage-workers. Using evidence from India, I seek to fill this gap by studying shrimp producers *as* wage laborers. When explored through a Marxist approach, the issue of shrimp wage laborers reveals the nature of a specific kind of 'metabolic rift' that is not talked about in the existing literature, a rift that characterizes the relation between wage labor and capital. This approach also shows how place-specific relations of difference along with biophysical conditions of production, influence the more general relations of capitalism, including those of the formal subsumption of labor.

The first section of this chapter briefly outlines the current state of the analysis of shrimp culture and offers Marxist criticisms of this analysis. The second section maps out the contours of a different framework. The third section introduces the geographical context of shrimp culture under study. In light of the conceptual ideas in the second section, I then present the empirical discussion on shrimp farm laborers, including their socio-geographical character, in the fourth and fifth sections. The final section summarizes the empirical findings and draws some conceptual conclusions.

1   Shrimp Aquaculture and the Missing Laborer

The shrimp aquaculture literature has usefully unpacked its ecological and economic aspects and effects. Scholars have studied the ecology of shrimp farming (Vandergeest et al., 1999). Research has shown how shrimp culture has caused the conversion of mangroves (Huitric et al., 2002; Martinez-Alier, 2001) and rice land into land for shrimp aquaculture (Islam, 2009). It has also shown how shrimp culture has led to soil salinization, water pollution, and depletion of soil nutrients (Flaherty and Karnjanakesorn, 1995), all of which contribute to a decline in the yield of staple crops (Ali, 2006). There is little on shrimp labor in this literature, however.

Scholars have also investigated the economic and developmental aspects of shrimp production at local and national scales. The globalization of shrimp culture, which includes trade in shrimps as well as the process of vertical integration within the industry, has already received attention (Goss et al., 2000). While some argue that this globalization process has produced positive effects on exports, income, consumption, nutrition, and equality, others are less sanguine about these effects (e.g. its effect on employment) (see Neiland et al., 2001; also Barraclough and Finger-Stich, 1996). The analysis of the economic aspects of shrimp culture, like that of the environmental aspects, is problematic, however. This is partly because serious theoretical attention is not paid to the issue of labor, or to class, more generally. When the literature looks at the impacts of shrimp culture on income and livelihood, it does not report on the class composition of income or the class character of that livelihood. Does the income of those engaged in shrimp culture come from profit, or from leasing out land for shrimp culture, or from smallholders' self-employment? Or does it come from *wages*? To the extent that there is any indication of the class aspects of income and livelihood, the focus has been on small-scale shrimp farmers in terms of their economic viability and other issues (Pradhan and Flaherty, 2008; Samal, 2003; Vandergeest, 1999). Undoubtedly, these studies have admirably shed useful light on the precarious nature of small-scale shrimp farmers. For example, Pradhan and Flaherty (2008) say that while Indian shrimp culture has benefited the country through increase in exports, it has hurt smaller shrimp farmers (pp. 71–72). Vandergeest et al. (1999: 584–585) are concerned with the viability of smaller farmers in Thailand based on their economic resilience, which is partly enabled by the particular ecology of shrimp culture. Samal (2003) has highlighted the competition for fishing areas (for both capture and culture of shrimp) between poorer traditional fishermen of lower castes and rich businesspersons of non-fishermen castes in one of the largest brackish-water lagoons in the world, Chilika Lagoon, which is located in eastern India.

However, some of this analysis tends to ignore the tendency that 'shrimp farms are witnessing increasing proletarianization' in well-known shrimp areas such as Thailand (Goss et al., 2001: 454). So the labor aspect of shrimp culture is relatively neglected.[2] An assumption underlying the promotion of export-oriented shrimp culture by national and international agencies is that the increased income from the sale of shrimps will allow rural people to buy the food they need which is no longer grown locally or nationally (Weeks, 1992: 7). Shrimp aquaculture is supposed to increase rural people's income through direct sales of shrimps and from wage employment (see World Bank, 2007: 60). But these assumptions are problematic if laborers earn wages that are so low as to compromise their ability to buy food and other necessaries. This I will show is the case.[3]

While acknowledging that sociologists, geographers, and others including those who adopt a political ecology approach, have made an enormous

---

2 However, the wage labor issue is not *entirely* ignored (see Pokrant and Reeves, 2007). Sometimes, it is mentioned in passing but in general it is not given much theoretically informed consideration. Stonich et al. (1997) mention 'a very modest number of low-paying, temporary jobs working on (shrimp) farms' (p. 170), but there is generally no *analysis* of the dynamics of the low-wage regime itself. In their very interesting work, Pradhan and Flaherty (2008: 69–70; also Islam, 2009: 73–74) mention low wages and irregularity of employment, but they do so briefly and descriptively.

3 Also: if shrimp aquaculture is a type of agricultural production, then the kind of attention that has been paid to relations between capital and labor within traditional agriculture by agrarian political economists (Byres, 1999; de Janvry, 1981; see also Buttel, 2001) must be paid to laborers on shrimp farms as well.

contribution towards our understanding of ecological and selected macro-economic/developmental aspects of shrimp-culture, this chapter claims that the story of shrimp-culture (indeed of aquaculture) has been, more or less, the story of the missing laborer.[4] The chapter therefore seeks to make a modest attempt to fill this gap. This chapter will only focus on the themes of wage and working day of laborers on shrimp-farms and in rural shrimp-be-heading depots (both of which are rural-based) as well as issues surrounding labor control in the sphere of production.[5]

---

4   While aquaculture work has neglected labor issues, labor studies – including the work of geographers and sociologists – suffer from an important problem. Much of this work has shed light on the conditions of work in automobile industries (Rutherford and Gertler, 2002) and cleaning industries (Aguiar and Herod, 2006) and on how workers' cultural practices are a barrier to getting and keeping a job (Bauder, 2005). There is also interesting research on temporary laborers in relation to labor intermediaries – temp agencies (Peck and Theodore, 2001) and 'labor contractors' (Breman, 1996) – and the regulatory role of the state (Peck, 1996). However, in much of the literature, and reflecting a wider tendency in social sciences, the materiality of capital – labor relation is displaced from its central position by a concern with issues of difference, identity, and unionization (Houston and Pulido, 2002: 404; Hudson 2001: 24; Rutherford, 2010: 774). Indeed, the defining aspect of what is called labor geography and new working class studies (Russo and Linkon, 2005) is the agency of organized labor in the making of the capitalist landscape (Castree, 2007; Herod, 2001: 33–37; Tufts and Savage, 2009) in the aquaculture context, see (Oseland et al., 2012). Of course, the materiality of labor is not entirely missing, but to the extent that it is discussed, it has a few problems. One is that the materiality of labor tends to be studied through a framework that does not require much serious theoretical attention to the issue of class exploitation in the spaces of production. Also, most of the work conducted in labor studies, including the geographic literature on labor, is focused on advanced capitalist countries and their cities. This spatial bias must be corrected. For a critique of the labor geography (type) literature, see Das, 2012a, and chapter 4 in Das, 2017a.

5   The life of a laborer cannot be reduced to how much money she receives and how long she toils every day. There are other important issues. These include: the effects of labor process on the working bodies used as 'a strategy of accumulation' (Harvey, 1998), as well as issues of labor control to which men and women are subjected in the hidden abode of production. In some cases, the labor process also involves a degree or violence against people, especially, child workers (see Das and Chen, 2019). It also includes: the discursive dimensions of laborers including their consciousness (which will be very briefly touched on as it relates to the wage-issue) and their 'class-identity' (and indeed various other identities including those that are regional, ethnic and gender-based) (see chapter 10 in Das, 2017a). There is, of course, the theme of class organization (which is stressed in the labor geography literature) (see chapters 11–12 in Das, 2017a).

2   A Labor-Based Approach to Nature-Dependent Commodity Production

Marx's philosophy emphasizes materiality. It also emphasizes relations and their contradictory character or rift-proneness. In terms of materiality, it is important to recognize that conditions for reproduction of life must be continuously produced. And for production to happen, nature and labor are necessary: indeed nature and labor are two sources of wealth (use-values). They are sources of the things we consume. In all forms of society, production requires relations between nature and humans, and relations among humans as they are related to production (these relations are the relations of production). And in a class society, there is always tension – rift – in these relations.

In a social-cultural system of large-scale profit-driven production, more is extracted out of nature in a specific place than is returned to it in that place within a given period of time. This process has been called a metabolic rift, a rift in the system of reciprocal exchanges between nature and society.[6]

That is not the only form of rift. There is a rift in 'human' relations as well. Marx assumes that laborers are paid a wage by the property owners that covers the cost of commodities that are necessary to satisfy their physiological needs as well as the needs that have a 'historical and moral element' (1977: 274–275). This is a useful assumption for investigating exploitation at the level of society, at a given spatial scale over a given period of time.[7] But in a specific place and at a specific time, wages for countless numbers of laborers do not allow them to satisfy their very basic needs, including food.[8] Marx *sometimes* recognizes

---

6   A country's soil nutrients are used to produce agri-commodities which are exported to other countries instead of being consumed and recycled in the place of their production; this causes the metabolic rift (Foster, 2007: 10). It is important to emphasize (pace Foster) that even if there is no export from a country, the metabolic rift can happen if nature is not used sustainably, i.e. if more matter (e.g. trees, or water, or soil nutrients, etc.) is extracted from nature than is given to it within a time period that nature needs to replenish – regenerate – itself) (Das, 2018b).

7   Note that this assumption can be criticized for ignoring unpaid labor performed mainly by women that contributes to the reproduction of labor power sold outside of the home for a wage (see Gimenez, 2005).

8   Marx *sometimes* recognizes this possibility. Indeed, in *Capital* itself, he says that: 'In the chapters on the production of surplus-value we constantly assumed that wages were at least equal to the value of labor power (which is roughly the cost in time of workers' maintenance). But the forcible reduction of the wage of labor below its value plays too important a role in the practical movement of affairs ... In fact, it transforms the worker's necessary fund for consumption ... into a fund for the accumulation of capital' (1977: 747–748). It is this possibility

this possibility, which has not received a lot of attention within political economy perhaps because of the 'Euro-centric'[9] tendency within post-Marx Marxism. In his *Wage, labor and Capital*, Marx says this: while it is true that 'the cost of production of simple labor power [of unskilled labor] amounts to the cost of the existence and propagation of the worker' and that 'The price of this cost of existence and propagation constitutes wages', this statement applies to the *whole* 'race' of laborers, for 'Individual workers, indeed, millions of workers, do not receive enough to be able to exist and propagate themselves' (1976: 27). Indeed, in *Capital* itself, he says that: 'In the chapters on the production of surplus-value we constantly assumed that wages were at least equal to the value of labor power (which is roughly the cost in time of workers' maintenance). But the forcible reduction of the wage of labor below its value plays too important a role in the practical movement of affairs...In fact, it transforms the worker's necessary fund for consumption ... into a fund for the accumulation of capital' (1977: 747–748). There are many reasons why wages may not cover the cost of workers' maintenance. These include: a reserve army of laborers (unemployment/under-employment), caused by constant technological change and independent small-scale producers being converted into wage-labor-dependent people, relative to demand for labor; economic crisis (over-production); and, a balance of power between capital and labor in favor of capital (Marx, 1977; Lebowitz, 2003). When and where wages are low in the specific sense mentioned above, a lot is taken out of 'laboring bodies' (and laboring bodies are a part of nature and have material needs) – in the form of work effort or energy – than is returned to them in the form of wages, resulting in *super*-exploitation, a process not hugely dissimilar to the metabolic rift.[10] In outlining a framework within which to understand these dynamics, one may start with three simple premises.

One is that production of wealth requires nature, and not just labor, as mentioned before. 'Labour is... not the only source of material wealth... As William

---

that the author seeks to investigate in the specific context of the production of the global 'white gold', shrimp.

9   This is 'Euro-centric' for a specific reason: in post-colonial societies, this phenomenon of millions of laborers barely being able to satisfy their bodily (food) needs with the wages they receive from capitalists is much more stark than in advanced capitalist countries of Europe and North America, where the wages received are not only higher, even holding productivity constant (consider per hour wages of a sweeper in India and a sweeper in the US), but are also supplemented with some social benefits from the government.

10   Note that even if wages cover the cost of workers' average needs, there will be still exploitation, a normal level of exploitation. When wages fail to cover workers' average needs, there is super-exploitation.

Petty says, labour is the father of material wealth, the earth is its mother' (Marx, 1977: 134). Capital uses natural forces as it finds them; it also directly transforms these forces to increase their productivity (Boyd, Prudham and Schurman, 2001). An important aspect of nature-dependent production is that it has a degree of inherent unpredictability (ibid.). To these insights must be added another process, one that is generally overlooked in the literature: the biophysical nature of the labor process influences the way labor itself is employed, exploited, and dominated.

The second premise is that labor is the other source of wealth (and indeed, labor is the only source of the capitalist form of wealth as value). Labor takes many forms, the most important of which is wage labor. This occurs where there is a high concentration of land and capital (a process of concentration that began with the original dispossession of peasants) and where the production of use values is driven by the production of value and surplus value. The fact that a large number of people must sell their labor power on a daily basis or for at least a significant part of their living, for an inadequate wage, defines the common fate of much of the global working class. The workplace, the hidden abode of production, and the labor marketplace (the wage relation) crucially affect how people live and work (Carter, 1995; Harvey, 1982: 106–119).

The third premise is that both nature and labor are subjected to relations of rift. Under private enterprise, those who control conditions of production extract more out of the environment in a specific place than they return to it in that place, within a given period of time. This process is called metabolic rift, defined as a rift in the reciprocal exchange between nature and society (Foster, 2007: 10). In the context of a nature-dependent process such as shrimp culture, this rift happens though mangrove destruction and chemical contamination of land and water. Now, laborers (the other source of wealth apart from nature) are *also* subjected to a rift: a lot more is taken out of them than is returned to them. Let us call this the Labor Metabolic Rift (LMR) or the second metabolic rift, to distinguish it from the metabolic rift mentioned above, which can be called environmental metabolic rift (EMR) or the first metabolic rift.

There are three forms of LMR. In LMR 1, capital takes a lot more out of labor than it gives in the form of wages with which to buy the means of subsistence. This is exploitation in its normal sense. This happens *even if* wages are adequate for the normal maintenance of labor. Exploitation in its normal sense can be expressed by presenting what is potentially the best sentence from *Capital* volume 1: 'The fact that half a day's labour is necessary to keep the labourer alive during 24 hours, does not in any way prevent him from working a whole day' (Marx, 1977: 300).

In LMR 2, wages *fall short* of what is needed for the normal maintenance of labor. This is super-exploitation, an above-normal level of exploitation. An extreme form of LMR 2 is LMR 3: the laboring bodies that enter into production are worse in quality than the bodies that had initially entered it. Marx (1977: 342–344) says that under specific conditions, even if workers are paid wages covering the cost of their reproduction, their laboring body (as a means of accumulation) is adversely affected. These conditions include: working longer-than-normal hours (which can reduce the length of the working life of a person by x%, while the daily/monthly wage received during his/her active working life is not increased by x%), a fast pace of work under strict surveillance, working under specific biophysical conditions including the use of hazardous chemicals, night work, and an absence of workplace safety. In its many forms, LMR draws attention to these issues concerning the labor process *as well as* the wage question which concerns the market for wage-labor.

Wages are low and working conditions are objectionable for a variety of conditions that we cannot discuss in detail here. Some of these factors are impacted by the specificity of the production regime, which, in the present context, includes the biophysical character of shrimp production. Very briefly, these conditions include: the level and strategy of accumulation (e.g. certain technologies – mechanical and biological – that are deployed to pump out more surplus value); a reserve army of labor, which reduces the bargaining power of the labor that is employed; the low level of consciousness of workers *vis-à-vis* capital, which adversely affects their bargaining power; and the absence or presence of state support for workers, which also adversely affects their political power. A very important condition for LMR is also the internal differentiation of the working class, based on such relations as gender, race, caste, age, and locational status. This means that: certain segments of the working class are defined as not worthy of the status of a full human being, having one unit of labor power and full citizenship. Such a construct, which is an attack on democratic rights of common toiling people, allows capital to depress their wages below the average, which is already inadequate.

3   The Local, National and the Global Contexts

Shrimp is a major world – commodity produced for a luxury internal and international market. Fewer than 30 countries, the majority of them in Asia, produce shrimp for export to the relatively advanced triad (the US, Japan, and the European Union). Shrimp production increased dramatically (by 650%) from 0.2 million tons in 1985 to about 1.5 million tons in 2002, according to the FAO

(Food and Agricultural Organization). A major shrimp-producing country, India accounts for 8.5% of world production (ibid.). Commercial shrimp aquaculture became a significant activity in India only in the early 1990s when the economic liberalization program was launched (IAA, 2001). Between 1996–97 and 2005–06, on an average, the area dedicated to shrimp farming was more than 155,000 hectares. The highest concentrations of shrimp farms in India are in the eastern coastal provinces of Andhra Pradesh, Tamilnadu, and Odisha; shrimp culture also happens in six other provinces (IAA, 2001). The empirical material for the present study is drawn from Odisha (shown on the map, Map 1: Orissa's name was changed to Odisha in 2010). Odisha has a potential area of more than 32,586 hectares that can be used for brackish-water shrimp culture, out of which 14,231 hectares in its seven coastal districts have been developed for shrimp farming.[11] In 2005–06, more than 8,000 hectares were being used for shrimp farming in Odisha, where shrimps are produced in ponds as well as within net barricades in the brackish-water Chilika Lagoon. The actual labor process in a pond environment is a little different from that in the lagoon, as I will discuss later.

During the period between 1996–97 and 2005–06, annual shrimp production in India averaged more than 105,000 tonnes. Between 2005 and 2007, India exported frozen shrimp worth one billion US dollars each year, most of which went to the US, Japan, and the EU (these data are from various tables in Indiastat.com, a user-fee-based database). According to Odisha's Directorate of Fisheries, shrimp production increased from 6,805 tonnes in 1996–97 to 9,739 tonnes in 2005–06. Odisha's productivity has been above the all-India average. In 2005–06, frozen shrimp worth US $56.94 million was exported from Odisha, most of which went to the US, Japan, the UAE, and European countries. It should be added that Odisha's shrimp culture is export-oriented like that in, say, Thailand, but its shrimp production is dominated more by wage labor than family labor.

Shrimp culture is being promoted by the state in order to increase export and earn dollars.[12] Odisha is not only an important shrimp-producing state; it is also one of the poorest states overall. Out of every 100 people, 36 cannot read or write. According to the 2011 census, it had a population of 42 million (which

---

11   Only 30% of the area consists of small farms (below two hectares) and 7.5% of the area consists of medium-size farms (two to five hectares). The vast majority of the shrimp aquaculture area (57%) is constituted by farms that are at least five hectares in size. 5.5% of the area is under the control of corporate farms. This information is provided in the India Aquaculture Authority report.

12   Also, with the withdrawal of support from the neoliberal governments for traditional farming, some farmers are inclined to switch capital investment to aquaculture.

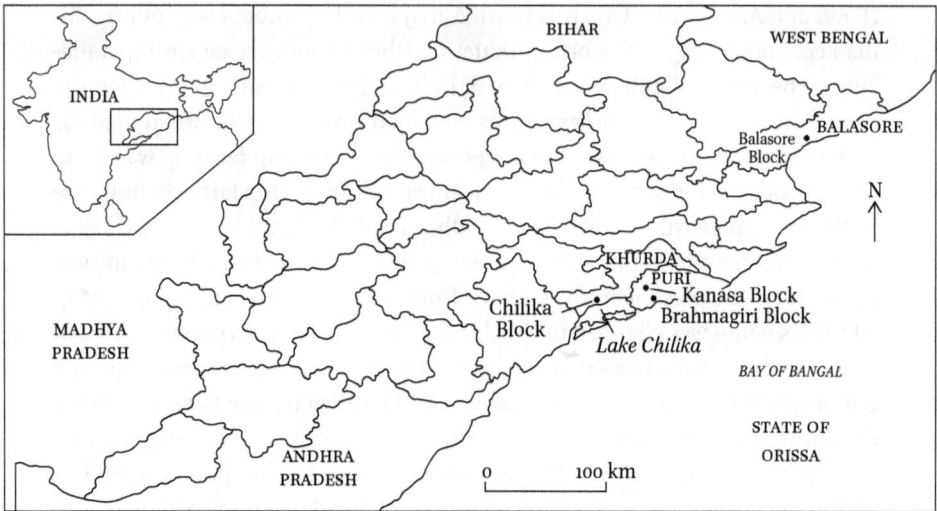

MAP 6.1   Four Blocks located in three shrimp districts
              SOURCE: AUTHOR

has increased to about 45 million in 2018), of which 85% lived in rural areas.
Odisha is divided into several districts, each of which comprises many Community Development Blocks (or Blocks). These are clusters of villages. The
present study was conducted in four Blocks located in three of the seven
shrimp districts (Puri, Khurda, and Balasore) (Map 6.1), which account for
more than half of the areas dedicated to shrimp production. The empirical
analysis in this chapter is predominantly based on the interviews with laborers
about their wages and working conditions, although I do not present too many
quotes.[13]

4   Working for Less and in Poor Conditions: 'Capital' Negated

There is a wide diversity of workers in the shrimp sector. This chapter deals
with workers involved in shrimp farming in Odisha, specifically in the ponds,
and in net barricades. It also deals with those employed in 'depots' where

---

13   The research reported in the chapter is based on 75 in-depth interviews and 5 focus group
       discussions (FGDs) conducted over a period of time (2006–2009) in the four Blocks. 36
       interviewees were wage laborers, including 6 women (note that the bulk of the work is
       done by males), and 3 of the FGDs consisted of wage laborers. The interviewees, selected
       on the basis of snowballing, also included 29 farmers (as well as 1 FGD) and 14 government
       officials and politicians (as well as 1 FGD). The majority of interviews were tape-recorded
       and transcribed. Some were manually recorded.

shrimps are sorted and beheaded. Located in close proximity to the farms, these depots can be seen as a geographical extension of the shrimp farms. The vast majority of laborers work for individual proprietors who own 1–7 ponds. There are less than half a dozen big farms, each of which has 10 to 16 ponds in the fieldwork area in the north. These farms are owned by city-based companies and are run by managers and supervisors on their behalf. I will mainly focus on the conditions that are common to these different kinds of workers, i.e. the workers who work in the ponds, the net barricades and in the depots. The social relations of production within which workers work are those of capitalism.

Shrimp workers work with two kinds of technology: biological (e.g. seeds; chemically contaminated water and medicines) and mechanical (e.g. tractors and spades for earth work; aerating machines; pumps; nets). Workers clear the land, dig ponds, construct and maintain embankments and dykes, release shrimp fingerlings, feed the shrimps, aerate the ponds, guard the farms, and harvest shrimps. Where shrimp culture happens within net barricades, people have to construct these barricades by dipping themselves in water.

Both men and women (including, aboriginal women) participate in earth work to prepare ponds. After the ponds are ready, the work is mainly done by males. Most are children or unmarried young adults. A number of the laborers are mothers, who sometimes bring their little children to the work-sites. They make a little resting place near the ponds for them to play. However, work on shrimp farms is not considered proper for women after the fingerlings have been released into the ponds, except for such work as carrying and breaking ice. Male pond owners do not want to employ women.[14] Women are employed on farms only when men are not available. Besides, working on shrimp farms requires night duty. Staying on the farms at night is not considered safe for women workers.

Most of the laborers are employed on either of two kinds of contract. Those hired on a daily basis do the pond preparation work. They also do the harvest work. The bulk of the work, however, is done by laborers, called 'permanent' staff, who are hired on seasonal contracts. They are employed on the basis of a monthly salary for one season of four to five months. On the few farms owned by city-based companies, which employ up to about 20 people per farm, annual contracts are offered to some people, who do repair work in the off season. Most of the permanent staff live on or near the shrimp-pond embankments. Several people live together in one small makeshift hut. Rainwater sometimes gets inside the huts, making them spend sleepless nights. Many child laborers are afraid to stay in these huts in stormy weather. In one season,

---

14   They fear that women's menstrual blood might affect the water quality in the pond.

two of them died due to lightning in one of the northern villages. Those who work in the net enclosures stay on boats if the enclosure is inside the lagoon, or live in a little hut if it is near the bank of the lagoon.

Permanent laborers are on duty around the clock (or for 16 hours, from 6 a.m. to 10 p.m., in case of company-owned farms). Workers eat and sleep on the farm (or on the boat, in case of the net barricades). These laborers are therefore *working* while eating, cooking, and sleeping. They take turns to sleep. Their 24-hour physical presence makes the theft of shrimps less likely. They stop people from throwing unwanted things in the ponds and protect the shrimps from birds. They have to go under water, even at night, to create waves to make the shrimps move; on big farms, aerating machines are used.

The shrimps have to be fed four times in 24 hours, including twice at night, as per a feed chart given by the owner or the supervisor. If the shrimps are not fed, the laborers are reprimanded. Thus, the biophysical nature of the labor process complements other ways of controlling labor, such as direct supervision (via, for example, the supervisors' gaze; unannounced checks at night) and a bureaucratic method (e.g. the feed chart). The biophysical conditions also have health implications: laborers catch cold and suffer from fever; chemically contaminated water spoils their skin.

Permanent workers receive wages in cash and in kind (i.e. in the form of food). Food comes from the owners' home or is cooked near the pond. In the case of net enclosures, the food is cooked on the boat, and the owner buys the groceries. On company farms, people eat in the company-run kitchen. The vast majority of adult laborers get between Rs. 1,500–2,000 a month for what are practically 24-hour working days. Even discounting the fact that they work while sleeping or eating in their huts, the working day is easily 16 hours. So, the *hourly* wage is Rs. 3–4 (approximately 7 to 9 cents USD). Daily wage workers get Rs. 50–70 a day without food (in 2008–2009). They get a little more during harvest time because of the greater workload. Those working in the net barricades earn a little more (i.e. Rs. 100 or so) because their work is a little harder.

Wages vary from one laborer to another. Women daily-wage earners get Rs. 5–10 less than men for similar work (e.g. earth work). Child workers receive anywhere from Rs. 800–1,200 with food. This is less than what adults get. Larger farms pay a little better than smaller owners. Those workers who are given supervisory duty, who are a little older than ordinary workers (called 'pond boys' on company-owned farms), get Rs. 300–500 more than others. Those who have worked with an employer continuously for more than a season get a little more than the 'first-timers', but even then their wages are not high.

Wages are usually paid *after* the sale of the harvest. As a result, migrants cannot send money home every month. Their family members live on credit, on which they have to pay an interest. Also, many get sick due to the effects of chemicals used in the ponds, so they have to spend money to get better. The net monthly wage (i.e. the gross wage minus the sum of interest payments just mentioned and the money spent on health-care) would be much lower. In all respects, the wage is low.

The wage is low relative to the amount of work performed. It is also low relative to profits made. These profits enhance the lifestyle of the owners. Laborers see or hear about the shrimp farmers' luxurious lifestyle (e.g. their ownership of big houses and motor vehicles). Interviews with owners suggest that a total investment on a one-acre farm, for one harvest of Rs. 300,000, including Rs. 20,000 spent on wages, may generate a total sale of Rs. 450,000. Approximately, this generates a rate of exploitation (profit relative to money spent on wages) of roughly 750% and a rate of profit-on-investment of about 50%. The wage is also low relative to people's needs (i.e. the value of their labor power). An average family needs Rs. 100–120 a day for food (rice or flour, groceries, and vegetables). But laborers do not make much more than Rs. 70–80, and work is not available every day.[15] They produce a delicacy that they can hardly afford to buy. The theoretical assumption in *Capital* that wages cover the cost of production of labor power is empirically negated. Capital extracts a lot more from labor than what it gives labor. Many permanent laborers do not even receive a wage at all or receive only a part of it. This is because of owners' and supervisors' fraudulent tricks. If laborers initially contract to work for the season but leave after a month or so, they are not paid for the days worked. Those who stay on also suffer: employers make deductions from wages saying they incur a loss. Some pay only a part of the arrears and promise to pay the remainder later. Many owners simply delay the payment of arrears. Many employees do not return to claim their arrears.

After the harvest, shrimps are taken to rural depots. As on the farms, there is a gender-based division of labor here. Shrimps are sorted and graded by men. The women's job is to behead the shrimps and to remove legs and shells from shrimps. Many women believe that men cannot sit for hours at a stretch to do this work. The gender division of labor at home may have an effect on that in the workplace.

Unlike men on the farms, women in the depots work for a piece wage. They get paid for filling a bowl with headless shrimps or on a weight basis (see Photo 6.1 below). Daily earnings, usually Rs. 50–70, fluctuate depending on

---

15   In 2004, a family of five in rural India needed approximately Rs. 95 to buy just enough food to provide the minimum of 2,400 calories necessary for normal bodily function (if one does not consume this many calories, one is considered poor) (Patnaik, 2007: 174).

PHOTO 6.1   Women in a shrimp-processing factory in Odisha, India
SOURCE: AUTHOR

how much work they do. Some days can fetch Rs. 100. In the early morning, they go to the supervisors' office to clean the kitchen utensils and sweep the floor, and this work is totally unpaid work. To be able to get the *paid* work, therefore, *unpaid* work must also be performed. Members of a group take turns to do this. *If* they complain or miss a day, they are threatened with the loss of paid work. It seems the household is not the only place of uncommodified, unpaid labor.

In the depots near the lagoon, women do night work. As a focus group discussion and interviews with farmers and politicians confirm, many traditional fishermen, including the husbands of these women, have migrated to cities, as the traditional fishing areas to which the locals had customary access are being increasingly taken over by the larger-scale businesses. So, being in the public places at night may not be safe, given the local conditions (females are usually accompanied by males in public places and at night). Night work is also not good for their health given their duties at home in the day. Also, in the depots, they have to squat for long hours on the wet ground (see Photo 6.1). Their waists, backs, and legs hurt. Their hands develop inflammations and wounds, and even bleed. Their nails are also affected. Like the men on the shrimp farms, they sometimes cannot eat with their hands. They burn newspapers and apply the ash to their wounds for relief. And they do this hard work under the gaze of male supervisors trying to maximize the work effort.

Thanks to the shrimp sector, women shrimp-laborers make substantial financial contributions to their families. This gives them some autonomy and some self-esteem. Although they are unceasingly superexploited, they have not stopped dreaming of a better life: as a woman worker said, she would like to have a house built with bricks, to pay for a good education for her children and to have a savings account in a bank. That the capitalist system has failed to fulfill these simple needs of common people is a cruel fact. There is a flip side, however. It is about the conditions of men. In the southern villages those men who have not migrated do not catch much fish to sell, due to overfishing in the lagoons by rich entrepreneurs, or do not get much wage-work. In the northern region, the use of indigenous migrant workers (and the preference for women laborers in the depots, as in the south), has meant limited work opportunity for men. Sometimes women earn more than their husbands. This creates conflicts, and some women face ill-treatment from their men. Interestingly, the difficult material situation (i.e. the lack of opportunities for earning a living by fishing on one's own account and the low wages offered for wage-work) is forcing a change in male consciousness: some men have accepted the importance of women's financial contribution. This suggests that capitalism seems to have some progressive effect on women's relation with men.

5   Making Sense of Low-Wage Capitalism: From the General
        to the Locally Specific

Why and how are wages in shrimp culture kept so low? Why are conditions of work so poor? And how are these conditions justified by owners and accepted by workers? Clearly, to make a profit, owners must extract a lot more net product out of workers than what they pay in wages. This is the fundamental aspect of the class relation. It is a power relation. It is a powerful imperative. This affects wages and working conditions directly. This class context also affects wages and working conditions indirectly and in complex ways, some of which are associated with neoliberalism.

First of all, the employment situation is fraught with insecurity. Capitalism is coercive. It is so because the majority are *compelled* to work for a wage for living, and whether they obtain wage-work depends on whether a profit can be made from it. Capitalism becomes doubly coercive where people cannot choose between employers. Shrimp workers accept low wages as there is no alternative (self- or wage-)employment. If they complain, they are told 'someone else will work if you don't'. Neo-liberalization of capitalism (relative withdrawal of government support to workers and poor peasants) has contributed to the situation by reducing (self- and wage-)employment opportunities. Employment insecurity can be acute *in specific places* (e.g. traditional fishing areas where people are losing rights to fishing and are relying on wage-work)[16] where owners have enhanced their power to drive down wages and impose poor conditions. Owners do not employ people continuously in part because continuously employed workers might demand an increase in wages.

The regime of overwork – extraction of a maximum amount of work effort in a given time and for a given wage – is indeed connected to the payment of low wages:

> If one man [working long hours] does the work of 1½ or 2 men, the supply of labour increases, although the supply of labour-power on the market remains constant. The competition thus created between the labourers allows the capitalist to beat down the price of labour, whilst the fall in the price of labour allows him, on the other hand, to force up the hours of work still further.
>
> MARX, 1977: 689

The prolongation of the working day increases the amount of work without increasing the number of workers hired. One does the work of two or three. It is this process of forcing workers to provide excessive amount of labor that keeps the commodity produced cheap and globally competitive. A 45-year-old shared his critical insight:

---

16   Trade liberalization has resulted in layoffs in cities, reducing employment opportunities for migrant rural workers. In rural areas, shrinking state investment in development projects has had a similar effect. When neoliberalism created an opportunity for shrimp exports, rich non-fishermen caste people have displaced poorer traditional fishermen in the Chilika Lagoon who increasingly have to depend on wage labor (rather than the direct sale of fish or shrimps). This adds to local unemployment, puts downward pressure on wages, and thus helps export-oriented capitalist shrimp culture. It is as if neoliberalism (= export-oriented high-value production) has secured some of its own conditions of reproduction (= low wages via unemployment through dispossession and state withdrawal of benefits). For a critical analysis of Indian neoliberalism, see chapter 4 of this book, and also Ahmed (2011) and Patnaik (2007).

> We are working at night. And in the day. But we get one salary. The owner
> makes money from this. The laborer is working twice over ... The work we
> do at night for that ... hmmm ... we are not getting any money. The salary
> we are getting is for the work in the day.

The regime of the long working day is associated with the biophysical character of the labor process. The labor process on shrimp farms is a continuous
process; it is like a biophysical assembly line. This means that shrimps have to
be attended to for 24 hours continuously for 4–5 months. The labor process
overlaps with the biophysical production process, unlike in crop farming. Also,
shrimp farming is a little risky: there can be a virus attack, for example, or a
sudden rainfall that can change the pond's salinity. Now, the biological nature
of the labor process contributes to consent to overwork (in Burawoy's sense).
Many, including child laborers, have come to accept this 'infantile' idea, that
shrimps are like little growing children needing care and protection.

However, it is *not* because of the nature-dependent and biological character
of the labor process as such that laborers work long hours. It is rather the *capitalist* character of this biophysical labor process, and further its neoliberal (unregulated) nature, that is behind the long working day, which contributes to
low wages. Surely, shrimps could be looked after in three shifts of eight hours
each, but this would increase wage costs and diminish the global competitiveness of the export-oriented sector. A statement from Marx in *Capital* seems to
accurately describe the situation: 'As soon as peoples ... are drawn into a world
market dominated by the capitalistic mode of production, whereby the sale of
their products for export develops into their principal interest, the civilized
horrors of over-work' begin (1977: 345).

The strategies of extraction of work effort in the depots that contribute to
low earnings are interesting. In the shrimp depots, workers (mostly women)
working on the basis of piece wages work very long hours. Their work intensity
is enhanced through strict supervision (i.e. bureaucratic labor control). This is
also done through the use of biological technology (i.e. technological labor
control) when, for example, chemicals are mixed with shrimps to help workers
process more shrimps. Work output is also maximized through the piece wage
system: the faster one works, the more money, one thinks, is earned. If workers
process more shrimps every hour, they will earn a little more, other things constant. However, workers barely receive the equivalent of a daily subsistence
wage. The piece-wage system acts more like a labor-control system within the
labor process, which allows the entrepreneurs to extract more work from workers, without having to pay more than what would be a daily time-wage. The
definition of the piece itself is contested and resolved in favor of the employer.

Workers are given shrimps in specific containers to behead and are paid by the container. Supervisors pack a lot more shrimps into each container than what they would normally contain, and this strategy reduces earnings. Thus the women workers in depots, like their male counterparts on the shrimp ponds, are subjected to capital's fraudulent tricks. No matter how fast women work, they still take home a wage that barely covers the costs of food. Since many of them do not know counting and they are paid once in many days, they generally depend on their supervisors to maintain the account. They say the wages they receive are less than what is due.

The method of wage payment and the form of wage contribute to the difficult situation as well. As mentioned, the majority of permanent workers are paid only *after* the harvest finishes. Women workers in the depots are also not paid daily. Withholding wages increases profits when arrears are not paid. One may not challenge low wages or bad conditions of work because of the fear of losing the arrears. Thus, withholding wages is also a way of making people stick around and work harder. Describing the situation of the *aqua*-laborers through an 'aqua' metaphor, one migrant worker said:

> [Sometimes] we return [home] without any money. We lack the courage to speak up ...Owners are water ... Labor-boys are thirsty. ... If they wish they will give water. Otherwise, not. If they wish, they will pay money. ... Maliks [owners] are locals. Workers are outsiders.

I now turn to what I have called *vulnerable workers*. The idea of difference is crucial here. Capitalist production, of course, requires labor. But the category 'labor' is a complex one at a concrete level, as suggested earlier, both geographically (local vs nonlocal labor) and socially (in terms of social relations of oppression based on gender, ethnicity, and age). Workers as a class that is subject to exploitation by capital become vulnerable workers when they also experience social relations of oppression. A large number of shrimp farm laborers are young adults or children, as young as 14 or 15 years. Farm owners recruit children from their villages by telling them that they are needed just to scare away crows from shrimp ponds; actually, they end up doing all kinds of work that adults do, including handling heavy aerating machines. When it comes to work, they are treated *as if* they are adults, so more work is expected of, and extracted from, them. But when it comes to wages, they are treated *as if* they are children, so wages can be kept at a low level. Younger workers are preferred to older adults because they can work for less (50–100% less). With no wives or children to look after, these young workers can be on duty for 24 hours. Finally, in a society where younger people are supposed to carry orders from, and respect, older people, younger workers, including children working for mature adults (i.e. the owners and supervisors), are also likely to be docile.

Apart from age, gender is another aspect of workers' social vulnerability. Most of the workers in rural beheading depots are women. Traditional gender norms contribute to their super-exploitation. As mentioned already, in many cases, women contribute substantially to family finances. Like women in other places, they must divide their labor time between home and paid workplace (McDowell, 2001). The crushing burden of work at home and in shrimp depots and the fact that their employment contracts are precariously temporary make collective protest against low wages and poor working conditions difficult. Even when they try to protest at times, male managers shout at them. Bear also in mind the fact, noted above, that the husbands of many of these women are not with them. True, their husbands, like their employers and supervisors, behave in a patriarchal manner, including in situations where their wives earn a little more than them. But often husbands *are* a source of support at home. The family is not only 'a place of unequal power and resources'; it is also a centre of 'elementary solidarities', '"a place" on which working-class people put an understandable value' (Barker, 2006: 73). When women protest, their honor can be at stake, especially in the absence of their husbands and in the absence of any workers' organization.

Many owners prefer to recruit migrants, although for initial pond preparation, locals are also hired: in other words *from where* laborers are recruited is important. For one thing, devoid of local social capital (access to social networks), migrants will not easily be able to steal the 'white gold' (that is, the crop of shrimps) and sell it to local friends and relatives. Given the biophysical character of production, ensuring the safety of the product is paramount: if there is a labor conflict, migrants are also less likely than locals to put poison or some unwanted material in the ponds. The biophysical production demands continuous attention, and locals are more able than migrants to leave work to see their family and friends and perform reproductive duties at home or quit before the harvest in search of a better job. It is generally easier to control non-local labor and extract more work effort and pay low wages. Furthermore, migrant workers do not have a permanent address in the villages where they work. They therefore lack access to a social wage in the form of government benefits, which would otherwise improve the relative power of labor. The way in which their labor power is bought in the marketplace further adds to their difficulty. Sometimes, owners and supervisors travel to the villages to look for workers, including young children. If one gets five but needs three, he gives two to another owner who saves on the recruitment costs. If the latter pays lower wages, laborers cannot protest because they have not entered into *direct* negotiation with their employer, nor can they complain to the person who recruited them but is not their employer.

Many migrant workers are from aboriginal communities. To the extent that wage relations *do* exist, wages *are* lower in these areas as compared to the relatively more developed areas of shrimp culture. This is in part because a portion of the value of these workers' labor power is covered by production on their own land or the sale of forest products. Culturally, people from aboriginal areas are perceived by others as having a simple life with a limited number of needs. So low wages have something to do with the low value of the labor power as well, in the uneven space-economy.[17] Thus the use of politically *vulnerable laborers* – migrants, aboriginal people, children and women – is partly responsible for the low-wage regime. These workers' identity has been constructed in a specific way by the wider population. Individual workers of oppressed groups are socially constructed as those who possess less than one unit of labor power (and indeed as people with less than one unit of citizenship, thus not having the rights that others can enjoy), and this fact allows and justifies the payment of low wages to them. Individuals from aboriginal communities are seen as the ones who lead a simple life (they are not 'modern' enough) and therefore need less to survive. So, they can be paid less than others. Marx assumes that the value of labor power is fixed at a point in time in a given country. This assumption needs to be relaxed where the labor market is characterized by a cultural geography, one where social-moral elements of the value of labor power vary between places.

Finally, there is the issue of the specific forms of workers' and employers' consciousness and political action through which the objective reality of the low-wage regime is reproduced. Employers deduct money from the arrears, citing the loss in business as a reason. Whether the loss in business is real or an excuse, workers will not know for sure, given that they, as workers, have no control over how the enterprises are run. But some of them tend to *believe* the owners. This belief may include an underlying feeling of empathy for the owner, a belief to which the biophysical labor process in shrimp farming contributes. Workers see that sometimes ponds are indeed flooded, and that this or that disease strikes. They also hear that the owner is 'exploited' by the seed and pharmaceutical companies. Many workers seem to have *internalized*

---

17   Marx assumes that the value of labor power is fixed at a point in time in a given country:
      'in a given country at a given period, the average amount of the means of subsistence
      necessary for the worker is a known *datum*' (Marx, 1977: 275). This assumption needs to be
      relaxed where, for example, the labor market is characterized by a cultural geography, one
      where social-moral elements of the value of labor power vary between places.

the business worries of the employer. There seem to be bourgeois instincts of workers rather than working class instincts.

The capital – labor relation is conflict-prone. Employers and supervisors are conscious that workers *can* protest against their condition. So they employ pre-emptive steps to stop any possible unity among workers. Conscious of their interests vis-à-vis workers', the employers thus deploy a micro-geographical strategy aimed at keeping them separated. Once again, the biophysical conditions of shrimp farming are crucial. Employers rely on these to justify their strategy: if workers from different sites mingle, owners say, a virus may spread from one pond to another. In general, there are serious barriers to workers developing solidarity. They are different from one another in terms of where they are from, their ethnic status, age, wages earned, and the fact that they are working on different farms that are geographically scattered. If the workers were allowed to mingle, these barriers might soften, and this is the unspoken logic of the employers' geographical strategy. The reproduction of capitalism, including the low-wage regime, happens through the reproduction of what Lebowitz (2003: 86) calls 'separation' among workers. Spatial separation is one form.

While workers work for low wages under difficult conditions, there is no union – not even a progressive civil society association – to unite them across space. This compounds laborers' difficulty and adds to employers' power, contributing to the regime of low wages and poor working conditions. Local Left parties (e.g. the Communist Party of India [Marxist] or CPM) are oblivious of the plight of, and political vulnerability of, shrimp workers, as it was clear during an interview with a major CPM leader. In northern Odisha villages, CPM members confine their activities to traditional agriculture in support of paddy farmers. In the southern villages around the lagoon, the communist parties, especially CPM and the Communist Party of India (Marxist-Leninist) or CPI (M-L) are focusing almost exclusively on the dispossession of fishermen from traditional fishing areas. That many of the traditional fishermen have become full-time or part-time laborers has not been registered on the Left radar. I had expected to see Left-based mobilization of laborers. The irony is that during the interviews, many shrimp workers themselves, who are not well-educated, said one after another that they *want* unions. A worker from the aboriginal community seemed to sum up my own analysis:

> Because there is not much work available, we are forced to accept whatever wages owners offer us ... If I bargain with the owner individually, he will not listen ... Laborers want to increase their wages. But the owner ... wants to give low wages. ... It would be good to have a union. People will join it. We want it. ... [But] No one is advising us about a union.

6   Conclusion

In an interesting way, the emphasis on agriculture and the neoliberal approach to development have come together. In the late 2000s, the World Bank's *World Development Report 2008* (World Bank, 2007) suggested that agriculture – commercial agriculture, that is – can deliver economic development and poverty-reduction in the Global South. And, internationally, neoliberal approach to development is promoted by the World Bank and other similar institutions. Neoliberalism (which is the main topic of Chapter 4) includes at least two inter-connected things. One is the state's relative withdrawal from welfare provision (which has implications for the social wage and the balance of power between capital and labor over wages, etc.).[18] Another is the promotion of a regime of relatively de-regulated production which is enabled by trade liberalization and which is based on a politically vulnerable non-unionized (mobile) working class to produce cheap commodities for export. These two approaches – stress on agriculture and a neoliberal approach – come together when export-oriented, de-regulated production of non-traditional agricultural goods from poorer countries (to richer countries but not just to richer countries) is encouraged. Shrimp aquaculture is a very important aspect of this process.[19] Shrimp production is a specific instance of a larger system of production. It is a form of 'New Agricultural Production' (NAP): the production of luxury (or high-value) non-traditional agri-commodities for export (Watts, 1996: 232–233). NAP fits in with, and is a part of, a larger process: neoliberalism, or, agrarian neoliberalism.

Social scientists, including economic geographers and sociologists, have critically analyzed the problems of shrimp farmers and the adverse environmental effects of shrimp aquaculture. But they have generally neglected a crucial dimension: the conditions under which men, women, and children *work* for a wage to produce shrimps. The story of shrimp culture has been, more or less, the story of the missing wage laborer. Drawing on in-depth interviews, this chapter has discussed the conditions of laborers in export-oriented shrimp

---

18   Expenditures on rural development as a percentage of national income have come down from 2.8 in 1993–94 to 2.3 in 1997–98 to 1.9 in 2000–01 (Patnaik, 2007: Table 2). Of course, aquaculture production, like production of other things, can happen within capitalist contexts, which may somewhat vary in terms of political power and working conditions of labor (on a comparison of aquaculture in social democratic and neoliberal contexts, see Phyne, 2010).

19   Note that with respect to aquaculture, there is much import and export within the global South as well (Belton et al., 2017).

culture. It shows how the export-oriented production of shrimps results in the reproduction of a working class that works for abysmally low wages and under very poor conditions.

Production of shrimp – like the production of all things – requires labor. In most cases, this labor takes the form of wage-labor. While all wage-laborers *are the same* at one level in that they all have a specific relation (of exploitation) with capital, at another level, wage-labor *is differentiated* along lines of social relations of gender, age, location and ethnicity. The exploitation and domination of aqua-laborers happens in ways in which capitalist relations[20] are mediated by place-specific relations of difference. The exploitation and domination of aqua-laborers are also shaped by the specificities of nature-dependent production (e.g. the biophysical character of labor process). Just as forces of nature such as land and water are 'exploited' in shrimp-culture, meaning that the shrimp-production process extracts a lot more out of nature than it returns to it, laborers on shrimp-farms are similarly exploited: the wage they receive to produce a 'cheap' commodity for export are less than the net value embodied in the shrimps that they produce. Nature and labor become the twin sources of this cheapness. Akin to the metabolic rift, this is a social rift. The two rifts are parts of the same process: relation between capital and the immediate producer.[21]

Shrimp culture is justified by what Bush (2008) calls 'development narratives' or by 'rhetoric of poverty alleviation'. This kind of development discourse around shrimp-farming is contradicted by the materiality of the real situation:

---

20   The capitalist relations in question may include in specific places what Belton et al. have chosen to call 'Quasi-capitalist operations' in Bangladeshi aquaculture that 'combine the use of labour based on both kinship and market relations' and that 'accumulate some surplus capital through the exploitation of wage labour, which may subsequently be deployed in the pursuit of further accumulation by, for instance, reinvestment in expansion, intensification, or diversification' (Belton et al., 2012: 907).

21   Political ecology of shrimp-culture – or what one may more properly refer to as the *political economy* of the environmental and social context of shrimp-farming – must deal with laborers, or laboring bodies of men, women and children, in a serious and a theoretically informed manner. Indeed, one may say that what is called political ecology as such must be concerned with not only the environment and small scale producers directly interacting with it but also wage-labor relations. Unfortunately, that is not the case. Given an anti-class approach in much political ecology, the political is without its class basis. And given its anti-materialist and idealistic approach, nature is treated as social/mental construction of nature, more or less, devoid of its materiality (for examples of this kind of work, see Castree and Braun, 2001; for a sympathetic critique, see Demeritt, 2002). So both the political and the natural/environmental remain under-theorized. In fact, a large part of what is called political ecology is neither political nor ecological.

those who produce shrimps, like millions of people performing other kinds of work, do not receive a decent wage, and are forced to experience all the three forms of LMR (Labor Metabolic Rift). The inadequacy of wages takes many forms. The 'gross wages' are low. Their *net* wages are also low because of the various hidden 'costs of work' (e.g. delayed payment of wages; deductions from wages; costs of illness that is caused by work). Real wages are low in relation to laborers' basic needs. Relative wages – wages relative to the profit – earned by entrepreneurs are also low (workers are aware of this class inequality in part from the lavish life style of the aqua-entrepreneurs). Laborers are working for more than 16 hours a day in inhumane conditions. Groups of four to five persons are herded together in tiny, unsafe huts that can break in rough weather, for four to five months (shrimp-farming season). To Kautsky's words (1988: 385), they work 'like beasts of burden by day [and are] housed worse than beasts of burden by night'. In spite of laws against child labor, a large number of children are employed who 'are far more defenseless than adults' (Kautsky, 1988: 352). Some of them are effectively unfree laborers, unable to negotiate with the private entrepreneurs over wages and working conditions. The conditions of aqua-laborers discussed here, including the ways in which their lives in the workplace and labor market are controlled, are similar those of the workers subjected to sweatshop conditions more generally (Mezzadri, 2016, 2018; Pattenden, 2016).

The regime of low wages and poor working conditions in shrimp areas, as elsewhere, is caused and reproduced by multiple concrete mechanisms. These include: the precarious employment situation. Increasingly divorced from the means of production such as land and access to water bodies, and without savings or secure long-term employment, workers, including women and child workers, rely on this or that capitalist for their social reproduction. Each owner presumes that the workers whom they employ only for 4–5 months will somehow survive for the rest of the year from family production, meager crumbs thrown at their families in their own villages from the government whose welfare commitment is dwindling, or from the employment by other owners. If employers have to employ certain workers on a more permanent basis, they might have *some* interest in their long-term social reproduction. This is not the case. Shrimp-workers are paid below-subsistence wages. The other concrete mechanisms behind the regime of low wages and poor working conditions include specific strategies on the part of the employers: deliberate delay in, and withholding of, the payment of wages; strict labor control regimes including use of chemicals maximizing work effort; the fraudulent tricks of employers; and capital's power to impose and define the 'piece' and the 'wage' in the piece-wage system, even in the face of occasional protests. Interestingly, these are some of the processes that Marx talks about in *Capital* volume 1.

There are also several subjective processes that reproduce low-wage capitalism. These include the specific form of working-class consciousness that suggests a form of empathy for the 'suffering' employers. This is a form of consciousness – a bourgeois consciousness of workers – that overlies an incipient 'anti-capital' consciousness, or consciousness in its 'embryonic form' as Lenin says in his *What is to be done?* (Lenin, 1977a: 113). Underlying workers' empathy for employers who pay low wages and commit what Marx would call 'fraudulent tricks' (cited in Lapides, 2008: 145, 208) is the mistaken idea that wages are paid to a laborer out of the sale of products of her labor. According to this idea the magnitude of wages depends on the actual price at which the employer is able to sell the shrimps, so if shrimps sell for less, wages will be less. Shared by both employers and laborers, this idea contributes to the reproduction of capitalist relations. Marx criticized it thus:

> Let us take any worker; for example, a weaver. The capitalist supplies him with the loom and the yarn. The weaver applies himself to work, and the yarn is turned into cloth. The capitalist takes possession of the cloth and sells it...Now are the wages of the weaver a share of the cloth..., of the product of his work? By no means. Long before the cloth is sold, ...the weaver has received his wages.
> MARX, 1976: 18

Therefore, 'Wages are not a share of the worker in the commodities produced by him. Wages are that part of already existing commodities with which the capitalist buys a certain amount of productive labour-power' (Marx, 1976: 36). The *fact* that wages are being paid *after* the shrimp-harvest is sold – note that this already represents delayed payment of wages – contributes to this *illusion* in the minds of workers.

Workers' spontaneous consciousness is generally contradictory. While there is evidence of illusion as just mentioned, there is also evidence that workers are conscious of the fact that their situation is objectionable, unjust and injurious. While many workers are conscious of the need to be organized against these conditions, some show more passive resistance. This is indicated by one person when he said (and it is worth repeating): 'No one should work in shrimp-culture in his or her life'. What if a large number of workers believe in this? What if local branches of Left parties suddenly have their veil over their eyes removed? Unfortunately, the reality is that the locally-based Left parties have failed to do anything to mobilize workers and raise the workers' consciousness. All this suggests the need for an investigation of the *absence* of workers' anti-capital agency, even in a trade-union form.

One can see that each of the processes underlying the low-wage regime discussed above is connected to the politics of wage-labor relations, i.e. to the issue of the balance of power between capital and labor. Even such economic factors as unemployment causing low wages are not just economic factors: unemployment makes political resistance against low wages difficult to launch, and hence wages tend to be low. But employers know that workers *can* resist. That is why they take pre-emptive steps to stop any possible unity among workers.

The relations between capital and labor are being mediated by specific social relations (and constructions) of gender, age, and ethnicity (one of whose local forms is 'tribality'). These are utilized by employers to create a vulnerable workforce, which makes it possible to superexploit without much political trouble. Importantly, relations between capital and labor are also mediated by the geographical character of labor. Generally, a social wage (e.g. government welfare) and local 'social capital' can tip the balance of power between the employer and the employee slightly, in favor of the employee. Migrant workers, however, are denied this advantage. At one level, capital's laborers do not have to be migrants or women or children. But in actual practice, in specific places and times, social difference makes a difference to capital.

It is also important to notice how the relation between capital and labor operates through the biophysical nature of the labor process. This happens in many ways. The shrimp production process is nature-dependent: it can be affected by unpredictable rains and floods. Shrimps can catch diseases. We need to, however, connect the nature of the nature-dependent production to its social (capitalist) nature. Consider how the unpredictability of the biophysical process as well as the fact that the production process is continuous (i.e. shrimps have to be looked after for 24 hours) contribute to a form of consent to the regime of long hours and difficult (night) work in the mind of laborers: people are made to believe that shrimps are like children, can become sick, and need to be constantly looked after through long hours of work. The biophysicality of the labor process acts as a mask to hide its capitalist character. It also acts as a form of labor control: if shrimps have not been fed well throughout the night at proper intervals, the employer will know this from a specific form of the physical movement of shrimps.[22] Aqua-labor is controlled in other

---

22   This form of labor control is in addition to other mechanisms being used: direct supervision; and 'bureaucratic' methods such as feed charts.

ways as well. For example, women laborers' work intensity is sought to be enhanced through the use of chemical technology when, for example, chemicals are mixed with shrimps to help the laborers de-head them faster. Ensuring the safety of the biological product (shrimp) is paramount; this leads the employers to hire nonlocals who are easier to discipline and who have limited ability to inflict Luddite style class revenge (e.g. by harming the shrimps in the event of a labor dispute). The biophysical process also affects laborers' health, producing what Fracchia (2008) would call the 'body in pain'. The men, women and children, who produce a popular delicacy for the national and global markets, cannot even eat with their hands the simple food (rice, etc., and not shrimp) that they can buy with their meager wages. Their hands have blisters due to the use of chemicals at the production and beheading sites. It is as if each shrimp, a commodity, records in its body the annals of low wages, unending night shifts, and long hours of work as well as the unfulfilled desire of the poor laborers, men and women, to enjoy a socially acceptable level of living.

Workers' conditions are of little concern to owners, however. If one worker is crippled, another can be hired. There are substitutes in plenty. There is a great deal of labor power in situ, whose production has no cost to individual employers. But if one shrimp is below the expected size or if it dies, what is lost for ever is value and surplus value (i.e. the amount of labor used), which have no substitute. When a use-value (e.g. edible shrimps) produced by the worker is lost, the value is also lost, and with that, any surplus value in it is also lost. If shrimps are not healthy, owners cannot sell them in the global market for an expected profit. So the health of the non-human living creatures is of much greater interest to the moneybags than the well-being of human beings. Human labor, in its metabolic relation with nature, produces shrimps, but shrimps, when turned into commodities, and the commodities for export, become more 'valuable' than human beings and their labor. A general point to note is that: the capitalists' interest in living beings is not because of their respect and care for life-forms, even if some of them could be animal rights activists, but because certain life-forms support the value-form of production, i.e. the production of value and surplus value.

Like many other export commodities from the countries of the periphery, shrimps are being produced dominantly under social relations of global capitalism.[23] This is capitalism based on formal subsumption of labor (which is the

---

23   And the story of shrimp laborers cannot be entirely their story. Indeed, their story is also
      that of most laborers producing other commodities for export in the periphery; it may be
      recalled here that euphoric accounts of export-oriented industrialization were even used

topic in Chapter 3), a mode of capitalist production based on long working days and the payment of low wages (i.e. wages that do not even cover subsistence needs). Formal subsumption of labor comprises what I called earlier in this chapter LMR 2 and LMR 3 (as well as LMR 1).[24] Wages and the working day are touching their physical minimum and physical maximum respectively. In the context of global demands for reduced state intervention in national economies, Third World comparative advantage supposedly lies in 'cheap' environmental and labor resources. 'Cheap', however, only signifies the relationship between exchanged commodities; hidden are the material realities of production, including the state's vital complicity, which permits such commodities to appear in the world market as 'cheap'. It is also unlikely that the low-wage regime described here is specific to the spatial context under study. It is likely to be common to most shrimp-exporting poorer regions in the world.[25] Export-oriented capitalist production of succulent shrimps results in, and is based on, the reproduction of a working class in its crippled state[26] that nonetheless continues to ensure the production of this global commodity. To the extent that natural resources and labor are used to produce subsistence goods for export to richer countries (more or less, of the imperialist bloc), this process potentially contributes to the decline in the value of labor power in the richer countries and higher rate of appropriation of surplus value in its relative form there.[27]

The conditions of work that low-wage aqua-workers experience as reported in this Chapter are similar to those of workers studied by other scholars. Basile (2013) discusses the low-wage capitalism in the context of the industrial district for silk production in rural South India. Pattenden (2016) talks about the harsh labor control regime in rural South India. Mazzadri (2016) reports

---

against radical development theory, which sought to analyze the limits of the extent to which capitalism could benefit workers in the periphery in a genuine sense.

24   The concept of subsumption is not always applied in a way Marx used it, as we have seen in chapter 3. In a study of aquaculture in China, Huang (2015: 403) says: the 'stage of "formal subsumption" [is] when agri-capital operates discretely through the monopoly of "inputs" and allows the continuation of individual labour'.

25   Economic globalization – development of the world market – is very democratic: it has a tendency to create a situation where all the human beings who must work for a wage, more or less, work and live under similar inhumane conditions.

26   The exact nature and magnitude of this state – in terms of mortality and morbidity and overall physical and mental health conditions – must be the topic of a separate detailed discussion.

27   This also represents the imperialist transfer of value (see Smith, 2016).

sweatshop conditions in garment production in multiple cities in India, shedding light on the interconnection between processes of class formation and patriarchal norms in globalized production circuits. Mazzadri's observations on the capitalist exploitation of women, including its effects on their bodies, reflect the conditions of child and women workers reported in this Chapter. Similarly, just as aqua-workers produce a high-value product which they cannot afford to consume, Mies's (2012) lace-workers produce a high-value product which they cannot use: Mies examines the ways in which women are used by capital to produce luxury goods for the Western market and simultaneously not counted as workers or as producers in their fragmented workplaces. Instead they are defined as 'non-working housewives'. This is similar to the fact that the perception of child workers being necessarily and always a secondary source of financial support for their families is a justification for why they are paid low wages in aqua-culture in the areas that I study. Bannerji (1995: 31) makes a general point: 'There is a direct connection between lower value of the labour [power] of women in general ... and the profit margin'.

Relevant here is Marx's (1977: 164) notion of commodity fetishism where relations between commodities produced (in different places) replace relations between people producing these, both in reality and in our consciousness, and where it appears as if being bought and sold for a profit is in the very DNA of a thing such as shrimp.[28] That a dollar can buy – or that a certain amount of a product can be exchanged for – several counts of cheap foreign shrimps, this relation of exchange, is not written in the body of this commodity-shrimp, how-much-ever we may twist and turn and pinch these edible creatures. Much rather, this relation of exchange is based on specific social relations under which the laboring creatures producing this commodity live, work and suffer. These are the social relations of property and of production, the class relations. These relations signify the fact that common men and women do not have control over social production, which is why the following is also a fact: the objective material interest of every laboring person is in buying as many counts of shrimp (or as much of any other commodity they need) for every dollar they have, which represents a certain amount of labor-time that

---

28   The argument is not that if people just understand that shrimps and other similar commodities are produced under inhumane conditions, these conditions will disappear and that there will be no commodity fetishism.

they themselves have sold under conditions that they, just like aqua-laborers, do not control. These conditions are given by the extant class relations, whether in India or elsewhere. And these class relations are defended by the state. In the next chapter, we will examine the class character of the Indian state, and whether it has been able to alleviate the conditions of workers.

Class Relations, Class Struggle, and the State in India

It is a truism that in order to understand the economic issues such as poverty and development that confront India (or any other country, for that matter), one must investigate the nature of the state, for the economic is a deeply political matter and the political is 'concentrated economics'.[1,2] It is not surprising that the state in a large, under-developed capitalist country such as India, has been the subject of much discussion. To gain an adequate understanding of the state, it is important to unpack the class context of the state, both in terms of class structure and the struggle of the lower classes who are not only exploited but are also social oppressed. And then there is the institutional materiality of the state itself, including its democratic and territorial form, that needs to be stressed. Like all relations, the relations between the state and its class context are potentially contradiction-ridden and the reasons for this need to be examined.

This chapter contains seven sections, of which the first examines how the Indian state has been examined by scholars and what is problematic about their views, setting the context for an alternative view of the state. Sections 2–3 show how the state has been influenced by its 'base' in the dominant classes, and how the relations between property-owning classes and between them and the upper bureaucracy work. Section 4 discusses the relation between the state and lower classes. Section 5 deals with the state-form (territorial and liberal-democratic form) and lower-class struggles. Implications of the politically contradictory nature of state intervention in relation to uneven development and neoliberalism are outlined in Section 6, while Section 7 contains a brief conclusion.

1   Existing Views on the Indian State: A Critical Review

Rudolph and Rudolph (1987), and indeed, many others who have followed them, look upon the state as a third actor which has seemingly marginalized

---

1 An earlier version of this chapter appeared as Das (2007).
2 Lenin (1921) says: 'politics is a concentrated expression of economics...'.

both capital and labor and plays an autonomous role.[3] There is a Marxist counter-part of the autonomous state: Lockwood (2014) argues that the Indian state is an autonomous agent as it is a part of production relations. However, the state autonomy approach, especially, that of the Rudolphs, substantially under-estimates the dominant class bias of the state. Bardhan (1998) characterizes the state as an 'above the fray' arbiter between dominant classes, responding to the interests of these 'classes'.[4] Adopting a problematic approach to class (within so-called analytical Marxism), this view does not say much about the actual exploitative class relations and the role of the Indian state in reproducing them.

Chibber (2003) seeks to conduct a class analysis of the Indian state. He says that: contrary to common belief, in the early years of post-colonial India, the Indian capitalist class did not embrace state planning, and that it did not allow the construction of a developmental state, which could have disciplined the capitalist class as in East Asia. The capitalist class accepted, and benefitted from, import-substituting industrialization, which ensured protection from external competition, and the capitalist class received subsidies from the state, but it thwarted state initiatives to regulate industrial activity which were thought necessary for rapid industrial transformation.

Chibber thus seeks to counter the perception that the Indian state was socialist before neoliberal policies began. It was not, he rightly says. The capitalist class was in favor of state intervention but it did not want to be told how to use the resources it received (Chibber and Usmani, 2013: 207). That class wielded tremendous power in making the state do what it wanted (e.g. scaling back the power of the planners). The Indian state always supported capital but its modalities of support changed. During Nehru's times, the state gave resources to the capitalist class as a whole but kept individual capitalists at arm's length. The state kept its instrumental autonomy, in other words. The planners thought that capitalism was necessary for development but capitalists were not to be trusted in the halls of power. After the mid-1980s, business class's proximity to policy-making grew. As well, the business houses which were new and which did not have much link to the state became more vocal and demanded liberalization.

It is not clear to me why any Marxist would expect the capitalist class to subordinate itself to the state to any significant extent and without complaint, except in exceptional cases.[5] Whether or not the Indian capitalist class refused

---

3   For recent reviews of the Rudolphs's work, see: Sarangi (2017), and Sinha (2016).

4   This is the standard neoclassical argument (see Caparaso and Levine, 1989).

5   These cases include South Korea. American imperialism used Korea (and Japan) as a battle-field against communism, so the USA supplied resources and bore the cost of their military

to be controlled and disciplined by the Indian state via the latter's planning mechanisms, becomes an important question, not for Marxists, but mainly for those – from the Right on the political spectrum – who take, and who took, the claim at its face value that the Indian state was a socialist state. Marxists do not need to be convinced that ultimately it is capital that decides what the state does or does not do and that the Indian state was – and is – an out-and-out capitalist state. And a capitalist class that funded the architect of anti-colonial struggle (Mr. Mohandas Gandhi) was not going to give away what it achieved (i.e. getting rid of some of the foreign shackles on its growth) by having to obey the disciplining rules of the new state at the cost of its interests, beyond a tolerable limit.

There are several other problems with Chibber's 'class' view of the state. (1) The state-class relation cannot be understood adequately within a framework such as Chibber's that abstracts from (a) the *totality* of the relations between the proprietary classes and the classes they exploit, *including in rural areas*, and (b) the global situation (e.g. imperialism's connection to an economy, both during colonial times and after formal de-colonization, a connection that imposes limits to economic development processes in the periphery). Chibber's view is more or less an instrumentalist view of the state. However, whether the instrumental control over the state happens – whether or not the capitalist class and/or its individual members direct the state and write its documents or initiate a legislation, and so on – is, more or less, beside the matter, as far as defining the capitalist character of the state is concerned. (2) To say that the state failed to become a developmental state because it failed to develop its political capacity to discipline the capitalist class, is to explain one political process in terms of another political process (Chibber, 2006), so the approach is more politicism that characterizes liberal/left-liberal thinking, and less class-analysis. In a capitalist society, it is normal to expect that the capitalist class would thwart being controlled, unless there are strong counter-vailing mechanisms (e.g. war; imperialism, etc.). What needs to be explained is why in certain cases the capitalist class agrees, however temporarily, to being controlled or why it can be controlled against its wish? (3) To say that India did not become another East Asia because appropriate state policies could not be in place is to assume that state policies as such could develop the productive

---

protection. American market was opened to exports from Korea. What the Korean case illustrates is this: individual members of the capitalist class could be persuaded to listen to the state (and thus regulate their tendencies towards anarchic competition) because the state, operating in an international environment that was made favorable by imperialism, ensure conditions for profit-making.

forces under capitalism, as if relations between capital and labor domestically and the imperialist context in which such relations exist, do not matter, i.e. as if the capital-labor relation in India, and imperialism as the global-level class relation between the big business of militarily powerful advanced countries and direct producers of India and similar other countries, do not create obstacles (limits) to the development process, whether in farming or industry in the periphery. The relationship between the state and class, or between the state and the capitalists, cannot be seen just from the standpoint of whether state can, or cannot, promote the development of productive forces. The matter of economic development is only partly determined by the success of state policy. To assign a greater role to state policy in capitalist development is another piece of liberal/left-liberal thinking that seeks to support the agenda of the reproduction of capitalism in slightly modified form (e.g. regulated capitalism). (4) Chibber's class analysis of the state implies a critique of the neoliberal ideas (that the state was socialist, that its socialist interventions were behind slow economic growth, and therefore the state must let private players do what they want), but that critique is from the standpoint of a left-liberal/social-democratic, or capitalist-state-developmentalist, framework like the one he prefers. In contrast, class analysis of the state must be from a thorough-going Marxist angle. The Marxist angle is one that prioritizes the relation between proprietary classes, and between them and the exploited classes, and sees the state and the capitalist class, more or less, as two arms[6] of capital-as-a-class-relation, within which disagreements, including over who should listen to whom and how much, are intra-family matters.[7]

As if to echo Chibber's views, Harriss (2013: 212) makes the following claim: 'failures of planning in India had to do with the attempt at combining it with accommodative democratic politics that actually gave power to the big bourgeoisie and to the dominant landowning peasants, who were able in effect, between them, to hold the state to ransom'. Harriss adds: 'The power structure of the Indian state still constrains redistribution', in spite of 'a second democratic upsurge' (i.e. protests by lower and middle castes). So here the implication is that it is democracy – politics – that has given power to the capitalist

---

6   In terms of agency, the two arms are: state actors (top officials and politicians) and members of the capitalist class organized in informal groups and chambers of commerce, etc. It is interesting that members of the capitalist class who authored the Bombay plan – the Indian capitalists' manifesto – also joined the National Planning Commission (Chandra, 1999: 217).

7   According to Naseemullah (2016), the Indian state is not weak or captured but internally divided and thus disarticulated, because of a deep and enduring political conflict between those who wish to use the state as a tool to transform society and those who see it as a means to preserve the current social relations.

class. Such a view under-conceptualizes the structural power of the capitalist class.

In the neoliberal approach to the state, the state apparatus invariably appears as oversized and too powerful.[8] This in turn permits it to be characterized as a barrier to the development of free enterprise, an approach which licenses the view that a minimalist state will be the one to ensure prosperity (see Tendulkar and Bhavani, 2007). However, as argued in Chapter 4, this minimalist apparatus, the neoliberal Indian state, is actually a maximalist one: it intervenes where and when necessary, so as to facilitate the exploitation of workers and small-scale producers by capital, whether domestic or foreign, rural or urban.[9]

In the institutional approach, the Indian state is seen in terms of the policy process, (i.e. in terms of what it does), and in terms of the differences between the branches of the state (Sinha, 2011: 50). But the question of the conditions of the existence of the state and of its power, which is expressed in its policy-making, remains under-theorized. Sinha says that the state is not to be seen as a homogeneous entity that constrains the bourgeoisie. The state is to be seen as segmented and porous: regional elites, provincial governments, the associations of the big business, bureaucracy of the federal government, all lobby for policies in their favor. Similarly, Sundar (2011) argues that every Act (law) of the state is ultimately a product of governmental bureaucracies, reflecting the *state's* imperatives at a point in time (e.g. to check Naxalism), and is subject to the acceptance of government officials at different levels, if it is to be implemented, even if 'there are interstices through which people can express their legislative power' (p. 187). In other words, for both Sinha and Sundar, the state is an autonomous institution whose roots in class relations are under-theorized.

The Indian state has also been examined by scholars who are, to varying degrees, influenced by the cultural turn (postmodernism/post-structuralism/post-colonialism) (Corbridge, 2001; Corbridge et al., 2004; Gupta and Sharma, 2006; Kaviraj, 1992, 2011). For exponents of this approach, the state is discussed in terms of its 'fragility' and 'fluidity', and of the meanings attached to it by citizens, including by villagers. Building on ethnographic studies, scholars point to 'the ways in which state institutions, practices, and discourses interact with cultural registers and modes of practice that lie outside formal institutional structures, thereby extending the influence of state institutions into everyday life but also transforming the experience of the state in the process' (Witsoe,

---

8 This is not to be confused with the concept of the 'over-developed' state (Alavi, 1972; also Saul, 1974).

9 On different aspects of the state under neoliberalism, see Sarmah and Barua (2014).

2011: 74; see also Premchand, 2017). They show how "the state" actually manifests itself within local contexts. They argue that there is a:

> need to take more account of the ways in which political practice shapes people's experience of the state – a move that necessarily leads to an awareness of the multiple ways in which the state is imagined.
>
> WITSOE, 2011: 74

They say that there are 'the specifically postcolonial ways in which state power is experienced in India, although wrought with insidiously direct forms of oppression and violence'. The ways in which the state works 'have also opened spaces for potentially radical democratic challenges to established power based on very different concepts of popular sovereignty and "social justice"' (ibid.).

The state is thus a collection of 'people' just as society itself is an aggregate of 'people', some of whom are poor or lower-income groups and interact with and 'see' the state.[10] The on-going and local-level interaction – inter-penetration – between the state and those who are called citizens is emphasized (Kruks-Wisner, 2018).[11] Out of sight in this conceptualization is the class character of the 'people', 'citizens' and 'state actors'.[12] The state's caste character is stressed.[13] But once again, the class relations underlying caste are cast away (see the excellent Marxist work on caste by Singh, 2014, who argues that the

---

10   The concept 'people' is always designed to hide class differences, especially when used interchangeably with 'the nation'. These Weberian categories, of 'people' who 'see' the state, are consistent with the Weberian view of the state as a mere organization. Class is doubly banished: from 'sight', and from those who do the seeing.

11   For example, Kruks-Wisner (2018) examines 'citizen-state relations, asking who makes claims on the state for social welfare, and why. The frequent, but varied ways in which citizens engage in claim-making reflect the state's deeper local penetration and, simultaneously, the increasing porousness of social and spatial boundaries. The state, through decentralization and a proliferation of social welfare programs, has become more visible while citizens have become more mobile, leading to a greater frequency and intensity of citizen – state encounters. Under these conditions, ... social and spatial exposure fosters claim-making. Those who traverse boundaries of community and locality are more likely to make claims on the state and to do so through a broader array of practices than are those for whom such boundaries remain more rigid' (p. 157).

12   On a critique of the culturalist framework, see Mannathukkaren (2011).

13   There are various studies on caste, from the standpoint of the state. Mosse (2019) talk about how caste has been studied in social sciences, including in terms of the effect of affirmative action policies in public-sector education and employment. De Zwart (2000) says that caste exists not as a fact of Hindu life but because of colonial and post-colonial governments: the government defines social categories (or official constructions) under

secret of caste lies not in Hindu religion but in political economy).[14] In the cultural approaches, the citizens who are supposed to be interacting with the state are not passive agents, and that is good, but citizens are seen as contesting, not the class aspects of the state and society but only/mainly relations of subordination or the relations between the governed and those who govern, and such contestation happens often outside of the sphere of formal rules and structures.[15] The underlying notion of the state is that it is merely a power relation, but why is there a need for state actors to exercise power relations and in whose interests they do so? Might there be a relation between power relations and the class character of the state?

This literature complements the macro, national level structuralist treatment of the state, in which the state appears to be disembodied and working without the involvement of social agents. But it comes at a cost: this literature, influenced by the post-turn (or the cultural or discursive turn) is largely silent on the materiality of the state, on its solidity, its coherence, all of which come mainly from its class logic. It is the latter which one should be able to infer from, and which in turn shapes, everyday interaction.

Linked to this literature is the recent social capital approach (Das Gupta et al., 2004; Krishna, 2002) which seeks to chart a middle path between the class (= societal) view of the state and a perception of it as 'autonomous'. Those who

---

which people must register in order to qualify for the material benefits such as jobs and education, a fact that has made these constructions real in their consequences.

14   Witsoe (2011: 74) says that: 'the experience of "the state" in India is *intimately* connected with the experience of caste, the changes associated with the politics of lower-caste empowerment have transformed the ways in which people imagine the postcolonial state'. Witsoe (2011) also says: 'The specificities of what could be meaningfully termed "postcolonial governmentality" in India are reflected in the ways in which these techniques of governance – exercised in relation to development discourse – are combined in practice with relations of dominance and subordination articulated in relation to caste, forming a hybrid mode of governance wherein the exercise of violence outside of the legitimated routines of "the state" is a standard aspect of political life. It is therefore not surprising that caste identities have profoundly shaped the ways in which people imagine the state, and vice versa' (p. 75).

15   Chatterjee (2004) argues, in India's postcolonial context, there is a distinction between the civil society of the elites (the realm of formal structures and rules which are inhabited by bureaucrats, technocrats and academic people, etc. imagining and interacting with the state) and the political society. The state's interaction with the majority happens within political society which comprises networks and groups, like slum dwellers' associations and (caste) mafias, whose very existence is predicated on illegality. 'Following this logic, one can differentiate between elite conceptions of "the state" emphasizing law-bound institutions of governance imagined as separate from "society" and imaginings of the state generated from political society' (Witsoe, 2011: 74). The class origin or the class aspect of caste is neglected.

hold this view maintain that relations of complementarity and synergy exist between on the one hand state officials, who are relatively insulated from dominant class pressures, and on the other the poor majority. The former are thus able to help the latter secure development inputs and benefits from an otherwise unsympathetic state. Such an over-optimistic view has been criticized by Das (2005) and Fine (2001). Here it is sufficient to note that, like the 'everyday state' literature, this view under-theorizes the class character of the state, and is therefore too sanguine about its development role vis-à-vis the poor.

Against such views is a historical materialist class-theoretic interpretation of the Indian state, which is deployed here. Just as political-economic processes discussed in earlier chapters are class processes and concern class relations, so do the fundamental aspects of the state. As I have said in Chapter 2, what is necessary is an emphatic reassertion of the validity of class analysis, now out of academic fashion, with particular reference to the formation, reproduction and agency of the state. Such an approach stresses that the state cannot but reflect – and is thus driven by – class interests, albeit in ways that are sometimes contradictory (Das, 2006). Even in apparently structurally autonomous quotidian behavior and relations, therefore, the material fact of class is the most important social context affecting the conditions under which lower classes (i.e. workers and small-scale producers of different castes in urban and rural areas) live and work.[16] Capitalist relations, along with what are taken to be 'pre-'/'non-'capitalist relations in rural areas where they exist, define this class context. Scholars in the 'post-tradition' are mistaken to *focus* on the formal and informal relations of political power between those who rule and those who are ruled. Such relations are not unimportant, theoretically or politically. But they need to be seen within the context of the relation between those who control society's productive resources and those who do not. This is the context which shapes the class character of the state, which in turn shapes its relation with those who are ruled. As Marx explains in *Capital* volume 3:

> The specific economic form, in which unpaid surplus-labour is pumped out of direct producers [i.e. specific ways in which class relations work], determines the relationship of domination and servitude [or, the relationship between rulers and ruled], as it grows directly out of production

16   Indian capitalism, like capitalism in other ex-colonial contexts, emerged out of the interaction between pre-capitalist society with capitalist colonialism. So there are classes other than workers and capitalists; as well, capitalism exists with pre-capitalist mechanisms in specific localities, and this situation affects the nature of the state (Mazumdar, 2016: 232).

itself and, in turn, reacts back on it as a determinant. ... It is in each case the direct relationship of the owners of the conditions of production to the immediate producers ... in which we find the innermost secret, the hidden basis of the entire social edifice, and hence also the political form of the relationship of sovereignty and dependence, in short, the specific form of the state in each case.

MARX, 1991: 927; parentheses added

However, there is more to the relation between class and the state than indicated above. The fact that the relation between classes shapes the state's relation with society in the general way that it does as indicated above:

does not prevent the same economic basis – the same in its major conditions – from displaying endless variations and gradations in its appearance, as the result of innumerable empirical circumstances, natural conditions, racial [or caste] relations, historical influences acting from outside [e.g. imperialism], etc. from showing infinite variations and gradations in appearance, and these can only be understood by analyzing these empirically given conditions.

MARX, 1991: 927–928; parentheses added

This is the perspective that is deployed here in this chapter. The class relation shapes the relation between the rulers and the ruled, and the latter relation, in turn, shapes the class relation, within a system of relations in which the class relation, ultimately, is fundamental. And the relation between classes and the state itself is shaped by various empirically-existing conditions, including mechanisms of social oppression (e.g. caste, gender),[17] external connections such as economic globalization, and so on. The class character of society and of the state does not (and cannot) operate in a vacuum: it is accordingly reproduced and impinged on – among other things – both by ideologies and practices of caste, ethnicity, religion, nationality, regionalism and gender, and by the political form of the state itself, which includes the democratic form and its geographical (e.g. federal form).[18] Since capitalism is the dominant mode of production in India, the state is predominantly a capitalist apparatus, and as

---

17   While many Indian feminists accept Marxists' class theory of the state, they also add that the Indian state is also patriarchal (Menon, 1999: 12).

18   On the state's relation not only with caste but also with ethnicity, nationality, regionalism and gender, see Beteille (2007), Chakrabarti (2001), Kumar (2017), Mohanty (2004), and Singh, 2014. On the state's democratic form, see Austin (2003), and on its geographical form, see Das (1998b), and Sinha (2003).

such an agent of capitalist development nationally and locally.[19] For this reason, the state and rural/urban capital are the two arms of what is an overarching capitalist social relationship. The actions of both capital and the capitalist state – class struggle from above – are in turn influenced politically by struggles conducted against them by lower classes.[20]

2   The Indian State and Its Class Base

It is a truism that classes which control the means of production also control state power. By controlling state power, these classes become, in turn, politically dominant.[21] The dominant classes are, in political terms, the fundamental 'support base' of the state and, in economic terms, its most important beneficiaries (two arms). The state protects their property rights when these are challenged, thereby protecting their political interests. It guarantees the reproduction of their accumulation project, the way in which wealth/value is generated, thus protecting their economic interests as classes, although specific members of these classes may lose out from this or that policy[22] or specific members of these classes may derive special benefits from certain policies because of their close connection to powerful actors within the state

---

19   As we have seen in Chapter 3, the view that Indian social formation is semi-feudal is held by many scholars (Bhaduri, 1973, 1983; Byres, 1996), and has been subjected to severe criticisms by Brass (2002) which I agree with. Also, simple fact is that capitalism – at least in the sense of formal, if not real, subordination of labor under capital – dominates non-capitalist class relations (where they exist) in the Indian social formation, including the 'rural social formation', which is politically managed by a capitalist state.

20   Mao, for example, defined these classes thus: 'poor peasants have to rent the land they work on and are subjected to exploitation, having to pay land rent and interest on loans and to hire themselves out to some extent'. And the worker 'as a rule owns no land or farm implements, though some do own a very small amount of land and very few farm implements. Workers make their living wholly or mainly by selling their labour power' (Mao, 1961).

21   'Because the state arose from the need to hold class antagonisms in check, but because it arose, at the same time, in the midst of the conflict of these classes, it is, as a rule, the state of the most powerful, economically dominant class, which, through the medium of the state, becomes also the politically dominant class, and thus acquires new means of holding down and exploiting the oppressed class', as Engels said (cited in Lenin, 1977c: 16).

22   They lose out because the perception by the state elite of the interests of specific capitalists may not exactly fit in with those of the latter, and also because of struggles within the state of capitalist fractions, including those based in specific regions and in rural areas. In these struggles, some capitalists but not others lose.

or to a party in power or because their enterprises are seen by the state as important to the nation, and so on.

As usually understood in the Indian context, the two main proprietary classes holding state power are urban capitalists and large rural landholders.[23] In this coalition, urban capitalists, especially the larger owners of capital with national and, under the neoliberal dispensation, international scale of operations, who exploit nominally free wage-labor, are not merely dominant but also increasingly so. Equally well known is the fact that the urban bourgeoisie has demanded, and benefited from, state policies, and such a favorable relationship had to be justified in the post-1917 and post-1947 situation on the basis of the *ideology* of socialism. Indeed, this relationship was cemented in the early years of independent India.

The Bombay Plan[24] was formulated in 1944 by the leaders of the big business (Birla, Tata, etc.), who also funded the anti-colonial struggle (Mukherjee, 2015). It envisaged a doubling of per capita income in 15 Years from 1944. Given its economic weakness, the big business authors of the Plan wanted the state to pay for infrastructural developments and the development of basic industries which were not profitable for the private enterprises (and which also needed bulky investment, something the private sector did not generally have). A manifesto of the Indian capitalist class, the Bombay plan was a document on what is to be done, from the standpoint of the interests of the capitalist class.[25] It connected the interests of the state, the masses and the capitalist class, within a whole, and this was the strategy of state-assisted capitalist development. The Plan did recognize inequality, in its own class interest though: inequality restricted the domestic market. So it allowed the state some redistributive role, but it made sure that egalitarian reforms (land redistribution) did not challenge the right to private property (this meant that class-based shackles on industrial development remained) (Prashad, 2015: 33).

Drafted in the last years of the World War II, which had prompted state interventionism in Britain itself, the 15-year Plan of the capitalists aimed to ensure that the new post-colonial state would protect Indian capitalists'

---

23   This is contrary to the view both that the state is a neutral arbiter between classes/groups, and that the state is controlled by 'intermediate classes' located between the exploited and the dominant classes. Note that while 'capitalist' signifies a relation of exploitation, 'landowner' usually indicates the nature of the property owned (that is, land) and says nothing about the form of exploitation that the landowner is engaged in.

24   It was formally known as 'A Brief Memorandum Outlining a Plan of Economic Development for India', or 'a Plan of Economic Development'.

25   The Indian capitalist class had made much progress under colonialism, even though colonialism constrained its growth (see Chandra, 1992 on pre-1917 Indian capitalism).

CHAPTER 7

interests vis-à-vis foreign capitalists (foreign competition) and domestic labor (Prashad, 2015: 32). The Plan even suggested that some measures of coercion were desirable (i.e. coercion vs anti-capitalist elements such as labor), and Nehru, a bourgeois-democrat, agreed to this (Prashad, 2015: 37). Yet, formulated during a time when the communist/democratic-socialist Left was organizing the masses and when the Russian Revolution of 1917 was fresh in people's memory, the Plan was shaped by the belief of capitalists that a policy of egalitarian reforms was 'the most effective remedy against social upheavals' and that 'socialist demands could be accommodated without capitalism surrendering any of its essential features' (Chandra, 1989: 384).[26]

So, the Plan was prepared to accept a 'temporary eclipse' in 'freedom of enterprise' in the interest of national development and even made friendly references to the Russian experiment (Sarkar, 1983: 408). The Plan even quoted the economist, Pigou, that socialism and capitalism were converging and that a dynamic economy needed to mix the best features of both (Guha, 2012: 134). Of course, it would be foolish not to believe that capitalists would listen to the state much less than they said they would, and that they would want to milk the new state (in a process of 'post-colonial' primitive accumulation) as much as possible in spite of all their love for the new independent nation for which they apparently fought. There was some kind of partnership between the two arms of capitalist relation: a partnership between the capitalist class, whose leaders authored the Bombay plan as their manifesto, and the top bureaucrats and the enlightened bourgeois politicians of the capitalist state, generally connected to the Congress party, which was financially and intellectually supported by the capitalist class and which made sure that anti-colonial struggle, i.e. the struggle against national oppression, did not grow over into a challenge to the private property, and class exploitation. The bureaucrats and politicians made use of capitalists' expertise, etc. (capitalists joined various committees of the state), and capitalists made use of the state. All this was done in the name of national development and anti-imperialism. Nothing major was done which would pose any fundamental obstacle to the fact that capitalist private property remained in the hands of the capitalists and that the vast majority would face a choice between starvation on the one hand and the sale of their labor power (as wage-earners), or the sale of the product of their labor (as small-scale producers) at a price that cannot even ensure a decent level of reproduction of their lives, on the other hand.

---

26   On the working class struggle and the potential threat of communism in pre-colonial India (see Bahl, 1995; Basu, 2004; Chandavarkar, 2009; Chowdhuri, 2007; Sahay, 2006).

In India, as we have discussed in Chapter 3, the capitalist form of exploitation is the dominant form of exploitation which is based on economic – and not extra-economic – coercion. This, in turn, allows the state to have a degree of autonomy vis-à-vis specific fractions of the capitalist class, an autonomy that allows the state to possess the flexibility with which to ensure the reproduction of the conditions of capitalist accumulation. Of course, there is nothing to guarantee that the state will succeed in doing what it is possible on its part to do. As well, nothing that has been said above means that there are no other processes which will shape the relation between the state and capital.

The Indian state firmly protects, not private property rights (consider the rights of self-employed peasants that are being crushed by the state), but capitalist property rights. An organic intellectual of the capitalist class, Gurcharan Das (2012: 158), writes: 'Capitalism depends on the right to property, which is one of India's advantages', especially since 1991, but, of course, the capitalist class demands that the state 'needs to do more to strengthen that right' (ibid.). This is necessary for the capitalist class to, for example, enlarge its property-base at the expense of self-exploiting small-scale property owners.

Of course, mere defense of private property would not be enough. The state has to promote capitalist economic development, which is a means of money-making for the capitalist class. The Bombay plan itself shaped the post-colonial state policies in relation to economic development.[27] Domestic markets were automatically protected, and state-owned industries provided cheap capital goods and state-owned banks continue to heap cheap money or indeed free money (loans given are pardoned) on private businesses. Close ties with the

---

27   Chibber says that the capitalist class did not embrace state planning, and that explains why industrial development did not happen. This is a little problematic. 1) It is mistaken to assume that correct developmental policy – including the disciplining of the capitalist class by state – *in itself* can result in the development of productive forces, especially in a very large and poverty-stricken low-income country such as India; there are obstacles to economic development that emanate from existing class relations that need to be transformed. 2) His thinking does considerably under-stress the fact that the capitalist economy was much more regulated in the early years than in more recent times. 3) For Chibber, it is a (neoliberal) myth that a weak bourgeoisie was shaped by developmental planning, a myth from which followed the claim that if industrial development did not occur, the blame must be on the state, a claim that was conducive to neoliberalism. For me, both the neoliberal myth and Chibber's critique of the myth share a common ground: the absence of a fundamental challenge to capitalism as a class relation, whether it is aided or un-aided by the state. To imply that capitalism is regulated or must be regulated by state power is not necessarily to challenge capitalism as such; whether that challenge happens depends on the dynamics of class struggle and on the matter of which class controls state power.

state allowed big business to ensure monopoly control of contracts (Prashad, 2015: 33). Concentration and centralization of capital went on.

Private sector companies (as well as public sector companies which have helped the former grow) have benefited enormously from the huge reserve army of labor in rural and semi-rural areas, which has been kept alive at near-subsistence level through various so-called development policies. In this respect, the strategy of locating industries in 'backward' (= aboriginal/semi-rural) areas in the name of promoting rural and/or regional development has been crucial. Recently, the neoliberal method of primitive accumulation encouraged by the state, including the sale of not only public sector companies – some of which are located in aboriginal/semi-rural areas – but also the land of indigenous peoples and other small-scale producers, to the urban capitalists at below-market prices, has deposited an enormous quantity of investible resources in their hands.[28] Indeed, those members of the capitalist class who have enjoyed close relations with influential politicians and bureaucrats have benefited hugely from this process.[29] There are some who think that the bourgeois class really had a bad time before the neoliberal times. Consider however what a former CEO of CII (Confederation of Indian Industries) says about those times: 'some of the larger business groups thrived within this system of controls by exercising their own influence and pre-empting capacities' (T. Das, 2018: 2) which constitute what Herring (1999) calls 'embedded particularism' (state's links to specific capitalists) that was responsible for what he calls 'India's failed developmental state'.

Members of the other arm of dominant class in India are the top ten percent of rural landholding families. They are involved in the appropriation of capitalist profit: mainly from farming, but also from non-farming activities, such as rural transportation and construction. These rural landowners appropriate ground rent, as well as mercantile profit and usurious interest. However, the actual mix of their portfolios may change from place to place, from time to

---

28   The post-colonial neoliberal state in India has acquired land on behalf of private companies by virtue of eminent domain' as outlined in the colonial-era Land Acquisition Act 1894. Several amendments to the 1894 Act have broadened the purview of the public purpose clause and have facilitated more state intervention in land acquisition on behalf of capitalists. The New Act of 2013 has expanded the ambit of public purpose to include public-private-partnership projects (Mallick, 2018; see also Chakravorty, 2016).

29   Therefore, the idea that free market policies will result in less corruption is no more than neoliberal propaganda. Interestingly, while every capitalist makes use of the state to accumulate their wealth, in public they and their well-paid intellectual supporters keep emphasizing how the free market – the invisible hand of the market and everyone obeying the law of dharma of the market (i.e. doing what is in one's self-interest and not cheating) (G. Das, 2012) – makes a nation prosperous.

time and from one member of the landed class to another. To some degree, the specifically capitalist elements of this class emerged in part due to what was predominantly a bourgeois land reform that removed some erstwhile pre-capitalist fetters (Das, 1999c; Djurfeldt and Sircar, 2017). The capitalist class in rural areas has benefited not only from the policy of exemption of taxation on agricultural incomes, but also – and more importantly – from the Green Revolution (discussed in Chapter 5), which was promoted by the state policy of providing cheap inputs and price support (Nanda, 1995). The economic importance of what may appear to be 'non-capitalist' elements of the dominant landowning class is an effect of the fact that the state considers it legitimate for them to extract extremely high rents (in cash, labor or kind), and charge usurious interest rates (which can be 50–60% a year) on loans.[30] These forms of exploitation are legal according to Indian bourgeois constitution (although bonded labor, which is widely used in rural areas, is not).[31] The rural propertied class still exercises substantial political power, through which it protects both its accumulation project and the sources of its capital/wealth.[32]

---

30   It is not clear why the level of rent/interest *per se* determines the nature of class relations, that is, whether these are capitalist or not (Das, 2001c: 164). Does the payment of wages below the value of labor power – which happens when the supply of labor outstrips demand – make the payment, and therefore the capital/labor relation, pre- or non-capitalist? To the extent that the nature of the state is conditioned by the relations of exploitation (whether and to what extent these are capitalist), and to the extent that the capitalist nature of the mode of exploitation is underemphasized (as in the much of the Indian mode of production debate), the capitalist nature of the state (which also happened to receive very little attention in that debate) will be also diluted.

31   Although the social base of the state is said to be formed by a coalition of proprietary classes, the state is a bourgeois state. According to Kaviraj (1988), this can be explained in three different senses. First, the logic of capitalism, no matter in what juridical form it appears (the public or the private sector), economically and politically subordinates the economic and political reproduction of 'non-capitalist' modes of production where they exist. That is, the society is dominated by the capitalist class, or a coalition dominated by that class. Second, the state-form is a parliamentary democratic one that 'arranges disbursing of advantages in a particular way; and the democratic mechanism works as a useful sensitive political index as to when the distribution of disadvantages, which is bound to happen and intensify in a capitalist economy, is becoming politically insupportable' (Kaviraj, 1988: 2430). And third, the state ensures the domination of the bourgeoisie and helps, through capitalist planning, in the reproduction of capitalist relations (Kaviraj, 1988: 2430).

32   Varshney (1994) almost reduces the power of 'the rural' and the countryside to the power of commercial farmers. Strictly speaking, rural power is that exercised by propertied class plus that of lower classes. Varshney correctly identifies some of the limits to the power of commercial farmers, but he misses the point that the real limit is that posed by the countervailing power of the lower classes.

Another beneficiary of state policies is what might be termed 'state elites', composed of high-ranking members of the bureaucracy plus senior officials engaged in the industrial management of public sector enterprises. In a country like India, where the overwhelming majority of the population are illiterate or primary school drop-outs, 'the educated elite' according to Bardhan (1998: 52), 'enjoy a high scarcity value (a rent) for their education and profession. By managing to direct educational investment away from the masses, they have been able to protect their scarcity rent', which is seen in their salary increases and perks. State elites have benefited considerably from the expansion of educational and administrative functions and the nationalization of industries, which created jobs for managers in the public sector, and subsidized collective consumption (which has actually made some of them members of an expanding consuming class). In the era before neoliberalism, the 'process of implementation of (policies) often generates rental income from disbursement of permits and favors which accrues to the bureaucratic elite' (Bardhan, 1998: 51). More recently, with neoliberalism, these elements have benefited – illegally – from the sale of public assets, the state-promoted method of primitive accumulation. In short, state elites have economic resources, as well as social and cultural capital. Since they occupy crucial positions in the state apparatus, they use state's 'autonomy' to implement policies in their own interest, akin to exercising powers of patronage. As long as the myth of state 'autonomy' circulates, this will confer an advantage on those who administer the economic resources and implement policies.[33]

At the local level, state elites (officials, and political leaders, especially, of ruling parties) represent the worst face of state power. Forming an alliance with the economically dominant classes at this level, they corner much of the development benefits that are supposed to go to the poor. Their high-handedness complements and reinforces that of the proprietary classes, not least because of the way urban capitalists disregard the legitimate trade unions rights of workers, and rural landowners keep rural sections of the lower classes in relations of servitude and 'hold' state power quite literally (they are the state itself in many areas). In effect, such actions blur the boundary between the state and the dominant classes at the local level.[34] All this renders problematic the sanguine social capital theory of the state, which pins hope on state – society synergy as a possible source of progress where lower classes are concerned.

---

33   Mukherji (2017, 2008) discusses how state autonomy in the form of state officials/ technocrats' autonomy matters, even if the state is weak.

34   The story of the 'hermeneutic divide' between the local/village-based and centrally-based officials is too well known to be narrated here (Kaviraj, 1992).

3   A Coalition/Alliance of Proprietary Classes

An obvious question to ask is why is the urban bourgeoisie said to find it necessary to share state power with landowners? Why is a *coalition* of large-scale
exploitative rural landowners (the landed) and the urban-industrial bourgeoisie said to exist in a social formation where capitalism is the dominant mode
of production and exchange?[35]
   One needs to understand the economic and political importance of the
landed. The landed includes those landowners who exploit the masses by appropriating ground rent (and sometimes, usurious interest) or surplus value or
a combination of the two. The relation between the landed class and the direct
producers, whether it is based on ground rent or surplus value, is a relation of
not only economic exploitation but also political power. The masses depend
on the landed for a little piece of land on rent, on loans, and for wage-
employment (in farming and non-farming activities). This dependence is economic. It can also have political effects: how much independence can the
masses whose lives depend on the landed class, have, when they themselves
are thoroughly unorganized? So economic control over the masses *is* a source
of political control. When the masses produce products (which, more or less,
take a commodity form) for the landed (indeed, for rural capitalists as such), in
the *same* process is reproduced a relation between the two classes, a relation
that is economic and political (as well as cultural/discursive).
   Besides, landowners actively exercise *de facto* control over the state apparatuses (e.g. police; civil administration that does some developmental work) at
the local scale through electoral and other mechanisms, especially at the local/
provincial scale.[36] Rural property owners – and rural capitalists as such – are

---

35   The 'coalition' concept in the sense in which it is used in the literature means that there
      are fundamental class differences (as well as overlaps of interests) between landowners
      and urban capitalists. Implicit in the concept is the idea, which is problematic and reso-
      nates with the semi-feudal thesis, that the nature of the surplus appropriated by land-
      owners is in a fundamental way different from that extracted by urban capitalists. It can
      be argued much rather that state power is held by a single bourgeoisie, composed of an
      urban component and a rural one. There are differences between individual capitalists
      and groups of capitalists, yet we do not use 'coalition of urban capitalists' in characterizing
      state power. So why *coalition* of landowners and urban capitalists? Strictly speaking, we
      should talk about the Indian capitalist class, a fraction of which comprises the rural capi-
      talists, a part of whose income comes from ground rent.
36   The Indian state is described as the capitalist-landlord state by many on the left (it is also
      described by Maoists as semi-colonial and semi-feudal). What is stressed in these various
      (confusing) characterizations is that the state redistributes value from smaller (national

not just a proprietary class. Rural politicians, who have an enormous control over the local administration, generally come from that class and/or from strata that are closely related to that class. They control and discipline the rural masses and punish them where necessary, through a judicious mixture of elections and extra-economic coercion and ideas, which are usually very regressive. The ideas that circulate in rural areas and that shape the thinking of the masses (for example, ideas about how to respond to society's problems; who to vote for, what should be the perception of the state?) are, typically, the ideas of the propertied class (from rural areas and also, increasingly from the cities)or are those that reflect the interests of this class. The rural property owners, including those who appropriate the surplus in the form of rent and interest and in the form of profit, are not just a class of economic exploiters. They are also social oppressors. The men, women and children who are economically exploited are also those who are socially oppressed. Usually, the large-scale property owners are not Dalits, but the direct producers often are. The property owners are typically men, but direct producers are both women and men. So the full force of caste and gender relations is made use of to control and shape the masses: not only to exploit them, but also to keep them subjugated. The rural masses (including those who have small plots of land), as a potential ally of the urban working class, are an enormous potential threat to the propertied class, whether in rural or urban areas. What makes them a potent force is not just the fact of their class-anger rooted in them being exploited and oppressed. It is also their number, given the fact that the majority of the people – majority of the direct producers – live in rural areas, unlike in, say, other parts of the Global South (e.g. Latin America). Given their potential as a threat to the propertied, it is important that they be prevented from launching any attack on the class character of the state or indeed on the urban capitalist class. The

---

or regional) enterprises to monopoly and overseas businesses, and that it protects relations generating ground rent, which hurts capitalist development. This is actually a critique of the excesses of the state activity (as opposed to its normal activity). This is because of a fractionalist approach to the state. As just mentioned, the Indian state is in my view best characterized simply as capitalist state. This is because it supports and reproduces, over any overt/covert class resistance, three things. First, the institution of private property and – most importantly – the form of capitalist private property. Second, and therefore, it supports the relations of exploitation between capital and labor in rural and urban contexts. And third, it supports capitalist accumulation, in the form of formal and real subsumption. Its support for ground rent is a consequence of its support for private property, without which ground rent as such could not exist. Therefore the state-promoted reproduction of the relations of ground rent, including 'pre-' or 'non-'capitalist forms where these exist, is predominantly a consequence of the state being capitalist.

urban bourgeoisie indeed needs the rural propertied class in a large, domi-nantly-rural country such as India, to control the masses. The rural proper-tied class is therefore regarded as functional to the political interests of the bourgeoisie.

The act of controlling and disciplining the rural masses by the rural proper-tied class also delivers an important *economic* advantage to the urban bour-geoisie: food and agri-materials consumed by industries are produced cheaply, because rural workers are remunerated well below the value of their labor-power and rural petty producers sell their products at a very low price, so the rural commodities are very 'competitively' priced. This kind of economic ad-vantage is not something that would be possible at the existing level of the development of the productive forces without the sort of control that rural property owners have over rural toilers. Besides, the continuing existence of rural landlords helps reproduce the idea of private property ownership and thereby the idea of capitalist private property, and this is beneficial to the ur-ban capitalist class. So in terms of the defense of private property and in terms of the defense of the capitalist market (note that both rural and urban prop-erty owners benefit from market transactions), they have the same interest. As well, any strong action (e.g. a properly-implemented land reforms policy) against the large-scale rural landowning class (whether they appropriate rent or profit and interest) would hurt the economic interests of the urban bour-geoisie because, as, the latter itself has been involved in the exploitation of peasants through its links with the rural landlord class and though its mercan-tile and usurious operations in villages, as just indicated (see also Davey, 1974: 102). It is important to note that just like most sections of the urban bourgeois class, the rural land-owning capitalists have also supported the liberalization of trade that the urban capitalists have demanded, because the rural capital-ists, generally speaking, have eyed making money from unregulated markets and from the exports of farm-products.

Some analyses include top state elites as a part of the coalition of classes holding state power. In line with his neoclassical economic approach, Bardhan (1998: 51) maintains that 'if physical capital can be the basis of class differentia-tion, so can be human capital in the form of education, skills and technical enterprise', which these top bureaucratic elites possess.[37] The latter have close links to intellectuals in India and abroad, and as a top bureaucrat in the rural

---

37   As Bardhan mistakenly thinks, the idea of the physicality of capital is consistent with a
     class approach. That approach to capital is firmly within mainstream, neoclassical eco-
     nomics (Fine, 2001).

development ministry of central government once informed me, 'all these IAS (Indian Administrative Service) officers want to be top class intellectuals, thinkers'. These bureaucratic elites also have connections with business groups, both in India itself and in the Indian diaspora, and thus constitute an important support base for the Indian capitalists at home and abroad. But are they part of the dominant class coalition? Not bourgeois in a productive sense, state elites have been affiliated to the bourgeoisie in cultural and ideological ways. It was in this sense that Nehru called himself a bourgeois. But they have had a degree of autonomy.

Even before independence, state elites were the repository of the intelligentsia, working out a development theory for Indian capitalism, often restraining more intensely bourgeois objectives and formulating policies that appeared to be more reformist and universal. They viewed 'their society as in need of basic change' (Kohli, 1987: 25), and charted a path of capitalist development that sought to resist, within limits, imperialist pressures, in a way that is consistent with the bourgeois conception of 'national' development. State elites are not wholly independent of capital, however, since its logic sets the limit within which state elites formulate specific strategies of accumulation and specific development discourses, both of which project the interests as well as the ideas of state elites. These ideas have included, at one time, belief that India should follow an independent capitalist path after 1947 and, more recently, the idea of neoliberal development. Much planning/policy discourse accordingly comes from these state elites who are always in interaction with the organic intellectuals of the capitalist class working in the academia, media, private consultancies, etc. This is effected through the various institutions/apparatuses of the state, and through their rules, procedures, discourses and strategies (see Baviskar, 2003; Ferguson, 1994; Williams, 2004) to which certain intellectuals contribute. In short, there is an ensemble of state institutions/apparatuses (e.g. National Institute of Rural Development; the Nehruvian Planning Commission or its present dwarfed neoliberal avatar), procedures, discourses and tactics of development – a Foucauldian might call this 'developmentality of the state' – that allows the state elites to govern the people, to exercise power over the millions of development-hungry, illiterate and semi-literate Indians in rural areas (and in impoverished urban spaces) in the name of development, although Foucauldians forget that these mechanisms do not of themselves *create* the power of state elites. The origin of that power is dominantly in the *class* nature of society and of the state.

I have mentioned the intellectual aspects (Bardhan calls these human capital) of the state bureaucracy. I should elaborate on this point. While one must acknowledge that the bureaucracy has included some very smart thinking minds from time to time, there are reasons to worry about its overall intellectual capacity which functions as the repository of knowledge that the state deploys to rule. One does not need to be a Weberian to unpack some of the reasons for this. The minimum requirement to be an IAS officer is an undergraduate degree, although a large number of officers are perhaps post-graduate drop outs. The quality of higher education in social sciences and humanities is simply poor and getting poorer. The content that students learn – memorize – is a set of ideas that are designed to support/justify an inegalitarian social order, and especially, a capitalist order, an order that is also oppressive of lower castes, of religious minorities, and of women.[38] To be an officer, one of the major requirements is memorizing a vast amount of raw information (e.g. who won the Olympic prize in sport x, in year y, from country z?): so what students do – i.e. memorizing – to get their under-graduate degree in order to be eligible for taking the recruitment examination, is what they do to get the job of an officer too. Many officers come from science and engineering backgrounds, and the nation does need officers with such backgrounds. But it is not clear how socially sensitive, both intellectually and practically, those people are. Given the way the officers live and work (generally pushing files, taking orders from politicians who often take orders from the business class), and indeed given the pressure of work, it is not clear if there is any significant scope for developing one's intellectual abilities whereby one can understand people's problems in a way that is scientific and critical.[39] Although they are known as civil servants, they are, more or less, uncivil masters of ordinary people: in a truly colonial style, the officers are perceived as mini-kings, and many of them probably perceive themselves as such (as brown sahibs).[40] To the extent that this is true, it is not even clear if they feel that they lack any knowledge, and if they do, they can always get someone by using their power to write a few things for them, just as politicians and prime ministers appear to be erudite by delivering speeches

---

38   That the scientific temper is being tampered with in recent times is a separate issue.

39   An approach is scientific when it is backed by evidence and reason, and not by belief, intuition or myth. An approach is critical when it is critical of the unequal power relations – between the property owners and the property-less or between the rich and the poor, between the oppressors and the oppressed, and between powerful state actors and ordinary citizens – and of how a society treats the physical environment. And, an approach is critical when it is critical of the ideas that support the exploitative and oppressive relations and the undermining of the material basis of society in the natural environment.

40   On Nehru's critical attitude towards the top bureaucratic layers (ICS/IAS), see Davey (1974: 224).

which are written by hired speech writers, etc. Let's assume that intellect is necessary for state-policy and it exists and that state-policy can contribute to the solution of people's problems. Then how is it that the Indian state is run by thousands of intellectually-capable men and women who are overseeing a society that fails to meet the basic needs of the vast majority, and is increasingly curtailing democratic rights of people? Given that the vast majority are suffering as much as they do, can one conclude that: there is limited intellect within the top layers of the bureaucracy or that policies are formed without being backed up by much intellectual work/rationale (consider demonetization that has hurt millions) or that to the extent that top layers of bureaucracy have a stock of intellect, it is ignored in policy-making, and that this is done in order to support an exploitative and oppressive order? When will 'the bureaucratic caste' understand that whether or not they have any intellectual abilities, they are, more or less, irrelevant as far as any significant improvement in the conditions of the toiling masses is concerned, because in spite of their self-grandeur about their intention to help the masses, they are tethered to the proprietary classes and their political representatives, both to serve these people and in their own interest (see Das, 2013b)? But surely, they are very relevant as far as ensuring conditions for exploitation and subjugation of the masses is concerned. In this sense, the top officers are close allies of the proprietary classes, and are a major obstacle to the self-emancipation of the toilers in whose name they administer.

Whether they have much 'human capital' or not, state elites *qua* elites are not a class, so they cannot be considered a part of the class coalition holding state power.[41] Unlike rural propertied class and urban capitalists, state elites cannot transfer property to their heirs. It is the ownership/control of the means of production that decides who ultimately has power in a society and the state.[42] State elites have a certain degree of autonomy, but this they exercise mainly on the basis of the fact that they coercively and ideologically defend capitalist property relations and implement capitalist accumulation projects: hence their activities – including rent-seeking – must be seen as contingent on

---

41   The idea – common in the 'political economy' literature – that state elites are a dominant class, and the idea – common in the neoliberal literature – that the activities of state elites are a reason for India's low level of development, are two sides of the same coin. The problems of society are located in the political realm, rather than in the sphere of class relations of exploitation. To accept that the state elites are a dominant class is also to accept that 'the rule of full-time corps of non-propertied officials is an unavoidable feature of modern society' (Post, 1999: 146).

42   In the African literature, state elites controlling the public sector industries and business are called a state bourgeoisie or a managerial bourgeoisie (Leftwich, 2000: 91). Pedersen (1992) says that Indian bureaucracy is not a class.

a state the structure of which is designed to pursue capitalist class interests. State elites qua state elites are *not* a class, and cannot therefore hold and exercise state power on their own behalf no matter how much they seek to elevate themselves.[43]

The dominant class-base of the state changes over time. Since the late 1960s, there has been a proliferation of members of the capitalist class (Chandrasekhar et al., 1999).[44] In more recent times, capitalist elements among the landed have become more powerful (Chattopadhyay, Sharma and Ray, 1987) and have been connected to urban capitalists. Under neoliberalism, there is greater corporate control over agriculture, and greater interaction with the landed through such mechanisms as contract farming. Also, a result of the competition between big corporations (domestic and foreign) and smaller-scale enterprises has been that many of the latter companies get slowly eliminated, causing an increasing level of centralization of the means of production in line with Marx's thinking (Marx, 1977: 777).[45] This same trend also manifests itself in another form within agriculture: the rising inequality in some areas of the distribution of operational land (land owned plus land leased in minus land leased out). So the class base of the state is narrowing in the sense that it is increasingly dominated by a powerful domestic urban bourgeoisie and rural property-owning class which are also linked to international circuits of capital, and as such, they are the main beneficiaries of the neoliberal globalization policy of the Indian state.[46]

4   The Indian State, Lower Classes, and Lower-Class Struggle

The above section outlines a more-or-less familiar story within political economy, one about control by elements composing the dominant classes over state power in India. But this is only one half of what is a larger story. A problem

---

43   The political implication of this is that replacing one set of state actors with another leads to no fundamental changes in the conditions under which workers and peasants live.

44   This suggests that: thanks to certain state intervention in the 1950s–1980s, new kinds of capitalists came into being (this constitutes the proliferation of the capitalist class), and then a changed capitalist class makes new demands on the state (e.g. liberalization).

45   This is something Patnaik (2001) has also commented on.

46   Also the top state elites as a 'consumption class', whose emergence state policies in the era before neoliberalism helped, along with the rural and urban propertied class, have acted as a great pressure for the liberalization of imported luxury items. They have also prompted the use of country's resources for the production of luxury non-wage goods, including new agricultural products (flowers, shrimps), a process which has further contributed to what Samir Amin has called 'disarticulation' of the economy.

with much radical theorization of the state and its class character has been its structuralist nature, and its near exclusive stress on the interests of the dominant classes.[47] This is un-dialectical. In a dialectical analysis of class, there are no capitalist interests or landowner interests that exist in abstraction from those of the lower classes. Rather obviously, class is a relationship of exploitation and power between classes. What the state is and does, and why, must accordingly also be investigated from the standpoint of the lower classes, and especially in terms of their struggle against the state and the propertied classes, no matter how weak and constrained that struggle is. In this dialectic, the fact that the Indian state is engaged in reproducing the political and economic interests of 'those above' does not go unchallenged by 'those below'.[48]

Class struggle is therefore not merely important but crucial to an analysis of the state. Accordingly, how the Indian state is perceived by the lower classes, who compose about 70% of the population is an essential part of the equation. As is well known, in the rural context, poor peasants and agricultural laborers are subordinated by a wide variety of regionally-specific production relations, extending from sharecropping and other kinds of tenancy arrangements, structuring conditional access to small plots of land, through to local/migrant/ seasonal forms of landless employment. Those compelled to rely mainly or wholly on the sale not of the product of their labor but rather of labor power itself are exploited by property owners, who appropriate surplus labor mainly in the form of profit. In the urban context, barely 10% of wage-earners have access to a regular wage and pension benefits. Everyone else is precariously employed.

For a large proportion of wage-workers, their employment is confined neither to given areas nor to one specific pattern of work. Forming a reserve army of labor, the size of which is swelling partly thanks to neoliberalism, they are also subject to exploitation by urban capitalists on a seasonal basis, when they migrate to towns and cities in search of off-farm work. Such workers are often paid below the value of labor power. In many instances they are deproletarianized (Brass, 1990, 1999, 2003) in the sense of not having the freedom personally to sell their own labor power, their only commodity.[49] Despite lip-service

---

47   For example, the Indian mode of production debate had very little to say about class struggle.

48   The critical approach which focuses simply on the power of the dominant class is therefore unhelpful from the standpoint both of lower-class interests and of macro-level change. Nilsen (2008) reflects on the possibilities for the state to function as an enabling space for the struggles of subaltern social groups.

49   This includes arrangements whereby migrants are recruited by a labor contractor, who then sells their labor power to a rich peasant or agribusiness enterprise.

to the eradication of bonded labor, this kind of unfreedom is a relation that the Indian state has failed to eliminate.[50]

Given the unequal distribution of resources, and the attendant exploitative conditions, class struggle is immanent. There is always a potential for struggle even if the potential is not always realized or manifested explicitly.[51] The history and geography of Indian society, like all class societies, is thus also a story about both the fact of and forms taken by lower-class struggle, a point underlined by numerous studies (Desai, 1986; Dhanagare, 1991; Mukherjee, 2004; Pathy, 1998; Shah, 2000; Singharoy, 2004).[52] The ideological impact of such class mobilization and agency in the specific context of the countryside, and especially struggle by poor peasants, is such as to have prompted Arvind Das (1982: 1) to observe: 'The spurts of writing on the agrarian question in India have quite remarkably followed the ebbs and tides of peasant movements'.

Forms of class struggle from below vary and are often place-specific. One can observe four inter-connected forms. The first is the struggle by proletarian and semi-proletarian elements as full-time or part-time wage-earners against capital, both in urban and in rural areas.[53] This 'from below' struggle also includes struggle against localized pre-capitalist exploitation. More importantly, the lower-class struggle, which is generally in the form of strikes (work-stoppage), is against the formal and real subsumption of labor under capital: that is, it is against low wages, oppressive labor practices, long hours and poor working conditions, precarity, and the introduction of, or subordination to,

---

50   Of a little more than a billion Indians, 836 million people – 82 per cent of whom are Dalits, the Scheduled Tribes, the Other Backward Classes and the poor Muslims – earn less than 20 rupees a day (note that a kilogram of rice costs more than 10 rupees in the market). If the sort of economic distress that afflicts the vast majority that is indicated by the above statistic does not show state failure, then what does? (Of course, the state has been very successful in ensuring that India has one of the highest number of millionaires and billionaires in the world.)

51   It is in this sense that class-in-itself is not entirely separate from class-for-itself.

52   See also the publications of the two major left-wing parties [CPI and CPI(M)], plus the various annual publications of peasants and laborers associations (including All Indian Kisan Sabha) affiliated to these parties. One does not have to approve of the theory underlying these struggles, or the tactics involved (the use of violence by armed squads), to appreciate the fact that generations of activists have given up everything in their lives to organize the lower classes/castes and fight against oppressive and exploitative conditions.

53   Recent literatures on class struggle include: Bhowmik, 2014; Dutta, 2018; Heller, 1996; Miyamura, 2010; Nathan, 1999; Pattenden, 2018, and Sheth, 2014. Chandramohan (1998) examines some of the theoretical explanations of agrarian unrest.

labor-saving technology, and so on.[54] Of necessity, this sort of struggle also becomes one aimed at the state which supports the propertied class against 'from
below' agency undertaken by workers and small-scale producers. The poor
people in rural and urban areas do fight for concessions from the capitalist
state, including in its role as an employer and provider of things that contribute to social reproduction.[55] Workers as a class have intra-class divisions: they
are divided on the basis of job security, occupation, wage-level, location, etc.
So their struggles include the struggles on the part of the informal labor (Agarwala, 2013) and not just the formally employed labor.[56] The fact that a large
proportion of those who must depend on the sale of labor power for a living
does not have access to regular employment has an implication for class
struggle: some fight against the employers for higher wages (trade union struggle) and others fight against the state for pro-poor policies (struggle in the political sphere). Besides, the trade union struggle itself also takes the form of
political struggle when trade unions demand a government-mandated minimum wage of Rs. 18,000 and linking the minimum wage to inflation.[57] Also,
workers have not only struck work; and they have also defended the public
sector (and fought against their privatization); and they have also built production and service-provision coops as a means of building working class power
(Kerswell and Pratap, 2019).

---

54 Consider the numerous accidents at work in rural areas, some of which are fatal (Nag and
    Nag, 2004), including those caused by tractors over-turning, one case of which I observed
    on a farm just outside of Delhi in the summer of 2007. The absence of any safety regula-
    tions is the main cause of these accidents.

55 Subadevan and Naqvi (2017) talk about how the urban poor seek to get concessions by
    pursuing informal and formal strategies.

56 Herring and Agarwala (2006) say that informal workers organize differently that stably
    employed workers. 'First, because capital takes the form of constantly changing employ-
    ers, who may even be unknown at the point of production, worker organizations take
    their demands to the state, rather than to capital. Second, demands for expansion of citi-
    zenship rights focus on welfare benefits (such as health and education), rather than work-
    ers' rights (such as minimum wage and job security). Third, because neither employers
    nor workplaces remain constant, informal workers organize around the neighborhood,
    rather than on the shop floor. These strategic changes have an impact on class identifica-
    tion: a unique class identity that simultaneously asserts workers' informality and their
    position within the working class. Informal workers employ a rhetoric of "citizenship"
    and mobilize votes to institutionalize rights' (p. 346).

57 Meyer (2016) says that only those workers who are in powerful structural locations, such
    as transportation and distribution workers, are in a position to take the economic route
    while the swelling ranks of the precariat have turned instead to the political sphere to
    press their demands for a better standard of living.

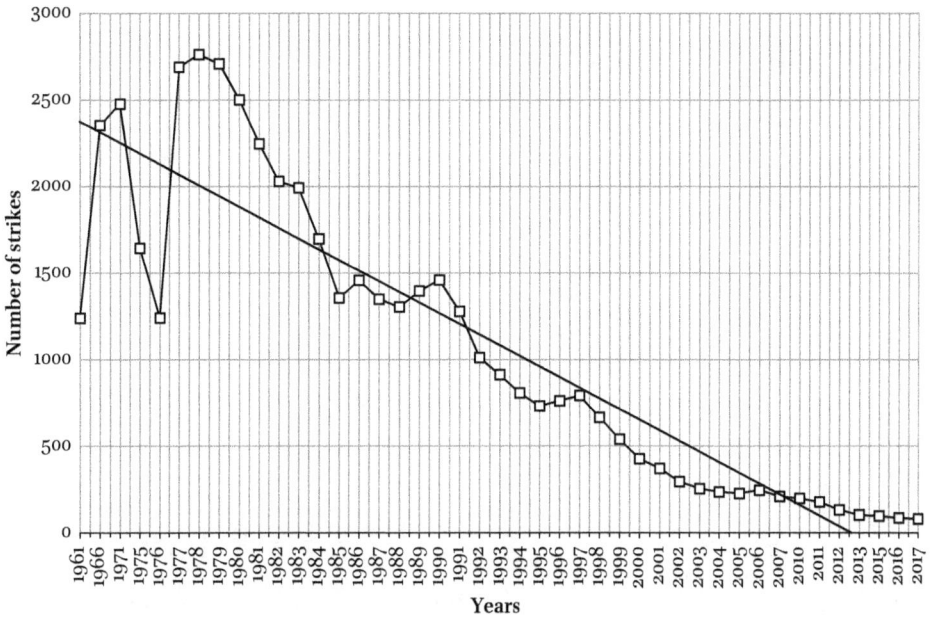

FIGURE 7.1   Number of strikes
SOURCES: HTTPS://THEOPENDATA.COM/SITE/2012/03/STRIKES-AND-
LOCKOUTS-IN-INDIA/; HTTPS://WWW.RESEARCHGATE.NET/FIGURE/
INDUSTRIAL-DISPUTES-IN-INDIA-19952006_TBL1_235622522; HTTPS://WWW
.FINANCIALEXPRESS.COM/ECONOMY/FEWER-STRIKES-LOCKOUTS-IN-LAST-
3-YEARS/1072233/; LABOUR BUREAU. 2015. SHIMLA: GOVERNMENT OF INDIA

I have mentioned in Chapter 4 the fact of regular workers' strikes in India, including under neoliberalism that began formally in 1991. My point has been to stress that workers have not been passive, even under neoliberalism which is supposed to have discouraged workers' struggle. Let us have a slightly long-term view of strikes. (1) There has been a decline in the number of strikes since the 1960s and 1970s, so the decline did not happen only since the onset of neoliberalism in mid-1980s and early-1990s (Figure 7.1). This requires an explanation which cannot be offered here. (2) Associated with the decline in the number of strikes has been a decline in person-days (called man-days, in official documents) that are lost due to the strike, which is a measure of the costs inflicted on the capitalist class. The decline in person-days is less steep and more uneven than the decline in the number of strikes (Figure 7.2). (3) However, and this is surprising, the ratio of person-days lost to the number of strikes has been increasing over time, especially since the onset of neoliberalism (Figure 7.3). As Kumar (2018) says, in the years between 2014 and 2017 only, there was a

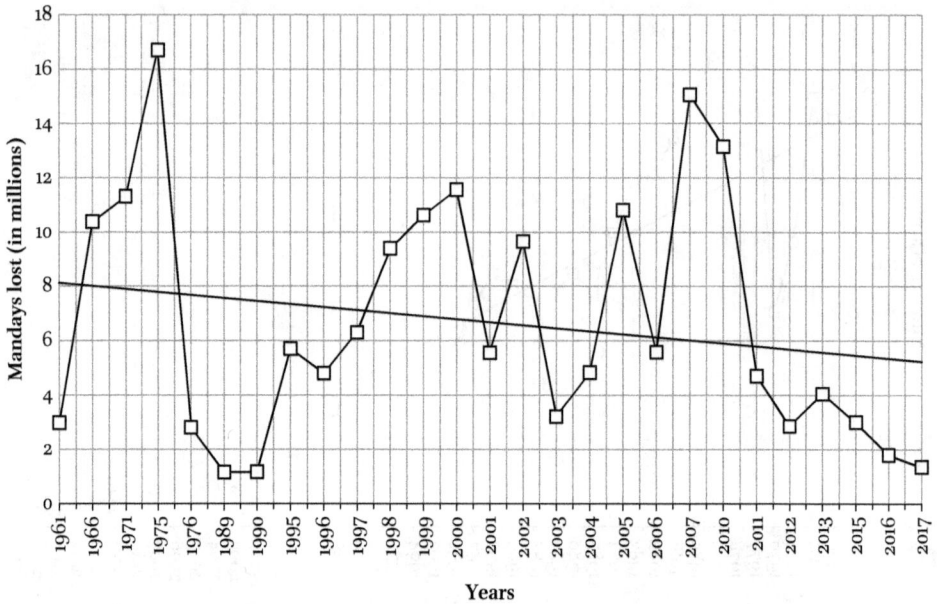

FIGURE 7.2   Mandays lost (in millions)
SOURCES: HTTPS://THEOPENDATA.COM/SITE/2012/03/STRIKES-AND-
LOCKOUTS-IN-INDIA/; HTTPS://WWW.RESEARCHGATE.NET/FIGURE/
INDUSTRIAL-DISPUTES-IN-INDIA-19952006_TBL1_235622522; HTTPS://WWW
.FINANCIALEXPRESS.COM/ECONOMY/FEWER-STRIKES-LOCKOUTS-IN-LAST-
3-YEARS/1072233/; LABOUR BUREAU. 2015. SHIMLA: GOVERNMENT OF INDIA

loss of 7.34 million person days, costing Rs. 14,350 million, including Rs. 5,500 million in 2017 only.

The second main form is 'from below' struggle against primitive accumulation:[58] the state assisting with, or facilitating, what Lenin called 'depeasantization' – smallholders being stripped of their means of production; the privatization of common property and public sector resources, again with the connivance of the state; and the withdrawal by the state of benefits meant for the poor.[59] Here again 'from below' agency targets the state (and not just the propertied classes) for its support for primitive accumulation – for example

---

58   There is a large amount of literature on protests/struggles against dispossession (see Levien, 2018; D'Costa, 2017; Nielson and Nilsen, 2016; Nilsen, 2010, 2016; Steur, 2014).

59   Marx discussed these processes with reference to England (Marx, 1977: Chapters 25–28). Modern interpretations of primitive accumulation are found in De Angelis (2004) and Harvey (2003), among others. On a critical analysis of Harvey's re-conceptualization of Marx's (and Luxemburg's) primitive accumulation, see Das (2017b).

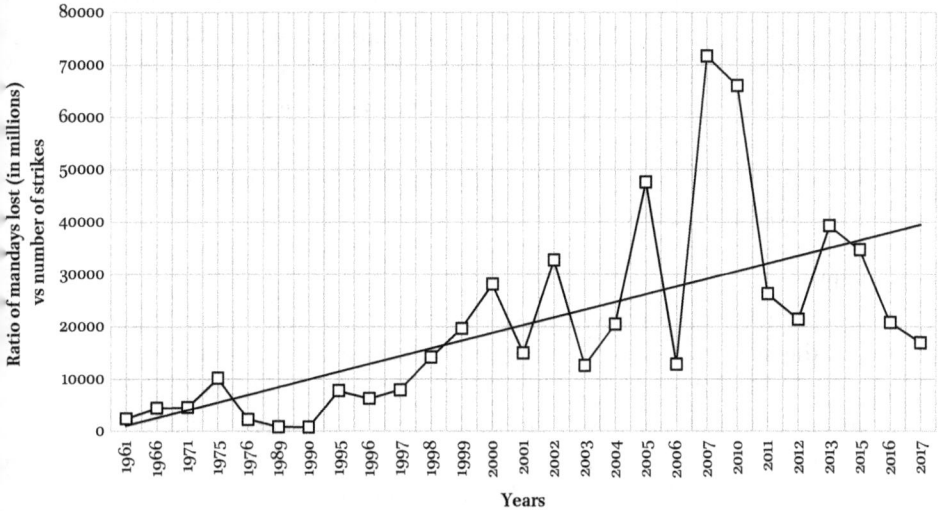

FIGURE 7.3   Ratio of mandays lost (in millions) versus number of strikes
SOURCES: HTTPS://THEOPENDATA.COM/SITE/2012/03/STRIKES-AND-
LOCKOUTS-IN-INDIA/; HTTPS://WWW.RESEARCHGATE.NET/FIGURE/
INDUSTRIAL-DISPUTES-IN-INDIA-19952006_TBL1_235622522; HTTPS://WWW
.FINANCIALEXPRESS.COM/ECONOMY/FEWER-STRIKES-LOCKOUTS-IN-LAST-
3-YEARS/1072233/; LABOUR BUREAU. 2015. SHIMLA: GOVERNMENT OF INDIA

when it privatizes the commons.[60] Connected to this form of struggles is the
struggle, launched by small-scale commodity producers for better farm prices
and lower farm inputs.[61]

In addition to these two forms of class struggle – aimed at capital and its
state – there are other kinds of conflict that have their roots in class inequality:
that are opposed to ecological degradation,[62] and gender/caste/ethnic/national

---

60   Lake Chilika is Asia's largest brackish water lake. For thousands of traditional fishermen
and women, it is a common property resource, which they use to obtain their livelihood.
The state is now allowing agribusiness enterprises to use parts of the lake for export-
oriented shrimp production. This hinders open access to the lake for traditional fishing,
and by polluting the lake, results in the depletion of the fish-stock adversely affecting the
economy of the traditional fishing community. All this has triggered a massive and often
militant movement, helped by the local left (CPI M-L/Liberation). Its targets are capitalists, some of whom are high level state officials themselves, and the provincial state
apparatus.
61   Of course, this struggle is often led by large-scale, capitalist farmers (on famers' movement, see Brass, 1995; Gupta, 2002).
62   See Guha (2002) on the environmental movements. On movements in aboriginal areas,
see Sinha (2002) and Singh (2002); on the Dalit movement, see Omvedt (2002); on

oppression. This is the third form of lower-class struggle. Indeed, adverse environmental change and non-class forms of oppression have, arguably, a disproportionate impact on the poor than on the better-off sections. To the degree that the propertied classes and the state bolster – either overtly or covertly – 'non-class' forms, moreover, they become the target of agency aimed at such oppressions. These are the struggles in which lower classes participate, although whether they do so always because they are conscious of the role of capitalism in the creation of ecological problems and social oppression, is doubtful.[63]

The fourth form of the lower-class struggle is one that is most clearly 'political': for the democratization of the state. Workers and small-scale producers join with the broad mass of the population in this kind of agency, not least because they are the ones who often experience in its most overt form the corrupt practices and patronizing attitudes of state elites, the 'brown sahibs' who treat them like slaves.[64] In so far as the undemocratic nature of the state – its lack of accountability to the lower classes in terms of policies, programs, and politics – derives from the fact that the main role of this apparatus in a society

---

women's movement, see Lingam (2002.) On the relation between the Marxist movement and the caste movement, see Teltumbde (2016) who says that there is an increasing divergence between the two. See Omvedt (1993) on the new social movement in relation to class agency.

63   These movements are portrayed as empowering alternatives – what Corbridge terms the 'politics of the feasible', echoing the words of the British Conservative Rab Butler (for whom politics was 'the art of the possible') – to 'bad' narrow-minded class-based leftist struggles (Omvedt, 1993). These movements often engage in the politics of neo-populism/ nationalism of the kind usually associated with the political right, such as the BJP. But these movements can have left-leaning elements in certain contexts. Indeed class based actors have been involved in these movements, and those involved in the latter – for example, Medha Patkar – sometimes show direct support for class struggles. Nilsen (2008) discusses accumulation by dispossession (in the Narmada Valley) in the larger context of the political economy of state-led capitalism in India, where state development strategies have in large part functioned as vehicles for the expropriation and enclosure of vital productive resources in favour of the country's dominant proprietary classes. But there are limits to the extent to which social movements can use the state as a neutral arbiter by ignoring the 'constraints' imposed by proprietary classes.

64   Attitudes towards corruption can be ambivalent. It is generally the case that leaders of communist parties are less corrupt than other leaders, and yet, apparently, some voters in Kerala think that if a leader is not corrupt they might not be able to help. I learnt this from my conversation with Professor Mohanakumar. Similarly, Witsoe (2011: 82–83) records that in the context of villages in Bihar in the 1990s: 'many people supported politicians not only despite perceptions that they were corrupt but also precisely because they were perceived as corrupt and therefore capable of using their positions for the benefit of their supporters'.

that is capitalist is to reproduce capitalist-class dominance over the direct producers, struggles over democracy are centrally linked to the fact of class. In
more recent times, struggles against the attack on democratic rights have focused on the attacks on religious minorities from fascistic forces.[65]

Apart from these four inter-connected forms of struggle of lower classes
against various forms of injustice that more or less emanate from the capitalist
character of the society and the state, the lower-class politics also takes forms
that directly reproduce and support the unjust conditions of their own existence. Partly given the constraints that class structure imposes on lower-class
politics and partly because of ruling class strategies to weaken potential lower-
class opposition, the lower classes have engaged in various forms of politics
that are ultimately not in their immediate or long-term interest and that are
shaped by their false consciousness: providing support to parties of the right
on the basis of identity politics of nationalism and religion; being a part of a
clientilistic structure in which some powerful property-owners-cum-politi-
cians provide limited assistance to lower classes in return for political support
(e.g. votes) from them;[66] and constantly reposing faith in the bourgeois parties
and indeed in the state as such as the set of institutions that one can appeal to
for the improvement of one's conditions.

5   State Form, State Policy, and Class Struggle

That such struggles are waged by 'those below', means in turn that both the
propertied classes and the state find it necessary to make concessions.[67] Many

---

65   It is important to stress that the map of lower-class struggles includes an inter-connected
      chain of struggles – the struggles against dispossession, disenfranchisement, and stigma
      or disrespect (Nilsen and Roy, 2015). Whether subalternity is the underlying factor under-
      lying these struggles is a different matter.
66   Pattenden (2011) says that: owing to fiscal decentralization to gram panchayats, some
      members of the dominant class have control over the financial resources spent at the
      local scale, which they use to gain support from workers: this process reproduces new
      patterns of workers' dependence upon the dominant class. This points to how class state
      relations are played out at the local scale.
67   Of course, these concessions are used by capital (and state elites) for its own benefit,
      generating demand for commodities (farm implements, fertilizers, cattle for small pro-
      ducers). State elites also benefit, since implementation of these policies is a source of
      bribes and influence. In terms of urban labor, the state has sometimes initiated pro-labor
      legislations not as a direct response to actual struggle but as a preemptive response to
      avoid having to face such struggle (on this see Teitelbaum, 2013). Yet, according to Teitel-
      baum (2006), workers are more united and powerful than assumed.

scholars have maintained that important anti-poverty policies, including agrarian reform programs, have indeed been the result of 'from below' class struggles (Desai, 1989).[68] Even such accumulation projects as the Green Revolution were driven in part by the fear that actual or potential famine conditions during the 1960s might constitute a threat to the political order from the lower classes.[69] It is undeniably the case that the Green Revolution was in part offered as an *anti-poverty* policy. Similarly, the recent policy aimed at ensuring 100 days of employment to those seeking manual work in villages – the National Rural Employment Guarantee Programme – for which the political left fought, is another example of concession by 'those above'.[70]

It is a mistake, however, to assume that the *only* response the Indian state can make to 'from below' struggle is a conciliatory or defensive response: giving concession. The state frequently launches 'from above' class struggle in support of capital's economic interests and in the interest of maintaining political order. This comes in many forms. One is the commodification of 'commons', or common property resources that pre-dated capitalism and were an important component of direct producers' subsistence. Commons also take the form of state provided subsistence (for example, subsidized food for the poor), an achievement won as a result of grassroots struggle by lower classes.[71] State actions aimed at commodifying the commons are designed to further two ends: not just promoting capitalist development but also preventing – or pre-empting – any move towards the project of *transcending* capitalism and

---

68   The Hindu (2007) reported that the Janadesh March on October 28, 2007, when thousands of rural poor and landless arrived in Delhi to press their demands, the Union government announced on October 29 the setting up of a National Land Reforms Council. The latter would take a 'holistic approach' to land reforms and will come out with a National Land Reforms Policy.

69   There are, of course, other interpretations as to the driving force behind the Green Revolution programme. An external one was identified by Cleaver (1972), who maintained that overproduction of chemical inputs by agribusiness, destined for the US markets, meant that these enterprises looked to foreign markets in the Third World as an outlet for their commodities. Hence the Green Revolution package (chemical inputs and irrigation).

70   Arjun Sengupta, Chairperson of the National Commission for Enterprises in the Unorganized Sector, candidly connected class struggle to state policy. His words (cited in Dhar, 2007) were as follows: 'We must realise that the voiceless groups have now started to assert themselves by seeking their rights. This (social engineering in the form of universal employment guarantee) is one way of doing it. The other way would be through naxalism (or more generally, 'from below' struggles). This is the dynamics of the situation that is pushing us towards a more inclusive economic development'.

71   This policy has been watered down (Swaminathan, 2000).

the capitalist state.[72] Another is a direct attack on working conditions in the form of policies that support exploitation of workers and small-scale producers by the property-owning class. And of course, when all else fails, repression is the response to class struggle.

Class struggles must additionally be seen as being influenced by the *form* taken by the Indian state, and not just by its actions. Hence the class character of Indian society, and the grassroots struggles arising from this, influence the nature of the state *form*, which in turn influences state *actions*. There are two dimensions to the state form: democratic and territorial. To begin with, therefore, is the double impact – as outcome of grassroots conflict and on the shape of such agency – of the fact that the Indian state currently exhibits a liberal democratic form.[73] Indeed, given severe forms of inequality and high level of poverty within the country, perhaps nowhere else in the world is the degree of the gap between substantive economic inequality and formal political equality as great as it is in India. This gap is decreasing though to the extent that the state-form is increasingly being more illiberal.

The existence and reproduction of the democratic form of the state itself must be seen partly as a product of continuing struggles by the lower classes in conjunction with other strata for democracy in the face of strong anti-democratic pressures from society.[74] The latter emanate from landlord elements that remain powerful in the countryside. More importantly, they also derive from the current nature of capitalism that depends increasingly on

---

72   One can even go further. The suppression by the Indian state of rural labor struggle against capital has, ironically, made it more vulnerable to capital. Among other things, this has enabled rich peasants, commercial farmers and agribusiness enterprises to conduct 'from above' forms of class struggle, including the reproduction and/or reintroduction of unfree labor (or what Brass calls deproletarianization). Misrecognizing the latter as evidence for the 'pre-' or 'non-capitalist' nature of the agrarian labor process has led to the epistemological confusion within the left about the nature of class contradiction. 'Feudal' or 'semi-feudal' landlords replace agrarian capitalists as the main target of 'from below' agency, and conflict between capital and labor gives way to a struggle between the broad masses and 'semi-feudal' landlords. Capitalism is as a result categorized as a desirable development, to be introduced by a 'progressive' bourgeoisie. This ideological mystification – arising from the fact that contemporary capitalist reality in rural India 'folds within itself a certain degree of falsity', to borrow a phrase from Eagleton (1999) – has contributed further to the disempowerment of agricultural labor and poor peasants.

73   India is unusual in this regard. It is similar to western developed countries in that the state has a liberal democratic form, but dissimilar in that a vast majority of the Indian population is dependent upon farming.

74   Although capitalism is compatible with liberal democracy, it does not necessarily need this.

various coercive measures that characterize primitive accumulation.[75] Threats to formal democracy also come from those (e.g. fascistic forces) who are opposed to gender equality and minority religions. Given the size of India, maintaining territorial and political order in half a million villages, 500 cities and thousands of towns amidst much deprivation is a difficult task for the class-state, which must constantly recycle/reinvent discourse about caste and religion so as to maintain order through the activities of political parties on the right and center of the political spectrum.

A liberal democratic capitalist state must not only promote accumulation but also legitimize this support by seeming to act on behalf of the whole nation, a strategy bolstered by making concessions. Arguably, the latter include the democratic form itself, which helps the state deflect or soften class antagonism by means of periodic elections. A secular form of religion for the masses, the capacity to exercise the vote at regular intervals provides lower classes with the illusion that it is they who exercise control over the state and the dominant classes. Not only does this fuel the hope that they gain material benefits from electoral patronage, but it also perpetuates the belief that if not this party/leader then the next one in power will address their problems.[76] The fetishistic worship of democracy is widely prevalent among the poor citizens and scholars. Indeed, thanks to the efforts of the state via educational institutions and publicity, etc., most people do not understand the following simple fact. Just as people are free to work for this or that capitalist employer but not free not to work under the control of a capitalist employer for a wage, similarly, people are free to choose this or that capitalist party, but not free not to vote for a capitalist party to power or a party that will fundamentally work within the constraints of capitalist property relations. Freedom to choose a party in elections, free or not, will not bring freedom from miseries: this is not understood by most people.[77]

The existence of the democratic form, of course, does not mean that it is the only form of class rule: indeed, when necessary the state will and does use coercion, increasingly so against the lower classes if they resist its accumulation policies beyond a certain limit. What is interesting to note is that the use of *coercion* against the lower classes is justified through the *democratic* form. Whichever party is in power, whether it is the 'centrist' Congress or the rightist

75   As Mandel (1969) notes, the state exercises coercion 'for maintaining the material interests of the strongest section of the exploiters'.

76   This is obviously a very different kind of hope to that referred to by Mandel (2002).

77   Roy says (2018) that India's democracy provides the country's poor with unique opportunities for political engagement and that the poor people are not, therefore, excluded from politics.

BJP (they are actually two factions of what could arguably be seen as a united party/front of the bourgeoisie, at least as far as economic policies are concerned), they tend to use violence against the lower classes if what the latter demand fundamentally challenges the dominant class elements. In fact, even the left front government has used repression against ordinary people protesting against the violation of their rights.[78]

When the state form is democratic, coercion is not seen as what it is – namely, suppression of lower classes by a class state acting on behalf of dominant class interests – but rather as what it appears to be. That is, it is merely seen as wrongful action carried out either by this or that political party in furtherance of an incorrect policy, or by officials/politicians who are misinformed as to what is really required. A corollary is that such agency by the state is in effect mistaken, an anomaly that can be rectified by changing the party in power, its leadership, or bureaucrats and officials carrying out the orders.[79] This is akin to Marx's theory of commodity fetishism, an ideological inversion (Ollman, 1993) whereby 'the relationships between producers [...] take on the form of a social relation between the products of labour' (Marx, 1977: 164, 165), when 'the definite social relation' among producers themselves assumes 'the fantastic form of a relation between things'. Similarly, what actually is a coercive relation between classes, enforced by the capitalist state, is mistakenly seen as a relation between voters/citizens on the one hand and parties, political leaders, and officials on the other. This is a relation that cannot be eliminated until the state is directly and socially regulated, in much the same way as commodity fetishism, as Rubin (1973) says, cannot be removed until labor power is directly and socially regulated.[80]

At the same time, however, excessive coercion can adversely affect political legitimacy of the parties in power and even of the state itself. In response to the numerous class struggles over the land issue during the 1960s, the federal government of India stated: 'It will be unrealistic to seek lasting solutions to a socioeconomic problem (i.e. unequal distribution of land)...through coercive measures alone' (Government of India, 1986). Thus the state is required to balance three processes: (i) accumulation; (ii) legitimation through material and non-material concessions, including the democratic form; and (iii) coercion.

---

78   Police have killed peasants resisting dispossession in CPM-ruled West Bengal and Congress ruled Andhra Pradesh.

79   The view that the state is an autonomous institution – popular among Weberian theorists – is consistent with this perception.

80   It is not just the rural poor who subscribe to this kind of reification. Both the postmodern 'left' and liberal political theorists do the same, as a result of which they endorse non-governmental organizational politics, aimed at putting pressure on the local-level state actors to change their ways.

The actual intervention over a period of time and over space must be seen as a mix of these three, the nature of which depends on the intensity of class struggle both inside and outside the state, as well as on the requirements of accumulation and the nature of a particular political regime that manages the affairs of the state.

The democratic state form also influences the shape taken by class struggle itself. On the one hand, it dissolves what are *classes* into *individuals* and – further – into *individual voters*. By giving opportunities for full expression to religious, casteist, ethnic and regional identities, the state fragments the lower classes into members of electoral groups, into supporters of this or that party (or fractions thereof), irrespective of their class position and interests, thereby weakening the power and agency as lower classes. Currently, democracy has enabled the property-owning class – including those who use unfree labor and are therefore *un*democratic in a substantive sense – to 'capture' specific parts of the state through liberal *democratic* elections. In some areas of India, therefore, proprietors are still able to compel lower class/caste members to vote as they (the landed) would like. Through their control over specific parts of the state – especially at the local/regional level – property owners appropriate the resources allocated by the state to the poor. On the other hand, by ensuring a limited degree of free association and speech, and through electoral procedures and the 'rule of law', the state in its democratic form has indeed allowed rural and urban workers who form the majority of the population, to voice limited opposition to economic exploitation and political domination. Within limits, they are permitted to exert pressure on the capitalist state to create conditions that favor the lower classes.[81]

The democratic state form has thus allowed competition between political parties which has contributed in varying degrees to the politicization of lower classes, and to the implementation of policies on their behalf such as land reform. Although much attention has been paid to competition between mainstream parties – see, for example, Chibber and Nooruddin (2004) – less has been said about the competition between these and leftist parties (see Bardhan and Mukherjee, 2005; Echeverri-Gent, 1995) and almost nothing about the competition *between* leftist parties. The latter is an important feature of India's liberal democracy, no matter how faulty democracy is and reformist many of

---

81   On the topic of how people's struggles have resulted in some developmental outcomes, see Williams (2009). It should be noted, however, that democracy, rather obviously, has not resulted in much reduction of substantive inequalities (Heller, 2000). It should be noted that the scope for egalitarian development has been shrinking within the neoliberal-capitalist phase that began since the early 1990s, which is why the state's response to lower-class struggles has been one of repression and ideological manipulation (e.g. the use of identity politics; lies, false promises, etc.), regardless of the political-party-regime.

these parties are. It was the *inter-communist* party competition – not electoral competition or democracy as such – and the consequent extraordinary combination of parliamentary and direct-action strategies by the two left parties that it fostered in Kerala, that was responsible in part for a higher degree of implementation there of 'radical' tenancy reforms.[82]

Many commentators, including Amartya Sen (1999), assume that by encouraging competition between parties and allowing a free press, democracy will lead to the implementation of pro-poor policies. He says that what the government does can be influenced by public pressures from below (Dreze and Sen, 1995). But much depends on what issues are politicized. What is, or is not, politicized depends on the visions and pre-occupations of *opposition* parties. Non-communist *opposition* parties do not *oppose* ruling parties on crucial issues such as payment of compensation to landlords in the land reform laws or privatization of state-owned companies or India's subjugation to the imperialist military-economic framework. In other words, on class-related issues that do matter to the lower classes, opposition parties do *not* matter. Parties in power and parties in opposition do not oppose the fundamental interests of the business class. Both ruling and opposition parties work within the framework of a state that supports the fundamental interests of the propertied classes and share an anti-lower-class ideology which, in turn, contributes to the depoliticization of the crucial issues. Dreze and Sen ignore the fact that the ideology of the propertied classes and the coercive character of the state, among other things, influence what enters into political debates and what does not. Sen's view is problematic because it is silent about the class character of the parties/regimes, which manage the common affairs of the state, which, in turn, manages the common affairs of the capitalist class. Sen's optimistic prognosis, which I mentioned in Chapter 2, cannot answer the question why it is that crucial development issues – such as unequal distribution of means of production (particularly land), extreme forms of income inequality, absence of high-quality and free state-provided health-care and education, and employment for all at an inflation-adjusted living wage – do not become important election issues, and are not much debated by competing mainstream parties (Das, 2001a). Democracy can help in the promulgation and implementation of policies favorable to the lower classes, but within limits. If these classes are to secure significant access to economic resources, including land, in the

---

82   It is significant that, with the exception of isolated pockets, these two left parties have more-or-less given up on extra-parliamentary actions. The resulting vacuum, in terms of class politics, has been filled in some areas – and especially in eastern India – by the parties/formations that are influenced by Maoism.

democratic process – so as to enjoy the health and educational freedoms which Sen rightly thinks all human beings should – then this at least requires the severe curtailment of political power exercised by dominant proprietary classes. And for this to happen, democracy must also involve competition and polemical struggle as well as a degree of collaboration between/among left parties, and democracy must allow genuine struggle between them and mainstream parties. Yet, the fact that remains that the (bourgeois) democratic state form itself poses severe limits to the capacity of lower classes to gain enough power to be able to secure resources from governments that must promote capitalist interests.

The other dimension of the state concerns its territorial or geographical form.[83] It is commonly agreed that the federal nature of the Indian state has meant that individual states possess some autonomy in framing and implementing policies (and this is especially so with respect to agriculture, police, education, health, etc.). A federal bourgeois state-form emerged mainly as a product of two processes. First, the struggle between members of the bourgeoisie at regional and national levels, over issues such as regional markets and labor reserves (Kosambi, 1957). And second, a similarly regional struggle conducted by lower classes (Vanaik, 1990). This territoriality of the state form provides regional components of the dominant class (regional bourgeoisie) of middle and higher castes some leeway, enabling them to pursue their class and caste interests by influencing the state at sub-national levels.

This form also creates – albeit unintentionally – spaces within the state structure that lower classes are able to use to their advantage within limits. It is this combination of territorial state form and class struggle that, in a context of uneven development nationally, results in regionally specific bourgeois-political-economies throughout India. The latter vary from regimes dominated by traditional landlords from the upper castes – such as, for example, Madhya Pradesh and Orissa – to one where their dominance has been challenged by capitalist farmers and rich peasant groups from middle caste backgrounds. Lower classes/castes are to a greater or lesser extent accommodated (Gujarat and Maharashtra being instances of the former, Bihar and Uttar Pradesh of the latter), while in yet other sub-national states their interests are better

---

83   The geographical form of the state includes: the central level; the provincial/State level; the local level (e.g. village or taluka or the district) interaction between state institutions and common citizens (mainly lower classes); relations between the central level and the provincial level; relations between provinces; relations between the local level and provincial/national levels; and relations between the different levels (especially, provincial and national levels) and the global-scale processes and institutions (Das, 1998; Sinha, 2011; also see Jacob, 2015).

represented, such as in Kerala. And there are similar variations within a province in terms of organization of lower classes and (institutionalization of) Left power.

Under certain conditions, therefore, lower classes 'ruling' at the sub-national level can formulate and implement area-specific policies that reflect their interests. Wherever this has occurred in the past – Kerala, West Bengal and Tripura, being obvious examples (Desai, 2003; Kohli, 1987; Heller, 2000; Pillai, 2003) – the following developments have resulted:

a)   The political legitimization of struggles by workers and small-scale producers in rural and urban areas, no matter how limited that acceptability is. This outcome is underlined by the decision of leftist governments not to allow the police to interfere in confrontations involving landlords and tenants in Kerala during the era of land reform;[84]

b)   The mitigation of class exploitation through anti-poverty policies in a relatively uncorrupt manner and social sector investment;

c)   A political decentralization which empowers lower classes at the village level;

d)   A stable environment where accumulation based on private property can proceed.[85]

Of significance has been the limited expansion of trade-union rights and, particularly, of broad civil rights and the legal prohibition of extra-economic coercive practices by landowners, at least, during the early period of the left regimes. Similarly important is the fact that at a sub-national level the left has facilitated the construction of an agrarian 'accumulation strategy'. For example, the devolution of power to lower classes has enabled – within limits – the provincial state to 'discipline' erstwhile landowners. As a result, there has been a decline in the share of the crop taken as rent, in the incidence of eviction, and some land has been redistributed. Limited financial support has also been provided to small holders (Bhattacharyya, 2001). What all this demonstrates, albeit tentatively, is that even a moderately reformist development strategy entailing redistribution of economic resources is in the end a reflection of the local balance of class forces: where state apparatuses are governed by left

---

84   For example, in Kerala the 'new police policy' prevented intervention in agrarian disputes in all cases except when life was in danger. Much the same happened in West Bengal during the 1960s when Mr. H. Konar was the land reform Minister in that state.

85   One should note that the last aspect of the left's social-democratic type regime (ensuring capitalist accumulation) sets limit to what can be achieved in terms of the first two. And indeed, the importance of the first two aspects has been reduced over time in the provinces where the Left has been in power.

parties, and where the left is well organized, lower-class input into these policies has been greater and the implementation of these policies in their interests has been better.

The lower classes have been able to win some concessions through their
parties (Left parties). However, since 2009, these parties (which are, more or
less, social-democratic in practice) have experienced drastic electoral decline,
and this is partly related to neoliberalism as discussed in Chapter 4. Two things
should be said about this. The political power of the Left cannot be reduced to
electoral success or defeat, however. While the Left's mobilizational power
may not be evident at the national scale, that does not mean that it is not powerful in specific areas within the country or a province. The fact that the Left is
not that powerful at the national and provincial scales is used by right-wing
people to say that the Left is irrelevant, that it is dead. And such a conclusion
helps to *legitimize* right-wing policies and thinking.

While capital – labor relation is everywhere, the ways in which that relation
is experienced are locally rooted. This is the case in the West (Cox, 1988) and in
India (Das, 2001b). In terms of the ways in which labor markets generally
function, they are quite localized. Similarly, relations between landlords and
moneylenders on the one hand and small-scale producers as tenants and debtors on the other hand, are locally rooted: their relations are experienced within
geographically circumscribed areas. If Left politics – organization of lower
classes – has to succeed, it has to begin in specific areas, and then scale up to
higher geographical levels such as district, province, etc. In other words, Left
organization has to be multi-scalar.

Indeed, state power in India is exercised at multiple scales. In the rural context, these are: central level (Delhi); States/provinces; districts within a State;
sub-districts/tehsil within a district; development block within a tehsil; cluster
of villages (Panchayat) in a development block; revenue or administratively
defined single villages; and wards/neighborhoods/hamlets. In terms of urban
India, there are: central level (Delhi); States/provinces; cities with their may-
ors, etc.; wards/neighborhoods within a city, and so on.

While left/radical/Marxist politics has lost some of its power at the Central
and provincial scales, there are literally hundreds of wards/hamlets, cities,
village-clusters or development blocks, villages, etc. where Marxists and radicals are relatively powerful, and they are exercising their power, however limited, to make the state and employers do what they would otherwise not do.
That there are serious limits to what Left parties can achieve – and these limits
are partly because of their limited ideological compass as mentioned in
Chapter 3 – is a separate topic (see Chapter 13).

6   The Indian State and the Class Contradictions of Economic Development

In view of its class character, the state is rather obviously a contradiction-ridden entity, and this in turn problematizes its development role. One consequence of having to manage conflicts is that the Indian state has been unable to play the same kind of developmental role (building infrastructure for agricultural and for industrial development) as the East Asian state (Amsden, 1998).[86] Another is the outcome of tax avoidance or evasion by the dominant classes: the shortfall in state revenues means that state expenditure is concentrated in specific regions. This creates a basis for regionally uneven economic development, which complements the inherent tendency towards uneven development under capitalism.

The most important outcome of this uneven economic development is, as noted earlier, a corresponding geographical unevenness to grassroots struggles (lower-class struggles).[87] Regional variations throughout India in terms of economic development shape the form and intensity of class conflict, along with factors such as the caste-class correlation, the nature and quality of lower class leadership, and the degree of left-wing unity.[88] This effect of uneven development is a geographically fragmented process of class formation and struggle, which is an important contributory factor in the weakness of a 'from below' challenge to the state at the national level, where the power of the dominant classes is concentrated and protected.

---

86   One should be careful not to over-stress this point: it is problematic to assume that the state under capitalism could play a positive role in promoting development on a sustainable long term basis, rural or urban. The positive role of the nation-state in, for example, East Asia has been overstated, and its negative role correspondingly understated (Burkett and Hart-Landsberg, 2003).

87   The state responds to unevenness of class struggle through a spatial fix. Urban workers, for example, tend to be more organized than rural workers, which permits income deflation through unfavorable terms of trade to operate against agriculture (Patnaik, 1995: 168). Class struggle in the urban areas reinforces this spatial fix, accentuating the rural-urban disparity. There are contradictions, however, as squeezing the countryside (and this really means squeezing its lower classes) creates the problem of agrarian backwardness which can be a fetter on industrial development.

88   It must be said that some of the most courageous left movements lack a coherent rigorous radical theory (applicable to the Indian social formation as opposed to its component local formations). Accordingly, they suffer politically from problems of empiricism (their views about society and tactics change according to locations) and from associated localization of the movements they lead (see Nathan, 1999).

When seen in terms of development policies for the lower classes/castes and in relation to class struggle, therefore, the Indian state is, once again, a deeply contradictory entity. If lack of grassroots power contributes to poverty, the process of regionally uneven development fostered by the capitalist state reproduces and entrenches that powerlessness: the state must therefore be seen as an important cause of lower-class poverty. This is one of the many reasons why one should be critical of those – among them postmodernists, supporters of NGOs and advocates of social capital – who regard decentralization of state power as part of the solution to poverty and underdevelopment, rather than as part of the problem.[89] Looked at differently, the issue of decentralization is one about the scale – and thus the efficacy – of opposition to the capitalist state.

In India, as elsewhere, scale is indeed central to the success or failure of the class struggle. Of significance, therefore, is the fact that the vast NGO sector, much favored as an 'alternative' form of development, grows out of, and is in tune with, neoliberal policies of the state (Petras, 1997). For its part, the neoliberal state is highly supportive of most NGOs, which act as its development subcontractors. While the left movement seeks to organize and formulate policy at the national and provincial levels, much NGO activity by contrast is resolutely small-scale, in terms both of issues addressed and the area covered. Although the work carried out by a few NGOs is of benefit to the poor, this kind of piecemeal approach to poverty tends to reinforce the fragmented nature of grassroots opposition to capitalism and its state, and to provide the latter with a semblance of ideological legitimacy, by fulfilling an ameliorating role (= 'survival') within the existing system.[90]

The three processes outlined above – the near-abrogation by the state of its development role, the sub-contracting of micro-level 'survival' projects to NGOs, and the organizational weakness of multi-scalar class-based opposition in the face of poverty and inequality – raise once again the following political question: can the Indian state face a legitimation crisis? In this context, the following points can be made.

To begin with, it is important to recall that, from the standpoint of lower classes, the colonial state did not discharge a developmental role; in part,

---

89   On the decentralization debate, see among many others Veron et al. (2006). On non-party
        grassroots politics (which does not aim to control power through electoral or by other
        means), see Kothari (2002), and Harriss (2011c).
90   Harriss (2011c) says that in neoliberal India, there is the popularity of a new politics: this is
        based in communities, not workplaces, on voluntary associations in civil society and not
        political parties, and on social movements and not trade unions (p. 91). The new politics
        excludes the poor as active agents. The organizations may work for the poor, but they are
        not of the poor (p. 92). New politics is against the state and not against the employer (p. 103).

therefore, the post-1947 state in India gained a degree of ideological legitimation from its promise to foster economic development, a break with the approach of the colonial state. About this Partha Chatterjee (1993: 203) observes:

> The new state represented the only legitimate form of the exercise of
> power because it was a necessary condition for the *development* of the
> nation. [...] (it) acquired its representativeness by directing a program of
> economic *development* on behalf of the nation.

Accordingly, the legitimacy of the state in the era of Independence 'had to flow
from ... the historical necessity of an independent state that would promote
national *development*' (Chatterjee, 1993: 205; emphasis added).[91]

Like the earlier colonial state, however, the current neoliberal state in India
is not fulfilling (and as importantly, not being seen to fulfill) a developmental
role. Hence the development process – both the material benefits and dis-
courses/rhetoric of development including such slogans as *garibi hatao* (eradi-
cate poverty) – no longer discharges for the state the legitimizing role to the
same extent it did earlier, in the more optimistic decades following Independence.[92] This is certainly true of the way the state is 'seen' by 'those below' in
many parts of eastern India, where there exist very strong radical militant organizations of the rural poor. There the reduction in spending by the neoliberal state on anti-poverty policies – a process termed the selective retreat of
the state – has indeed eroded its legitimacy in the eyes of the vast majority of
the rural population in terms of promoting development. For lower classes,
therefore, the state is not perceived as a 'caring' state to the same extent it was
earlier, both materially and discursively. If capital says to labor 'perform or per-
ish', cannot labor say the same to capital's state?

The potential legitimation crisis arising from the failure of the state to fulfil
its development role – i.e. to act as a 'developmental state' – also has a scale
aspect. Previously, and however misguidedly, citizens in the vast rural periphery subscribed to the belief that that higher-level state institutions really

---

91   Some scholars say that the colonial state was characterized by a dominance without he-
      gemony while the postcolonial state is characterized by a passive revolution (Chatterjee,
      2017).

92   Roy (2018) says that poor people are central to Indian politics in that the poor engage with
      their elected representatives, political mediators and dominant classes in varied ways in
      order to advance their claims, and that public policy and political parties, and develop-
      ment plans and elected representatives derive their legitimacy in the name of the poor.
      The point is: if the poor (lower classes) can be a source of legitimacy at one time, they can
      be a source of its opposite – the crisis of legitimacy – at another time.

wanted to help the poor, and that it was only the local scale officials/politicians that were mismanaging the resources.[93] A villager confirmed this to Akhil Gupta (2000) in the following manner: 'Although the government has many good schemes, the officials in the middle eat it all'. I too have come across this type of responses from the lower classes in Orissa as well in my research on the state, social capital and poverty (Das, 2005). Thus the potential crisis of legitimation used to be confined largely to the local state. Now, however, with central government – even the judiciary at the provincial and national scales – openly espousing neoliberalism (and its twin, authoritarianism), all levels of the state apparatus are vulnerable in this respect.

Of additional relevance is that the ideological illegitimacy of the colonial state derived from its being 'other' economically: that is, it was seen as serving the external ('foreign', 'non-Indian') interests in furtherance of which it licensed the exploitation of Indian workers and peasants. The ideological legitimacy of the post-1947 state, and a central emplacement of Indian nationalist discourse, emanated from the fact that it would be independent of an international capitalism. Hence the legitimacy of the Indian state 'had to flow from the nationalistic criticism of colonialism as an alien and unrepresentative power' (Chatterjee, 1993: 205). The point is that now – and once again – the state is creating the conditions for the transfer of profits to the foreign capital: indeed, the neoliberal Indian state is actively encouraging international capital to exploit its own lower classes, a process in which domestic capitalists – urban and rural – are invited to participate. Under neoliberalism, capital has no nation. Even capitalists from a poor nation such as India, in pursuit of profit, are investing capital in the richest countries such as Canada, the US and the UK, and indeed thousands of dollar millionnaires from India are leaving India (6000 left in 2016 and 7000 in 2017). To this has to be added the fact that many smaller business units are going under because of neoliberal competition and withdrawal of state protection, thereby narrowing the class/social basis of the capitalist state. The nationalistic dream – the idea that there is a nation and what the state does is good for the nation – may be on the way out. If the concept of nation has any significance, it must, first of all, be the 'nation' of workers and small-scale producers, yet the neoliberal state is increasingly alienating itself from *this* 'nation'. And this is why, there is a need to construct another nation, one that is based on religious etc. identity. This strategy creates internal enemies of the fake nation (e.g. religious minorities and politically progressive

---

93   For a similar case of mistrust in the local state combined with trust in the central state, in
        the context of China, see So (2007). On the 'development state' in Latin America, see
        Petras and Veltmeyer (2007).

people defending democratic rights), so the real nation is divided and weakened and does not concentrate the real enemies of the nation. The real enemies are (a) the capitalist class in whose interest policies are being formed by all kinds of governments, and (b) all those who support this class and all those who are creating disunity within *the nation of toiling masses* in the name of religion (hard or soft Hindutva), and by using a false sense of history, and so on.

Another contributory factor in this delegitimization process is that action by the neoliberal state is perceived to lack rationality. The colonial state was exporting wheat from India to the UK when in India itself the population did not have sufficient food to eat. In a similar vein, the neoliberal state is now seen as irrational in promoting the production of luxury commodities, such as flowers, shrimps and animal feed for export to imperialist/rich countries, when millions are malnourished and hungry at home.[94] The state-promoted export of these new agricultural commodities is itself based on cheap labor and cheap land. 'Cheap', however, hides the ecological and social conditions under which these commodities are produced by peasants and workers, many of whom are lower-caste women. Cheapness is not a characteristic innate to India, either to the (tattered) bodies of its workforce or to its (degraded) nature, both of which are deployed by neoliberal capitalist accumulation (this issue is discussed in the last chapter).[95]

The perceived difference between the colonial state and its post-1947 counterpart – a crucial ideological one – thus no longer holds.[96] This is because the state is no longer able to sustain even the fiction of carrying out policies designed to benefit large swathes of the Indian polity – the 'people' who form 'the nation', in other words. The failure is more drastic with the turn to neoliberalism, and to right-wing politics associated with the rise of BJP as a hard-right governing party. In fact, the neoliberal state-form and state intervention (the state's relative withdrawal from welfare-provision, and a certain degree of control over the business class) were justified on the basis that the neoliberal state is good for the masses but as we have seen, this has turned out to be a lie. Neoliberalization has hurt the masses, including by dispossessing them of their small-scale property, so the neoliberal form of the state cannot have the legitimacy in the minds of the ordinary people.[97]

---

94   As others have argued, per capita food availability has declined to levels experienced during the 1943 Bengal famine (Patnaik, 2002, 1999).

95   See Harvey (1998) and Smith (2007) for discussions about the body, nature and capitalism.

96   There are many other aspects of the difference between the colonial and the post-colonial state than those discussed here (see Murphy and Jammaulamadaka, 2017).

97   Chacko (2018) says that there is a long-term crisis of the state because successive governments have been unable to establish legitimacy for the post-1990s policies of

While neoliberalism is deeply against the interests of the masses, the state and the business class justify neoliberalism on the ground that it helps and will help the poor. Apart from the differences/contradictions between the colonial state and the post-colonial state, there are important differences/contradictions between the pre-neoliberal state and the neoliberal state. While the personnel of the state before the mid-1980s, often drawn from lower strata of society (e.g. petty-bourgeois strata), maintained some distance between them and the capitalist class, now the personnel of the state revel in their connections with, and take pride from their work for, the business class. The social legitimacy of the state clearly is at stake because the state, at least, has to give the appearance that it is neutral, that it is for everyone, for all classes. But maintaining such an appearance is difficult because a distinctive change in the class character of the personnel of the state, as Prabhat Patnaik (2018) eloquently describes, prior to neoliberalism:

> The State personnel drawn from the ranks of the petty bourgeoisie were generally skeptical about, and even to a degree hostile to, the capitalist class and were committed to State capitalism which they also saw as a means of self- advancement in the new situation of de-colonization. The State was a bourgeois State, laying the foundations for capitalist development. But the motivation, the ideological inclinations, and the class background of the State personnel ensured that the State had a degree of autonomy both vis a vis imperialism and also vis a vis the domestic capitalists.

However, something has changed with the turn to neoliberalism:

> The "neo-liberal State" too is a bourgeois State like the *dirigiste* State, but the personnel of the former differ fundamentally from the personnel of the latter, not just in their ideological predilections, which are closely aligned to the views of the Bretton Woods institutions, *but also in their being deeply enmeshed with the world of finance and big business.* What we find in today's State personnel is not just a different set of ideologues, World Bank ideologues, as distinct from the Nehruvian ideologues that manned the *dirigiste* bourgeois State, but a set whose motivation is no different from that of the big bourgeoisie and financial interests and

---

neoliberalization. Similarly, Levien (2013) argues that while the pre-neoliberal state dispossessed small-scale producers like the neoliberal state does now, the latter has been unable to achieve the ideological legitimacy of its predecessor, leading to more widespread struggles against state-enabled dispossession.

which therefore has no compunctions about being closely integrated with the latter.[98]

This is something Harsh Mander (2016), a former top civil servant also remarks on:

> in my time no official would be seen spending time with businesses. If an official socialised with the rich and the powerful, the official was considered someone who lacked integrity. Today you can claim to be doing it in the name of nation-building and advancing the economy.

As a result of this, there has been an 'undermining of the social legitimacy of the State', and this 'especially in the context of the tremendous increase in wealth and income inequalities associated with the pursuit of the neo-liberal strategy' (Patnaik, 2018).

Whether all these structural conditions will actually result in a legitimation crisis, and to what extent, will, of course, depend on how the lower classes and their political parties and their organic intellectuals at home and internationally, respond to these conditions politically.[99] And to the degree that the crisis does take shape, much also will depend on how the state reacts, in particular its deployment of coercive power at its disposal, and in turn how lower classes respond to this. There is also a possibility that the crisis of the state will be manifested as the crisis of parts of the state.[100]

---

98   Patnaik adds: 'The matter relates not just to anti-poverty programmes. The personnel of the neo- liberal State have little interest in running the public sector, which is one reason why the public sector becomes financially unviable over time, and provides grist to the mill of those who want it privatized. Even normal government functions are not carried out by the bureaucracy, which is more interested in networking with patrons in the world of corporates and foreign donors, or in attending World Bank-sponsored training programmes, than in the nitty-gritty of administration. More and more government functions as a result are "outsourced" to private agencies, which promises profits for all'. (Patnaik, 2018). It is however important not to over-emphasize this change in personnel which concerns instrumentalist control of the bourgeois. It is the capitalist class character of neoliberalism that has led to the state being managed by bourgeois personnel (people who either include members of the bourgeoisie or who are shaped by bourgeois ideas and aspirations), and that in turn is responsible for the on-going reproduction of the capitalist-neoliberal order.

99   For a different view of the crisis of the Indian state, one that stresses ethnic politics, see Mukherji (2014).

100   According to Kaviraj (2011): governments, bureaucracy, army, etc. – the parts that make the state – are seen by people as corrupt or inefficient or dreaded, while the state 'as a powerful regulatory idea' continues to exist in their mind, an idea that is involved in every

7   Conclusion

In the analysis of the state, including the state in a specific country, the class character of the state is generally obscured or mystified. To do a class analysis of the state often prompts a charge of analytical bias (because the state is assumed by most to work as a neutral agent), as well as the charge of economism and 'classism'. The latter charge implies that a class analysis of the state reduces the state to class relations and to its economic imperatives, and thus ignores non-class social relations such as caste and gender, etc.

The main aim of this chapter has been to implicitly respond to these charges and to explicitly re-assert the class character of the state. It is a truism, albeit a crucial one, that class relations and the attendant material conditions constitute the most important context for all forms of intervention by the state and for the very form (territorial and political form) of the state itself. Of course, within this class context other social relations – i.e. those of caste, religion, ethnicity, region and nation – operate and influence the state and its class character at a concrete level.

So reasserted in this chapter is the class view of the Indian state. Because capitalism is the dominant mode of production in India, the state is a capitalist state, and thus an agent of capitalist development, both in pre-neoliberal and neoliberal times, and both in rural and urban areas. The relation of partnership between the two arms of capital relation – the state and the capitalist class – has been justified in terms of two major ideologies: one is of state control and socialism, and another is one of free market (and its twin, communal-hyper-nationalistic authoritarianism). Ideology does not mean total lies. Ideology refers to ideas that are partly true and partly false and that contribute to the reproduction of an exploitative and oppressive order (Eagleton, 1991). The ideology of state control over the business world in India in the early years of the post-1947 period was not entirely a lie. There *was* a degree of state control. There was a degree of state intervention on behalf of the masses. Even the ruling class understood from the very beginning (since the 1940s) that a small degree of state control and a small degree of pro-poor re-distribution is a remedy to potential social upheaval. In the neoliberal times, the ideology of free market has justified serious intervention in the interest of capital while it seeks to make common people believe that it lacks the resources to help them in any

_____

demand for justice. In other words, there is no crisis of legitimacy of the state, although its parts have 'lost some of their legitimacy, in a rising tide of undirected and uncontrollable social aspiration ... There is no end in sight of the Indian society's strange enchantment with the modern state' (p. 46).

significant manner. In other words, the state has always worked, more or less, in the interest of the capitalist class (see Sen, 2017; Das Gupta, 2016). Its policies (as well its form – federal-liberal-democratic form) have been accordingly influenced by the interests/actions of the dominant classes, although they have also been, to some extent, shaped by the lower-class struggles, actual or potential.

Like any capitalist state, the state in India must sustain the myth that capitalist accumulation (which goes by the name of 'growth') benefits not just the already-better-off entrepreneurs, and that the poor also gain some advantages from it. The myth needed is that the exploiters (misnamed as employers and wealth-creators) and the exploited benefit from the same process. The legitimacy of the post-1947 state derived in no small measure from two assumptions: that, unlike colonial government which served 'foreign' interests, it would serve domestic ones; and that, to this end, it would promote economic development from which the nation as a whole benefited. Increasingly, however, the distinction between the pre-1947 and post-1947 development projects is being eroded, as the neoliberal state not only facilitates the dispossession and exploitation of the poor by international and domestic capital, but also encourages the latter to undertake export-oriented cultivation. Farm crops are once again being seen to be produced mainly for an elite (= 'foreign') market, much as they were during the colonial era. This can contribute to the broader process of delegitimizing the development state, a situation which in turn intensifies class struggle 'from below', and the repressive 'from above' response by the neoliberal state protecting the interests of the capitalist class in India.

Because of a continuing failure on the part of the state to promote development in the interest of workers and small-scale producers and because of its current neoliberal policies supportive of domestic and foreign capital, this apparatus may face a legitimation crisis, especially in rural areas and in urban slums. Might the economic crisis of accumulation, including crisis of livelihood, and the legitimation crisis of the state (or its political crisis), lead to a larger crisis, i.e. a crisis of democracy itself and of the bourgeois system as a whole, which might be manifested as the strengthening of fascistic tendencies? Whether the potential for such a systemic crisis, that affects both the ruling class the masses, will be realized depends on how the lower classes and their organizations respond to the situation politically. Indeed, the topic of how the lower classes fight for their rights and how the state responds, is an important one. This will be discussed in the next two chapters.

Processes Influencing the Balance of Power between Capital and Labor

The first process is the *availability* – and economic affordability – of a given productivity-raising technology (which can be mechanical, chemical, bio-technical, etc.). Secondly, and in the context of nature-dependent production, favorable ecological conditions are particularly important.[1] These do not exist everywhere. Thirdly, for accumulation and struggle against employers to happen in any significant manner, there must be a substantial amount of concentration of property in the hands of a few owners. Unless there are a few property owners with a sufficient amount of means of production under their control, and even if wage-labor relations dominate, accumulation by private owners, and especially, via technological change, will be inhibited, and class struggle against the employers over wages and working conditions may not be particularly intense because of the absence of strong economic-cultural differences between laborers and property owners who are operating as relatively small-scale capitalists. Fourthly, there is the issue of inter-sectoral relations in terms of production of consumer demand: for example, the development of non-agricultural economic activities in rural areas and associated increase in the total amount of investment, expands the market for farm goods and may increase the demand for (farm-) labor. The latter can enhance labor's bargaining power resulting in higher wages, to which capital can respond by introducing technology, with the real subsumption of labor as the result. Finally, there is the issue of capitalist state interventions. Government assistance including subsidized food and employment generation on public projects – which partly reflects struggle of direct producers – leads to the tightening of the labor market and covers a part of the reproduction of labor power, including sections of the reserve army. All this enhances the bargaining power of labor. From the standpoint of capital itself, state interventions also matter. The state intervention on behalf of the working class and poor peasantry creates an internal market for capital. And by manipulating relative prices, the state can make the terms of trade between two sectors (e.g. agriculture and industry) favorable for one. This can increase the amount of capital in the hands of property owners in the favored sector and therefore may make technology

---

1   Money invested cannot be got back before a certain time period (e.g. until a crop matures), which is determined by nature's time rather than capital's time. This means that capitalists can be slow to sink money in farming, making the development of agrarian capitalism over time a slow process (Mann and Dickinson, 1978).

affordable by it. It should be noted that all these contextual factors (including the ways in which ecological conditions are made use of) are connected to the overall *capitalist* development of the country, directly or indirectly, and this overall *capitalist* nature of development indirectly defines the context within which capital-labor confrontation takes places and which affects the possibility of the transition from formal subsumption. This transition as a spatially uneven process contributes to uneven (and combined) development.

A Suggested Research Program on Agrarian Neoliberalism

1. Why does neoliberalism impact labor and environmental resources in rural areas?

    1.1. How do production processes, wages, and employment differ amongst different types of subsistence and commercial farms, and between places, and why?

    1.2. Does neoliberalism promote change from formal subsumption of labor (deployment of labor on the basis of low wages and long hours) to real subsumption of labor (deployment of labor on the basis labor-saving technology), and how?

    1.3. Is there greater interaction between agriculture and industry and between rural and urban areas, under neoliberalism, and with what consequences for the different classes in rural areas? How do economic development processes and state interventions within a given 'city-region' (a large city and its surrounding rural areas) impact the possibilities for a political alliance between urban workers and rural non-exploiting petty-producers to demand radical concessions and to challenge capitalist relations?

    1.4. How do agricultural production relations transform local ecologies and lead to (adverse) consequences for the environment and laboring bodies?

2. How does neoliberalism lead to new patterns of deployment of labor and land in rural areas specifically in the form of what is called 'new agriculture'?

    2.1. With respect to 'new agriculture', which refers to the conversion of land-use to production and export of luxury crops, how do production/labor processes differ across different types of farms, and between places, and why?

    2.2. How closely is 'new agriculture' related to food availability, employment, wages, and poverty over time and across regions?

    2.3. How do new agricultural production relations transform local ecologies and lead to (adverse) consequences for the environment and laboring bodies?

3. Why does neoliberalism, promising to promote fast economic growth and benefit the masses, turn out to be a contradiction-prone and problematic development project?

3.1. How is the state's selective 'withdrawal' from the economy under neoliberalism related to rural economic development, food security and poverty?

3.2. How does neoliberalism create and intensify conflicts (e.g. between workers and employers; and between different users of natural resources)?

3.3. By spatially concentrating investment and laborers, might new agriculture enable political organization of the masses over social and ecological issues?

3.4. How do state and agribusinesses respond to various conflicts? What material and discursive strategies are employed to promote social norms supportive of agrarian neoliberalism?

3.5. How are conflicts expressed within state institutions, and between the state and civil society at large? How does the democratic state justify support for agribusiness whilst reducing subsidies for poor populations, as under WTO rubric? Is a legitimacy crisis emergent in rural areas for a state no longer appearing as guarantor of welfare in the everyday lives of the poor? What connection might there be between agrarian neoliberalism and growing influence of fascistic tendencies among certain classes and groups in rural areas?

Bibliography

Adduci, M. 2017. "Neoliberalism, mining and labour in the Indian state of Odisha: Outlining a political economy analysis." *Journal of Contemporary Asia* 47, no. 4: 596–614.

Agamben, G. 2005. *The state of exception*. Chicago: University of Chicago Press.

Agarwala, R. 2006. "From work to welfare: A new class movement in India." *Critical Asian Studies* 38, no. 4: 419–444.

Agarwala, R. 2013. *Informal labor, formal politics and dignified discontent in India*. Cambridge: Cambridge University Press.

Agarwala, R. 2019. "Using legal empowerment for labour rights in India." *Journal of Development Studies* 55, no. 3: 401–419.

Aguiar, L., and Herod, A., eds. 2006. *The dirty work of neoliberalism: Cleaners in the global economy*. Oxford: Blackwell.

Ahluwalia, M.S. 1978. "Rural poverty and agricultural performance in India." *Journal of Development Studies* 14, no. 3: 298–323.

Ahluwalia, M.S. 2002. "Economic reforms in India since 1991: Has Gradualism worked?" *Journal of Economic Perspectives* 16, no. 7: 67–88.

Ahmad, A. 2013. "Communalisms: Changing forms and fortunes." *The Marxist* XXIX, no. 2.

Alauddin, M., and Tisdell, C. 1991. *The Green Revolution and economic development: The process and its impacts in Bangladesh*. Basingstoke: Macmillan.

Alauddin, M., and Tisdell, C. 1995. "Labour absorption and agricultural development Bangladesh experience and predicament." *World Development* 23, no. 2: 281–295.

Alavi, H. 1965. "Peasant and Revolution." In *The Socialist Register 1965*, eds. R. Miliband and J. Saville, 241–277. London: The Merlin Press.

Alavi, H. 1972. "The State in Post-colonial Societies: Pakistan and Bangladesh." *New Left Review*, no. 74: 59–81.

Albright, M. 2018. "Will we stop Trump before it's too late?" *New York Times*. https://www.nytimes.com/2018/04/06/opinion/sunday/trump-fascism-madeleine-albright.html.

Ali, A. 2006. "Rice to shrimp: Land use land cover changes and soil degradation in Southwestern Bangladesh." *Land Use Policy* 23, no. 4: 421–435.

Allinson, J., and Anievas, A. 2009. "The uses and misuses of uneven and combined development: an anatomy of a concept." *Cambridge Review of International Affairs* 22, no. 1: 47–67.

Ambani, M. 2018. "Building a global-scale corporation in India." In *India Transformed*, ed. R. Mohan, 554–566. Washington D.C.: Brookings Institution Press.

Amin, S. 2005. "India: A great power?" *Monthly Review* 6, no. 9: 1–13.

Amsden, A. 1998. *Asia's next giant: South Korea and late industrialization.* Oxford: Oxford University Press.

Anandan, S. 2018. "4 years of Modi: Dalits are being stripped of their dignity." *National Herald.* https://www.nationalheraldindia.com/opinion/4-years-of-modi-dalits-are -being-stripped-of-their-dignity.

Anandhi, S., and Kapadia, K. 2017. *Dalit women: Vanguard of an alternative politics in India.* Abingdon, Oxon: Routledge.

Anderson, L., and Seligson, M.A. 1994. "Reformism and radicalism among peasants." *American Journal of Political Science* 38, no. 4: 944–972.

Anderson, P. 1980. *Arguments within English Marxism.* London: Verso.

Anievas, A., Saull, R., Davidson, N., and Fabry, A. 2014. *The longue durée of the far right: An international historical sociology.* London: Routledge.

Ansari, A. 2011. *Communalisation of Indian society.* Delhi: Aakar.

Arun, M. 2017. "Demonetisation shook the economy. Did it break it, or leave it healthier?" *India Today.* https://www.indiatoday.in/magazine/msn-it/story/20171113-dem onitisation-note-ban-bjp-modi-economy-arun-jaitley-gdp-1077353-2017-11-04.

Ashman, A. 2009. "Capitalism, Uneven and Combined Development and the Transhistoric." *Cambridge Review of International Affairs* 22, no. 1: 29–46.

Aston, T., and Philpin, C. 1985. *The Brenner Debate: Agrarian class structure and economic development in pre-industrial Europe.* Cambridge: Cambridge University Press.

Auvinen, J. 1997. "Political conflict in less developed countries 1981–89." *Journal of Peace Research* 34, no. 2: 177–195.

Avakian, B. 2008. *Away with gods.* Chicago: Insight Press.

Azam, J., and Bhatia, K. 2017. "Provoking insurgency in a federal state: Theory and application to India." *Public choice* 170, no. 3–4: 183–210.

Bagchi, S. 2017. "Naxalbari at 50." *The Hindu.* https://www.thehindu.com/society/naxal bari-at-50/article18514656.ece.

Bahl, V. 1995. *The making of the Indian working class: A case of the Tata Iron and Steel Company, 1880–1946.* New Delhi: Sage.

Baker, D. 2006. "The political economy of fascism: Myth or reality, or myth and reality?" *New Political Economy* 11, no. 2: 227–250.

Baker, K., and Jewitt, S. 2007. "Evaluating 35 years of the green revolution technology in villages of Bulandshahr district, western UP, north India." *Journal of Development Studies* 43, no. 2: 312–339.

Balagopal, K. 2006. "Chattisgarh: The physiognomy of violence." *Economic and Political Weekly* 41, no. 21: 2183–2186.

Banaji, J. 2003. "The fictions of free labor: Contract, coercion, and the so-called unfree labor." *Historical Materialism* 11, no. 3: 69–95.

Banaji, J. 2010. "The ironies of Indian Maoism." *International Socialism*, issue 128. http://isj.org.uk/the-ironies-of-indian-maoism/.

Banaji, J., ed. 2016a. *Fascism: essays on Europe and India,* Gurgaon: Three Essays Collective.

Banaji, J., ed. 2016b. "Preface." In *Fascism: Essays on Europe and India,* ed. J. Banaji. Gurgaon: Three Essays Collective.

Banaji, J., ed. 2016c. "Postscript." In *Fascism: Essays on Europe and India,* ed. J. Banaji. Gurgaon: Three Essays Collective.

Banaji, J., ed. 2016d. "Trajectories of fascism: Extreme-right movements in India and elsewhere." In *Fascism: Essays on Europe and India,* ed. J. Banaji. Gurgaon: Three Essays Collective.

Bandyopadhyay, D. 1994. "Reflections on Land Reforms in India since Independence." In *Industry and Agriculture in India since Independence*, ed. T. Sathyamurthy. New Delhi: Oxford University Press.

Banerjee, S. 1980. *In the wake of Naxalbari: A history of the Naxalite Movement in India.* Calcutta: Subarnarekha.

Banerjee, S. 1984. India's simmering revolution: The Naxalite uprising. London: Zed.

Banerjee, S. 1986. "Rural scene." In *Agrarian Struggles after Independence,* ed. A.R. Desai. New Delhi: Oxford University Press.

Banerjee, S. 1999. "Strategy and forms of political participation among left parties." In *Class formation and political transformation in post-colonial India*, ed. T. Sathyamurthy, 202–237. Delhi: Oxford University Press.

Banerjee, S. 2002. "Naxalbari: between past and future." *Economic and Political Weekly* 37, no. 22: 2115–2116.

Banerjee, S. 2006. "Beyond Naxalbari." *Economic and Political Weekly* 41, no. 29: 3159–3163.

Banerjee, S. 2008a. "On the Naxalite movement: a report with a difference." *Economic and Political Weekly* 43, no. 21: 10–12.

Banerjee, S. 2008b. "A Political cul-de-sac: CPI(M)'s tragic denouement." *Economic and Political Weekly* 43, no. 42: 12–15.

Banerjee, S. 2012. *Marxism and the Indian left: From 'interpreting' India to 'changing' it.* Kolkata: Purbalok.

Banerjee, S. 2017. "Half-a-century of Maoist journey in India from Naxalbari to Chhatisgarh." *Economic and Political Weekly* 52, no. 21.

Bannerji, S. 2000. "Organized business and politics in India." In *Politics in India,* ed. R. Chatterji. Kolkata: Levanta Books.

Banerjee-Guha, S. 2009. "Neoliberalising the 'urban': New geographies of power and injustice in Indian cities." *Economic and Political Weekly* 44, no. 22: 95–107.

Bannerji, H. 1995. *Thinking through: Essays on feminism, Marxism, and anti-racism.* Toronto: Women's press.

Bannerji, H. 2006. "Making India Hindu and male – cultural nationalism and the emergence of the ethnic citizen in contemporary India." *Ethnicities* 6, no. 3: 362–390.

Bansil, P. 1992. *Agricultural statistics compendium,* vols. 1–2. Technical and Economic Research Institute, New Delhi.

Barbier, E., and Suthawan, S. 2004. *Shrimp farming and mangrove loss in Thailand.* Cheltenham: Edward Elgar.

Bardhan, P. 1984. *Land, labour and rural poverty: Essays in development economics.* Oxford University Press, Delhi.

Bardhan, P. 1990. *Political Economy of Development in India.* Delhi: Oxford University Press.

Bardhan, P. 1998. *The political economy of India's development.* New Delhi: Oxford University Press.

Bardhan, P. 2005. "Nature of opposition to economic reforms in India." *Economic and Political Weekly* 40, no. 48: 4995–4998.

Barker, C. 2006. "Capital and revolutionary practice." *Historical Materialism* 14, no. 2: 55–82.

Barraclough, S., and Finger-Stich, A. 1996. *Some ecological and social implications of commercial shrimp farming in Asia.* UN Research Institute for Social Development #74, Geneva.

Basile, E. 2013. *Capitalist development in India's informal economy.* New York: Routledge.

Basole, A. 2016. "The agrarian question in India." *In contemporary readings in Marxism: A critical introduction,* ed. R. Kumar. Delhi: Aakar Books.

Basu, A. 2013. "The changing fortunes of the Bharatiya Janata Party." In *Routledge handbook of Indian politics,* eds. A. Kohli and P. Singh, 81–90. London: Routledge.

Basu, D. 2009. "Analysis of classes in India: A preliminary note on the industrial bourgeoisie and Middle class." *Sanhati* http://sanhati.com/excerpted/1919/.

Basu, P. 2002. *Towards Naxalbari.* Calcutta: Progressive Publishers.

Basu, S. 2004. *Does class matter? Colonial capital and workers' resistance in Bengal (1980–1937).* Delhi: Oxford University Press.

Basu, D., and Das, D. 2013. "The Maoist Movement in India: Some political economy considerations." *Journal of Agrarian Change* 13, no. 3: 365–381.

Basu, T., Datta, P., Sarkar, S., and Sen, S. 1993. *Khaki shorts and saffron flags.* Hyderabad: Orient Longman.

Baviskar, A., 2003. "Between violence and desire: Space, power, and identity in the making of metropolitan Delhi." *International Social Science Journal* 55, no. 175: 89–98.

Bear, L. 2017. "'Alternatives' to austerity: A critique of financialized infrastructure in India and beyond." *Anthropology today* 33, no. 5: 3–7.

Beck, T. 1995. "The green revolution and poverty in India: A case study of West Bengal." *Applied Geography* 15, no. 2: 161–181.

Beeson, M. 2009. "Developmental states in East Asia: A comparison of the Japanese and Chinese experiences." *Asian Perspective* 33, no. 2: 5–39.

Behera, C. 2002. "India: Prospects for Conflict and Peace." *Swisspeace and Swiss Agency for Development and Cooperation.* www.isn.ethz.ch/researchpub/publihouse/fast/crp/2000/crp_india_2000.htm.

Belton, B., and Little D. 2008. "The development of aquaculture in Central Thailand: Domestic demand versus export-led production." *Journal of Agrarian Change* 8, no. 1: 123–143.

Belton, B., Haque, M., and Little D. 2012. "Does size matter? Reassessing the relationship between aquaculture and poverty in Bangladesh." *Journal of Development Studies* 48, no. 7: 904–922.

Belton, B., Padiyar, A., Ravibabu G., and Rao, G. 2017. "Boom and bust in Andhra Pradesh: Development and transformation in India's domestic aquaculture value chain." *Aquaculture* 470: 196–206.

Bentall, J., and Corbridge, S. 1996. "Urban rural relations, demand politics and the new agrarianism in North West India: the Bharatiya Kisan union." *Transactions of the Institute of British Geographers* 21, no. 1: 27–48.

Bernstein, H. 1996. "Agrarian questions then and now." *Journal of Peasant Studies* 24: 22–59.

Bernstein, H. 2007. *Capital and labor from centre to margins.* Keynote address at conference on Living on the Margins. Vulnerability, Exclusion and the State in the Informal Economy, Cape Town. http://pdf.steerweb.org/WFP%20ESSAY/Bernstein_dsi .pdf.

Beteille, A. 2000. *Chronicles of our time.* Delhi: Penguin Books.

Beteille, A. 2007. *Marxism and class analysis.* New Delhi: Oxford University Press.

Berti, D., Jaoul, N., and Kanungo, P. 2011. *Cultural entrenchment of Hindutva: Local meditations and forms of convergence.* New Delhi: Routledge.

Bhaduri, A. 1973. "A study in agricultural backwardness under semi-feudalism." *The Economic Journal* 83, no. 329: 120–137.

Bhaduri, A. 1983. *The economic structure of backward agriculture.* London: Academic Press.

Bhaduri, A., Rahman, H.Z., and Arn, A. 1986. "Persistence and polarization: A study in the dynamics of agrarian contradiction." *Journal of Peasant Studies* 13, no. 3: 82–89.

Bhagwati, J. 1998. "The design of Indian development." In *India's economic reforms and development: Essays for Manmohan Singh,* eds. I.J. Ahluwalia and I.M.D. Little, 23–39. New Delhi: Oxford University Press.

Bhagwati, J. 2001. "Growth, poverty and reforms." *Economic and Political Weekly* 36, no. 10: 843–846.

Bhalla, G.S. 2007. *Indian agriculture since Independence.* Delhi: National Book Trust.

Bhalla, S. 1995. "Development, poverty and policy: The Haryana experience." *Economic and Political Weekly* 30, no. 41–42: 2619–2621, 2623–2625, 2627–2631, 2633–2634.

Bhalla, S. 1999. "Liberalisation, rural labour markets and the mobilisation of farm workers: The Haryana story in an all-India context." *Journal of Peasant Studies* 26, no. 2–3: 25–70.

Bhandari, R. 2008. "The disguises of wage-labor: Juridical illusions, unfree conditions and novel extensions." *Historical Materialism* 16, no. 1: 71–99.

Bhardwaj, A. 2015. "RSS mouthpiece defends Dadri lynching: Vedas order killing of sinners who kill cows." *The Indian Express.* https://indianexpress.com/article/india/india-news-india/rss-mouthpiece-defends-dadri-vedas-order-killing-of-sinners-who-kill-cows/.

Bharadwaj. K. 1982. "Regional Differentiation in India." *Economic and Political Weekly* 17:14–16.

Bhat, M., and Bhatta, R. 2004. "Considering aquacultural externality in Coastal Land allocation decisions in India." *Environmental & Resource Economics* 29: 1–20.

Bhatia, B. 2006. "On armed resistance." *Economic and Political Weekly* 41, no. 29: 3179–3183.

Bhatia, R. 2017. "The Year of Love Jihad in India." *New Yorker.* https://www.newyorker.com/culture/2017-in-review/the-year-of-love-jihad-in-india.

Bhattacharya, D. 2017. "50 years of Naxalbari: With Sangh in power, a new political energy needed now." *Catch News.* http://www.catchnews.com/politics-news/50-years-of-naxalbari-with-sangh-in-power-a-new-political-energy-needed-now-60954.html.

Bhattacharyya, S. 2001. "Capitalist development, peasant differentiation and the State: Survey findings from West Bengal." *The Journal of Peasant Studies* 28, no. 4: 95–126.

Bhattacharyya, S. 2013. *Two decades of market reform in India: Some dissenting views.* New York: Anthem Press.

Bhattacharyya, A., and Basu, S. 2018. *Marginalities in India: Themes and perspectives.* Singapore: Springer Verlag.

Bhelari, K. 2003. "Partners in progress: Maoist Naxals are trying out all ways to win the hearts of people." *The Week*, 22 June.

Bhowmik, S. 2014. *The state of labour: The global financial crisis and its impact.* India: Routledge.

Bidwai, P. 2015. *The Phoenix moment: Challenges confronting the Indian left.* New Delhi: Harper Collins.

Block, F., and Polanyi, K. 2003. "Karl Polanyi and the Writing of 'The Great Transformation.'" *Theory and Society* 32, no. 3: 275–306.

Bobbio, N. 2005. *Liberalism and democracy.* London: Verso.

Boer, R. 2009. *Criticism of heaven.* Chicago: Haymarket.

Boer, R. 2011. *Criticism of religion.* Chicago: Haymarket.

Boer, R. 2012. *Criticism of theology.* Chicago: Haymarket.

Boer, R. 2013. *Criticism of earth.* Chicago: Haymarket.

Boer, R. 2014. *In the vale of tears.* Chicago: Haymarket.

Bond, P. 2014. "BRICS and the tendency to sub-imperialism." *Pambazuka News.* https://www.pambazuka.org/governance/brics-and-tendency-sub-imperialism.

Bond, P., and Desai, A. 2006. *Explaining uneven and combined development in South Africa.* http://146.230.128.54/ccs/files/Bond%20Desai%20Uneven%20and%20Combined%20Development.pdf.

Bordoloi, Sudarshana, and Das, R. "Modernization Theory." In *International Encyclopedia of Geography: People, the Earth, Environment and Technology,* eds. Douglas Richardson, Noel Castree, Michael F. Goodchild, Audrey Kobayashi, Weidong Liu, and Richard A. Marston. Hoboken, NJ: John Wiley & Sons.

Borooah, V.K. 2008. "Deprivation, Violence, and Conflict: An Analysis of Naxalite Activity in the Districts of India." *International Journal of Conflict and Violence* 2, no. 2: 317–333.

Bownas, R. 2016. "Lost in transnationalism? GMOS in India and the eclipse of equitable development discourse." *Journal of South Asian Development* 11, no. 1: 67–87.

Boyd, W., Prudham, S., and Schurman, R. 2001. "Industrial dynamics and the problem of nature." *Society and natural resources* 14, no. 7: 555–570.

Brass, P.R. 1997. *Theft of an idol: Text and context in the representation of collective violence,* Princeton, NJ: Princeton University Press.

Brass, T. 1990. "Class struggle and the deproletarianization of agricultural labour in Haryana (India)." *Journal of Peasant Studies* 18, no. 1: 36–67.

Brass, T. 1994. "Some observations on unfree labor, capitalist restructuring, and de proletarianization." *International Review of Social History* 39, no. 2: 255–275.

Brass, T. 1995a. "Reply to Utsa Patnaik: If the Cap Fits..." *International Journal of Social History Review* 40, no. 1: 93–117.

Brass, T. 1995b. "The Politics of Gender, Nature and Nation in the Discourse of the New Farmers' Movements." In *New Farmers' Movements in India,* ed. T. Brass. London: Frank Cass Publishers.

Brass, T. 1999. *Towards a comparative political economy of unfree labour.* London and Portland: Frank Cass Publishers.

Brass, T. 2000. "Labour in post-colonial India: A response to Jan Breman." *The Journal of Peasant Studies* 28, no. 1: 126–146.

Brass, T. 2002. "Rural labour in agrarian transitions: The semi-feudal thesis revisited." *Journal of Contemporary Asia* 32, no. 4: 456–473.

Brass, T. 2003. "Why unfree labour is not "so-called": The fictions of Jairus Banaji." *The Journal of Peasant Studies* 31, no. 1: 101–136.

Brass, T. 2011. "Primitive accumulation, capitalist development and socialist transition: Still waiting for Godot?" *Journal of Contemporary Asia* 41, no. 1: 1–24.

Brass, T. 2012. *Labor regime change in the 21st century*. Leiden: Brill.

Brass, T. 2017a. "Class struggle and unfree labor: The (Marxist) road not taken." *Science & Society* 81, no. 2: 197–219.

Brass, T. 2017b. "Who these days is not a subaltern? The populist drift of global labor history." *Science & Society* 81, no. 1: 10–34.

Breman, J. 1985. *Of peasants, migrants and paupers: Rural labor circulation and capitalist production in West India*. Oxford: Oxford University Press.

Breman, J. 1989. "The disintegration of the Hali system." In *South Asia*, eds. H. Alavi and J. Harriss. New York: Monthly Review Press.

Breman, J. 1990. "Even dogs are better of the ongoing battle between capital and labor in the cane fields of Gujarat." *Journal of Peasant Studies* 17, no. 4: 546–608.

Breman, J. 1996. *Footloose labor: Working in India's informal economy*. Cambridge: Cambridge University Press.

Breman, J. 2003. *The labouring poor in India: Patterns of exploitation, subordination, and exclusion*. New Delhi: Oxford University Press.

Brenner, R. 1982. "The agrarian roots of European capitalism." *Past and Present* 97: 16–113.

Brenner, R. 1985. "Agrarian class structure and economic development in pre-industrial Europe." In *The Brenner Debate*, eds. T.H. Aston and C. Philipin, 10–63. Cambridge: Cambridge University Press.

Brenner, R. 1986. "The Social Basis of Economic Development." In *Analytical Marxism*, ed. J. Roemer, 23–53. Cambridge: Cambridge University Press.

Bridi, R. 2017. *The political-economy of science and (bio)technology: The emergence of agricultural biotechnology in the Canada*. (Ph.D. dissertation). York University, Toronto, Canada.

Brohman, J. 1996. "Postwar development in the Asian NICs: Does the neoliberal model fit reality?" *Economic Geography* 72, no. 2: 107–130.

Bukharin, N.I. 1933. "The theory of Capitalism." *Marxist.org.* https://www.marxists.org/archive/bukharin/works/1933/teaching/3.htm.

Burkett, P. 1996. "Value, capital and nature: some ecological implications of Marx's critique of political economy." *Science and Society* 60, no. 3: 332–359.

Burkett, P. 1999. *Marx and nature: A red and green perspective*. New York: St. Martin's Press.

Burkett, P., and Hart-Landberg, M. 2003. "A critique of 'catch-up' theories of development." *Journal of Contemporary Asia* 33, no. 2: 147–171.

Burkhart, R.E. 2002. "The capitalist political economy and human rights: Cross-national evidence." *Social Science Journal* 39, no. 2: 155–170.

Bush, S. 2008. "Contextualising fisheries policy in the Lower Mekong Basin." *Journal of Southeast Asian Studies* 39, no. 3: 329–353.

Byres, T. 1972. "The dialectic of India's Green Revolution." *South Asian Review* 5, no. 2: 99–116.

Byres, T. 1981. "The new technology, class formation and class action in the Indian countryside." *Journal of Peasant Studies* 8, no. 4: 405–454.

Byres, T. 1983. *The Green Revolution in India.* Milton Keynes: The Open University Press.

Byres, T. 1989. "Agrarian structure, the new technology and class action in India." In *South Asia,* eds. H. Alavi and J. Harriss. New York: Monthly Review Press.

Byres, T. 1991. "Agrarian question and differing forms of capitalist agrarian transition: An essay with reference to Asia." In *Rural Transformation in Asia,* eds. J. Breman and S. Mundle. Delhi: Oxford University Press.

Byres, T. 1996. *Capitalism from above and capitalism from below.* London: Macmillan.

Byres, T., ed. 1997. *The state, development planning & liberalisation in India.* Delhi: Oxford University Press.

Byres, T. 2003. "Structural change, the agrarian question and the possible impact of globalization." In *Work and well-being in the age of finance,* eds. J. Ghosh and C. Chandrasekhar, 171–211. New Dehli: Tulika.

Byres, T. 2013. "Development planning and the interventionist state versus liberalization and the neoliberal state: India, 1989–1996." In *Two decades of market reform in India: Some dissenting views,* ed. S. Bhattacharayya, 27–54. New York: Anthem Press.

Callinicos, A. 1988. *Making history: Agency, structure and change in social theory.* Cornell: Cornell University Press.

Callinicos, A. 1993. *Race and class.* London: Bookmarks.

Callinicos, A. 2004. *Making history: Agency, structure in social theory.* Leiden: Brill.

Callinicos, A. 2010. "Editor's introduction." *International Socialism.* http://isj.org.uk/the-ironies-of-indian-maoism/.

Caparaso, J., and Levine, D. 1991. *Theories of political economy.* Cambridge: Cambridge University Press.

Carchedi, G. 2010. *Behind the crisis.* Leiden: Brill.

Carling, A., and Wetherly, P., eds. 2006. "Rethinking Marx and history (a special issue)." *Science & Society* 70, no. 2: 46–154.

Carroll, M. 2017. "The sticky materiality of neoliberal neonatures: GMOs and the agrarian question." *New Political economy* 22, no. 2: 203–218.

Carter, B. 1995. "A growing divide: Marxist class analysis and the labor process." *Capital & Class* 19, no. 1: 33–72.

Castell, M. 1983. *The city and the grassroots: A Cross-cultural theory of urban social movements.* Berkeley: University of California Press.

Castree, N. 2001. "Commodity fetishism, geographical imaginations and imaginative geographies." *Environment and Planning A* 33: 1519–1525.

Castree, N. and Braun, B. 2001. *Social Nature: Theory, Practice and Politics.* Oxford: Blackwell.

Center for Monitoring Indian Economy (CMIE). 1987. *Basic statistics relating to the Indian economy,* vol. 2. Bombay.

Chacko, P. 2018. *Marketizing Hindutva: The state, society, and markets in Hindu nationalism.* Cambridge: Cambridge University Press.

Chadha, G. 1984. "The landless and the poor in green revolution regions of India." *Agricultural Situation in India* 39, no. 5.

Chadha, G. 1994. *Employment, earnings and poverty.* New Delhi: Sage.

Chakrabarti, A. 2012. "The Indian communist movement at a crossroads: A Marxian assessment." *Rethinking Marxism* 24, no. 3: 458–474.

Chakrabarti, A., and Cullenberg, S. 2003. *Transition and development in India.* New York: Routledge.

Chakrabarti, A., Chaudhury, A., and Cullenberg, S. 2009. "Global order and the new economic policy in India: The (post)colonial formation of the small-scale sector." *Cambridge Journal of Economics* 33, no. 6: 1169–1186.

Chakrabarti, S. 2009. *Red sun: Travels in Naxalite country.* New Delhi: Penguin Books.

Chakrabarty, B. 2008. *Indian politics and society since independence: Events, processes and ideology.* London: Routledge.

Chakrabarty, B. 2014. *Communism in India: Events, processes and ideologies.* New York: Oxford University press.

Chakrabarty, B. 2015. *Left radicalism in India.* Abington: Routledge.

Chakravarti, A. 2001. *Social power and everyday class relations: Agrarian transformation in North Bihar.* New Delhi: Sage.

Chakravarti, A. 2018. *Is this Azaadi? Everyday lives of Dalit agricultural laborers in a Bihar village.* Delhi: Tulka.

Chakravarty, M. 2016. "The richest 1% of Indians now own 58.4% of wealth." *Livemint.* https://www.livemint.com/Money/MML9OZRwaACyEhLzUNImnO/The-richest-1-of-Indians-now-own-584-of-wealth.html.

Chakravorty, S. 2016. "Land acquisition in India: The political-economy of changing the law." *Area Development and Policy* 1, no. 1: 48–62.

Chancel, L., and Picketty, T. 2017. "Indian income inequality, 1922–2015: From British Raj to billionaire Raj?" *World Inequality Database.* https://wid.world/document/chancelpiketty2017widworld/.

Chandan, A. 1979. "Victims of green revolution." *Economic and Political Weekly* 14, no. 25.

Chandavarkar, R. 2009. *Origins of industrial capitalism in India.* Cambridge, GBR: Cambridge University Press.

Chandra, B. 1989. *India's struggle for independence.* New Delhi: Penguin.

Chandra, B. 1992. "The Indian capitalist class and imperialism before 1947." In *Class, state and development in India,* B. Berberoglu. New Delhi: Sage.

Chandra, B. 2008. *Communalism: A primer.* Delhi: National Book Trust.

Chandra, N. 1974. "Farm efficiency under semi-feudalism – a critique of marginalist theories and some Marxist formulations." *Economic and Political Weekly* 9, no. 32–33–34.

Chandra, U., and Taghioff, D. 2016. *Staking claims: The politics of social movements in contemporary rural India.* New Delhi: Oxford University Press.

Chandramohan, C. 1998. "Political economy of agrarian conflicts in India." *Economic and Political Weekly* 33, no. 41: 2647–2653.

Chandrasekhar, C. 2018. "Neoliberal anti-populism." *Frontline* https://www.frontline .in/columns/C_P_Chandrasekhar/neoliberal antipopulism/article6279859.ece.

Chandrasekhar, C., and Ghosh, J. 2006. *The market that failed: A decade of neoliberal economic reforms in India.* New Delhi: Leftword Books.

Chandrasekhar, C., Patnaik, P., and Sen, A. 1999. "The proliferation of the bourgeoisie and economic policy." In *Class formation and political transformation in post-colonial India,* ed. T. Sathymurthy. Delhi: Oxford University Press.

Chang, D. 2003. *Demystifying the developmental state: A critique of the theories and practices of the state in the development of capital relations in Korea.* (Ph.D. thesis). University of Warwick, England.

Chang, D. 2013. "Labour and 'developmental state': A critique of the developmental state through of labour." In *Beyond the development state: Industrial policy into the twenty-first century,* eds. B. Fine, D. Tavasci, and J. Saraswati, 85–109. London: Pluto.

Chari, S. 2004. *Fraternal capital: Peasant-workers, self-made men, and globalization in provincial India.* Stanford: Stanford University Press.

Chatterjee, I. 2012. "Feminism, the false consciousness of neoliberal capitalism? Informalization, fundamentalism, and women in an Indian city." *Gender, Place and Culture* 19, no. 6: 790–809.

Chatterjee, P. 2000. "Development planning and the Indian state." In *Politics and the State in India,* ed. Z. Hasan. New Delhi: Sage.

Chatterjee, P. 2004. *The politics of the governed: Reflections on popular politics in most of the world.* New York: Columbia University Press.

Chatterjee, P. 2005. "Making autonomous geographies: Argentina's popular uprising and the unemployed workers movement." *Geoforum* 36, no. 5: 545–561.

Chatterjee, P. 2017. "Gramsci in India: Capitalist hegemony and subaltern politics." *Studi Storici* 58, no. 4: 963–986.

Chattopadhyay, B., Sharma, S.C., and Ray, A.K. 1987. "Rural/Urban terms of Trade, Primary Accumulation and the Increasing Strength of the Indian Farm Lobby." In *Food Systems and Society in Eastern India,* eds. B. Chattopadhyay and P. Spitz. Geneva: UNRISD.

Chattopadhyay, P. 1990a. "On the question of the mode of production in Indian agriculture: A preliminary note." In *Agrarian relations and accumulation: The mode of production debate in India,* ed. U. Patnaik. Delhi: Oxford University Press.

Chattopadhyay, P. 1990b. "An anti-kritik." In *Agrarian relations and accumulation: The mode of production debate in India,* ed. U. Patnaik. Delhi: Oxford University Press.

Chattopadhyaya, D. 2013. *Religion and society.* Delhi: Aakar.

Chauhan, B.R. 2003. "Village community." *The Oxford Companion to Sociology and Social Anthropology Volume 1,* ed. V. Das, 409–457. Delhi: Oxford University Press.

Chaudhuri, K. 2001. "A Naxalite Offensive in Orissa." *Frontline* 18, no. 18. https://www.frontline.in/static/html/fl1818/18180400.htm.

Chhibber, P. 2010. *Democracy without associations transformation of the party system and social cleavages in India.* Ann Arbor: University of Michigan Press.

Chhibber, P., and Nooruddin, I. 2004. "Do party systems count? The number of parties and government performance in the Indian States." *Comparative Political Studies* 37, no. 2: 152–187.

Chibber, V. 2003. *Locked in place: State building and late industrialization in India.* Princeton: Princeton University Press.

Chibber, V. 2006. "On the decline of class analysis in South Asian studies." *Critical Asian Studies* 38, no. 4: 356–387.

Chibber, V. 2017. "Our road to power." *Jacobin.* https://www.jacobinmag.com/2017/12/our-road-to-power.

Chibber, V., and Usmani, A. 2013. "The state and the capitalist class in India." In *Routledge handbook of Indian politics,* eds. A. Kohli and P. Singh, 204–210. London: Routledge.

Chossudovsky, M. 1999. *The globalization of poverty: Impacts of IMF and World Bank Reforms.* London: Zed Books.

Clarke, K. 2017. "Social forces and regime change beyond class analysis." *World Politics.* 69, no. 3: 569–602.

Clarke, S. 1991. *The state debate.* New York: St. Martin's Press.

Cleaver, H. 1972. "The contradictions of the Green Revolution." *American Economic Review* 62, no, 2: 177–186.

Cohen, D. 2014. "Is India about to elect its Reagan?" *The Hindu.* https://www.thehindu.com/opinion/op-ed/Is-India-about-to-elect-its-Reagan/article11640720.ece.

Cohen, G. 2000 (1978). *Karl Marx's theory of history: A defence.* Princeton: Princeton University Press.

Communist Party of India (Marxist-Leninist-Liberation). 2008. "CAG audit interim report: NREGA being mocked in spirit?" *Communist Party of India (Marxist-Leninist Liberation).* http://www.cpiml.net/liberation/2008/02/cag-audit-interim-report-nrega-being-mocked-spirit.

Cook, N. 1996. "Population and poverty in classical theory: testing a structural model for India." *Population Studies A Journal of Demography* 50, no. 2: 173–185.

Corbridge, S. 1993. "Marxisms, modernities, and moralities: Development praxis and the claims of distant strangers." *Environment and Planning D* 11, no. 4: 450–471.

Corbridge, S., and Harriss, J. 2000. *Reinventing India: Liberalization, Hindu nationalism and popular democracy.* New Delhi: Oxford University Press.

Corbridge, S., Williams, G., Srivastava, M., and Veron, R. 2004. *Seeing the State: Governance and Governmentality in Rural India.* Cambridge: Cambridge University Press.

Cox, K. 1990. "Territorial structures of the state: Some conceptual issues." *Tijdschrift voor economische en sociale geografie* 81, no. 4: 251–266.

Cowan, T. 2018. "The urban village, agrarian transformation, and rentier capitalism in Gurgaon, India." *Antipode* 50, no. 5: 1244–1266.

Cowen, M., and R. Shenton. 1996. *Doctrines of development.* London: Routledge.

CPI(M). 2017. 'Thinking together'; People's Democracy. http://peoplesdemocracy. in/2017/0402_pd/thinking-together.

CPI(M). 2018. "Press Communique. March 30." Party Central Office, New Delhi.

CPI-ML (Liberation). 2008. "CAG audit interim report: NREGA being mocked in spirit?" http://www.cpiml.net/liberation/2008/02/cag-audit-interim-report-nrega-being -mocked-spirit.

CPI(Maoist). 2014. Strategy and tactics of Indian revolution. http://www.banned thought.net/India/CPI-Maoist-Docs/Founding/StrategyTactics-pamphlet.pdf.

CPI-ML. 2011. "POSCO Project: No to corporate corruption and loot!" *Communist Party of India (Marxist-Leninist) Liberation.* http://www.cpiml.net/liberation/2011/06/ posco-project-no-corporate-corruption-and-loot.

CPI(ML). 2018. General Programme of CPI(ML); http://cpiml.net/documents/10th- party-congress/general-programme-of-cpiml.

Crowley, T. 2014. "The Many Faces of the Indian Left." *Jacobin.* https://www.jacobin mag.com/2014/05/the-many-faces-of-the-indian-left/.

D'Costa, A. 2005. *The long march to capitalism: Embourgeoisment, international and industrial transformation in India.* New York: Palgrave MacMillian.

D'Costa, A. 2011. "Geography, uneven development and distributive justice; The political economy of IT growth in India." *Cambridge Journal of Regions Economy and Society* 4, no. 2: 237–251.

D'Costa, A. 2013. "Globalization, the middle class and the transformation of the Indian state in the new economy." In *Two decades of market reform in India: Some dissenting views,* ed. S. Bhattacharyya, 125–142. New York: Anthem Press.

D'Costa, A. 2017. *The land question in India: State, dispossession, and capitalist transition.* Oxford: Oxford University Press.

D'Mello, B. 2018. *India after Naxalbari: Unfinished history.* New York: Monthly Review Press.

Da Corta, L., and Venkateshwarlu, D. 1999. "Unfree relations and the feminisation of agricultural labour in Andhra Pradesh, 1970–95." *Journal of Peasant Studies* 26, no. 2–3: 71–139.

Dale, G. 2010. Karl Polanyi: The limits of the market. Cambridge: Polity Press.

Damas, M. 1991. *Approaching Naxalbari.* Calcutta: Radical Impression.

Damodaran, H. 2018. "Labour markets: The 'puzzle' of rural wages." *Indian Express.* https://indianexpress.com/article/india/labour-markets-the-puzzle-of-rural-wages -5019670/.

Dantawala, M. 1987. "Growth and equity in agriculture." *Indian Journal of Agricultural Economics* 42, no. 2.

Das, A.N. 1982. *Agrarian movements in India: Studies on 20th century Bihar.* London: Frank Cass.

Das, A.N. 1997. *Swami and Friends: Sahajananda Saraswati and Those who Refuse to Let the Past of Bihar's Peasant Movements Become History.* Paper for the Peasant Symposium, University of Virginia, May 1997. Charlottesville, Virginia.

Das, G. 2012. *India grows at night: A liberal case for a strong state.* New Delhi: Penguin.

Das, K. 2000. "Informal Sector." In *Alternative Economic Survey.* Delhi: Rainbow Publishers.

Das, R. [Raju]. 1995. "Poverty and agrarian social structure: A case-study in rural India." *Dialectical Anthropology* 20, no. 2: 169–192.

Das, R. [Raju]. 1996. "State theories: A critical analysis." *Science and Society* 60, no. 1: 27–57.

Das, R. [Raju]. 1998a. "The green revolution, agrarian productivity and labour." *International Journal of Urban and Regional Research* 22, no. 1: 122–135.

Das, R. [Raju]. 1998b. "The social and spatial character of the Indian state." *Political Geography* 17, no. 7: 787–808.

Das, R. [Raju]. 1999a. "Politicism and idealism in state theory." *Science and Society* 63, no. 1: 97–104.

Das, R. [Raju]. 1999b. "Geographical unevenness of India's green revolution." *Journal Contemporary Asia* 29, no. 2: 167–186.

Das, R. [Raju]. 1999c. "The spatiality of class and state power: The case of India's land reforms." *Environment and Planning A* 31, no. 12: 2103–2216.

Das, R. [Raju]. 2000. "The state society relations: The case of an anti-poverty policy." *Environment and Planning C* 18, no. 6: 631–650.

Das, R. [Raju]. 2001a. "The political economy of India." *New Political Economy* 6, no. 1: 103–117.

Das, R. [Raju]. 2001b. "The spatiality of social relations: An Indian case-study." *The Journal of Rural Studies* 17, no. 3: 347–362.

Das, R. [Raju]. 2001c. "Class, capitalism and agrarian transition: A review and critique of some recent arguments." *Journal of Peasant Studies* 29, no. 1: 155–174.

Das, R. [Raju]. 2002. "The Green Revolution and poverty: A theoretical and empirical examination of the relation between technology and society." *Geoforum* 33, no. 1: 55–72.

Das, R. [Raju]. 2004. "Social capital and poverty of wage labourers: Problems with the social capital theory." *Transactions Institute of British Geographers* 29, no. 1: 27–45.

Das, R. [Raju]. 2005. "Rural society, the state and social capital in Eastern India: A critical investigation." *Journal of Peasant Studies* 32, no. 11: 48–87.

Das, R. [Raju]. 2006. "Marxist theories of the state." In *Alternative theories of the state*, ed. S. Pressman, 64–90. New York: Palgrave Macmillan.

Das, R. [Raju]. 2007. "*Looking, but not seeing: State* and/as class in rural India." *Journal of Peasant Studies* 34, no. 3–4 (Special issue on Peasant, State and Class): 408–440.

Das, R. [Raju]. 2009. "What's the Left to do in India." *A Socialist Project Review*, no. 26: 58–61.

Das, R. [Raju]. 2010. "Radical peasant movements and rural distress in India: A Study of the Naxalite Movement." In *India's New Economic Policy*, eds. W. Ahmad, A. Kundu, and R. Peet, 281–306. New York: Routledge.

Das, R. [Raju]. 2012a. "From labor geography to class geography: Reasserting the Marxist theory of class." *Human Geography: A New Radical Journal* 5, no. 1: 19–35.

Das, R. [Raju]. 2012b. "Academia as a site of class struggle." *Radical Notes.* http://radical notes.com/journal.

Das, R. [Raju]. 2012c. "Reconceptualizing capitalism: Forms of *subsumption of* labor, class struggle, and uneven development." *Review of Radical Political Economics* 44, no. 2: 178–200.

Das, R. [Raju]. 2012d. "The dirty picture of neoliberalism." *Links: International Journal of Socialist Renewal.* http://links.org.au/node/2818.

Das, R. [Raju]. 2013a. "The relevance of Marxist academics." *Class, Race and Corporate Power* 1, no. 1.

Das, R. [Raju]. 2013b. "Capitalism and regime change in the (globalizing) world of labour." *Journal of Contemporary Asia* 43, no. 4: 709–723.

Das, R. [Raju]. 2013c. "The market for education, civil servants and the India state." *Sanhati.* http://sanhati.com/excerpted/8813/.

Das, R. [Raju]. 2015. "Critical observations on neoliberalism and India's New Economic Policy." *Journal of Contemporary Asia* 45, no. 4: 715–726.

Das, R. [Raju]. 2016. "The attack on democracy and secularism in India." *Bullet: Socialist Project E-Bulletin, No. 1252.* http://www.socialistproject.ca/bullet/1252.php.

Das, R. [Raju]. 2017a. *Marxist class theory for a sceptical world.* Leiden/Boston: Brill.

Das, R. [Raju]. 2017b. "David Harvey's Theory of Accumulation by Dispossession: A Marxist Critique." *World Review of Political Economy* 8, no. 4: 590–616.

Das, R. [Raju]. 2017c. "David Harvey's theory of uneven geographical development: A Marxist critique." *Capital and Class* 41, no. 3: 511–536.

Das, R. [Raju]. 2018a. "Contradictions of India's Right-wing Government, and Growing Disenchantment." *Journal of Contemporary Asia* 49, no. 2: 313–328.

Das, R. [Raju]. 2018b. "A Marxist perspective on sustainability: Brief reflections on ecological sustainability and social inequality." *Links: International Journal of Socialist Renewal.* http://links.org.au/marxism-ecological-sustainability-social-inequality.

Das, R. [Raju]. 2019. "Politics of Marx as non-sectarian revolutionary class politics: An interpretation in the context of the 20th and 21st centuries." *Class, Race and Corporate Power*, March issue.

Das, R.J. and Chen, A. 2019. "Towards a Theoretical Framework for Understanding Capitalist Violence Against Child Labour." *World Review of Political Economy* 10, no. 2: 191–219.

Das, R. [Raju], and Mishra, D. 2019. "Industrialization and Geographically Uneven Development." Unpublished manuscript.

Das, R. [Ritanjan]. 2018. Neoliberalism and the transforming left in India: A contradictory manifesto. London: Routledge.

Das, T. 2018. "Changing colours of government-business relations." In *India Transformed,* ed. R. Mohan, 224–236. Washington, DC: Brookings Institution Press.

Das, R. [Ritanjan], and Mahmood, Z. 2015. "Contradictions, Negotiations and Reform: The Story of Left Policy Transition in West Bengal." *Journal of South Asian Development* 10, no. 2: 199–229.

Das Gupta, C. 2016. *State and capital in independent India: Institutions and accumulations.* Cambridge: Cambridge University Press.

Das Gupta, M., Grandvoinnet, H., and Romani, M. 2004. "State-community synergies in community-driven development." *Journal of Development Studies* 40, no. 3: 27–58.

Dasgupta, A. 2012. "Reverse pessimistic climate and boost investor sentiment." *The Hindu.* https://www.thehindu.com/business/Economy/reverse-pessimistic-climate-and-boost-investor-sentiment-pm/article3577372.ece.

Dasgupta, A. 2018. "Technological change and political turnover: The democratizing effects of the Green Revolution in India." *American Political Science Review* 112, no. 4: 918–938.

Dasgupta, B. [Biblab]. 1977. *Agrarian change and the new technology in India united nations research institute for social development.* Geneva: United Nations Research Institute for Small Development.

Dasgupta, B. [Biblab]. 1998. *Structural adjustment, global trade and the new political economy of development.* New Delhi: Vistaar.

Dasgupta, B. [Byasdeb]. 2017. "Flexible labour and capital accumulation in a postcolonial country." In *Accumulation in post-colonial capitalism,* eds. I.K. Mitra, R. Samaddar, and S. Sen, 27–57. Singapore: Springer.

Dasgupta, A., Gawande, K., and Kapur, D. 2017. "(When) do antipoverty programs reduce violence? India's rural employment guarantee and Maoist conflict." *International organization* 71, no. 3: 605–632.

Datt, G., and Ravallion, M. 2010. "Shining for the poor too." *Economic and Political Weekly* XLV, no. 7: 55–60.

Datta, A., 1998. *Land and labour relations in Southwest Bangladesh.* London: Macmillan.

Davenport, C. 2004. "The promise of democratic pacification: An empirical assessment." *International Studies Quarterly* 48, no. 3: 539–560.

Davey, B. 1974. *The economic development of India.* Nottingham: Spokesman Books.

Davidson, R. 2012. *The emotional life of your brain.* New York: Hudson Street Press.

Davidson, R. 2016. "The Four Keys to Well-Being." *Greater Good Magazine.* https://greatergood.berkeley.edu/article/item/the_four_keys_to_well_being.

De, S., and Saha, P. 2002. "BJP's politics of expediency: permeating Hindutva and legislating neo-liberal reforms." In *Class, ideology, and political parties in India,* ed. A. Jana and B. Sarmah. New Delhi: South Asian Publishers.

De Angelis, M. 2004. "Separating the doing and the deed: capital and the continuous character of enclosures." *Historical Materialism* 12, no. 2: 57–87.

De Zwart, F. 2000. "The logic of affirmative action: Caste, class and quotas in India." *Acta Sociologica* 43, no. 3: 235–249.

Demeritt, D. 2002. "What is the 'social construction of nature'? A typology and sympathetic critique", *Progress in Human Geography* 26, no. 6: 767–790.

Della Porta, D. 1995. *Social movements, political violence, and the state: A comparative analysis of Italy and Germany.* New York: Cambridge University Press.

Della Porta, D. 2014. "On violence and repression: A relational approach." *Government and Opposition* 49, no. 2: 159–187.

Desai, A.R. 1975. *State and Society in India.* Bombay: Popular Prakashan.

Desai, A.R., ed. 1986. *Agrarian struggles in India since Independence.* Delhi: Oxford University Press.

Desai, A.R. 1989. "Rural development and human rights in Independent India." *Economic and Political Weekly* 12, no. 31: 1291–1296.

Desai, M. 2003. "From movement to Party to Government: Why social policies in Kerala and West Bengal are so different." In *States, Parties and Social Movements,* ed. J. Goldstone, 170–196. Cambridge: Cambridge University Press.

Desai, R. 2002. *Slouching towards Ayodhya.* Gurgaon: Three Essays Collective.

Desai, R. 2011. "Gujarat's Hindutva of capitalist development." *South Asia: Journal of South Asian Studies* 34, no. 3: 354–381.

Deshmane, A. 2017. "Selling spirituality." *Frontline.* https://frontline.thehindu.com/the-nation/selling-spirituality/article9870620.ece?homepage=true.

Dev, S.M. 2000. "Economic reforms, poverty, income distribution and employment." *Economic and Political Weekly* 35, no. 10: 823–835.

Dhanagare, D.N. 1991. *Peasant movements in India, 1920–1950.* Delhi: Oxford University Press.

Dhar, A. 2007. "The approach to planning should change." *The Hindu.* https://www.thehindu.com/todays-paper/tp-opinion/ldquoThe-approach-to-planning-should-changerdquo/article14829064.ece.

Dhar, A. 2009. "Atrocities on SCs/STs disturbing." *The Hindu.* https://www.thehindu.com/todays-paper/tp-national/Atrocities-on-SCsSTs-disturbing-Manmohan/article16510646.ece.

Dhawale, A. 2000. "The Shiv Sena: Semi-fascism in action." *The Marxist* 16, no. 2. https://www.cpim.org/marxist/200002_marxist_sena_dhawle.htm.

Ding, X., and Ying, X. 2015. "The uneven and crisis-prone development of capitalism: A review of the tenth forum of world association for political economy." *World Review of Political Economy* 6, no. 4: 583–601.

Dias, W. 2005. "One-day general strike in India exposes need for socialist-internationalist strategy." *World Socialist Web Site.* http://www.wsws.org/en/articles/2005/09/indi-s29.html.

Dirlik, A. 2014. "Mao Zedong thought and the Third World/Global South." *Interventions-International Journal of Postcolonial Studies* 16, no. 2: 233–256.

Djurfeldt, G., and Sircar, S. 2017. *Structural transformation and agrarian change in India.* London: Taylor & Francis Group.

Dixon, C., 1990. *Rural Development in the Third World.* London: Routledge.

Dobkowski, M., and Walliman, I., eds. 2003. *Radical perspectives on the rise of fascism in German.* Kharagpur (India): Cornerstone (Original work published in 1989, by New York: MR Press).

Dollar, D., and Kraay, A. 2000. "Growth is good for the poor." *World Bank.* http://www.worldbank.org/research/growth/absddolakray.htm.

Donnelly, J. 1989. "Repression and development: The political contingency of human rights tradeoffs." In *Human Rights and Development: International Views,* ed. D.P. Forsythe, 305–328. New York: St. Martin's Press.

Doshi, S., and Ranganathan, M. 2017. "Contesting the unethical city: Land disposses-sion and corruption narratives in urban India." *Annals of the American Associations of Geographers* 107, no. 1: 183–199.

Draper, H. 1977. *Karl Marx's theory of revolution: State and bureaucracy.* New York: Monthly Review Press.

Dreze, J., Sen, A. 1995. *India: Economic development and social opportunity.* Delhi: Oxford University Press.

Dreze, J., Sen, A. 2002. *India: Development and participation.* Delhi: Oxford University Press.

Dryzek, J.S. 1996. "Political inclusion and the dynamics of democratization." *American Political Science Review* 90, no. 3: 475–487.

Dudley, R., and Miller, R.A. 1998. "Group Rebellion in the 1980s." *Journal of Conflict Resolution* 42, no. 1: 77–96.

Duménil, G., and Lévy, D. 2005. "The neoliberal (counter-)revolution." In *Neoliberalism: A critical reader,* eds. A. Saad-Filho and D. Johnston, 9–19. London: Pluto Press.

Dutta, A. 2018. "BJP Is trying hard to undercut Congress's soft Hindutva in Madhya Pradesh." *The Wire.* https://thewire.in/politics/bjp-is-trying-hard-to-undercut-congresss-soft-hindutva-in-madhya-pradesh.

Dutta, M. 2018. "Against All Odds: Tracing the Struggles of Workers to Form a Union Inside a Special Economic Zone in Tamil Nadu, India." In *Workers' movements and strikes in the twenty-first century: A global perspective,* eds. J. Nowak, M. Dutta, and P. Birke, 97–114. London: Rowman and Littlefield International.

Dyer, G. 1997. "Output per acre and size of holding: The logic of peasant agriculture under semi feudalism." *Journal of Peasant Studies* 24, no. 1–2: 103–131.

Eagleton, T. 1999. *Ideology.* London: Verso.

Earl, J. 2003. "Tanks, tear gas, and taxes: Toward a theory of movement repression." *Sociological Theory* 21, no. 1: 43–68.

Earl, J., Soule, S.A., and McCarthy, J.D. 2003. "Protest under fire? Explaining the policing of protest." *American Sociological Review* 68, no. 4: 581–606.

Earl, J., Martin, A., McCarthy, J., and Soile. S. 2004. "The use of newspaper data in the study of collective action." *Annual Review of Sociology* 30: 65–80.

Echeverri-Gent, J. 1995. *The state and the poor: Public policy and political development in India and the United States.* New Delhi: Vistaar Publications.

Eicher, C.K. 1995. "Zimbabwe maize based green revolution preconditions for replication." *World Development* 23, no. 5: 805–818.

Engels, F. 1883. "Frederick Engels' Speech at the Grave of Karl Marx." *Marxists.org.* https://www.marxists.org/archive/marx/works/1883/death/burial.htm.

Engels, F. 1848. "Principles of communism." In *Communist Manifesto,* K. Marx and F. Engels. https://www.marxists.org/archive/marx/works/download/pdf/Manifesto.pdf.

Engels, F. 1890. "Letter to J. Bloch." *Marxists.org.* https://www.marxists.org/archive/marx/works/1890/letters/90_09_21.htm.

Engels, F. 1894/1951. "The Peasant Question in France and Germany." In *Selected Works,* vol. 2, K. Marx and F. Engels. Moscow: Foreign Languages Publishing House.

Escobar, A. 1992. "Imagining a post-development era? Critical thought, development and social movements." *Social Text,* no. 31/32: 20–56.

Farid, H. 2005. "Indonesia's original sin: Mass killings and capitalist expansion, 1965–66." *Inter-Asia Cultural Studies* 6, no. 1: 3–16.

Ferguson, J. 1994. *The anti-politics machine: 'Development', depoliticisation and bureaucratic power in Lesotho.* Cambridge: Cambridge University Press.

Fernandes, L. 1994. "Contesting class- gender, community, and the politics of labor in a Calcutta jute mill." *Bulletin of Concerned Asian Scholars* 26, no. 4: 29–43.

Fernandes, L. 2014. *Routledge handbook of gender in South Asia.* Routledge: Milton Park.

Fernandes, L. 2016. "India's middle classes in contemporary India." In *Routledge handbook of contemporary India,* ed. K.A. Jacobsen, 232–242. London: Routledge.

Fernandez, B. 2018. "Dispossession and the depletion of social reproduction." *Antipode* 50, no. 1: 142–163.

Fields, G. 1995. "Income distribution in developing economies: conceptual, data and policy issues in broad based growth." In *Critical issues in Asian development: Theories, experience and policies*, ed. M.G. Quibria. New York: Oxford University Press.

Financial Express. 2018a. "Modi's minister makes bizarre claim; PM never said demonetisation was about black money, says MoS Shukla." *Financial Express*. https://www .financialexpress.com/economy/modis-minister-makes-bizarre-claim-pm-never -said-demonetisation-was-about-black-money-says-mos-shukla/1297529/.

Financial Express. 2018b. "Ease of doing business ranking 2019: know what worked for India and what didn't in its 23 notch leap to 77th slot." *Financial Express*. https:// www.financialexpress.com/economy/ease-of-doing-business-ranking-2019-know -what-worked-for-india-and-what-didnt-in-23-notch-leap-to-77th-slot/1368596/.

Findlay, A. 1995. "Population crises: The Malthusian spectre." In *Geographies of global change*, eds. R. Johnston, P. Taylor, and M. Watts. Oxford: Blackwell.

Fine, B. 2001. *Social capital versus social theory: Political economy and social science at the turn of the millennium*. London: Routledge.

Fine, B., and Saad-Filho, A. 2017. "Thirteen things you need to know about neoliberalism." *Critical Sociology* 43, no. 4–5: 685–706.

Flaherty, M., and Karnjanakesorn, C. 1995. "Marine shrimp aquaculture and natural resource degradation in Thailand." *Environmental Management* 19, no. 1: 27–37.

Flaherty, M., Vandergeest, P., and Miller, P. 1999. "Rice paddy or shrimp pond: Tough decisions in rural Thailand." *World Development* 27, no. 12: 2045–2060.

Foley, B. 2018. "Intersectionality: A Marxist Critique." *Science & Society* 82, no. 2: 269–275.

Fominaya, C.F., and Wood, L., eds. 2011. "Repression and Social Movements." *Interface: A Journal for and About Social Movements* 3, no. 1: 1–11.

Foucault, M. 1979. *Discipline and punish: The birth of the prison*. New York: Vintage Books. Translated from the French by Alan Sheridan.

Fracchia, J. 2008. "The capitalist labour-process and the body in pain: The corporeal depths of Marx's concept of immiseration." *Historical Materialism* 16, no. 4: 35–66.

Franke, R., and Chasin, B. 1991. "Kerala state, India: Radical reform as development." *Monthly Review* 42, no. 8: 1–23.

Frankel, F. 1971. *India's Green Revolution: Economic gains and political costs*. Princeton: Princeton University Press.

Frankel, F. 1990. "Caste, land and dominance in Bihar: Breakdown of the Brahminical order." In *Dominance and state power*, vol. 1, eds. F. Frankel and M. Rao, 46–132. Delhi: Oxford University Press.

Frankel, F. 1994. *Dominance and state power in modern India: Decline of a social order*, volume 1. Delhi: Oxford University Press.

Frankel, F. 2005. *India's political economy, 1947–2004 The gradual revolution.* New Delhi: Oxford India.

Freebairn, D. 1995. "Did the green revolution concentrate incomes? A quantitative study of research reports." *World Development* 23, no. 2: 265–279.

Friedmann, H. 1993. "The political economy of food: A global crisis." *New Left Review* 197: 29–56.

Frontier. (n.d.). www.frontierindia.scriptmania.com/V15PAGE5.htm.

Fuller, C., and Véronique, B., eds. 2001. *The everyday state and society in Modern India.* London: Hurst.

Gabriel, M. *Love and capital.* New York: Back Bay Books.

Ghertner, D.A. 2014. "India's urban revolution: Geographies of displacement beyond gentrification." *Environment and Planning A* 46, no. 7: 1554–1571.

Ghose, D. 2018. "Rahul Gandhi tests 'soft Hindutva' in poll-bound Madhya Pradesh as Congress borrows heavily from BJP's electoral strategy." *Firstpost.* https://www.first post.com/politics/rahul-gandhi-tests-soft-hindutva-in-poll-bound-madhya-pradesh-as-congress-borrows-heavily-from-bjps-electoral-strategy-5283511.html.

Ghosh, J. 1998. "Liberalization Debates." In *The Indian economy since independence*, ed. T. Byres. New Delhi: Oxford University Press.

Gibson-Graham, J.K. 2006. *A post-capitalist politics.* Minneapolis: Minnesota University Press.

Giddens, A. 1981. *A contemporary critique of historical materialism.* London: Macmillan.

Gidwani, V. 2008. *Capital, interrupted: Agrarian development and the politics of work in India.* Minneapolis: University of Minneapolis Press.

Gill, S. 1988. "Contradictions of Punjab model of growth and search for an alternative." *Economic and Political Weekly* 23, no. 42: 2167–2173.

Gill, S. 1994. "The farmers movement and agrarian change in the green revolution belt of North West India." *Journal of Peasant Studies* 21, no. 3–4: 195–211.

Gimenez, M. 2005. "Capitalism and the oppression of women: Marx revisited." *Science & Society* 69, no. 1: 11–32.

Gimenez, M. 2017. "Intersectionality." *Science & Society* 81, no. 2: 261–269; no. 3: 450–452.

Gimenez, M. 2018. Intersectionality: Marxist critical observations. *Science & Society* 82, no. 2: 261–269.

Goldman, A., and Smith, J. 1995. "Nature of green revolutions." *World Development* 23, no. 2.

Gomes, J. 2015. "The political economy of the Maoist conflict in India: An empirical analysis." *World Development* 68: 96–123.

Gonzalez, O., Beltran, L., Caceres-Martinez, C., Ramirez, H., Hernandez-Vazquez, S., Troyo-Dieguez, E., and Ortega-Rubio, A. 2003. "Sustainability Development Analysis of Semi-Intensive Shrimp Farms in Sonora, Mexico." *Sustainable Development* 11, no. 4: 213–222.

Goss, J., Burch, D., and Rickson, R. 2000. "Agri-food restructuring and Third World transnationals: Thailand, the CP Group and the Global Shrimp Industry." *World Development* 28, no. 3: 513–530.

Goss, J., Skladany, M., and Middendorf, G. 2001. "Dialogue: Shrimp aquaculture in Thailand: A response to Vandergeest, Flaherty, and Miller." *Rural Sociology* 66, no. 3: 451–460.

Goodman, D., and Watts, M., eds. 1997. *Globalising food: Agrarian questions and global restructuring.* London: Routledge.

Government of India. 1969. "Home ministry, research and policy division, 1969." In *The Causes and Nature of Current Agrarian Tensions*, ed. A. Desai. New Delhi.

Government of India. 1986. "The Causes and Nature of Current Agrarian Tension." In *Agrarian struggles in India since Independence,* ed. A.R. Desai. Delhi: Oxford University Press.

Government of India. 1998. *Rural Development Statistics, 1998.* Hyderabad: National Institute of Rural Development.

Government of India. 1998. Union Home Minister Shri L.K. Advani's Speech. The High Level Meeting of Chief Ministers and Police Chiefs on Naxalism, Hyderabad, June 15, 2009.

Government of India. 2003. India: *Rural Development Statistics, 2002–2003.* Hyderabad: National Institute of Rural Development.

Government of India. 2005. *India: Rural Development Report.* Hyderabad: National Institute of Rural Development.

Government of India. 2007. *Rural Development Statistics: 2005–2006.* Hyderabad: National Institute of Rural Development.

Government of India. 2008. *Rural Development Statistics: 2007.* Hyderabad: National Institute of Rural Development.

Government of India. 2015. "Ministry of labour and employment. Annual Report." *Government of India.* https://labour.gov.in/sites/default/files/Chapter%20-%204.pdf.

Grabowski, R. 2005. "Agricultural revolution, political development, and long-run economic growth." *Canadian Journal of Development Studies* 26, no. 3: 393–408.

Griffin, K. 1974. *The political economy of agrarian change: An essay on the Green Revolution.* London: Macmillan.

Griffin, K. 1989. *Alternative strategies for economic development.* New York: St. Martin's Press.

Grossman, H. 1929. *Law of the accumulation and breakdown.* https://www.marxists.org/archive/grossman/1929/breakdown/

Gudavarthy, A. 2005. "Dalit and Naxalite Movements in AP: Solidarity or Hegemony?" *Economic and Political Weekly* 40, no. 51: 5410–5418.

Guha, R. 1983. *Elementary aspects of peasant insurgency in colonial India.* Delhi: Oxford University Press.

Guha, R. 2002. "Chipko: Social history of an 'environmental' movement." In *Social movements and the state,* ed. G. Shah. Delhi: Sage.

Guha, R. 2006. "The guru of hate." *The Hindu.* https://www.thehindu.com/todays-paper/tp-features/tp-sundaymagazine/the-guru-of-hate/article3232784.ece.

Guha, R. 2007. "Adivasis, Naxalites and democracy." *Economic and Political Weekly* 42, no. 32: 3305–3312.

Guha, R. 2012. *Patriots and partisans.* New Delhi: Penguin Books.

Gupta, A. 2000. "Blurred boundaries: The discourse of corruption, the culture of politics and the imagined state." In *Politics and the State in India,* ed. Z. Hasan. New Delhi: Sage.

Gupta, A., and A. Sharma, 2006. "Globalization and Postcolonial States." *Current Anthropology* 47, no. 2.

Gupta, A. and Sivaramakrishnan, K. 2011. "Introduction: The state in India after liberalization." In *The State in India after Liberalization: Interdisciplinary Perspectives,* eds. A. Gupta, and K. Sivaramakrishnan, 1–28. New York: Routledge.

Gupta, D., and Sriram, K. 2018. "Impact of security expenditures in military alliances on violence from non-state actors: evidence from India." *World Development* 107: 338–357.

Gupta, T.D. 2003. "Recent developments in the Naxalite movement – Communists in India." *Monthly Review* 45, no. 4: 8–24.

Gupta, T.D. 2006. "Maoism in India." *Economic and Political Weekly* 41, no. 29: 3172–3176.

Gurr, T. 1986. "Persisting Patterns of Repression and Rebellion: Foundations for a General Theory of Political Coercion." In *Persistent Patterns and Emergent Structures in a Waning Century,* ed. M. Karns, 149–170. New York: Praeger.

Gurr, T. 1988. "War, revolution, and the growth of the coercive state." *Comparative Political Studies* 21, no. 1: 45–65.

Habib, I. 2014. "Major historical problems in the light of Marxism." In *Marx, Gandhi and Modernity,* ed. A. Bilgrami. Delhi: Tulika Books.

Habib, I. 2015. *Religion in Indian history.* Delhi: Tulika Books.

Habib, I. 2017. "Seventy years on, India cannot allow the divisive forces to triumph again." *The Wire.* https://thewire.in/history/bjps-fascist-character-grave-danger-democracy-civil-rights-india.

Hale, A., and Opondo, M. 2005. "Humanizing the cut flower chain: Confronting the realities of flower production for workers in Kenya." *Antipode* 37, no. 2: 301–323.

Hansda, R. 2017. "Small-scale farming and gender-friendly agricultural technologies: the interplay between gender, labour, caste, policy and practice." *Gender, Technology, and Development* 21, no. 3: 189–205.

Haragopal, G. 2017. "Maoist Movement: Context and Concerns." *Economic & Political Weekly* 52, no. 21.

Hardin, C. 2014. "Finding the 'neo' in neoliberalism." *Cultural Studies* 28, no. 2: 199–221.

Harris, R., and Seid, M., eds. 2000. *Critical perspectives on globalization and neoliberalism in the developing countries.* Leiden: Brill.

Harriss, J. 1988. "A review of South Asian studies." *Modern Asian Studies* 22, no. 1: 43–56.

Harriss, J. 1991. "The green revolution in North Arcot: Economic trends, household mobility, and the politics of an awkward class." In *The Green Revolution Reconsidered,* eds. P.B. Hazell and C. Ramaswamy. Baltimore: The John Hopkins University Press.

Harriss, J. 1992. "Does the 'Depressor' Still Work? Agrarian Structure and Development in India: A Review of Evidence and Argument." *Journal of Peasant Studies* 19, no. 2: 189–227.

Harriss, J. 2011a. "What is Going on in India's 'Red Corridor'? Questions about India's Maoist Insurgency-Literature Review." *Pacific Affairs* 84, no. 2: 309–327.

Harriss, J. 2011b. "How far have India's economic reforms been 'guided by compassion and justice'? Social policy in the neoliberal era." In *Understanding India's New Political Economy: A Great Transformation?*, eds. S. Ruparelia, S. Reddy, J. Harriss, and S. Corbridge, 127–140. New York: Routledge.

Harriss, J. 2011c. "'New politics' and the governmentality of the post-liberalization state in India: an ethnographic perspective." In *The state in India after liberalization: Interdisciplinary perspectives,* eds. A. Gupta and L. Sivaramakrishnan, 91–108. London: Routledge.

Harriss, J. 2013. "Politics and redistribution in India." In *Routledge handbook of Indian politics*, eds. A. Kohli and P. Singh. London: Routledge.

Harriss White, B., and Janakarajan, S. 1997. "From green revolution to rural industrialization in South India." *Economic and Political Weekly* 32, no. 25: 1469–1477.

Harriss-White, B., and Janakarajan, S. 2004. *Rural India facing the twenty-first century: Essays on long-term village change and recent development policy.* London: Anthem Press.

Harvey, D. 1974. "Population, resources, and the ideology of science." *Economic Geography* 50, no. 3: 256–277.

Harvey, D. 1978. "The urban process under capitalism." *International Journal of Urban and Regional Research* 2, no. 1–4: 101–131.

Harvey, D. 1982. *Limits to capital.* Chicago: Chicago University Press.

Harvey, D. 1990. "Between space and time: Reflections on the geographical imagination." *Annals of the Association of American Geographers* 80, no. 3: 418–434.

Harvey, D. 1996. "Justice, nature and the geography of difference." Oxford: Blackwell.

Harvey, D. 1998. "The body as an accumulation strategy." *Environment and Planning D: Society and Space* 16, no. 4: 401–421.

Harvey, D. 2000. *Spaces of hope*. Edinburgh: Edinburgh University Press.

Harvey, D. 2003. *The New Imperialism*. Oxford: Oxford University Press.

Harvey, D. 2005. *A brief history of neoliberalism*. New York: Oxford University Press.

Harvey, D. 2006. *Spaces of global capitalism*. London: Verso.

Harvey, D. 2016. "Neoliberalism is a political project (an interview)." *Jacobin*. https://www.jacobinmag.com/2016/07/david-harvey-neoliberalism-capitalism-labor-crisis-resistance/.

Harwood, J. 2013. "Development policy and history: Lessons from the green revolution." *History and Policy*. http://www.historyandpolicy.org/policy-papers/papers/development-policy-and-history-lessons-from-the-green-revolution.

Heble, A. 1979. "The green revolution: its social and economic consequences." *How*.

Heller, P. 1995. "From class struggle to class compromise: redistribution and growth in a South Indian state." *Journal of Development Studies* 31, no. 5: 645–672.

Heller, P. 1999. *The labor of development: Workers and the trans formation of capitalism in Kerala, India*. Ithaca & London: Cornell University Press.

Heller, P., and Fernandes, L. 2006. "Hegemonic aspirations: New middle class politics and India's democracy in comparative perspective." *Critical Asian Studies* 38, no. 4: 495–522.

Heller, P., and Fernandes, L. 1996. "Social capital as a product of class mobilization and state intervention: Industrial workers in Kerala, India." *World Development* 24, no. 6: 1055–1071.

Heller, P., and Fernandes, L. 1999. *The labour of development: Workers and the transformation of capitalism in Kerala, India*. Ithaca: Cornell University Press.

Henderson, C.W. 1991. "Conditions affecting the use of political repression." *Journal of conflict resolution* 35, no. 1: 120–142.

Herath, G., and Jayasuriya, S. 1996. "Adoption of HYV technology in Asian countries." *Asian Survey* 36, no. 12: 1184–1200.

Herod, A. 1994. "On workers' theoretical (in)visibility in the writing of critical urban geography: A comradely critique." *Urban Geography* 15, no. 7: 681–693.

Herod, A. 1999. "Reflections on interviewing foreign elites: Praxis, positionality, validity, and the cult of the insider." *Geoforum* 30, no. 4: 313–327.

Herring, R. 1999. "Embedded Particularism: India's failed developmental state." In *The developmental state*, ed. M. Woo-Cumings. Ithaca, NY: Cornell University Press.

Herring, R. 2006. "Why did "operation cremate Monsanto" fail? Science and class in India's great terminator-technology hoax." *Critical Asian Studies* 38, no. 4: 467–493.

Herring, R. 2013. "Class politics in India: Euphemization, identity, and power." In *Routledge handbook of Indian politics*, eds. A. Kohli and P. Singh. London: Routledge.

Herring, R.J., and Agarwala, R. 2006. "Introduction – Restoring to class: Puzzles from the subcontinent." *Critical Asian Studies* 38, no. 4: 323–356.

Herring, R., and Paarlberg, R. 2016. "The political economy of biotechnology." *Annual Review of Resource Economics* 8: 397–341.

Hess, D., and Martin, B. 2006. "Repression, backfire, and the theory of transformative events." *Mobilization* 11, no. 2: 249–267.

Hilton, R., ed. 1978. *The transition from feudalism to capitalism.* London: Verso.

Hindustan Times. PTI. 2002. "Major Naxalite Outfits." *Hindustan Times.* https://www .hindustantimes.com/india/major-naxalite-outfits/story-oveBIOPZoV4Hd B5La2w7dM.html.

Holloway, J. 2005. "No." *Historical Materialism* 13, no. 4: 265–284.

Houston, I., and Pulido, L. 2000. "The work of performativity." *Environment and Planning D: Society and Space* 20, no. 4: 401–424.

Houtzager, P. 2000. "Social movements amidst democratic transitions: Lessons from the Brazilian countryside." *Journal of Development Studies* 36, no. 5: 59–88.

Hristov, J. 2005. "Indigenous Struggles for land and culture in Cauca, Colombia." *Journal of Peasant Studies* 32, no. 1: 88–117.

Huang, Y. 2015. "Can capitalist farms defeat family farms? The dynamics of capitalist accumulation in shrimp aquaculture in South China." *Journal of Agrarian Change* 15, no. 3: 392–412.

Huitric, M., Folke, C., and Kautsky, N. 2002. "Development and government policies of the shrimp farming industry in Thailand in relation to mangrove ecosystems." *Ecological Economics* 40, no. 3: 441–455.

Human Rights Watch. 1999a. *Broken People: Caste violence against India's 'untouchables'.* New York: Human Rights Watch.

Human Rights Watch. 1999b. "The pattern of abuse: Rural violence in Bihar and the state's response." *Human Rights Watch.* http://www.hrw.org/reports/1999/india/In dia994-06.htm.

Ilaiah, K. 2000. "Caste, or class or caste-class: a study in Dalitbahujan consciousness and struggles in Andhra Pradesh in 1980s." In *Class, caste, and gender*, ed. M. Mohanty, 227–255. Delhi: Sage.

India Together. 2007. "NREGA battling cancerous corruption in Orissa." *India Together.* http://www.india together.org/2007/oct/gov-nregs.htm.

Indian Aquaculture Authority (IAA). 2001. "Shrimp Aquaculture and the Environment." http://aquaculture.tn.nic.in/pdf/farming.pdf.

Indian Express. 2017. "BJP-RSS new enemies of Naxalite movement, say leaders." *The Indian Press.* https://indianexpress.com/article/india/bjp-rss-new-enemies-of-nax alite-movement-say-leaders-4678690/.

Indian National Congress. 2017. "Modi govt. diluting MNREGA." *Indian National Congress.* https://www.inc.in/en/in-focus/the-systematic-strangulation-of-mgnre ga-under-modi-s-watch.

International Communist League. 2014. "India: Hindu far right sweeps elections: For a socialist federation of South Asia!" *International Communist League.* https://www .icl-fi.org/english/wh/227/india.html.

Islam, M. 2008. "In search of "white gold": Environmental and agrarian changes in rural Bangladesh." *Society and Natural Resources* 22, no. 1: 66–78.

Ismi, A. 2013. "Maoist Insurgency Spreads to Over 40% of India. Mass Poverty and Delhi's Embrace of Corporate Neoliberalism Fuels Social Uprising." *Global Research.* http://www.globalresearch.ca.

Jacob, S. 2015. "Towards a comparative subnational perspective on India." *Studies in Indian Politics* 3, no. 2: 229–246.

Jaffrelot, C. 2011. *Religion, caste, and politics in India.* New York: Columbia University Press.

Jaffrelot, C. 2013. "Caste and political parties in India." In *Routledge handbook of Indian politics*, eds. A. Kohli and P. Singh. London: Routledge.

Jain, H.K. 2010. *Green revolution: history, impact and future.* Houston: Studium Press.

Jairath, V. 2014. "Studying communal riots in India: Some methodological issues." In *Political sociology of India,* ed. A. Kumar. Delhi: Sage.

Jal, M. 2014. *The new militants.* Delhi: Aakar.

Jalal, A. 1995. *Democracy and authoritarianism in South Asia.* Cambridge: Cambridge University Press.

Jamieson, M. 2002. "Ownership of sea-shrimp production and perceptions of economic opportunity in a Nicaraguan Miskitu Village." *Ethnography* 41, no. 3: 281–298.

Jamil, G. 2017. *Accumulation by segregation: Muslims localities in Delhi.* Delhi: Oxford University Press.

Jannuzi, F. 1996. *India's persistent dilemma: The political economy of agrarian reform.* London: Orient Longman.

Jawed, S. 2017. "Fact check: Are rural roads constructed in 2016–17 at an all-time high as claimed by BJP?" *Altnews.* https://www.altnews.in/fact-check-rural-roads-construc ted-2016-17-time-high-claimed-bjp/.

Jeffrey, C. 1997. "Richer farmers and agrarian change in Meerut District, Uttar Pradesh, India." *Environment and Planning A* 29, no. 12: 2113–2127.

Jeffrey, C., Jeffery, P., and Jeffery, R. 2005. "Reproducing difference? Schooling, jobs, and empowerment in Uttar Pradesh, India." *World Development* 33, no. 12: 2085–2101.

Jeffrey, C., and Lerche, J. 2000. "Stating the difference: State, discourse and class reproduction in Uttar Pradesh, India." *Development and Change* 31, no. 4: 857–878.

Jenkins, S. 2011. "The politics of India's special economic zones." In *Understanding India's new political economy*, eds. S. Ruparelia, S. Reddy, J. Harriss, and S. Corbridge. London: Routledge.

Jessop, B. 2002. *The future of the capitalist state.* Cambridge: Polity Press.

Jha, A., Gupta, S., and Ramaswamy, S. 2017. "India risk survey 2017." *Pinkerton/FICCI.* http://www.ficci.in/Sedocument/20416/India-Risk-Survey-2017-Report.pdf.

Jha, S.K. 2003. "Jharkhand: Anti-naxal strategy and use of POTA." *Institute for Conflict Management,* no. 1021, 2003. http://www.ipcs.org/article/naxalite-violence/jharkh and-anti-naxal-strategy-and-use-of-pota-1021.html.

Jodhka, S., Rehbein, B., and Souza, J. 2017. *Inequality in capitalist societies.* London: Routledge.

Jones, H. 1990. *Population geography.* London: Paul Chapman.

Jones, K. 2018. "Indian court dismisses Maruti Suzuki workers' bail application." *World Socialist Website.* https://www.wsws.org/en/articles/2018/10/23/mswu-023.html.

Jones, S. 2014. "US corporate profits soar as productivity rises and wages stagnate." https://www.wsws.org/en/articles/2014/12/04/wage-d04.html.

Jose, A. 1988. "Agricultural wages in India." *Economic and Political Weekly* 23.

Josh, B. 2011. *A history of the Indian communists: from united front to left front.* New Delhi: Sage.

Judge, P., ed. 2014. *Towards sociology of Dalits.* Delhi: Sage.

Kallis, A. 2003. *The fascism reader.* London: Routledge.

Kannan, K. 1999. "Rural labour relations and development dilemmas in Kerala: Reflections on the dilemmas of a socially transforming labour force in a slowly growing economy." *Journal of Peasant Studies* 26, no. 2–3: 140–181.

Kapadia, K. 1997. "Mediating the meaning of market opportunities – Gender, caste and class in rural South India." *Economic and Political Weekly* 32, no. 52: 3329–3235.

Kapadia, K. 2002. *The violence of development: The politics of identity, gender and social inequalities in India.* London: Zed.

Kar, G. 2018. "The enduring prevalence of semi-feudal agrarian relations in India." *Journal of Labour and Society* 21, no. 2: 193–213.

Karat, P. 1992. "BJP: A reactionary response." *The Marxist* x, no. 3.

Karat, P. 2000. "CPI(M) programme: Basic strategy reiterated." *The Marxist* 16, no. 3. http://www.cpim.org/marxist/200003_marxist_progrm_pk.htm.

Karat, P. 2004. "Implications of BJP rule: The election battle ahead." *The Marxist* 20, no. 1.

Karat, P. 2014. "The rise of Narendra Modi: A joint enterprise of Hindutva and big business." *The Marxist* xxx, no. 1.

Kautsky, K. 1988. *The Agrarian Question.* Winchester, Massachusetts: Zwan Publications.

Kaviraj, S. 1988. "A critique of the passive revolution." *Economic and Political Weekly* 23, no. 45/47: 2429–2433, 2436–2441, 2443–2444.

Kaviraj, S. 1991. "On state, society and discourse in India." In *Rethinking Third World Politics,* ed. J. Manor, 72–99. Harlow: Longman.

Kaviraj, S. 2011. "On the enchantment of the state: Indian thought on the role of the state in the narrative of modernity." In *The state in India after liberalization: Interdis-*

ciplinary perspectives, eds. A. Gupta and L. Sivaramakrishnan, 31–48. London: Routledge.

Kennedy, J., and Purushotham. S. 2012. "Beyond Naxalbari: A comparative analysis of Maoist insurgency and counterinsurgency in Independent India." *Comparative Studies in Society and History* 54, no. 4: 832–862.

Kerswell, T., and Pratap, S. 2019. *Worker Cooperative in India.* Singapore: Springer Singapore.

Khanna, G., and Zimmerman, L. 2017. "Guns and butter? Fighting violence with the promise of development." *Journal of Development Economics* 124: 120–141.

Khatkhate, D. 2006. "Indian economic reform, a philosopher's stone." *Economic and Political Weekly* 41, no. 22: 2203–2205.

Khera, R. 2008. "Empowerment guarantee act." *Economic and Political Weekly* 43, no. 35: 8–10.

Khilnani, S. 2017. *The idea of India.* New York: Farrar, Straus and Girour.

Kishor, C.S. 1998. "Poverty alleviation after post liberalisation: Study of a tribal block in Orissa." *Economic and Political Weekly* 33, no. 28: 1846–1851.

Klak, T., and Myers, G. 1997. "The discursive tactics of neoliberal development in small third world countries." *Geoforum* 28, no. 2: 133–149.

Kodras, J.E. 1997. "The changing map of American poverty in an era of economic restructuring and political realignment." *Economic Geography* 73, no. 1: 67–93.

Kohli, A. 1987. *The state and poverty in India: The politics of reform.* Cambridge: Cambridge University Press.

Kohli, A. 2012. *Poverty amid plenty in the new India.* Delhi: Cambridge University Press.

Kosambi, D. 1957. *Exasperating essays: Exercises in the dialectical method.* Poona: Bhagawat.

Kotovsky, G. 1964. *Agrarian Reforms in India.* New Delhi: People's Publishing House.

Krishna, A. 2002. "Enhancing Political Participation in Democracies – What is the Role of Social Capital?" *Comparative Political Studies* 35, no. 4: 437–460.

Krishna, C. 2003. *Fascism in India: Faces, fangs, and facts.* New Delhi: Manak Publications.

Krishna, S. 2015. "Number fetish: Middle-class India's obsession with the GDP." *Globalizations* 12, no. 6: 859–871.

Krishnan, S. 2017. "The engineering India's middle-class politics." *Contemporary South Asia* 25, no. 4: 364–379.

Kruks-Wisner, G. 2018. "The pursuit of social welfare: citizens claim making in rural India." *World Politics* 70, no. 1: 122–163.

Kujur, R. 2006. "Under development and Naxal movement." *Economic and Political Weekly* 41, no. 7: 557–559.

Kumar, A. 1999. "Massacres by landlord militia rock India's second most populous state." *World Socialist Website.* http://www.wsws.org/articles/1999/feb1999/ind2-f24.shtml.

Kumar, A. 2008. "Dissonance between economic reforms and democracy." *Economic and Political Weekly* 43, no. 1: 54–60.

Kumar, C. 2018. "India lost 11.73 lakh man days to strikes in 2017." *Times of India.* https://timesofindia.indiatimes.com/india/india-lost-11-73-lakh-man-days-to-strikes-in-2017/articleshow/62539692.cms.

Kumar, S. 2017. "After silent revolution: Most marginalized Dalits and local democracy in Uttar Pradesh, North India." *Studies in India Politics* 5, no. 1: 18–31.

Kumar, V. 2002. "Dalits." *Alternative economic survey.* New Delhi: Rainbow Publishers.

Kumara, K. 2017. "Indian economy in a downward spiral." *World Socialist Website.* https://www.wsws.org/en/articles/2017/10/11/inec-o11.html.

Kumara, K. 2018a. "India: Modi government accelerates anti-worker privatization drive." *World Socialist Website.* https://www.wsws.org/en/articles/2018/04/09/modi-a09.html.

Kumara, K. 2018b. "Indian Prime Minister Modi to tout pro-business record at World Economic Forum." *World Socialist Website.* https://www.wsws.org/en/articles/2018/01/23/modi-j23.html.

Kumara, K. and Kumar, A. 2016. "Indian government's demonetisation causes mass hardship and economic chaos." *World Socialist Website.* https://www.wsws.org/en/articles/2016/11/21/inde-n21.html.

Kumbamu, A. 2019. "The Naxalite movement, the oppressive state, and the revolutionary struggle in India." In *The Palgrave handbook of social movements, revolution, and social transformation,* ed. B. Berberoglu, 233–247. Cham: Palgrave.

Kundu, S. 2018. "RBI Working Paper Series No. 03 Rural Wage Dynamics in India: What Role does Inflation Play?" *Reserve Bank of Canada.* https://www.rbi.org.in/Scripts/PublicationsView.aspx?id=18117#C7.

Kunnath, G. 2006. "Becoming a Naxalite in rural Bihar: Class struggle and its contradictions." *Journal of Peasant Studies* 33, no. 1: 89–123.

Kunnath, G. 2013. "Anthropology's ethical dilemmas reflections from the Maoist fields of India." *Current Anthropology* 54, no. 6: 740–752.

Lebowitz, M. 2003. *Beyond Capital: Marx's political economy of the working class.* New York: Palgrave Macmillan.

Lebowitz, M. 2005. "The politics of assumption and the assumption of politics." *Historical Materialism* 14, no. 2: 29–487.

Leftwich, A. 2000. *States of development: On the primacy of politics in development.* Cambridge: Polity.

Lenin, V. 1899. The *development of capitalism in Russia, volume of collected works.* Moscow: Progress Publishers.

Lenin, V. 1901. "What is to be done?" *Marxists.org.* https://www.marxists.org/archive/lenin/works/1901/witbd/iii.htm.

Lenin, V. 1908. "Marxism and revisionism." *Marxists.org.* https://www.marxists.org/archive/lenin/works/1908/apr/03.htm.

Lenin, V. 1913. "The three sources and three component parts of Marxism." *Marxists. org.* https://www.marxists.org/archive/lenin/works/1913/mar/x01.htm.

Lenin, V. 1914a. "Tactics of the class struggle of the proletariat." https://www.marxists .org/archive/lenin/works/1914/granat/ch05.htm.

Lenin, V. 1914b. "Summary of dialectics." *Marxists.org.* https://www.marxists.org/ar chive/lenin/works/1914/cons-logic/summary.htm.

Lenin, V. 1917. "On compromises." *Marxists.org.* https://www.marxists.org/archive/len in/works/1917/sep/03.htm.

Lenin, V. 1918. "The proletarian revolution and the renegade Kautsky." Marxists.org. https://www.marxists.org/archive/lenin/works/1918/prrk/democracy.htm

Lenin, V. 1919a. "A great beginning." *Marxists.org.* https://www.marxists.org/archive/ lenin/works/1919/jun/19.htm.

Lenin, V. 1919b. "The state." *Marxists.org.* https://www.marxists.org/archive/lenin/ works/1919/jul/11.htm.

Lenin, V. 1920. ""Left-wing" communism: An infantile disorder: No compromises." *Marxists.org.* https://www.marxists.org/archive/lenin/works/1920/lwc/ch08.htm.

Lenin, V. 1921. "Once again on the trade unions: The current situation and the mistakes of Trotsky and Buhkarin." *Marxists.org.* https://www.marxists.org/archive/lenin/ works/1921/jan/25.htm.

Lenin, V. 1922. "On the Significance of Militant Materialism." *Marxists.org.* https:// www.marxists.org/archive/lenin/works/1922/mar/12.htm.

Lenin, V. 1977a. *Selected Works*, vol. 1. Moscow: Progress Publishers.

Lenin, V. 1977b. *The state and revolution.* Moscow: Progress Publishers.

Lenin, V. 1977c. *Selected works*, vol. 3. Moscow: Progress Publishers.

Lenin, V. 1978. *Revolutionary adventurism.* Moscow: Progress Publishers.

Lerche, J. 1999. "Politics of the poor: Agricultural labourers and political transforma- tions in Uttar Pradesh." *Journal of Peasant Studies* 26, no. 2–3: 182–241.

Lerche, J., Shah, A., and Harriss-White, B. 2013. "Introduction: Agrarian questions and left politics in India." *Journal of Agrarian Change* 13, no. 3: 337–350.

Levien, M. 2011. "Special economic zones and accumulation by dispossession in India." *Journal of Agrarian Change* 11, no 4: 454–483.

Levien, M. 2012. "The land question: Special economic zones and the political economy of dispossession in India." *Journal of Peasant Studies* 39, no. 3–4: 933–969.

Levien, M. 2013. "Regimes of dispossession: From steel towns to special economic zones." *Development and Change* 44, no. 2: 381–407.

Levien, M. 2017. "Gender and land dispossession: A comparative analysis." *Journal of Peasant Studies* 44, no. 6: 1111–1134.

Levien, M. 2018. *Dispossession without development: Land grabs in neoliberal India.* Ox- ford: Oxford University Press.

Liberation. 2003. "Women agricultural labour struggles: Key issues." http://www.cpiml .org/liberation/year_2003/february/aadhi%20zameen%202.htm.

Liodakis, G. 1997. "Technological change in agriculture: A Marxist critique" *Sociologia Ruralis* 37, no. 1: 61–78.

Lipton, M. 1989. *New seeds and poor people.* London: Unwin Hyman.

Lockwood, D. 2014. The *Indian bourgeoisie: A political history of the Indian capitalist class in the early twentieth century.* London: I.B. Tauris.

Lofgren, H. 2016. "The Communist Party of India (Marxist) and the Left government in West Bengal, 1977–2011: Strains of governance and socialist imagination." *Studies in Indian Politics* 4, no. 1: 102–115.

Lokniti. 2018. "Lokniti-CSDS-ABP News Mood of The Nation Survey-3." http://www .lokniti.org/pdf/Lokniti-ABP-News-Mood-of-the-Nation-Survey-Round-3-May-2018 .pdf.

Louis, P. 2000. "Shankarbigha revisited." *Economic and Political Weekly* 35, no. 7: 507–509.

Louis, P. 2005. "Jehanabad II: Viewing Bihar." *Economic and Political Weekly* 40, no. 51: 5371–5372.

Lowy, M. 2010. *The politics of combined and uneven development.* Chicago, IL: Haymarket Books.

Luxemburg, R. 2009. *The Rosa Luxemburg Reader,* eds. P. Hudis and K. Anderson. New York: MR Press.

MacCulloch, R. 2005. "Income Inequality and the Taste for Revolution." *Journal of Law & Economics* 48, no. 1: 93–123.

Mackel, K.A. 2010. "Fascism: A political ideology of the past." *Inquiries Journal* 2, no. 11. http://www.inquiriesjournal.com/articles/317/fascism-a-political-ideology-of-the -past.

Maitra, K. 2012. *Marxism in India: From decline to debacle.* New Delhi: Lotus Collection.

Maitra, P. 1997. "Globalization of capitalism, agriculture and the negation of nation states." *International Journal of Social Economics* 24: 237–254.

Mallick, C. 2018. "Public-private discord in the land acquisition law: Insights from Rajarhat in India." *Singapore Journal of Tropical Geography* 39, no. 3: 401–420.

Mallick, R. 1994. *Indian communism: Opposition, collaboration, and institutionalization.* Oxford: Oxford University Press.

Malreddy, P.K. 2014. "Domesticating the 'New Terrorism': The case of the Maoist insurgency in India." *European Legacy-Toward New Paradigms* 19, no. 5: 590–605.

Mandel, E. 1969. "Marxist theory of the state." *Marxists.org.* https://www.marxists.org/ archive/mandel/1969/xx/state.htm.

Mandel, E. 2002. "Anticipation and hope as categories of historical materialism." *Historical* Materialism 10, no. 4: 245–259.

Mander, H. 2016. "The poor have been forgotten more and more." *Governance Now.* https://www.governancenow.com/views/columns/the-poor-have-been-gotten-more-more- harsh-mander-economic-reforms.

Mann, M. 2004. *Fascists.* Cambridge: Cambridge University Press.

Mann, S.A., and Dickinson, J.M. 1978. "Obstacles to the development of a capitalist agriculture." *Journal of Peasant Studies* 5, no. 4: 466–481.

Mannathukkaren, N. 2011. "Redistribution and recognition: Land reforms in Kerala and the limits of culturalism." *The Journal of Peasant Studies* 38, no. 2: 379–411.

Mao T. 1926. "Analysis of classes in Chinese society." *Marxists.org.* https://www.marxists.org/reference/archive/mao/selected-works/volume-1/mswv1_1.htm.

Mao T. 1961. "Selected Works." *Marxists.org.* https://www.marxists.org/reference/archive/mao/selected-works/index.htm.

Martinez-Alier, J. 2001. "Ecological conflicts and valuation: Mangroves versus shrimps in the late 1990s." *Environment and Planning C: Government and Policy* 19, no. 5: 713–728.

Marx, K. 1843. "A contribution to the critique of Hegel's philosophy of right: Introduction." *Marxists.org.* https://www.marxists.org/archive/marx/works/1843/critique-hpr/intro.htm.

Marx, K. 1845. "Theses on Feuerbach." *Marxists.org.* https://www.marxists.org/archive/marx/works/1845/theses/theses.htm.

Marx, K. 1873. "Political Indifferentism." *Marxists.org.* https://www.marxists.org/archive/marx/works/1873/01/indifferentism.htm.

Marx, K. 1967. *The eighteenth Brumaire of Louis Napoleon.* Moscow: Progress.

Marx, K. 1976. *Wage-labour and capital.* New York: International Publishers.

Marx, K. 1977. *Capital,* vol. 1. New York: Vintage.

Marx, K. 1991. *Capital,* vol. 3. London: Penguin Books.

Marx, K. 2000. *Selected Writings,* ed. by D. McLellan. New York: Oxford University Press.

Marx, K. 2010. *The first international and after.* London: Verso.

Marx, K., and Engels, F. 1845. "Theses on Feuerbach." *Marxists.org.* https://www.marxists.org/archive/marx/works/1845/theses/theses.htm.

Marx, K., and Engels, F. 1848. "The Communist Manifesto." *Marxists.org.* https://www.marxists.org/archive/marx/works/download/pdf/Manifesto.pdf.

Marx, K., and Engels, F. 1850. "Address of the central committee to the Communist League." *Marxists.org.* https://www.marxists.org/archive/marx/works/1847/communist-league/1850-ad1.htm.

Marx, K., and Engels, F. 1964. *On religion,* ed. R. Niebuhr. Atlanta: Scholars Press.

Marx, K., and Engels, F. 1976. *Collected works,* vol. 6. New York: International Publishers.

Marx, K., and Engels, F. 1977. *Selected works.* Moscow: Progress Publishers.

Marx, K., and Engels, F. 1978. *The German Ideology,* ed. C. Arthur. New York: International Publishers.

Marx, K., and Engels, F. 1982. *Selected correspondence.* Moscow: Progress Publishers.

Mason, T. 1995. *Nazism, Fascism and the working class.* Cambridge: Cambridge University.

Mazumdar, S. 2016. "Theorizing the capitalist state." In *Contemporary readings in Marxism*, ed. R. Kumar. Delhi: Aakar.

Mazzadri, A. 2017. *The sweatshop regime: Labouring bodies, exploitation, and garments made in India.* Cambridge: Cambridge University Press.

McAdam, D., McCarthy, J.D., and Zald, M.N., eds. 1996. *Comparative perspectives on social movements: Political opportunities, mobilizing structures, and cultural framings.* New York: Cambridge University Press.

McCartney, M. 2013. "Going, going, but not yet quite gone: the political economy of the Indian intermediate classes during the era of liberalization." In *Two decades of market reform in India: Some dissenting views,* ed. S. Bhattacharyya. New York: Anthem Press.

McDowell, L. 2001. "Father and Ford revisited: gender, class and employment change in the new millennium." *Transactions of the Institute of British Geographers* 26, no. 4: 448–464.

McDowell, L. 2008. "Thinking through class and gender in the context of working class Studies." *Antipode* 40, no. 1: 20–24.

McMichael, P. 2000. "A global interpretation of the rise of the East Asian food import complex." *World Development* 28, no. 3: 409–424.

Mehta, J. 2002. "Give poverty a face, please." *Alternative Economic Survey: 2000–2001,* 29–34. Delhi: Rainbow Publishers.

Menon. N., ed. 1999a. *Gender and politics in India.* Delhi: Oxford University Press.

Menon, N., ed. 1999b. "Introduction." In *Gender and politics in India,* ed. N. Menon. Delhi: Oxford University Press.

Meyer, R. 2016. "Precarious workers' movements and the neoliberal state." *Working USA – The Journal of Labor and Society* 19, no. 1: 37–55.

Mezzadri, A. 2016. "Class, gender and the sweatshop: On the nexus between labour commodification and exploitation." *Third World Quarterly* 37, no. 10: 1877–1900.

Mezzadri, A. 2017. *The sweatshop regime: Labouring bodies exploitation, and garments made in India.* Cambridge: Cambridge University Press.

Mezzadri, A., and Fan, L. 2018. "'Classes of labour' at the margins of global commodity chains in India and China." *Development and Change* 49, no. 4: 1034–1063.

Mies, M. 2012. *The lace makers of Narsapur: Indian housewives produce for the world market.* Victoria, Australia: Spinifex Press.

Miliband, R. 1983. "State power and class interests." *New Left Review* 1/138, March–April.

Miller, B.A. 2000. *Geography and Social Movements.* Minneapolis: University of Minnesota Press.

Misra, A. 1994. "Bihar changing peasant struggle." *Economic & Political Weekly* 29, no. 19.

Misra, V., and Hazell, P. 1996. "Terms of trade, rural poverty, technology and investment: the Indian experience, 1952–53 to 1990–91." *Economic and Political Weekly* 31, no. 13: A2-A13.

Mitra, S. 2011. *Politics in India: Structure, process and policy.* London: Routledge.

Mittal, S. 2018. "Rise of the new entrepreneurial classes and the emergence of a high-growth economy." In *India Transformed,* ed. R Mohan, 567–574. Washington, DC: Brookings Institution Press.

Miyamura, S. 2010. "Diverse trajectories of industrial restructuring and labor organising in India." *Third World Quarterly* 37, no. 10: 1921–1941.

Moberg, L. 2015. "The political economy of special economic zones." *Journal of Institutional Economics* 11, no. 1: 167–190.

Mohammad, N. 2018. "How Many Jobs are really being created by the Modi govt's Mudra Scheme?" *The Wire.* https://thewire.in/labour/modi-mudra-loan-scheme-job-creation-reality.

Mohanty, M. 1977. *Revolutionary violence: A Study of the Maoist Movement in India.* New Delhi: Allied.

Mohanty, M. 2004. "Introduction: Dimensions of power and social transformation." In *Class, caste, and gender,* ed. M. Mohanty. Delhi: Sage.

Mohanty, M. 2006. "Challenges of revolutionary violence." *Economic and Political Weekly* 41, no. 29: 3163–3168.

Mohanty, M. 2017. "Adivasi Swaraj is the answer to violence." *Economic and Political Weekly* 52, no. 21.

Moore, B. 1993. *Social origins of dictatorship and democracy: Lord and peasant in the making of the modern world.* Boston: Beacon Press.

Morris, A. 2000. "Charting futures for sociology: Reflections on social movement theory." *Contemporary Sociology – A Journal of Reviews* 29, no. 3: 445–454.

Mosse, D. 2018. "Caste and development: Contemporary perspectives on a structure of discrimination and advantage." *World Development* 110: 422–436.

Mukherjee, A. 2015. "Imperialism, nationalism and the making of the Indian capitalist class, 1920–1947." In *SAGE series in modern Indian history,* eds. B. Chandra, M. Mukherjee, and A. Mukherjee. Los Angeles: Sage.

Mukherjee, M. 2004. *Peasants in India's non-violent revolution: Practice and theory.* New Delhi: Sage.

Mukherji, N. 2012. *The Maoists in India: Tribal under siege.* London: Pluto.

Mukherji, P. 1984/2000. "Naxalbari movement and the peasant Revolt in North Bengal." In *Social movements in India,* ed. M.S.A. Rao, 17–90. Delhi: Manohar.

Mukherji, P. 2014. "The Indian state in crisis? Nationalism and nation-building." In *Sociology of India,* ed. A. Kumar. Delhi: Sage.

Mukherji, R. 2008. "The political economy of India's economic reforms." *Asian Economic Policy Review* 3, no. 2: 315–331.

Mukherji, R. 2017. "Governance reform in a weak state: Thirty years of Indian experience." *Governance – An International Journal of Policy Administration and Institutions* 30, no. 1: 53–58.

Mullings, B. 1999. "Insider or outsider, both or neither: Some dilemmas of interviewing in a cross-cultural setting." *Geoforum* 30, no. 4: 337–350.

Murali, K. 2002. "Andhra Pradesh: Continuing militancy in Telengana." *Economic and Political Weekly* 37, no. 8: 692–695.

Murali, K. 2017. *Caste, class, and capital: The social and political origins of economic policy in India.* Cambridge: Cambridge University Press.

Murphy, J. 2011. "Indian call centre workers: Vanguard of a global middle class?" *Work Employment and Society* 25, no. 3: 417–433.

Murphy, J., and Jammaulamadaka, N. 2017. *Governance, resistance and the post-colonial state: Management and state building social movements.* New York: Routledge.

Murthy, N. 2018. "The impact of the 1991 economic reforms on Indian businesses." In *India Transformed,* ed. R. Mohan, 609–618. Washington, DC: Brookings Institution Press.

Nadkarni, M. 1976. "Tenants from the dominant class: A developing contradiction in land reforms." *Economic and Political Weekly* 11, no. 52: A137, A139–A146.

Nadkarni, M. 1991. "Review: The mode of production debate: A review article." *Indian Economic Review* New Series 26, no. 1: 99–104.

Nag, P.K., and Nag, A. 2004. "Drudgery, accidents and injuries in Indian agriculture." *Industrial Health* 42, no. 2: 149–162.

Naher, F. 1997. "Green revolution in Bangladesh production stability and food self- sufficiency." *Economic and Political Weekly* 32, no. 26: A84–A89.

Nair, S. 2018. "Farmers badly hit by demonetisation, admits Agriculture Ministry." *The Hindu.* https://www.thehindu.com/news/national/farmers-badly-hit-by-demonetisation-admits-agriculture-ministry/article25550924.ece?homepage=true.

Nanda, M. 1995. "Transnationalization of third world state and undoing of Green Revolution." *Economic and Political Weekly* 30, no. 4: PE 20–30.

Nanda, M. 2005. *The wrongs of the religious Right.* Gurgaon: Three Essays Collective.

Nanda, M. 2007. *Postmodernism and religious fundamentalism.* Pondicherry: Navayana.

Nanda, P. 2015. "Industrial strikes and lockouts see steep decline in India." *Livemint.* https://www.livemint.com/Politics/tjP4DiG7Uro95iNCiebrAO/Industrial-strikes-and-lockouts-see-steep-decline-in-India.html.

Nandy, A. 2003. *The romance of the state and the fate of dissent in the tropics.* New Delhi: Oxford University Press.

Naruzzaman, M. 2005. "Economic liberalization and poverty in the developing countries." *Journal of Contemporary Asia* 35, no. 1: 109–127.

Naseemullah, A. 2016. "The contested capacity of the Indian state." *Indian Review* 16, no. 4: 407–432.

Nathan, D. 1999. "Agricultural labour and poor peasant movement in India." In *Class Formation and Political Transformation in Post-colonial India*, ed. T. Sathyamurthy. New Delhi: Oxford University Press.

Navlakha, G. 2006. "Maoists in India." *Economic and Political Weekly* 41, no. 22: 2186–2189.

Nayar, B. 2001. *Globalization and nationalism: The changing balance in India's economic policy 1950–2000*. New Delhi: Sage Publications.

Nayyar, R. 1996. "New initiatives for poverty alleviation in rural India." In *Economic reforms and poverty alleviation in India*, eds. C. Rao and H. Linnemann. New Delhi: Sage.

NCRB. 2016. "Crime in India." *National Crime Records Bureau*. http://ncrb.gov.in/Stat Publications/CII/CII2016/pdfs/NEWPDFs/Crime%20in%20India%20-%202016% 20Complete%20PDF%20291117.pdf.

Neiberg, M. 2018. *Fascism*. London: Routledge.

Neiland, A., Soley, N., and Varley, J. 2001. "Shrimp aquaculture: economic perspectives for policy development." *Marine Policy* 25, no. 4: 265–279.

Nelson, L. 2003. "Decentering the movement: Collective action, place, and the 'sedimentation' of radical political discourses." *Environment and Planning D-Society and Space* 21, no. 5: 559–581.

Niclas- Tölle, B. 2015. *The socialist opposition in Nehruvian India, 1947–1964*. Frankfurt am Main: Peter Land Edition.

Nielsen, K.B. 2016. "The everyday politics of India's "land wars" in rural eastern India." *Focaal-Journal of Global and Historical Anthropology* no. 75: 105–118.

Nielsen, K.B., and Nilsen, A.G. 2016. *Social movements and the state in India: Deepening democracy?* London: Palgrave Macmillan.

Nigam, A. 2006. *The insurrection of little selves: The crisis of secular-nationalism in India*. Delhi: Oxford University Press.

Nilsen, A.G. 2008. "Political economy, social movements and state power: A Marxian perspective on two decades of resistance to the Narmada dam projects." *Journal of Historical Sociology* 21, no. 2–3: 303–330.

Nilsen, A.G. 2010. *Dispossession and resistance in India: The river and the rage*. London: Routledge.

Nilsen, A.G., and Roy, S. 2015. *New subaltern politics: Reconceptualizing hegemony and resistance in contemporary India*. New Delhi: Oxford University Press.

O'Connor, J. 2017. "Marxism and the three movements of neoliberalism." *Critical Sociology* 36, no. 5: 691–715.

Oberoi, R. 2018. "4 years of Modi govt: 8 charts that show why the euphoria is gone & next big positive missing." *Economic Times*. https://economictimes.indiatimes.com/ markets/stocks/news/4-years-of-modi-8-charts-that-show-why-the-euphoria-is-gone-next-big-positive-missing/articleshow/64314349.cms.

O'Brien, P. 2007. "Global economic history as the accumulation of capital through a process of combined and uneven development: an appreciation and critique of Ernest Mandel." *Historical Materialism* 15, no. 1: 75–108.

Odisha Government. 2004. *Odisha human development report*. Bhubaneswar: Odisha Government: Planning and Coordination Department.

Odisha Government. 2005. *District statistical handbook: Puri*. Bhubaneswar: Odisha Government: Directorate of Economics and Statistics.

Ollman, B. 1993. *Dialectical Investigations*. New York: Routledge.

Ollman, B. 2003. *Dance of the dialectic*. Urbana: University of Illinois Press.

Omvedt, G. 1993. *Reinventing revolution: New social movements and the socialist tradition in India*. Armonk, NY: M.E. Sharpe.

Ondetti, G.A. 2006. "Repression, opportunity, and protest: Explaining the take-off of Brazil's landless movement." *Latin American Politics and Society* 48, no. 2: 61–94.

Oommen, T.K. 1971. "Green revolution and Agrarian conflict." *Economic and Political Weekly* 6, no. 26: A99, A101–A103.

Oseland, E., Håvard Haarstad, H., and Fløysand, A. 2012. "Labor agency and the importance of the national scale: Emergent aquaculture unionism in Chile." *Political Geography* 31, no. 2: 94–103.

Oslender, U. 2004. "Fleshing out the geographies of social movements: Colombia's Pacific Coast black communities and the 'aquatic space.'" *Political Geography* 23, no. 8: 957–985.

Ostry, J., Loungani, P., and Furceri, D. 2016. "Neoliberalism: Oversold?" *IMF: Finance and Development*. https://www.imf.org/external/pubs/ft/fandd/2016/06/pdf/ostry.pdf.

Otsuka, K., Gascon, F., and Asano, S. 1994. "Green revolution and labour demand in rice farming the case of Central Luzon, 1966–1990." *Journal of Development Studies* 31, no. 1: 82–109.

Oxfam. 2018. "Richest 1 percent bagged 73 percent of wealth created last year." OXFAM *India*. https://www.oxfamindia.org/pressrelease/2093.

Oya, C. 2005. "Agrarian neoliberalism." In *Neoliberalism: A critical Reader*, ed. A. Saad-Filho. London: Pluto.

Page, B. 1993. *Marxism and spirituality: An international anthology*. Westport, Connecticut, and London: Bergin and Garvey.

Paige, J.M. 1975. *Agrarian revolution*. New York: Free Press.

Palmer-Jones, R. 1993. "Agricultural wages in Bangladesh what the figures really show." *Journal of Development Studies* 29, no. 2: 277–300.

Palshikar, S., Kumar, S., and Lodha, S. 2017. *Electoral politics in Indi: The resurgence of the Bharatiya Janata Party*. London: Routledge, Taylor and Francis.

Panitch, L., and Albo, G., eds. 2016. *Socialist Register 2016: The politics of the right*. London: Merlin Press.

Parker, J. 2012. "Unravelling the neoliberal paradox with Marx." *Journal of Australian Political Economy* 70, no. 70: 193–213.

Parthasarathy, D. 2015. "The poverty of (Marxist) theory: peasant classes, provincial capital, and the critique of globalization in India." *Journal of Social History* 48, no. 4: 816–841.

Parthasarathy, G. 1987. "Changes in the incidence of rural poverty." *Indian Journal of Agricultural Economics* 42, no. 1.

Parthasarathy, G. 1995. "Public intervention and rural poverty: case of non-sustainable reduction in Andhra Pradesh." *Economic and Political Weekly* 30, no. 41/42: 2573–2575, 2577–2581, 2583–2586.

Parsai, G. 2007. "Manmohan to head land reforms council." *The Hindu.* https://www.thehindu.com/todays-paper/Manmohan-to-head-land-reforms-council/article14866257.ece.

Patel, R., and McMichael, P. 2008. "Third worldism and the lineages of global fascism: The regrouping of the global South in the neoliberal era." *Third World Quarterly* 25, no. 1: 231–254.

Pathy, J. 1998. "Contemporary struggles of the tribal peoples of India." *Indian Journal of Social Work* 59, no. 1.

Patnaik, P. 1995. *Whatever happened to Imperialism.* New Delhi: Tulika.

Patnaik, P. 2010. "The state under neo-liberalism." *MRZine.* http://mrzine.monthlyreview.org/2010/patnaik100810.html.

Patnaik, P. 2011. "Future of Marxism." In *Another millennium?,* ed. R. Thapar. New Delhi: Penguin.

Patnaik, P. 2016. "Nationalism, Hindutva and the assault on thought." *Communist Party of India: Marxist,* XXXII 1. http://www.cpim.org/content/nationalism-hindutva-and-assault-thought.

Patnaik, P. 2017a. "Neoliberalism and inequality are inseparable." *News Click.* https://newsclick.in/neoliberalism-and-inequality-are-inseparable.

Patnaik, P. 2017b. "Why India needs the Left." *The Wire.* https://thewire.in/196923/india-left-future-economy-social-policy/.

Patnaik, P. 2018a. "The dramatic rise in wealth inequality." *People's Democracy.* http://peoplesdemocracy.in/2018/0128_pd/dramatic-rise-wealth-inequality.

Patnaik, P. 2018b. "The state under neoliberalism." http://citeseerx.ist.psu.edu/viewdoc/download?doi=10.1.1.527.9907&rep=rep1&type=pdf.

Patnaik, U. 1972. "Development of capitalism in agriculture – I." *Social Scientist* 1, no. 2: 15–31.

Patnaik, U. 1983. "Classical theory of rent and its application to India: Some preliminary thoughts on sharecropping." *Journal of Peasant Studies* 10, no. 2–3: 71–87.

Patnaik, U. 1986. "The agrarian question and development of capitalism in India." *Economic and Political Weekly* 21, no. 18: 781–793.

Patnaik, U. 1990a. *Agrarian relations and accumulation: The mode of production debate in India.* Delhi: Oxford University Press.

Patnaik, U. 1990b. "Capitalist development in agriculture: Note." In *Agrarian relations and accumulation: The mode of production debate in India,* ed. U. Patnaik. Delhi: Oxford University Press.

Patnaik, U. 1990c. "Capitalist development in agriculture: Further comment." In *Agrarian relations and accumulation: The mode of production debate in India,* ed. U. Patnaik. Delhi: Oxford University Press.

Patnaik, U. 1990d. "On the mode of production in Indian agriculture: Reply." In *Agrarian relations and accumulation: The mode of production debate in India,* ed. U. Patnaik. Delhi: Oxford University Press.

Patnaik, U. 1990e. "Some economic and political consequences of the green revolution in India." In *The Food Question: Profits versus people,* eds. H. Bernstein, B. Crow, M. McKintosh, and C. Martin. New York: Monthly Review Press.

Patnaik, U. 1991. "Food availability and famine: a longer view." *The Journal of Peasant Studies* 19, no. 1: 1–25.

Patnaik, U. 1995. "On capitalism and agrestic unfreedom." *International Review of Social History* 40, no. 1: 77–92.

Patnaik, U. 1999. *The long transition: Essays on political Economy.* New Delhi: Tulika.

Patnaik, U. 2002. "Deflation and Deja vu: India's Agriculture in the World Economy." In *Agrarian studies: Essays on agrarian relations in less developed countries,* eds. V. Ramachandran and M. Swaminathan. New Delhi: Tulika.

Patnaik, U. 2003. "On the inverse relation between primary exports and food absorption in developing countries under liberalized trading regimes." In *Work and well-being in the age of finance,* eds. J. Ghosh and C. Chandrasekhar, 256–287. New Delhi: Tulika.

Patnaik, U. 2007. *The republic of hunger.* Gurgaon: Three Essays Collective.

Patnaik, U. 2013. "Theorizing food security and poverty in the era of economic reforms." In *Two decades of market reform in India: Some dissenting views,* ed. S. Bhattacharyya, 93–124. New York: Anthem Press.

Patnaik, U. 2016. "Growing inequalities in the South in the Present Era of primitive capitalist accumulation." *Studies in Peoples History* 3, no. 1: 59–70.

Patnaik, P., Chandrasekhar, C.P., and Ghosh, J. 2004. "The political economy of the economic reform strategy: The role of the Indian capitalist class." In *Class, caste, and gender,* ed. M. Mohanty. Delhi: Sage.

Pattenden, J. 2011. "Gatekeeping as accumulation and domination: Decentralization and class relations in rural south India." *Journal of Agrarian Change* 11, no. 2: 164–194.

Pattenden, J. 2016. "Working at the margins of global production networks: local labour control regimes and rural-based labourers in South India." *Third World Quarterly* 37, no. 10: 1809–1833.

Pattenden, J. 2018. "The politics of classes of labour: Fragmentation, reproduction zones and collective action in Karnataka, India." *Journal of Peasant Studies* 45, no. 5–6: 1039–1059.

Paul, S. 1990. "Green revolution and poverty among farm families in Haryana, 1969/70–1982/83." *Economic and Political Weekly* 25, no. 39: 1809–1833.

Paul, S, and Sarma, V. 2017. "Industrialization-led displacement and long term-welfare: Evidence from West Bengal." *Oxford Development Studies* 45, no. 3: 240–259.

Paulini, T. 1979. *Agrarian movements and reforms in India: The case of Kerala.* Breitenbach: Verlag Stuttgart.

Paxton, R. 2004. *The anatomy of Fascism.* New York: Vintage.

Pearse, A. 1980. *Seeds of plenty, seeds of want: Social and economic implications of the Green Revolution.* London: Clarendon Press.

Peck, J., and Theodore, N. 2001. "Contingent Chicago: Restructuring the spaces of temporary labor." *International Journal of Urban and Regional Research* 25, no. 3: 471–496.

Peck, J., and Tickell, A. 2002. "Neoliberalizing space." *Antipode* 34, no. 3: 380–404.

Pedersen, J.D. 1992. "State, bureaucracy and change in India." *Journal of Development-Studies* 28, no. 4: 616–639.

Peet, R. 1983. "Relations of production and the relocation of United States manufacturing industry since 1960." *Economic Geography* 59, no. 2: 112–143.

People's Democracy. 2017. "Thinking together." *People's Democracy.* https://peoplesdemocracy.in/2015/0712_pd/thinking-together.

Pereira, A. 2016. "BJP tops list of reelected MPs in terms of assets and criminal cases." *Firstpost.* https://www.firstpost.com/politics/bjp-tops-list-of-reelected-mps-in-terms-of-assets-and-criminal-cases-1557703.html.

Petras, J. 1997. "Imperialism and NGOs in Latin America." *Monthly Review* 49, no. 7.

Petras, J., and Veltemeyer, H. 2007. "The 'development state' in Latin America: Whose development, whose state?" *Journal of Peasant Studies* 34, no. 3–4: 371–407.

Phyne, P. 2010. "A comparative political economy of rural capitalism salmon aquaculture in Norway, Chile and Ireland." *Acta Sociologica* 53, no. 2: 160–180.

Pillai, P. 2003. *Left Movement and Agrarian Relations, 1920–1995.* New Delhi: South Asian Publishers.

Plahe, J., Wright, S., and Marmbo, M. 2017. "Livelihood crises in Vidarbha, India: Food sovereignty through traditional farming systems as a possible solution." *South Asia: Journal of South Asian Studies* 40, no. 3: 600–618.

Plekhanov, G. 1971. *Fundamental problems of Marxism.* New York: International Publishers.

Poe, S.C., and Tate, C.N. 1994. "Repression of human rights to personal integrity in the 1980s." *American Political Science Review* 88, no. 4: 853–872.

Pokrant, B., and Reeves, P. 2007. "Work and labor in the Bangladesh brackish-water shrimp export sector." *South Asia: Journal of South Asian Studies* 26, no. 3: 359–389.

Polanyi, K. 1944/2001. *The great transformation: The political and economic origins of our time*, 2nd ed. Boston: Beacon Press.

Post, C. 1999. "Ernest Mandel and the Marxist theory of bureaucracy." In *The Legacy of Ernest Mandel*, ed. G. Achcar. London: Verso.

Poulantzas, N. 1968. *Political Power and Social Classes*. London: New Left Books (cited from the English Translation, NLB, London, 1973).

Pradhan, D., and Flaherty, M. 2008. "National initiatives, local effects: Trade liberalization, shrimp aquaculture, and coastal communities in Odisha, India." *Society & Natural Resources* 21, no. 1: 63–76.

Pramanik, S., and Nandi, N. 2001. Women fishworkers and their role in the inshore fishing areas of Sundarban. *Man in India* 81, no. 1: 169–177.

Prasad, P. 1989. *Lopsided growth: Political economy of Indian development*. Delhi: Oxford University Press.

Prasad, P. 1990. "Reactionary role of usurer's capital in Rural India." In *The mode of production debate in India*, ed. U. Patnaik. Delhi: Oxford University Press.

Prasad-Aleyamma, M. 2018. "Cards and carriers: migration, identification and surveillance in Kerala, South India." *Contemporary South Asia* 26, no. 2: 191–205.

Prashad, V. 2015. *No free left: The futures of Indian communism*. New Delhi: Leftword.

Pratt, G. 2004. *Working Feminism*. Edinburgh: Edinburgh University Press.

Pred, A. 1984. "Place as historically contingent process: Structuration and the time-geography of becoming places." *Annals of the American Association of Geographers* 74, no. 2: 279–297.

Premchand, A. 2017. *Contemporary India: Society and its governance*. Milton: Taylor and Francis.

Pressman, S., ed. 2006. *Alternative theories of the State*. New York: Palgrave.

Pushpendra. 2000. "Liberalization and Agrarian reforms: some recent controversies." In *Land reforms in India: Volume 5*, eds. B.N. Sinha, and Pushpendra, 45–63. New Delhi: Sage.

Qazi, M. 2018. "Malnutrition ravages India's children." *The Asian Age*. http://www.asianage.com/india/all-india/030118/malnutrition-ravages-indias-children.html.

Radice, H. 2008. "The developmental state under global neoliberalism." *Third World Quarterly* 29, no. 6: 1153–1174.

Rahul, N. 1995. "Green revolution and subsistence agriculture you reap as you sow." *Economic and Political Weekly* 32, no. 18: 930–932.

Rai, P. 2007. "NREGA battling cancerous corruption." *India Together*. http://www.indiatogether.org/nregs-government--2.

Rao, C. 1994. *Agricultural growth, Rural poverty and environmental degradation in India*. Delhi: Oxford University Press.

Rao, J.M. 1998. "Agricultural development under state planning." In *The State, Development Planning and Liberalisation in India*, ed. T. Byres. Delhi: Oxford University Press.

Rao, J.M. 1999. "Agrarian power and unfree labour." *Journal of Peasant Studies* 26, no. 2–3: 242–262.

Rao, S. 2018. "Gender and class relations in rural India." *Journal of Peasant Studies* 45, no. 5–6: 950–968.

Ram, N. 1972. "Development of Capitalism in Agriculture." *Social Scientist,* vol. 1, no. 5: 51–57.

Ramakrishnan, V. 1999. "A history of massacres." *Frontline* 16, no. 5. https://www.front line.in/static/html/fl1605/16050300.htm.

Ranganathan, S. 2018. *Hinduism: A contemporary philosophical investigation.* New York: Routledge.

Ray, R. 2002. *The Naxalites and their ideology.* Delhi: Oxford University Press.

Rediff. 2006. "Naxalism single biggest internal security challenge: PM." *Rediff India Abroad.* http://www.rediff.com/news/2006/apr/13naxal.htm.

Renton, D. 2007. *Fascism: Theory and practice.* Delhi: Aakar (originally published by Pluto).

Rieman, R. 2018. *To fight against this age: Fascism and humanism.* New York: W.W. Norton & Company.

Rigg, J. 1989. "The green revolution and equity: Who adopts the new rice varieties and why?" *Geography* 74, no. 2: 144–150.

Roberts, D. 2011. "Reconsidering Gramsci's interpretation of Fascism." *Journal of Modern Italian Studies* 16, no. 2: 239–255.

Roberts, M. 2016. *The long depression.* Chicago: Haymarket.

Roberts, M. 2017. "Modi rules, Harvard doesn't." *Michael Roberts Blog.* https://thenext recession.wordpress.com/2017/03/14/modi-rules-harvard-doesnt/.

Roberts, M. 2018. "China workshop: Challenging the misconceptions." *Michael Roberts Blog.* https://thenextrecession.wordpress.com/2018/06/07/china-workshop -challenging-the-misconceptions/.

Robinson, W., and Barrera, M. 2012. "Global capitalism and twenty-first century fascism: a US case-study." *Race and Class* 53, no. 3: 4–29.

Ronnback, P., Troell, M., Zetterstrom, T., and Babu, D. 2003. "Mangrove dependence and socio-economic concerns in shrimp hatcheries of Andhra Pradesh, India." *Environmental Conservation* 30, no. 4: 344–352.

Routledge, P. 1997. "Space, mobility, and collective action: India's Naxalite movement." *Environment and Planning A* 29, no. 12: 2165–2189.

Roy, A. 2011. *Broken republic.* New Delhi: Penguin Books.

Roy, A. 2009. "The heart of India is under attack." *The Guardian.* https://www.theguard ian.com/commentisfree/2009/oct/30/mining-india-maoists-green-hunt.

Roy, B. 2002. "Naxalite violence: Legacy of another era." *Times of India.* https://timeso findia.indiatimes.com/edit-page/Naxalite-Violence-Legacy-of-Another-Era/article show/15602206.cms.

Roy, I. 2018. *Politics of the poor: Negotiating democracy in contemporary India.* Cambridge: Cambridge University Press.

Roy, M.S. 2011. *Gender and radical politics in India: Magic moments of Naxalbari (1967–1975).* New York: Routledge.

Roy, T. 2005. *Rethinking economic change in India: Labour and livelihood.* London: Routledge.

Roy Chowdhury, S. 2015. "Bring class back in: Informality in Bangalore." *Socialist Register* 51: 73–92.

Rubin, I. 1973. *Essays on Marx's theory of value.* Montreal: Black Rose Books.

Rudolph, L.I., and Rudolph S.H. 1987. *In pursuit of Lakshmi: The political economy of the Indian State.* Chicago: Chicago University Press.

Rudra, A. 1983. "Mode of production in Indian agriculture." *Economic and Political Weekly* 18, no. 12: 421.

Rudra, A. 1988. "Emerging class structure in rural India." In *Rural poverty in South Asia,* eds. T. Srinivasan and P. Bardhan. New York: Columbia University Press.

Rudra, A., Majid, A., and Talib, B. 1990 (1969–70). "Big farmers of Punjab." In *Agrarian Relations and Accumulation: The mode of production debate in India,* ed. U. Patnaik. Delhi: Oxford University Press.

Rukmini, S. 2017. "On religious hostilities, India ranked just slightly better than Syria: Pew study." *Huffpost.* https://www.huffingtonpost.in/2017/04/13/on-religious-hosti lities-india-ranked-just-slightly-better-than_a_22037994/.

Rummel, R.J. 1984. "Libertarianism, violence within states, and the polarity principle." *Comparative Politics* 16, no. 4: 443–462.

Ruparelia, S., Reddy, S., Harriss, J. and Corbridge, S., eds. 2011. *Understanding India's new political economy,* London: Routledge.

Rutherford, T. 2010. "De/Re-centering work and class?: A review and critique of labor geography." *Geography Compass* 4, no 7: 768–777.

Rutherford, T., and Gertler, M. 2002. "Labor in lean times: geography, scale and national trajectory of work place change." *Transactions of the Institute of British Geographers* 27, no. 2: 195–212.

Sackley, N. 2015. "The road from serfdom: economic storytelling and narratives in the rise of neoliberalism." *History and Technology* 31, no. 4: 397–419.

Sagar. 2006. "The spring and its thunder." *Economic and Political Weekly* 41, no. 29: 3176–3178.

Sahay, S. 2006. *The Indian working class movement during freedom struggle.* Patna: Janaki Prakashan.

SAHRDC (South Asia Human Rights Documentation Centre). 2002. "Emerging state of insecurity: India's war against Itself." *SAHRDC.* www.hrdc.net/sahrdc/hrfeatures/ HRF51.htm.

Sainaith, P. 2001. "Age of inequality." In *India: Another millennium?*, R. Thapar, 152–168. New York: Penguin.

Sainaith, P. 2009. "Neo-liberal terrorism in India: The largest wave of suicides in history." *Counterpunch.* http://www.counterpunch.org/sainath02122009.html.

Sainaith, P. 2013. "Farmers' suicide rates soar above the rest." *The Hindu.* https://www.thehindu.com/opinion/columns/sainath/farmers-suicide-rates-soar-above-the-rest/article4725101.ece.

Samal, K. 2003. "Fishing communities on Chilika Lake." *Economic and Political Weekly* 38, no. 31: 3319–3325.

Samanta, A. 1984. *Left extremist movement in West Bengal.* Calcutta: Firma KLM Private Ltd.

Samuel, V. 2019. "What is inequality?" *Oxfam India.* https://www.oxfamindia.org/blog/what-inequality.

Sanchez, A., and Strumpell, C. 2014. "Anthropological and historical perspectives on India's working classes." *Modern Asian Studies* 48, no. 5: 1233–1241.

Sanyal, K. 2013. *Rethinking capitalist development: Primitive accumulation, governmentality and post-colonial capitalism.* London: Routledge.

Sarangi, A. 2017. "State formation and political economy of India: The Rudolphian paradigm." *Indian Review* 16, no. 3: 344–356.

Sarkar, R., and Sarkar, A. 2016. "The rebel's resource curse: A theory of insurgent-civilian dynamics." *Studies in Conflict and Terrorism* 40, no. 10: 870–898.

Sarkar, S. 1983. *Modern India: 1885–1947.* Delhi: Macmillan.

Sarkar, S. 2016. "The fascism of the Sangh Parivar." In *Fascism: Essays on Europe and India,* ed. J. Banaji. Gurgaon: Three Essays Collective.

Sarmah, B., and Baurua, J., eds. 2014. *Neoliberal state and its challenges.* Delhi: Aakar.

Sass, R. 2000. "Agricultural 'killing fields': The poisoning of Costa Rican Banana Workers." *International Journal of Health Services* 30, no. 3: 491–514.

Sathyamurthy, T. 1996. "State and society in a changing political perspective." In *Class formation and political transformation in post-colonial India,* ed. T.V. Sathyamurthy. Delhi: Oxford University Press.

Saul, J. 1974. "The State in postcolonial societies: Tanzania." In *The Socialist Register 1974,* eds. R. Miliband and J. Saville. London: The Merlin Press.

Saull, R. 2015. "Capitalist development and the rise and 'Fall' of the far-right." *Critical Sociology* 41, no. 4–5: 619–639.

Saxton, A. 2007. *Religion and the human impact.* Delhi: Aakar.

Sayer, A. 1992. *Method in social science: A realist approach.* London: Routledge.

Sayer, A. 2000. *Realism and social science.* London: Sage.

Schatzman, C. 2005. "Political challenge in Latin America: Rebellion and collective protest in an era of democratization." *Journal of Peace Research* 42, no. 3: 291–310.

Schiller, B. 1998. *The economics of poverty and discrimination.* Eaglewood Cliffs: Prentice Hall.

Schultz, K. 2018. "Indian children's book lists Hitler as leader 'who will inspire you.'" *The New York Times.* https://www.nytimes.com/2018/03/17/world/asia/india-hitler-chil drens-book.html.

Science & Society. 2018. "Intersectionality: A symposium." *Science & Society* 82, no. 2: 248–291.

Sen, A. [Amartya]. 1999. *Development as Freedom.* New Delhi: Oxford University Press.

Sen, A. [Amartya]. 2005. *The argumentative India: Writings on Indian history, culture and identity.* London: Allen Lane.

Sen, A. [Anupam]. 2017. *The state, industrialization and class formations in India: A Neo-Marxist perspective on colonialism, underdevelopment and development.* London: Routledge.

Sen, A. [Arindam]. 2017. "The movement-party dialectics: Tebhaga-Telangana to Naxalbari-CPI(ML)." *Economic and Political Weekly* 52, no. 21.

Sen, S., Debabrata, P., and Lahiri, A. 1978. *Naxalbari and after: A frontier anthology.* Calcutta: Kathashilpa.

Sengupta, M. 2008. "How the state changed its mind: Power, politics & the origins of India's market reforms." *Economic & Political Weekly* 43, no. 21: 35–42.

Shah, A. 2006. "Markets of protection – The terrorist Maoist Movement and the state in Jharkhand, India." *Critique of Anthropology* 26, no. 3: 297–314.

Shah, A. 2013. "The agrarian question in a Maoist guerrilla zone: Land, labour and capital in the forests and hills of Jharkhand, India." *Journal of Agrarian Change* 13, no. 3: 424–450.

Shah, A. 2017. "Humaneness and Contradictions: India's Maoist-inspired Naxalites." *Economic and Political Weekly* 52, no. 21.

Shah, A., and Jain, D. 2017. "Naxalbari at its golden jubilee: Fifty recent books on the Maoist movement in India." *Modern Asian Studies* 51, no. 4: 1165–1219.

Shah, G. 1988. "Grass-roots mobilization in Indian politics." In *India's democracy*, ed. A. Kohli, 262–304. Hyderabad: Orient Longman.

Shah, G. 2004. *Social movements in India.* New Delhi: Sage.

Shah, G., Mander, H., Thorat, S., Deshpande, S., and Beviskar, A. 2006. *Untouchability in rural India.* Delhi: Sage.

Shakir, M. 1986. *State and politics in contemporary India.* New Delhi: Ajanta Publications.

Shantha, S. 2018. "In Dantewada's Naxal area, 'political participation' looks completely different." *The Wire.* https://thewire.in/politics/chhattisgarh-elections-dantewada -naxals.

Shariff, A. 1999. *India: Human development report.* New Delhi: Oxford University Press.

Sharma, D. 2017. "Farm output may have increased in three years, but farmers welfare has not." *The Wire.* https://thewire.in/agriculture/modi-three-years-farmers-agriculture.

Sharma, H.R. 1992. "Agrarian relations in India since independence." *Journal of Indian School of Political Economy* 4, no. 2: 201–262.

Sharma, T. 1992. *Technical change, income distribution and rural poverty.* New Delhi: Shirpa Publications.

Sharma, U. 2002. *Caste.* Delhi: Viva Books.

Sharma, R., and Poleman, T. 1993. *The new economics of India's Green Revolution: Income and employment diffusion in Uttar Pradesh.* Ithaca: Cornell University Press.

Sheth, N. 2014. "Trade unions in India: A sociological approach." In *Political sociology of India,* ed. A. Kumar. Delhi: Sage.

Shiva, V. 1991. *The violence of the green revolution: Third world agriculture, ecology and politics.* London: Zed Books Ltd.

Shiva, V. 2000. *Stolen harvest: The hijacking of the global food supply.* Cambridge: South End Press.

Shiva, V., Jafri, A., Emani, A., and Pande, M. 2002. *Seeds of suicide: The ecological and human costs of globalisation of agriculture.* New Delhi: Navdanya.

Shrestha, N., and Patterson, J., 1990. "Population and poverty in dependent states Latin America considered." *Antipode* 22, no. 2: 121–155.

Shrimali, R. Forthcoming. *Corporate hijack of agriculture: Case of contract farming in India.* Singapore: Palgrave.

Simeon, D. 1986. "Communalism in modern India: a theoretical examination." *Mainstream.* http://www.sacw.net/article2760.html.

Simeon, D. 2016. "The law of killing: A brief history of Indian fascism." In *Fascism: essays on Europe and India,* ed. J. Banaji. Gurgaon: Three Essays Collective.

Singer, W. 2012. *Independent India, 1947–2000.* London: Pearson.

Singh, H. 2014. *Recasting Caste: From the sacred to the profane.* New Delhi: Sage.

Singh, I. 1990. *The great ascent: The rural poor in South Asia.* Baltimore: The John Hopkins University Press.

Singh, P. 1995. *The Naxalite Movement in India.* Delhi: Rupa Publication.

Singh, R. 2010. *On nationalism and communalism in India.* Delhi: Aakar.

Singh, S. 2002. "Agricultural labourers." In *Alternative economic survey.* New Delhi: Rainbow Publishers.

Singh, S. [Supriya]. 2017. *Commercialization of Hinterland and dynamics of class, caste and gender in rural India.* Newcastle: Cambridge Scholars Publishing.

Singhal, S., and Nilakantan, R. 2016. "The economic effects of a counterinsurgency policy in India: a synthetic control analysis." *European Journal of Political Economy* 45: 1–17.

Singharoy, D. 2004. *Peasant movements in post-colonial India.* New Delhi: Sage.

Sinha, A. 2011. "An institutional perspective on the liberalization state in India." In *The state in India after liberalization: Interdisciplinary perspectives*, eds. A. Gupta and K. Sivaramakrishnan, 49–68. London: Routledge.

Sinha, A. 2016. "A distinctive Indian political economy: New concepts and a synthesizing framework." *Studies in Indian Politics* 4, no. 2: 266–273.

Sinha, S. 2009. "Workers and working classes in contemporary India." In *Beyond Marx: Theorizing the global relations of the 21st century*, eds. M. van der Linden and K. Roth. Leiden: Brill.

Sinha, S. 2017. "Histories of power, the 'Universalization of Capital' and India's Modi government: Between and beyond Marxism and post-colonial theory." *Critical Sociology* 43: 4–5.

Sitton, J. 1996. *Recent Marxian theory.* Albany: State University of New York Press.

Skocpol, T. 1982. "What makes peasants revolutionary?" *Comparative Politics* 14, no. 3: 351–375.

Smith, J. 2016. *Imperialism in the twenty-first century: Globalization, super-exploitation, and capitalism's final crisis.* New York: Monthly Review Press.

Smith, J. 1979. "Jayprakash Narayan dies." *Washington Post.* https://www.washington post.com/archive/local/1979/10/09/jayaprakash-narayan-dies/5a363a02-4138-49e2-8a4e-d977f8304104/?utm_term=.caef13d50dbe.

Smith, M. 2018. *Invisible leviathan: Marx's law of value in the twilight of capitalism.* Leiden: Brill.

Smith, N. 2007. "Nature as an accumulation strategy." In *The Socialist Register 2007*, eds. C. Leys and L. Panitch. London: The Merlin Press.

Smith, T. 2010. "Technological change in capitalism: Some Marxian themes." *Cambridge Journal of Economics* 34, no. 1: 203–212.

So, A. 2007. "Peasant conflict and the local predatory state in the Chinese countryside." *Journal of Peasant Studies* 34, no. 3–4: 560–581.

Song, H. 2013. "Marxist critiques of the developmental state and the fetishism of national development." *Antipode* 45, no. 5: 1254–1276.

Spacek, M. 2017. "Internal borderlands: Architectures of force and state expansion in India's central 'frontier'." *Conflict Security and Development* 17, no. 2: 163–182.

Spivak, G. 2000. "Discussion: An afterword on the new subaltern." In *Subaltern Studies 11*, eds. P. Chatterjee and P. Jeganathan, 305–334. New Delhi: Permanent black.

Sreeraj, A.P., and Vakulabharanam, V. 2015. "High growth and rising inequality in Kerala since the 1980s." *Oxford Development Studies* 44, no. 4: 367–383.

Srinivas, N. 1998. "Explaining small scale organization forms in Kerala fisheries." In *Entrepreneurship and Innovation: Models of Development*, ed. R. Kanungo. Delhi: Sage.

Srinivas, M.N. 2012. "Sociology in India and its future." In *Indian sociology: Issues and Challenges*, ed. L. Bhai. Delhi: Sage.

Srivastava, A. 1997. "Bihar to check leak of government funds to Naxals." *Indian Express*.

Srivastava, R. 1999. "Rural labour in Uttar Pradesh: Emerging features of subsistence, contradiction and resistance." *Journal of Peasant Studies* 26, no. 2–3: 263–315.

Srujana, B. 2017. "British Raj to billionaire Raj—India's journey into neoliberalism." *Newsclick.* https://newsclick.in/british-raj-billionaire-raj-indias-journey-neoliberalism.

Stanley, D. 2003. "The economic impact of mariculture on a small regional economy." *World Development* 31, no. 1: 191–210.

Steger, M., and Roy. 2010. *Neoliberalism: A very short introduction.* Oxford: Oxford University Press.

Stern, R. 2000. *Democracy and dictatorship in South Asia: Dominant classes an political outcomes in India, Pakistan, and Bangladesh.* Santa Barbara: ABC-CLIO.

Stern, R. 2011. *Changing India: Bourgeois revolution on the subcontinent.* Cambridge: Cambridge University Press.

Steur, L. 2014. "An 'expanded' class perspective: Bringing capitalism down to earth in the changing political lives of Adivasi workers in Kerala." *Modern Asian Studies* 48, no. 5: 1334–1357.

Stonich, S. 1995. "The environmental-quality and social-justice implications of shrimp mariculture development in Honduras." *Human Ecology* 23: 143–168.

Stonich, S., Bort, J., and Ovares, L. 1997. "Globalization of shrimp mariculture: The impact on social justice and environmental quality in Central America." *Society & Natural Resources* 10, no. 2: 161–179.

Storper, M. and Walker, R. 1989. *The capitalist imperative.* New York: Blackwell.

Subadevan, S., and Naqvi, I. 2017. "Contesting urban citizenship: the urban poor's strategies of state engagement in Chennai, India." *International development planning review* 39, no. 1: 77–95.

Subramanian, A., ed. 2008. *India's turn: Understanding the economic transformation.* New Delhi: Oxford University Press.

Subramanian, D. 2015. "No room for class struggle in these undertakings: Providing social welfare for Indian state sector industrial workers (circa 1950–2000)." *Modern Asian Studies* 49, no. 5: 1526–1579.

Subramanian, K. 2004. "The Naxalite Movement and government response: A critical assessment." *Mainstream* XLII, no. 52.

Subramanian, S. 1998. "Combating Naxalite violence." http://www.aapssindia.org/articles/art2/naxalite.html.

Subramanian, S. 2008. "Control and access: The everyday dimensions of property." *Contributions to Indian Sociology* 42, no. 1: 93–122.

Sud, N. 2014. "The state in the era of India's sub-national regions: liberalisation and land in Gujarat." *Geoforum* 51: 233–242.

Sugden, F. 2017. "A mode of production flux: the transformation and reproduction of rural class relations in lowland Nepal and North Bihar." *Dialectical Anthropology* 41, no. 2: 129–161.

Sugden, F., and Punch, S. 2014. "Capitalist expansion and the decline of common property ecosystems in China, Vietnam and India." *Development and Change* 45, no. 4: 656–684.

Sundar, N. 2006. "Bastar, Maoism and Salwa Judum." *Economic and Political Weekly* 41, no. 29: 3187–3192.

Sundar, N. 2011. "The rule of law and the rule of property: law-struggles and the neoliberal state in India." In *The state in India after liberalization: Interdisciplinary perspectives,* eds. A. Gupta and L. Sivaramakrishnan, 175–194. London: Routledge.

Sundar, N. 2014a. "Mimetic sovereignties, precarious citizenship: state effects in a looking-glass world." *Journal of peasant Studies* 41, no. 4: 469–490.

Sundar, N. 2014b. "No surprises here: Modi's Naxalite policy." http://nandinisundar .blogspot.ca/2014/09/no-surprises-here-modis-naxalite-policy.html.

Sunilraj, B., and Heath, O. 2017. "The historical legacy of party system stability in Kerala." *Studies in Indian Politics* 5, no. 2: 193–204.

Surjeet, H.S. 1986. *What the AIKS Stands For.* New Delhi: All India Kisan Sabha.

Surjeet, H.S. 1992. *Land reforms in India.* New Delhi: National Book Centre.

Swaminathan, M. 2000. "Consumer food subsidies in India: Proposals for reform." *The Journal of Peasant Studies* 27, no. 3: 92–114.

Sweezy, P.M. 1986. "Feudalism-to-Capitalism revisited." *Science & Society* 50, no. 1: 81–84.

Tagore, R. 1913. *Gitanjali.* http://www.spiritualbee.com/media/gitanjali-by-tagore.pdf.

Teitelbaum, E. 2006. "Was the Indian labor movement ever co-opted? Evaluating standard accounts." *Critical Asian Studies* 38, no. 4: 389–417.

Teitelbaum, E. 2013. "Labour regulation, trade unions and unemployment." In *Routledge handbook of Indian politics,* eds. A. Kohli and P. Singh. London: Routledge.

Teltumbde, A. 2010. *The persistence of caste.* Delhi: Navayana.

Teltumbde, A. 2016. *Dalits: Past, present and future.* Abingdon, Oxon: Taylor and Francis.

Tendulkar, S., and Bhavani, T. 2007. *Understanding reforms.* New Delhi: Oxford University Press.

Tendulkar, S., and Jain, L. 1995. "Economic reforms and poverty." *Economic and Political Weekly* 30, no. 23: 1373–1375, 1377.

Teubal, M. 2000. "Structural adjustment and social disarticulation: The case of Argentina." *Science and Society* 64, no. 4: 460–489.

Thapar, R. 2016. *Indian society and the secular.* Gurgaon: Three essays collective.

Thara, K. 2016. "Protecting caste livelihoods on the western coast of India: An intersectional analysis of Udupi's fisherwomen." *Environment and Urbanization* 28, no. 2: 423–436.

The Economic Times. 2008. "Jyoti Basu supports Buddhadeb's view on capitalism." *The Economic Times.* https://economictimes.indiatimes.com/jyoti-basu-supports-bud dhadebs-view-on-capitalism/articleshow/2676957.cms?from=mdr.

The Hindu. 2017. "'Unforgiveable': The Hindu's editorial on December 7, 1992 on Babri Masjid demolition." *The Hindu.* https://www.thehindu.com/news/national/unfor givable-editorial-on-the-babri-masjid-demolition-published-by-the-hindu-on-de cember-7-1992/article21272508.ece.

The Hindu. 2018a. "Who is an urban Naxal, asks Romila Thapar." *The Hindu.* https:// www.thehindu.com/news/national/who-is-an-urban-naxal-asks-romila-thapar/ar ticle25088465.ece.

The Hindu. 2018b. "Need for an employment policy to solve jobless growth." *The Hindu.* https://www.thehindu.com/news/national/need-for-an-employment-policy-to- solve-jobless-growth/article25041745.ece.

The Indian Express. 2018. "Why a new report agrees with Piketty on inequality, blames policy." *The Indian Express.* https://indianexpress.com/article/explained/pay-gap -income-inequality-policy-sc-st-religion-bias-5074635/.

Thompson, E.P. 1966. *The making of the English working class.* New York: Vintage Books.

Thorner, A. 1982. "Semi-feudalism or capitalism: Contemporary debate on classes and modes of production in India." *Economic and Political Weekly* 17, no. 51: 2061–2066.

Thorner, D. 1969. "Maliks and money-lenders – Their role." In *Rural Sociology in India,* ed. A.K. Desai. Bombay: Popular Prakashan.

Thorner, D. 1973. *Agrarian prospect in India.* Delhi: Allied Publishers.

Tilly, C. 2005. "Repression, mobilization and explanation." In *Repression and mobiliza- tion,* eds. C. Davenport, H. Johnston, and C. Muller, 211–226. Minneapolis: University of Minnesota Press.

Times of India. 2016. "Five women die every hour during childbirth, according to World Health Organization." *Times of India.* https://timesofindia.indiatimes.com/india/5- women-die-every-hour-during-childbirth-in-India-WHO/articleshow/52781552. cms.

Times of India. 2018. "Shashi Tharoor warns of 'Hindu Pakistan' under BJP rule, Sambit Patra hits back." *Times of India.* https://timesofindia.indiatimes.com/india/if-bjp- wins-2019-ls-polls-it-will-pave-the-way-for-creation-of-hindu-pakistan-shashi-thar oor/articleshow/64951115.cms.

Tisdell, C., Maitra, P., eds. 2018. *Technological change, development, and the environ- ment: Socio-economic perspectives.* Milton: Routledge.

Tiwana, B., and Singh, P. 2015. "Nation state, marketization of social services and uncer- tainty of livelihood in India." *World Review of Political Economy* 6, no. 1: 33–57.

Toye, J., and Jackson, C. 1996. "Public expenditure policy and poverty reduction: Has the world bank got it right?" *Institute of Development Studies Bulletin* 27, no. 1: 56–66.

Trotsky, L. 1928. "The Third International after Lenin: 11. Strategy and tactics in the imperialist epoch (Part 3)." *Marxists.org.* https://www.marxists.org/archive/trotsky/ 1928/3rd/ti06.htm#p2-08.

Trotsky, L. 1929. "Leon Trotsky's Writings on Britain: The Anglo-Russian Committee: Trotsky on the struggle in Britain in retrospect." *Marxists.org*. https://www.marxists .org/archive/trotsky/britain/v2/ch02g.htm.

Trotsky, L. 1930. "The Turn in the Communist International and the Situation in Germany." *Marxists.org*. https://www.marxists.org/archive/trotsky/germany/1930/3009 26.htm.

Trotsky, L. 1931a. "Germany, the key to the international situation." *Marxists.org*. https:// www.marxists.org/archive/trotsky/germany/1931/311126.htm.

Trotsky, L. 1931b. "Permanent Revolution." *Marxists.org*. https://www.marxists.org/ar chive/trotsky/1931/tpr/prge.htm.

Trotsky, L. 1932a. "Bourgeoisie, petty bourgeoisie and proletariat." *Marxists.org*. https:// www.marxists.org/archive/trotsky/1932/08/onlyroad2.htm.

Trotsky, L. 1932b. "Bureaucratic ultimatism." *Marxists.org*. https://www.marxists.org/ archive/trotsky/1932/01/whatnext5.htm.

Trotsky, L. 1932c. "Centrism 'in general' and the centrism of the Stalinist bureaucracy." *Marxists.org*. https://www.marxists.org/archive/trotsky/1932/01/whatnext9.htm.

Trotsky, L. 1932d. "Democracy and fascism I." *Marxists.org*. https://www.marxists.org/ archive/trotsky/1932/01/whatnext2.htm.

Trotsky, L. 1932e. "Democracy and fascism II." *Marxists.org*. https://www.marxists.org/ archive/trotsky/1932/01/whatnext3.htm.

Trotsky, L. 1932f. "Germany: The Only Road (Part 1)." *Marxists.org*. https://www.marx ists.org/archive/trotsky/germany/1932/onlyroad1.htm.

Trotsky, L. 1932g. "Germany: The Only Road (Part 2)." *Marxists.org*. https://www.marx ists.org/archive/trotsky/germany/1932/onlyroad2.htm#s9.

Trotsky, L. 1932h. "Strike strategy." *Marxists.org*. https://www.marxists.org/archive/ trotsky/1932/01/whatnext11.htm.

Trotsky, L. 1932i. "What next? Vital questions for the German proletariat. Part I." *Marx ists.org*. https://www.marxists.org/archive/trotsky/germany/1932-ger/next01.htm.

Trotsky, L. 1932j. "What next? Vital questions for the German proletariat. Part II." *Marxists.org*.   https://www.marxists.org/archive/trotsky/germany/1932-ger/next02 .htm.

Trotsky, L. 1932k. "What next? Vital questions for the German proletariat. Part III." *Marxists.org*.   https://www.marxists.org/archive/trotsky/germany/1932-ger/next03 .htm.

Trotsky, L. 1932l. "What they say in Prague about the united front." *Marxists.org*. https:// www.marxists.org/archive/trotsky/1932/09/onlyroad7.htm.

Trotsky, L. 1933a. "The German Catastrophe: The Responsibility of the Leadership." *Marxists.org*. https://www.marxists.org/archive/trotsky/germany/1933/330528.htm.

Trotsky, L. 1933b. "What is national socialism?" *Marxists.org*. https://www.marxists.org/ archive/trotsky/germany/1933/330610.htm.

Trotsky, L. 1934a. "Bonapartism and fascism." *Marxists.org.* https://www.marxists.org/archive/trotsky/germany/1934/340715.htm.

Trotsky, L. 1934b. "Whither France." *Marxists.org.* https://www.marxists.org/archive/trotsky/1936/whitherfrance/choo.htm.

Trotsky, L. 1938. "Transitional program." *Marxists.org.* https://www.marxists.org/archive/trotsky/1938/tp/transprogram.pdf.

Trotsky, L. 1939. "Three conceptions of the Russian Revolution." *Marxists.org.* https://www.marxists.org/archive/trotsky/1939/xx/3concepts.htm.

Trotsky, L. 1940. "Bonapartism, fascism and war." *Marxists.org.* https://www.marxists.org/archive/trotsky/1940/08/last-article.htm.

Trotsky, L. 1944. "Fascism what it is and how to fight it." *Marxists.org.* https://www.marxists.org/archive/trotsky/works/1944/1944-fas.htm.

Trotsky, L. 1974. *Writings of Leon Trotsky*: 1938–1939. New York: Pathfinder.

Ullrich, O. 1992. "Technology." In *Development Dictionary*, ed. E. Sachs. London: Orient Longman.

Upadhya, C. 1997. "Social and cultural strategies of class formation in coastal Andhra Pradesh." *Contributions to Indian Sociology* 31, no. 2: 169–193.

Upadhyay, S. 2018. "Workers and the right wing: The situation in India." *International Labor and Working-class History* 93: 79–90.

Vaddiraju, A.K. 1999. "Emergence of backward castes in South Telengana agrarian change and grass roots politics." *Economic Political Weekly* 34, no. 7: 425–430.

Vaidyanathan, A. 1986. "Labour use in rural India: A study of spatial and temporal variations." *Economic and Political Weekly* 21, no. 52: A130–A146.

Vakulabharanam, V., and Motiram, S. 2011. "Political economy of agrarian distress in India since the 1990s." In *Understanding India's new political economy*, ed. S. Ruparelia, S. Reddy, and S. Corbridge. London: Routledge.

Vakulabhranam, V., Zhong, W. and X. Jinjun. 2009. "Patterns of Wealth Disparities in India during the Era of Liberalization." Working Paper, Graduate Economics Research Center, Nagoya University.

Vanaik, A. 1990. *The painful transition: Bourgeois democracy in India.* London: Verso.

Vanaik, A. 2011. "Subcontinental strategies." *New Left Review*, no. 70.

Vanaik, A. 2017. *The rise of Hindu authoritarianism: Secular claims, communal realities.* London: Verso.

Vanaik, A. 2018. "India's two hegemonies." *New Left Review*, 112. https://newleftreview.org/II/112/achin-vanaik-india-s-two-hegemonies.

Vanden, E. 2018. "Targets of violence: evidence from India's Naxalite conflict." *Economic Journal* 128, no. 609: 887–916.

van der Linden, M. 2007. "The 'law' of uneven and combined development: some underdeveloped thoughts." *Historical Materialism* 15, no. 1: 145–165.

Vandergeest, P., Flaherty, M., and Miller, P. 1999. "A political ecology of shrimp aquaculture in Thailand." *Rural Sociology* 64, no. 4: 573–596.

Varadarajan, S. 2009. "Modi's 'action-reaction' quote." *Reality, one bite at a time: India, Asia and the World.* http://svaradarajan.blogspot.com/2009/10/modis-action-reaction-quote.html.

Varma, S. 2018a. "Indian millionaires up 20%, while 670 million Indians' income rises 1%." *News Click.* https://newsclick.in/indian-millionaires-20-while-670-million-indians-income-rises-1.

Varma, S. 2018b. "Glimpses of four years of Modi's Achche Din." *News Click.* https://newsclick.in/glimpses-four-years-modis-achche-din.

Varma, S. 2019. "Agri workers' wages grew just 3% per year during Modi rule." *News Click.* https://www.newsclick.in/agri-workers-wages-grew-just-3-year-under-modi-rule.

Varshney, A. 1993. "Self-limited empowerment: Democracy, economic development and rural India." *Journal of Development Studies* 29, no.4: 177–215.

Varshney, A. 1994/1998. *Democracy, development and the countryside: Urban rural struggles in India.* Cambridge: Cambridge University Press.

Vasudevan, R. 2008. "Accumulation by dispossession in India." *Econmomic and Political Weekly* 43, no. 11: 41–43.

Velaskar, P. 2016. "Theorising the interaction of caste, class and gender: A feminist sociological approach." *Contributions to Indian Sociology* 50, no. 3: 389–414.

Veltmeyer, H. 1997. "New social movements in Latin America." *Journal of Peasant Studies* 25, no. 1: 139–169.

Veltmeyer, H., Petras, J., and Vieux, S. 1997. *Neoliberalism and class conflict in Latin America: A comparative perspective on the political economy of structural adjustment.* New York: St. Martin's Press.

Verma, H.S. 2005. *The OBCs and the ruling classes in India.* Jaipur: Rawat Publications.

Veron, R., Williams, G., Corbridge, S., and Srivastava, M. 2006. "Decentralized Corruption or Corrupt Decentralization? Community Monitoring of Poverty-alleviation Schemes in Eastern India." *World Development* 34, no. 11: 1922–1941.

Vicol, M. 2019. "Potatoes, Petty Commodity Producers and Livelihoods: Contract farming and agrarian change in Maharashtra, India." *Journal of Agrarian Change* 19, no. 1: 135–161.

Vidyasagar, K. 2005. *Communist politics in India: Struggle for survival.* Delhi: Academic Excellence.

Vidyasagar, R. 1999. "New agrarianism and the challenges of the left." In *Class formation and political transformation in post-colonial India,* ed. T. Sathyamurthy, 202–237. Delhi: Oxford University Press.

Vijayabaskar, M., and Menon, A. 2018. "Dispossession by neglect: Agricultural land sales in southern India." *Journal of Agrarian Change* 18, no. 3: 571–587.

Vogel, L. 2014. *Marxism and social oppression.* Leiden/Boston: Brill.

Volodin, A. 2018. "The logic of directed development in postcolonial India." *Herald of the Russian Academy of Sciences* 88, no. 1: 96–103.

Vyas, V.S., and Bhargava, P. 1995. "Public intervention for poverty alleviation." *Economic and Political Weekly* 30, no. 41/42: 559–2561, 2563–2565, 2567–2569, 2571–2572.

Walker, K. 2008. "Neoliberalism on the ground in rural India: predatory growth, agrarian crisis, internal colonization, and the intensification of class struggle." *Journal of Peasant Studies* 35, no. 4: 557–620.

Wallace, H.S. 2017. "American Fascism, in 1944 and Today." *The New York Times.* https://www.nytimes.com/2017/05/12/opinion/american-fascism-trump.html.

Watts, M. 1996. "Development III: The global agrofood system and late twentieth-century development, (or Kautsky redux)." *Progress in Human Geography*, 20, no. 2: 230–245.

Webster, N. 1990. "Agrarian relations in Burdwan District, West Bengal: From the economics of Green Revolution to the politics of Panchayat Raj." *Journal of Contemporary Asia* 20, no. 2: 177–211.

Weeks, J. 1981. *Capital and exploitation.* Princeton: Princeton University Press.

Weeks, P. 1992. "Fish and people: Aquaculture and the social sciences." *Society & Natural Resources* 5, no. 4: 345–357.

Whitehead, J. 2007. "Hegemony and the decline of the Narmada Bachao Andolan in Gujarat, 1998–2001." *Critical Asian Studies* 39, no. 3: 399–421.

Whitehead, J. 2010. *Development and dispossession in the Narmada Valley.* Delhi: Pearson.

Wickremasinghe, N., and Jones, K. 2004. "India: Stalinists to promote Congress power bid." *World Socialist Web Site.* http://www.wsws.org/en/articles/2004/05/ind-m13.html.

Williams, G. 2004. "Evaluating participatory development: Tyranny, power and (re-) politicisation." *Third World Quarterly* 25, no. 3: 557–578.

Williams, M. 2009. *The roots of participatory democracy: Democratic communists in South Africa and Kerala, India.* New York: Palgrave Macmillan.

Wilson, K. 1999. "Patterns of accumulation and struggles of rural labour: Some aspects of agrarian change in central Bihar." *Journal of Peasant Studies* 26, no. 2–3: 316–354.

Witsoe, J. 2011. "Corruption as power: Caste and the political imagination of the postcolonial state." *American Ethnologist* 38, no. 11: 73–85.

Wood, E. 1995. *Democracy against capitalism.* New York: Cambridge University Press.

Wood, E. 1997. "The non-history of capitalism." *Historical Materialism* 1, no. 1: 5–21.

Wood, E. 2003. *The empire of capital.* Delhi: Leftword.

Wood, E. 2007. "A reply to critics." *Historical Materialism* 15: 143–170.

World Bank. 1997. *India: Achievements and challenges in reducing poverty.* The World Bank, Washington.

World Bank. 2007. *World development report: Agriculture for development.* The International Bank for Reconstruction and Development/The World Bank, Washington.

World Economic Forum. 2018. "The inclusive development index." *World Economic Forum.* http://www3.weforum.org/docs/WEF_Forum_IncGrwth_2018.pdf.

Wright, E. 1995. "The class analysis of poverty." *International Journal of Health Services* 25, no. 1: 85–100.

Wright, E. 2015. *Understanding class.* London: Verso.

Yapa, L.S. 1979. "Ecopolitical economy of the green revolution." *Professional Geographer* 31, no. 4: 371–376.

Yapa, L.S. 1993. "What are improved seeds: An epistemology of improved seeds." *Economic Geography* 69, no. 3: 254–273.

Yapa, L.S. 1996. "What causes poverty? A postmodern view." *Annals of the Association of American Geographers* 86, no. 4: 707–728.

Yechury, S. 1993. "Communalism, religion and Marxism." *The Marxist* 10, no. 4; 11, no. 1.

Yuval, N.H. 2018. *21 lessons for the 21st century.* London: Jonathan Cape.

Zizek, S. 2008. *Violence.* New York: Picador.

Index

Keywords below include concepts that reflect social processes at a more general level and in the Indian context.

www.ingramcontent.com/pod-product-compliance
Lightning Source LLC
Chambersburg PA
CBHW070902030426
42336CB00014BA/2289